This book is a reassessment of British performance in manufacturing since 1850 in the light of new evidence on international comparisons of productivity. Using a novel analytical framework of technological evolution, Stephen Broadberry uncovers new ways of looking at Britain's relative economic decline while debunking a number of misapprehensions regarding the nature and causes of the decline. The book analyses productivity levels in Britain, the United States and Germany and provides detailed case studies of all the major manufacturing industries, broken down into three periods: 1850–1914, 1914–50 and 1950–90. Broadberry offers a wide coverage of industries, with invaluable country-specific information; by combining a multitude of detailed productivity measurements with qualitative industrial and business history, he provides a major contribution to our understanding of British economic performance over the last 150 years.

The productivity race

The productivity race

British manufacturing in international perspective, 1850–1990

S.N. Broadberry

University of Warwick

CAMBRIDGE
UNIVERSITY PRESS

PUBLISHED BY THE PRESS SYNDICATE OF THE UNIVERSITY OF CAMBRIDGE
The Pitt Building, Trumpington Street, Cambridge CB2 1RP, United Kingdom

CAMBRIDGE UNIVERSITY PRESS
The Edinburgh Building, Cambridge, CB2 2RU, United Kingdom
40 West 20th Street, New York, NY 10011-4211, USA
10 Stamford Road, Oakleigh, Melbourne 3166, Australia

First published 1997

Printed in the United Kingdom at the University Press, Cambridge

Typeset in 10/12 Monotype Times

A catalogue record for this book is available from the British Library

Library of Congress Cataloguing in Publication data
Broadberry, S. N.
    The productivity race: British manufacturing in international
perspective 1850–1990 / S.N. Broadberry
        p.   cm.
    ISBN 0 521 58440 X
    1. Industrial productivity – Great Britain–History – 19th century.
    2. Industrial productivity – Great Britain–History – 20th century.
    3. Industrial productivity – United States–History – 19th century.
    4. Industrial productivity – United States–History – 20th century.
    5. Industrial productivity – Germany–History – 19th century.
    6. Industrial productivity – Germany–History – 20th century.
    7. Competition. International – History.   I. Title.
    HC260.I52B76   1997   338.4'767'0941–dc21   96-49929   CIP
ISBN 0 521 58440 X hardback

For Mary and in memory of Caroline

Contents

Figures

Tables

Acknowledgements

During the course of researching for and writing this book, I have incurred many debts. I owe a particular debt to Nick Crafts, who has offered constructive criticism over many years and who patiently read the manuscript as it emerged. Many colleagues and seminar participants have also given encouragement, advice and constructive criticism. In particular, I wish to thank without implicating in any way Moses Abramovitz, Bart van Ark, Stuart Bennett, Paul David, Charles Feinstein, James Foreman-Peck, Rainer Fremdling, Les Hannah, Knick Harley, Mark Harrison, Herman de Jong, Peter Law, Angus Maddison, Andy Marrison, Bob Millward, Geoffrey Owen, Peter Solar, Richard Tilly, Gianni Toniolo, Karin Wagner, Gavin Wright and Jonathan Zeitlin.

Parts of the book draw on joint work with Nick Crafts, Rainer Fremdling and Karin Wagner. Other parts use unpublished material kindly made available by Herman de Jong, Mary O'Mahony, the National Institute of Economic and Social Research, the Engineering Employers' Federation and the Chartered Institute of Accountants in England and Wales. I am indebted to the editors and publishers of the following journals for permission to include material which has appeared in their publications: *Economic Journal* (Blackwell Publishers), *Explorations in Economic History* (Academic Press), *Journal of Economic History* (Cambridge University Press). Excellent research assistance was provided by Jeanette Ellicott, Carsten Johnson, Martin Judge, Claus Olsen, Karina Ransby, Christopher Skak-Nielsen, Jackie Swanton and Adam Wright. Financial support was provided by the University of Warwick through its Innovations and Research Fund, and by the Commission of the European Communities under its SPES Programme via the Centre for Economic Policy Research. The staff of Warwick University Library were most helpful, particularly Finola Osborn of the Statistics section on the fourth floor. Patrick McCartan of Cambridge University Press provided much patient encouragement and advice. I thank them all.

I have already made one acknowledgement to my wife Mary O'Mahony for access to unpublished material. However, the debt I owe her is much greater than this; without her, the book would simply not have been possible. This book is dedicated to her and to the memory of our daughter Caroline.

Glossary of terms and company names

AACP	Anglo-American Council on Productivity
AEG	Allgemeine Elektrizitäts Gesellschaft
AEI	Associated Electrical Industries
AFVG	Anglo-French Variable Geometry fighter
AG	Aktien Gesellschaft
ALM	Associated Lead Manufacturers Limited
APCM	Associated Portland Cement Manufacturers
APOC	Anglo-Persian Oil Company
AVC	American Viscose Corporation
BAC	British Aircraft Corporation
BAe	British Aerospace
BASF	Badische Anilin und Soda Fabrik
BAT	British–American Tobacco Company
BISF	British Iron and Steel Federation
BSC	British Steel Corporation
BISF	British Iron and Steel Federation
BLMC	British Leyland Motor Corporation
BMC	British Motor Corporation
BMH	British Motor Holdings
BMW	Bayerische Motoren Werke
BNS	British Nylon Spinners
BOS	Basic Oxygen Steelmaking
BSC	British Steel Corporation
BT	British Telecom
BTH	British Thomson–Houston Company
BTM	British Tabulating Machine Company
BTR	British Tyre and Rubber Company
BSA	Birmingham Small Arms Company
CAMRA	Campaign for Real Ale
CEM	Combined English Mills
CMA	Cable Makers' Association
CWS	Cooperative Wholesale Society

DCL	Distillers Company Limited
DE	Department of Employment
ECSC	European Coal and Steel Community
EE	English Electric
EEC	European Economic Community
EEF	Engineering Employers' Federation
EFA	European Fighter Aircraft
EFTA	European Free Trade Area
ELMA	Electric Lamp Manufacturers' Association
EMI	Electrical and Musical Industries Limited
ENIAC	Electrical Numerical Integrator and Calculator
EPOS	Electronic Point of Sale
ESC	English Sewing Cotton
FDT	food, drink and tobacco
FSD	Fine Spinners and Doublers
GATT	General Agreement on Tariffs and Trade
GDP	gross domestic product
GE	General Electric Company (US)
GEC	General Electric Company (UK)
GNP	gross national product
GWB	Gesetz gegen Wettbewerbsbeschränkungen
HSA	Hawker Siddeley Aviation
IBM	International Business Machines
ICI	Imperial Chemical Industries Limited
ICL	International Computers Limited
ICT	International Computers and Tabulators
IDAC	Import Duties Advisory Committee
IG	Interessengemeinschaft
IMF	International Monetary Fund
IRC	Industrial Reorganisation Corporation
ISCGB	Iron and Steel Corporation of Great Britain
ISHRA	Iron and Steel Holding and Realisation Agency
ITT	International Telephone and Telegraph Company
LCC	Lancashire Cotton Corporation
LME	London Metal Exchange
MB	Metal Box
MLH	Minimum List Heading
MMB	Milk Marketing Board
MMC	Monopolies and Mergers Commission
m.p.g.	million proof gallons
MUPS/WSA	Manpower Utilisation and Payment Structure/Weekly Staff Agreement

NEB	National Enterprise Board
NGA	National Graphical Association
NHS	National Health Service
NIC	Newly Industrialised Country
NRDC	National Research Development Corporation
OPEC	Organisation of Petroleum Exporting Countries
R&D	research and development
RTB	Richard Thomas and Baldwins
RTZ	Rio Tinto Zinc
SIB	Shipbuilding Industry Board
SIC	Standard Industrial Classification
SOGAT	Society of Graphical and Allied Trades
STC	Standard Telephone and Cables
TFI	total factor input
TFP	total factor productivity
TRC	Therapeutic Research Corporation
TSR	Tactical Strike and Reconnaissance
UCS	Upper Clyde Shipbuilders
VER	voluntary export restraint
VPRS	voluntary price regulation scheme

1 Introduction and overview

Introduction

Given the relative decline in British living standards over the period since the mid-nineteenth century, well known from Angus Maddison's (1982, 1991, 1995) work on national income statistics, it might be expected that British manufacturing productivity would exhibit a similar relative decline. In fact, however, as we can see from figure 1.1, this is not the case. Since the mid-nineteenth century British labour productivity in manufacturing has been about half the American level, and about the same as the German level. There have been some fairly sustained fluctuations around these levels, particularly around major wars, but in the long run these levels have been restored. Part 1 of this book is concerned with the establishment of these productivity patterns.

Part 2 then turns to the explanation of these productivity patterns in manufacturing. The key factor is the parallel development of different production techniques on the two sides of the Atlantic which, following Piore and Sabel (1984), Tolliday and Zeitlin (1991) and others, I have described as 'mass production' and 'flexible production', although, as I also stress, this is not inconsistent with producers having access to the same technology on both sides of the Atlantic. The key features of the two systems that I focus on concern (a) the degree of standardisation or customisation of output and (b) the skill of the shopfloor labour force. With mass production, standardised products are produced with special purpose machinery, requiring a relatively unskilled shopfloor labour force, while with flexible production, customised products are produced with general purpose machinery, requiring a highly skilled shopfloor labour force.

Part 2 works mainly at the level of manufacturing as a whole. However, to be convincing, any explanation of manufacturing productivity performance must be able to stand up to scrutiny at a finer level of disaggregation. Accordingly, in part 3 a detailed evaluation of productivity performance is provided for a large number of industries, covering all the major branches of manufacturing. This helps to counter the tendency in much of the existing literature to dwell on the failures and ignore the

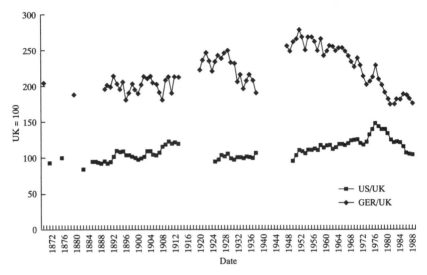

1.1 Comparative labour productivity in manufacturing, 1869–1989

successes, which has resulted in an overly negative view of British manufacturing performance over the long run.

Comparative labour productivity in manufacturing

In chapters 2 and 3, levels of comparative labour productivity in manufacturing are provided for Britain, the United States and Germany. Chapter 2 establishes benchmark levels of comparative labour productivity in manufacturing for the US/UK and Germany/UK comparisons on a highly disaggregated basis, covering up to 77 industries at regular intervals since 1907. The benchmarks are based on value added converted at purchasing power parity (PPP) adjusted price ratios for the postwar period and physical indicators for the prewar period, following the methodology of Paige and Bombach (1959) and Rostas (1948a) respectively. These figures form the basis of the industry studies in part 3.

The benchmark estimates for individual industries can be aggregated up to produce benchmark estimates of comparative labour productivity for manufacturing as a whole for census years. In chapter 3, the comparative labour productivity position for manufacturing as a whole is extended to other years, using time series of output and employment for extrapolation. The extrapolations from benchmarks around the middle of the sample period can be checked against additional benchmark estimates, to provide a reconciliation between time series and cross-sectional evidence.

Figures for comparative labour productivity in manufacturing can be compared with figures for comparative productivity at the whole economy level for Britain, the United States and Germany, derived from Maddison (1991). There are some striking differences in levels and trends. First, there has been no clear trend over about the last 120 years in comparative labour productivity performance in manufacturing between these three major exporting nations. Labour productivity in US manufacturing has fluctuated around a level of about twice the British level, while German manufacturing labour productivity has fluctuated around a level broadly the same as the British one. This contrasts strikingly with the position at the whole economy level, where the United States has pulled substantially ahead of Britain from a position of broad equality in 1870, and Germany has come from a productivity level less than 60 per cent of the British level to a small productivity advantage over Britain.

Sustained deviations from the 2:1 US/UK productivity lead in manufacturing (lasting a decade or more) seem to be associated with the two world wars, and interestingly enough, looking back into the nineteenth century the United States did badly across the Civil War. During the post-Second World War period, Germany began to pull ahead of Britain in manufacturing, although the major divergence between Britain and Germany in this sector did not occur until the 1970s, and was very much reversed during the 1980s.

Chapter 4 then extends the measurement of comparative labour productivity in manufacturing as a whole to cover another nine industrialised countries, building up a total sample of twelve countries. I find that there have been a number of convergence clubs, even amongst the advanced industrialised countries. As suggested by the findings for Britain and Germany compared with the United States, there has been a persistent transatlantic labour productivity gap in manufacturing throughout the twentieth century.

Chapter 5 returns to the theme of the different trends and levels of comparative labour productivity at the manufacturing and whole economy levels. Clearly, the United States forging ahead between 1870 and 1950 at the whole economy level cannot be explained simply in terms of productivity growth in manufacturing. Rather, it is seen to reflect trends in other sectors and the effects of structural change, with the latter including the growing importance of manufacturing. Similarly, Germany's catching up of Britain at the whole economy level cannot be explained by trends in manufacturing, but must be attributed to trends in other sectors and sectoral reallocation of labour, particularly the declining importance of agriculture.

Technical choice

Part 2 seeks to explain the persistent labour productivity gap in manufacturing between the United States on the one hand and Britain and Germany on the other in terms of path dependence in technology. This involves going back in chapter 6 to the Habakkuk debate on British and American technology in the nineteenth century. The basic idea in Habakkuk's (1962) model was that land abundance in America caused labour scarcity and led to the use of capital-intensive production methods in manufacturing. This would be sufficient to generate the observed result of higher labour productivity in US manufacturing, with higher output per worker determined by higher capital per worker via a conventional production function.

In fact, there was a great controversy at the time of the original debate since, in general, land abundance means capital scarcity as well as labour scarcity (Temin, 1966a, 1971). The issue was resolved to most people's satisfaction by Ames and Rosenberg's (1968) argument that there was a complementarity between capital and natural resources, with which America was abundantly endowed. The model used here retains the complementarity between resources and capital, but distinguishes between two types of capital: human capital and physical capital. This modification is particularly important for bringing the story forward into the twentieth century.

In the nineteenth century, US firms used technology which was very resource-intensive and machinery-intensive, but which saved on the use of skilled shopfloor workers, who were in very scarce supply in America. In Britain and Germany, however, resource and factor endowments were rather different, which meant that the American techniques could not be adopted profitably. European production was intensive in the use of skilled shopfloor labour and economised on the use of resources and machinery.

However, it is usual to note a demand reinforcement effect in the emergence of American mass production technology (Hounshell, 1984; Chandler, 1990; Frankel, 1957; Rostas, 1948a). Mass production of standardised output can only be profitable if markets can be found for undifferentiated items. Most authors are agreed on the greater willingness of American consumers to accept standardised goods, and as the nineteenth century wore on, the large size of the US home market became important. By contrast, European producers are usually seen as dependent on fragmented national markets stratified by class differences, coupled with greater reliance on differentiated export markets.

Suppose, now, that there is technical progress over time. Should the two technologies be expected to converge? In the brilliant first chapter of his

1975 book, Paul David argued that initial factor proportions would tend to be preserved over time so long as technical progress can be characterised by 'local learning'. This can be thought of as a kind of trial and error process, or what Joel Mokyr (1990) has more recently called 'micro inventions'. The basic idea is that trial and error adaptations never stray too far from the original design.

Note that once different techniques have been selected, in a way they are in competition with each other. Thus it is possible to have the coexistence of the mule and the ring frame in cotton spinning, for example. It may be perfectly rational at a point in time to use the ring in America and the mule in Britain, given different relative factor prices in the two countries, as Sandberg (1974) argued. But now suppose that by trial and error American producers improve the ring and succeed in lowering input requirements. So long as British mule spinners can also find ways of lowering costs, perhaps through imitation, then the mule will remain profitable.

Suppose now, however, that the British mule spinners have exhausted all possibility of improvement. Eventually, if improvements continue on the ring, there must come a point where mule spinning will be unprofitable in Britain at any factor prices. At that point, it may at first sight appear that it would pay simply to switch to the American technique in Britain. But even here, however, it is unlikely that the American technology will be simply copied without adaptation to local circumstances. After all, factor endowments will still be different.

Indeed, the fact that accumulation of physical capital and human capital takes place around specific techniques helps to ensure that initial differences in factor proportions are preserved through time. In the spinning example, it is clear that after a period in which mules have been used in Britain and rings in America, Britain will be left with a stock of skilled shopfloor workers and America with an unskilled labour force in cotton spinning, simply because the mule uses skilled labour and the ring uses unskilled labour. It should be clear, then, that what Mokyr (1990) would call 'macro inventions' like the ring frame, although at first sight appearing to offer a fresh start, in practice do not do so.

This model helps in understanding the long-run stability in the comparative productivity ratios noted in part 1. When there were 'macro inventions' in the United States leading to the development of mass production technology, British craft-based flexible production methods were able to survive so long as they more or less matched the American productivity growth. To the extent that British methods were unable to keep up with US productivity improvements, however, those industries found their survival threatened, and indeed in some cases, such as cotton and shipbuilding, were effectively wiped out.

For a sustained deterioration in British productivity performance to occur, it would be necessary for the failing industries to be able to interfere with the operation of market forces through, for example, protection or subsidies. Only then could those industries survive. When market forces are allowed to operate more or less freely, as in the 1980s, a return to the long-run productivity ratios would be expected.

Having set out the theoretical framework in chapter 6, the next step is to examine the empirical evidence on the transatlantic differences in technology and accumulation strategy. Chapter 7 begins the process with a look at the role of resource endowments and demand factors. There is widespread agreement on the importance of resources for American economic development during the nineteenth century. Furthermore, the autarky of the interwar period meant that this American advantage persisted into the twentieth century (Nelson and Wright, 1992). Although it seems likely that the impact of resources has lessened as the world economy has become more integrated since the Second World War, it remains the case that energy is relatively cheap in the United States, and continues to affect the choice between machinery and labour in the way suggested by Melman (1956).

Turning to the issue of demand, clearly mass production may be expected to work better when producing for a homogeneous market, and the importance of the greater differentiation of demand in Europe than America, which was always seen as important in the Habakkuk (1962) debate on the nineteenth century, has already been alluded to. However, from the end of the nineteenth century, these trends were reinforced by the increasing division of the world into separate spheres of influence. The business history literature in particular documents a rising trend of deals allocating North America to US firms, Europe to German firms and the British Empire to British firms, and avoiding head-to-head competition. From about 1870 there was a clear upward trend in the share of British exports going to Empire markets. At the same time, there was a strong retreat of British producers from the main continental European markets. The scale of the movements was very large, with the share of exports going to Empire markets rising from about a quarter in 1870 to more than a half by 1951. And as late as 1970, more of Britain's exports went to 'British' countries than to the original European Economic Community (EEC) Six.

Whether this concentration on Empire markets is seen as illustrating an unwillingness to compete and a seeking out of 'soft markets', or simply as an inevitable response to rising protectionism elsewhere, it is clear that British industry faced a tough period of reorientation of trade away from the Commonwealth after the Second World War as the world economy re-integrated.

Turning to accumulation strategy in chapter 8, the simplest way in which technological differences might be expected to show up on the two sides of the Atlantic might be in capital intensity. In fact, however, there are some serious measurement difficulties here. The first problem concerns asset lives, about which surprisingly little is known. The problem is that statistical offices in different countries use very different assumptions, based on very thin evidence. This is important, because in the perpetual inventory method, capital stocks are obtained by cumulating past investments and subtracting retirements as assets reach the end of their useful lives. Thus, for example, since asset lives are usually taken as much longer in Britain than in the United States, Britain appears to have a large capital stock despite not investing very much. Consequently if official asset lives are used, there is the odd outcome that in the late nineteenth century capital per worker was higher in Britain, even though output per worker was much higher in the United States. One way around this problem is to take the investment data for each country and recalculate capital stocks on the basis of standardised asset lives (Maddison, 1993; O'Mahony, 1996). This can be done for the post-Second World War period, and indeed results in quite a close correspondence between the capital per worker and output per worker ratios for the US/UK and Germany/UK comparisons.

However, there are real problems in extending this technique back before the Second World War because for some assets insurance valuations of the stocks were used rather than the perpetual inventory method of adding up investment flows (Feinstein, 1972, 1988). Hence for the prewar period, it may be more instructive to look at an alternative indicator of capital intensity of production which was widely collected during the first half of the twentieth century, horse-power per worker. Again, there is quite a high degree of correspondence between labour productivity and horse-power per worker ratios for the US/UK and Germany/UK comparisons. In fact, this measure also has the advantage of being restricted to machinery, which is of some importance because machinery is a surprisingly small proportion of capital, as Field (1985) points out.

However, in many ways I would see bigger transatlantic differences in human capital than in physical capital accumulation. Again, however, there are measurement problems. If attention is restricted to years of education, the most widely used human capital indicator in the recent economics literature, then there is little difference between the major industrialised countries (Maddison, 1987). However, this can be supplemented with more specific data on shopfloor skills, managerial skills and research skills. Different technological systems in different countries have different balances of these skills.

Perhaps the most obvious transatlantic difference can be seen in the area of the training of shopfloor workers. Apprenticeships were widespread in Britain and Germany before the Second World War and almost non-existent in American manufacturing. This reflects the reliance of European flexible production methods on skilled shopfloor labour, but American mass production on unskilled labour on the shopfloor. After the Second World War there was a decline in apprenticeships in British and German engineering, as a response to the technological leadership of American mass production technology. However, the decline was greater in Britain than in Germany, reflecting the greater enthusiasm for American production methods in Britain. This was undoubtedly influenced by the integration of the British and American economies during the Allied war effort.

During the 1970s, a revival of apprenticeships occurred in Germany, which I would see as reflecting the need for skilled shopfloor workers with the return of technological leadership to flexible production methods. These developments can in turn be seen as resulting from the information revolution, rejuvenating production methods geared to catering for customised rather than standardised demand (Piore and Sabel, 1984; Tolliday and Zeitlin, 1991). This has resulted in something of a crisis in American manufacturing, and the emergence of a literature akin to that dealing with British relative decline after 1870 (Baily and Chakrabarti, 1988; Dertouzos *et al.*, 1989). Although formal apprenticeships have continued to decline in Britain during the 1980s, there has been an expansion of other forms of training, which suggests that British firms have moved back towards a more skilled labour-intensive strategy, drawing on German and Japanese flexible production methods. Nevertheless, there is still a large 'intermediate skills gap' in Britain relative to Germany, and British industry may continue to be hampered by skill shortages for some time to come (Prais, 1993).

Following Chandler (1990), greater investment in the managerial aspects of human capital would be expected in the United States, at least in the first half of the twentieth century, and this does seem to be borne out by data on the educational attainments of managers. Britain and Germany had about the same proportion of top managers with degrees in the 1950s as the United States had in the 1920s, and although there is quite a range of estimates for the post-1950 period, depending on sampling error and definitional problems, there does seem to be a small continued American advantage in this area.

The growth of R&D can be seen as allied to the growth of managerial capabilities, since as skill is taken off the shopfloor there is a greater need to develop new products and processes in laboratories. Again, the data suggest that there has been a big gap between Britain and the United States, but not between Britain and Germany for much of the twentieth century, a point recently made by Edgerton and Horrocks (1994) on the basis of firm level data for the interwar period.

In chapter 9, the role of competition is considered. Although competition is not an accumulation strategy in itself, it may make the transition away from a strategy that has become unsuccessful easier to achieve. High levels of labour productivity necessarily depend upon previous investment in human and physical capital. If the specific investments have not been made in one country, then no amount of liberalisation can lead to higher labour productivity than in countries with higher levels of human and physical capital. Thus no simple correlation should be expected between the degree of competition and labour productivity performance at a point in time. Nevertheless, I would see barriers to competition as inimical to adjustment. If the world changes, then shielding the economy from market forces may make the necessary adjustments harder to achieve. It should be noted that this conclusion runs directly counter to the claims of Elbaum and Lazonick (1986) and other 'corporatist' writers such as Chandler (1990), who see British industry as failing to substitute the 'visible hand of coordinated control' for the 'invisible hand of the self-regulating market'. Chapter 9 establishes the fact that for much of the twentieth century, far from being too competitive, the British economy has been too corporatist, with high levels of concentration, large plant size, widespread collusion and high levels of protection in product markets and high levels of union density in labour markets.

Industry studies

Part 3 of the book turns to individual industry case studies, split into three chapters covering the periods 1850–1914, 1914–50 and 1950–90. Where possible, estimates of comparative labour productivity levels have been obtained at benchmark intervals, and this has been supplemented with time series of output, capital and labour inputs and productivity in Britain. An attempt has also been made to integrate the discussion of productivity trends and levels with the large secondary literature on the performance of individual industries, although inevitably space constraints must limit the extent to which this should be seen as a general history of British manufacturing.

The rise of competition from abroad, 1850–1914

Chapter 10 looks at the response of British manufacturing to the rise of competition from abroad before the First World War. For this period, there is only one reasonably full set of benchmark productivity level estimates for the US/UK comparison for 1909/07, together with some incomplete additional figures for 1912/14, since the 1912 *Census of Production* was never fully written up. There are a few additional calculations for the Germany/UK case for 1907. For the pre-1914 period, data on output and productivity trends within Britain are also necessarily more limited than for later periods.

The first thing that stands out from these estimates is the high degree of variation in the comparative productivity performance of individual industries. It is instructive to consider the industries in which Britain did relatively well, i.e. where the US/UK productivity ratio was below the 209 for manufacturing as a whole. The first type of industry in which Britain did relatively well was where British craft-based flexible production methods continued to remain competitive despite the adoption of high throughput mass production methods in the United States. Britain clearly did relatively well in textiles, with productivity not far below American levels. As a result, given lower wages, Britain dominated world markets. In these industries, despite the use of high throughput techniques in America such as ring spinning and the automatic loom in cotton, British firms continued to make improvements through trial and error and raised productivity sufficiently to remain competitive. Claims by Lazonick and Mass (1984) that productivity stagnated in British cotton before the First World War are shown to be the result of incorrect adjustments of the raw data, which as Sandberg (1974) noted, continue to show labour productivity growth through to 1913. British production in small-scale vertically specialised firms was efficient, leading to relatively high labour productivity through Marshall's acclaimed external economies of scale. Clearly, however, it was highly dependent on a liberal trading environment. If there was any ominous trend for Lancashire before 1914 it was the growing threat of protection in overseas markets.

The second type of industry where Britain also achieved productivity levels not dissimilar to American levels was where mass production techniques were difficult to apply, so that flexible production methods had to be used on both sides of the Atlantic, giving Britain an advantage because of the supply of skilled labour. The clearest example here was shipbuilding, where much as in cotton, a large number of small British firms utilised a skilled labour force to attain external economies of scale. Pollard and Robertson (1979) claim that British production methods were more labour-intensive even compared with other European countries, and that this enabled British firms to survive in cyclical downturns by reducing their dependence on fixed costs. Although there were other parts of the engineering and metal industries where mass production methods had still not been applied successfully before 1914, the data for direct productivity level comparisons are not available, largely as a result of the bizarre decision to report the quantities of many British engineering goods only in tons in the *Census of Production*.

The third type of industry in which Britain achieved relatively high levels of labour productivity was where there was no noticeable lag in the adoption of high throughput techniques, due to the absence of demand constraints. These industries, such as seedcrushing, coke, sugar and tobacco (before cigarettes became the major product) produced relatively homogeneous products. Although information on German productivity levels at this time is sketchy, it is possible to infer from the qualitative literature, together with quantitative information from the interwar period, that Britain was a long way ahead of Germany in the application of high throughput techniques in the food, drink and tobacco industries. This would further support the importance of demand constraints through the lower levels of urbanisation in Germany before 1914. The high levels of labour productivity in the British food, drink and tobacco sector are worth emphasising, since they are rarely considered when attempting an evaluation of manufacturing performance overall.

The industries with a relatively poor British labour productivity performance tended to be mass production industries where demand conditions or resource and factor endowments simply prevented the adoption of American techniques in Britain. The classic example here is motor vehicles, where there was no question of building a mass production car industry in Britain because of the absence of a mass market for cars at this time. Again, there are undoubtedly other examples, for example in electrical goods, but the British *Census of Production*, with its quantity information limited to tonnage, precludes the calculation of productivity level estimates.

The picture of the pre-1914 British economy that emerges from chapter 10 is thus one of a country adapting rationally to the rise of competition from abroad. In general, the continued use of flexible production techniques in Britain despite the adoption of mass production techniques in the United States should not be seen as irrational technological conservatism, but rather as profit maximisation under different demand conditions and with different resource and factor endowments. As McCloskey and Sandberg (1971) note, in most industries conditions were competitive, acting as a spur to efficiency, with existing rivals or new entrants ready to take up opportunities neglected by incumbent producers. It is significant that the one widely accepted case of failure to adopt the efficient technology was the retention of the Leblanc process by the United Alkali Company, and this occurred in a cartelised industry (Lindert and Trace, 1971).

War and depression, 1914–1950

The years between 1914 and 1950 were highly disturbed, covering two world wars and a world slump of unprecedented severity. Over the period as a whole, Britain's manufacturing labour productivity position relative to the United States deteriorated somewhat, but there was no deterioration relative to Germany. Attempts to adjust accumulation strategy in the light of the American innovations of the Second Industrial Revolution did not close the transatlantic productivity gap at this time, and even permitted it to widen. Although it is possible to see demand and resource and factor endowments as preventing a full elimination of the productivity gap, I would also see lack of competition weakening the pressure on firms to adjust.

As the world economy became increasingly protectionist, British exporters became increasingly dependent on Empire markets. Although this had short-run advantages, helping to maintain output and employment during the 1930s, it also had adverse long-run consequences; head-to-head competition with Germany and the United States was avoided, and marketing investments were made in remote areas which would not be natural British markets in a more integrated postwar world, although the latter was by no means foreseeable. Also, within Britain cartelisation and collusion became commonplace to avoid cut-throat price competition during the world slump, and this became institutionalised through the rapid growth of trade associations. Again, although it is possible to see short-run gains from such behaviour, this was to store up productivity problems for the future (Broadberry and Crafts, 1990b).

For the interwar period, there is a relatively full sample of Anglo-German comparative labour productivity level estimates to put alongside the Anglo-American comparisons. There is also a much more complete quantitative picture of the growth of output and productivity (both labour productivity and total factor productivity) by industry within Britain.

In general, the comparative productivity level estimates reveal a high degree of continuity with the pre-1914 position, with British performance better in the lighter textiles and food, drink and tobacco industries, and lagging particularly in the heavier metals and engineering industries. Following the literature, and seeking a difference between new and old industries is not particularly helpful. Although some new industries such as rayon and fertilisers performed well in terms of labour productivity levels, others such as radios, electric lamps, motor vehicles and aircraft performed very poorly. And although some old industries such as blast furnaces performed badly in terms of labour productivity levels, others such as cotton and shipbuilding continued to perform well.

Clearly, the figures on comparative productivity levels need to be supplemented with information on trends in output and employment for a full evaluation of performance. Thus, for example, it would be wrong to conclude that cotton was very successful in interwar Britain on the basis of the productivity level figures, since output and employment declined. The point is rather that the contraction of the industry occurred in such a way as to maintain Britain's relative productivity position before the Second World War. It was only moving across the Second World War that the external economies of scale disappeared and Britain's comparative productivity position in cotton moved close to that for manufacturing as a whole. It would be hard to read this into the writings of someone like Lazonick (1986).

In shipbuilding, Britain also retained a strong comparative labour productivity level position through to 1950, although in this case it is possible to see capacity utilisation effects during the 1920s, when the US/UK productivity gap rose to about 50 per cent. The reason for the continued strong British productivity showing in shipbuilding was that mass production techniques were not really applied on a large scale in this industry until the 1950s (Lorenz, 1991a).

In the new industries, cartels were strong in electrical goods, shoring up inefficient producers, helping to explain the very large productivity gaps in products such as electronic tubes, radios, household appliances and electric lamps. Lewchuk's (1987) work on the motor vehicle industry is important in showing how the industrial relations problems arising from craft unionism could affect new as well as old industries, although his attempt to explain the difference between British and American production methods in the interwar period largely in terms of industrial relations systems surely understates the role of demand conditions through the absence of a mass market for cars in Britain (Tolliday, 1987b; Bowden, 1991).

Perhaps the most important message to take away from the Anglo-German productivity level comparisons for the interwar period is that Britain did not lag behind Germany in manufacturing as a whole at this time. Although Germany had higher labour productivity in some heavy industries such as blast furnaces and sulphuric acid, this was offset by a British labour productivity lead in other industries such as cotton weaving, beet sugar, brewing and tobacco. Britain and Germany were much more evenly matched before the Second World War than a reader of Chandler (1990) would expect.

Changing markets and technology, 1950–1990

British industry emerged from the Second World War highly dependent on home and Commonwealth markets, and the continued belief in the importance of the Commonwealth was an important part of the business environment in postwar Britain. As well as colouring the attitudes of businessmen, keen to return to the prewar cartels and avoid direct competition with the United States and Germany, it coloured the attitudes of politicians, who remained ambivalent about participation in supra-national European institutions such as the European Coal and Steel Community (ECSC) and the EEC. Thus until Britain joined the EEC in 1973, British industry was to some extent shielded from international competition. Since anti-trust policy was also applied rather hesitantly during the early postwar period, domestic competition was also relatively restrained. The strengthening of competitive forces in Britain on both the international and domestic fronts during the 1970s and 1980s represents a major change in the business environment.

The Second World War also left its mark on technology in British industry. During the war, many British industrialists were brought face to face with the much higher labour productivity achieved in American industry, as the two economies were integrated in the Allied war effort. Wartime visits by British industrialists to the United States were followed up after the war by the Anglo-American Council on Productivity (AACP), which sponsored visits by productivity teams made up of managers and trade unionists in a wide range of industries. However, attempts to adopt American technology in British conditions were not very successful. As well as meeting the inevitable opposition of craft workers, who saw the value of their skills being eroded, American technology was unpopular with managers, who were not used to exercising the degree of shopfloor control needed to make it profitable (Lewchuk, 1987; Tolliday and Zeitlin, 1991). The antagonistic industrial relations that emerged during this period of technological upheaval formed an important part of the postwar industrial culture, and came to be seen as one of the major symptoms of the 'British disease' in the literature on economic decline. This was much less of a problem in Continental Europe because of a supply of unskilled labour from the countryside as agriculture contracted and from abroad in the form of temporary guest workers (Bardou *et al.*, 1982).

These two problems of markets and technology came to a head in the 1970s. Although Imperial Preference had been removed and tariffs reduced under GATT during the 1950s and 1960s, EEC entry in 1973 produced a severe competitive shock, while industrial relations, which had been simmering throughout the postwar period, exploded in the 1970s. The situation was exacerbated by the oil shocks of 1973–4 (OPEC I) and 1979–80 (OPEC II). The increase in the price of a major input inevitably hit manufacturing profitability, already reeling from the effects of increased competition within the EEC. Furthermore, OPEC II had an additional damaging effect on the competitiveness of British manufacturing through exchange rate appreciation. Since Britain was a net exporter of oil by the end of the 1970s, the increase in the price of oil improved the current account of the balance of payments and hence put upward pressure on the pound (Bean, 1987). After the recession of the 1980s, British manufacturing emerged substantially reduced in size, but as the decade progressed, it became clear that much of the deterioration in comparative labour productivity that had occurred in the 1970s was being reversed.

In some industries, the turn-round of productivity performance during the 1980s was staggering. In iron and steel, for example, German productivity rose from 125 per cent of the British level in 1973 to 263 per cent in 1979, before falling back to 89 per cent in 1989. In motor vehicles, German relative productivity peaked at 186 per cent of the British level before falling back to 124 per cent by 1989. In aerospace, the British improvement between 1979 and 1989 was even more dramatic, from 200 per cent to 101 per cent. By the end of the 1980s, labour productivity in British manufacturing was once again approaching German levels. Manufacturing then accounted for about 20 per cent of employment in Britain, about average for Europe. Germany and Japan, with substantially larger shares of employment in manufacturing, remained outliers in this respect.

The shake-out of labour that occurred during the recession of the early 1980s was largely unskilled (O'Mahony and Wagner, 1994). However, although there is now a renewed emphasis on shopfloor skills, Britain still lags behind much of Continental Europe in the provision of skilled shopfloor workers as a result of the deskilling during the Fordist era. Nevertheless, Britain now competes effectively in a number of skilled labour-intensive sectors, including general chemicals, pharmaceuticals, aerospace, motor vehicles and electronics.

Conclusions

British labour productivity performance in manufacturing over the last 120 years or so has not been as disastrous as is sometimes thought. In fact, poor productivity performance has really been confined to the period 1950–79, when a substantial gap opened up between Britain and most other West European countries (typified by Germany). This poor performance can be seen largely as a result of a failure in standardised mass production. Attempts to apply American-style mass production methods in Britain led to a serious deterioration in industrial relations. There were also problems in securing the markets to accept the high volume of standardised output produced by the new methods. Constraints imposed by the size and variability of the British market were compounded by fundamental changes in the world economy, leading to a decline in the importance of Britain's traditional Commonwealth markets and requiring a reorientation towards Continental Europe, traditionally seen as Germany's natural market.

Adjustment to these trends, which would have been difficult anyway, was delayed by a reluctance to allow competitive forces to direct the allocation of resources, a reluctance which was not fully overcome until the 1980s. By the time that the corporatist approach was finally abandoned in 1979, technological trends had moved back in Britain's favour. In the era of information technology, American-style mass production techniques were no longer seen as appropriate, and manufacturing technology moved back in the direction of flexible production methods, with an emphasis on customisation and skilled shopfloor labour.

Part 1

Measuring comparative productivity performance

2 International comparisons of productivity in manufacturing: benchmark estimates by industry

Introduction

There exist a number of studies comparing labour productivity in British manufacturing with the United States and Germany at a number of points in time since the 1930s. Some of these studies have become integrated into the economic history literature and are widely cited (Rostas, 1948a; Paige and Bombach, 1959). In this chapter, these existing estimates are gathered together on a common basis and extended with a number of additional new estimates going back as far as the first British *Census of Production* for 1907.

As well as discussing the methodology underlying these estimates, this chapter uses the individual industry estimates to shed some light on the growth process by identifying the particular strengths and weaknesses of countries, and showing how their comparative advantages have evolved over time. Detailed data are presented for up to 77 industries in appendix tables A2.1 and A2.2 (pp.28 and 31). To help in identifying patterns, the data are also presented at an intermediate level of disaggregation. The figures for these six industry groups are gathered together in tables 2.3 and 2.4 (p.26). The chemicals, metals and engineering industries are conventionally seen as 'heavy', or large-scale industries, while textiles and clothing, food, drink and tobacco and other industries are seen as 'light' or smaller-scale industries.

The benchmark estimates

Estimation methods for individual industries

There are basically two approaches to the establishment of comparative labour productivity levels in an industry. For the pre-1945 period, benchmarks are based on a direct comparison of physical output per worker, following the methodology of Rostas (1948a). Post-1945 estimates, however, follow the methodology of Paige and Bombach (1959), based on comparisons of net output per employee converted at price ratios obtained from

19

comparisons of factory gate prices reported in the production censuses of each country.

It is worth emphasising that these benchmark comparisons do not rely on exchange rates to convert output values in different currencies. Indeed, the methods of Rostas and Paige and Bombach can be seen as solutions to the pitfalls that plagued early attempts at comparative productivity analysis in manufacturing by Flux (1924, 1933). Differences in the value of net output per worker could be due to differences in prices or quantities. The use of a single market exchange rate implies that all the differences are due to quantity differences, an unwarranted assumption (Gilbert and Kravis, 1954). Flux was aware of the problem, and experimented with comparisons of physical output per worker for a number of industries. These figures were made available to and later published by Taussig (1924). The results, mainly for a number of metals and food industries, appeared to be broadly consistent with Flux's findings of a substantial US productivity lead, but the unrepresentativeness of the sample meant that this conclusion remained insecure. Rostas (1943; 1948a) extended Flux's method and provided estimates of comparative physical output per worker for a wider range of industries. There were a number of methodological innovations, including adjustments for coverage and weighting schemes for heterogeneous outputs, and we shall examine the details of these calculations in some specific examples below.

The next major development was the use of data on net output by Paige and Bombach (1959). Net output is defined in the British *Census of Production* as gross output *minus* the cost of materials and fuel used and the amount paid for industrial services. Whereas with the physical indicators a direct comparison between countries of labour productivity in an industry is straightforward because units are the same (say tons), with net output data the units are not directly comparable. Price ratios are needed to convert values in different currencies. Paige and Bombach solved the problem by deriving unit values from the Census data. The *Census of Production* provides data on both the quantity of sales in physical units and the value of those sales. Hence the factory gate price or unit value of a product can be obtained through dividing the value of sales by the quantity. If the average price of a product is say £1 in the United Kingdom and $2 in the the United States, then the appropriate price ratio is £1=$2. In general, such a price ratio, or purchasing power parity (PPP), will differ from the exchange rate, which is determined in foreign exchange markets, and may be subject to movements that are not closely related to movements in the relative price of manufactured goods, at least in the short run. This methodology has been used in most postwar studies of productivity in manufacturing (Maddison and van Ark, 1988; van Ark, 1993).

Table 2.1. *The tinplate industry, 1907–09*

	UK 1907	US 1909
Quantity (tons)	672,000	595,854
Value	£8,745,000	$46,335,611
Unit value (per ton)	£13.01	$77.76
Value of total output	£9,167,000	$47,969,645
Operatives in the trade	20,059	5,352
Estimated operatives	19,136	5,170
Output per operative (tons)	35.1	115.3

Sources: UK *Census of Production* (1907); US *Census of Manufactures* (1909).

It will be useful to look at some specific examples of the comparative labour productivity calculations, taken from the US/UK comparison for 1909/07 in Broadberry (1994b). Table 2.1 presents data for the tinplate industry, which is representative of industries where output can be aggregated relatively straightforwardly, in this case in tons produced. In the first line, physical output is taken directly from the Census, together with the value of this output, recorded in the second line. This information is sufficient to calculate the unit value in the third line. The value of total output for the trade is given in the fourth line. This usually differs from the value of output in the second line because physical volumes are not recorded for all items produced (say because there are by-products or secondary lines of output). The ratio of the second to the fourth line gives the proportion of the trade covered, and this ratio is then used to deflate the number of operatives in the trade to obtain the estimated number of operatives producing the main output in the sixth line. Dividing output from the first line by estimated operatives from the sixth line yields output per operative in the final line. The comparative labour productivity ratio for tinplate is thus 328.5. The unit value ratio of £1 = $5.98 can also be obtained from the third line, and can be used to check that the deviation from purchasing power parity is not implausibly large.

Table 2.2 presents information on the cars, cycles and motorcycles industry, which is representative of industries where aggregation of output is difficult because of the heterogeneity of production. In part (a), output is converted to automobile equivalents using relative unit values. Since relative unit values are different in the two countries, aggregate output can be calculated at both UK and US prices. Thus, for example, in British prices a car is worth 9.4 motorcycles, while in American prices a car is worth 8.0

Table 2.2. *The cars, cycles and motorcycles industry, 1907–09*

(a) Output UK 1907	Cars	Bicycles	Motorcycles
Number	10,300	615,300	3,700
Value (£000)	3,585	3,396	137
Unit value (£)	348.06	5.519	37.03
US 1909			
Number	126,593	168,824	18,628
Value ($000)	164,269	2,437	3,016
Unit value ($)	1,297.62	14.35	161.91

(b) Labour productivity	UK 1907	US 1909
Output in car equivalents:		
at UK prices	21,248	131,433
at US prices	17,607	130,795
Operatives in the trade	47,664	47,874
Estimated operatives	29,299	45,735
Output per operative:		
at UK prices	0.725	2.874
at US prices	0.600	2.860

Sources: UK *Census of Production* (1907); *US Census of Manufactures* (1909).

motorcycles. In part (b) the output in car equivalents can be combined with employment data (again suitably adjusted to take account of coverage) to obtain output per operative. Since output per operative is available at both British and American prices (Laspeyres and Paasche indices, respectively), the two estimates can be combined by taking the geometric mean (a Fisher index), to yield an overall US/UK labour productivity ratio of 434.7 for cars, cycles and motorcycles.

Most of the benchmark estimates from the pre-Second World War period have been calculated using the methods illustrated in tables 2.1 and 2.2, and developed by Rostas (1948a). The exception to this is machinery, where for 1937/35 Rostas used net output converted at a purchasing power parity exchange rate rather than the market exchange rate. For the other pre-Second World War years, I have used the average unit value ratio for the whole sample to compare net output in machinery.

Aggregation procedures

The aggregation method used in the pre-Second World War period has been to weight the individual industries by their shares in employment. This yields two estimates, depending on whether home country or foreign country weights are used, and the usual procedure to obtain a single estimate is to take the geometric mean (to obtain a Fisher index).

For the post-Second World War period the approach has been to convert net output at unit value ratios specific to each industry, following Paige and Bombach (1959). Aggregation is then via net output weights, again taking the geometric mean of home country and foreign country results. As production has become more complex and coverage ratios have fallen from over 40 per cent to under 20 per cent during the post-Second World War period, researchers at the University of Groningen have devoted more attention to the aggregation procedure (Maddison and van Ark, 1988; van Ark, 1993). They propose a stage-wise aggregation procedure, distinguishing between products, industries (broadly speaking SIC MLH level) and branches (broadly speaking SIC order levels). The first stage is to obtain unit value ratios for particular products. These are then aggregated up to industry level using gross output weights. The second stage is to obtain unit value ratios at branch level from the industry level unit values ratios, using net output weights. The third stage is to obtain the unit value ratio for aggregate manufacturing from the branch level unit value ratios, again using net output weights. The stage-wise aggregation procedure helps to prevent a product or an industry that is well represented in the sample from dominating the aggregate result. Thus, for example, if a large industry has very low coverage and a small industry has very high coverage, a simple aggregation procedure using weights based on the products sampled will assign too high a weight to the small industry. The stage-wise aggregation procedure will ensure that the large industry has a larger weight.

Double deflation

For the post-Second World War period, the comparative productivity ratios have been obtained by calculating net output per employee in the two countries and converting them to a common currency using a single unit value ratio. This is known as single deflation, and means assuming that the ratio of output prices is the same as the ratio of input prices. The theoretically correct procedure would be to obtain data on gross output and material inputs in both countries and to convert them to a common currency using separate price ratios for output and material inputs. This is known as double deflation. In practice, however, there is insufficient data on input prices to obtain reliable double deflated estimates and all the figures reported in this study are single deflated (Paige and Bombach, 1959: 82; van Ark, 1993: 41).

Product quality

The results are clearly highly dependent on the accurate matching of products and industries between countries. This naturally raises the issue of differences in product quality. For example, with the 1909/07 US/UK benchmark, is it possible that British goods were twice as good rather than that American productivity was twice as high? In fact, there are good grounds for believing that quality adjustments could not be that important. First, acceptance of the proposition that American manufacturers made greater use of mass production techniques to produce standardised products while British producers concentrated on flexible production of customised products does not automatically mean that we should make large adjustments for quality. We know that mass production techniques are associated with economies of scale and different factor proportions so that we should expect labour productivity differences. This is consistent with the well known wage differences between Britain and America at this time. I prefer to see the strategy of concentrating on mass production or flexible production as explaining these productivity differences rather than adjusting for quality differences to remove them.

Second, arguments for the importance of quality differences are usually based on an unrepresentative sample of consumer products, which accounts for only a small part of manufacturing. Third, even here, there is often a confusion between horizontal and vertical product differentiation. Vertical product differentiation is where consumers all have the same preferences but consume different brands because of, say, income constraints. Thus, for example, most people would agree that a Rolls Royce is better than a Ford Escort, but few people can afford a Rolls Royce. If one country was producing all Rolls Royces and another country producing all Ford Escorts, but both countries consumed both cars in the same proportions, clearly there would be a bias if comparative productivity was measured in terms of the number of cars produced per worker in each country.

However, horizontal product differentiation is where consumers have different preferences and hence choose to consume different brands. Suppose in country *A* consumers buy only check shirts that are made locally while in country *B* consumers buy only floral shirts that are made locally, but that there is free trade between the two countries. Suppose also that check shirts require more hand-finishing than floral shirts, so that labour productivity is higher in the production of floral shirts. If consumers in country *B* were prepared to pay a premium for the check shirts, it would be appropriate to make an adjustment for quality. However, if consumers in country *B* are not prepared to pay a premium, adjustment is inappropriate; the floral shirts are not regarded as vertically differentiated (higher quality), but merely horizontally differentiated (due to differences in tastes or fashion).

The standard approach in the benchmark studies has been to check for obvious cases of vertical product differentiation, which are normally indicated in the production census data, and to make adjustments accordingly. This can be seen very clearly in the detailed data appendices in Rostas (1948a), where careful consideration is given to the proportions of output in various classes.

Fourth, any substantial adjustment to the unit value ratios for quality would mean implausibly large deviations of the exchange rate from purchasing power parity. And fifth, although it was usually claimed that British goods were of superior quality in the early twentieth century, it has been more usual since about the 1960s to argue that British goods have been of inferior quality. And yet, as we shall see in chapter 3, time series and benchmark comparisons between Britain, the United States and Germany can be reconciled over the period 1850–1989 without making additional adjustments for quality despite the alleged shift of Britain from a high quality to a low quality producer.

A recent study by Mason et al. (1994) suggests a substantial allowance for quality in an international comparison of labour productivity in biscuits. However, some of this is an inappropriate adjustment for horizontal differentiation. Although different types of biscuits are consumed in Britain and Germany, there is free trade in biscuits between the two countries. British consumers have tastes for biscuits which can be made with less labour than German biscuits, and German preferences explain the need to tie up large amounts of labour in biscuit production in Germany. There is no extra boost to German living standards from this, since there are virtually no exports; foreigners are not prepared to pay the price premium for German biscuits. Furthermore, even if the adjustment were accepted for biscuits, there would be no reason to believe that this is representative of manufacturing as a whole. Indeed, in a study involving a range of industries in the United States, Germany and Japan, McKinsey Global Institute (1993) found that for a large range of products the Census data provide a reasonably good guide to comparative productivity, even after a very detailed analysis of product quality. Although for individual products there are sometimes quality adjustments of the order of 10 to 20 per cent, these adjustments are not all in the same direction, so that the adjustments for manufacturing as a whole, and even for major industrial sectors, tend to be fairly small, of the order of about 5 per cent. Most writers appear to believe that quality differences have become more important over time, so it is unlikely that the earlier benchmarks would require larger adjustments.

Table 2.3. *US/UK manufacturing output per employee, 1909/07 to 1987
(UK=100)*

	1909/07	1937/35	1950	1967/68	1975	1987
Chemicals	143	227	356	281	227	152
Metals	288	192	274	261	251	166
Engineering	203	289	337	294	191	186
Textile/Cloth	151	145	198	225	223	174
FDT	144	204	215	246	208	233
Other	227	211	285	276	275	208
Total	209	218	273	276	225	187

Source: Appendix table A2.1.

Table 2.4. *Germany/UK manufacturing
output per employee, 1935–87 (UK=100)*

	1935	1967/68	1987
Chemicals	123	124	88
Metals	116	137	96
Engineering	120	117	112
Textile/Cloth	97	108	109
FDT	41	94	114
Other	102	141	132
Total	102	119	113

Source: Appendix table A2.2.

Comparative productivity and comparative advantage

For the twentieth century we can examine comparative productivity ratios
in up to 77 manufacturing industries for the US/UK comparison and in up
to 32 industries for the Germany/UK comparison. Using the six industry
groups in tables 2.3 and 2.4, it appears that for most of the twentieth
century, between 1909/07 and 1967/68, British productivity performance
was better in the lighter industries, especially food, drink and tobacco
(FDT) and textiles. This is apparent from both the US/UK and
Germany/UK comparisons.

To what extent does this variation in comparative labour productivity
performance across industries reflect comparative advantage? Clearly,
there is no one-to-one mapping between variations in comparative labour
productivity and comparative advantage, since labour is not the only factor
of production. However, in manufacturing as a whole, labour's share of

Table 2.5. *Employment, by sector, in British manufacturing, 1907–89 (%)*

	1907	1924	1935	1948	1973	1989
Chemicals	2.8	3.5	3.7	5.1	5.6	11.2
Metals	6.9	6.7	6.5	7.5	6.5	2.8
Engineering	26.6	29.0	28.6	39.3	44.0	43.0
Textile/Cloth	38.6	34.6	29.8	20.8	14.1	10.8
FDT	8.8	9.5	11.1	10.0	10.5	12.1
Other	16.3	16.7	20.3	17.2	19.3	20.1
Total	100.0	100.0	100.0	100.0	100.0	100.0

Source: Appendix table A2.3.

value added has varied between about two-thirds and three-quarters over the twentieth century. It would clearly have been difficult for an industry with below average labour productivity performance to thrive, because the existence of a national unified labour market severely limited the extent to which low wages could be paid to offset low labour productivity (Salter, 1960). Hence it is not surprising to find a correspondence between industries in which a country has a relatively good labour productivity performance and a relatively strong export performance. Broadberry and Crafts (1992: 542), for example, note that for the 1930s there is a strong relationship between comparative labour productivity performance in Rostas'(1948a) sample and revealed comparative advantage as measured by Crafts and Thomas (1986).

The German productivity strength and export success in heavy industry, especially chemicals, is also apparent at this time. The US productivity advantage before the 1970s was also strongest in heavy industry, especially engineering. Since the 1970s, however, there seems to have been a change in comparative advantage, accompanied by a reduction in the dispersion of comparative productivity ratios around the aggregate manufacturing ratio. Most notably, British performance has dramatically improved in heavy industry, with very rapid productivity gains in chemicals, metals (especially steel) and engineering (notably motor vehicles).

These shifting patterns of comparative advantage are also reflected broadly in the data on sectoral shares of employment and net output in tables 2.5 and 2.6. Before the First World War, British manufacturing was highly specialised in textiles and clothing, which accounted for 38.6 per cent of manufacturing employment in 1907 and 29.3 per cent of net output. Since the First World War, however, there has been a steady decline in the importance of this sector, with a corresponding growth in importance of engineering and chemicals, particularly across the Second World War. The

Table 2.6. *Net output, by sector, in British manufacturing, 1907–89 (%)*

	1907	1924	1935	1948	1973	1989
Chemicals	5.0	6.1	7.0	7.0	10.5	17.1
Metals	8.4	6.6	7.0	8.2	7.1	3.7
Engineering	26.6	25.7	27.3	36.5	39.4	40.0
Textile/Cloth	29.3	27.3	19.9	17.9	9.6	5.6
FDT	14.7	16.2	17.7	12.9	12.9	12.9
Other	16.0	18.1	21.1	17.5	20.5	20.7
Total	100.0	100.0	100.0	100.0	100.0	100.0

Source: Appendix table A2.4.

1980s has seen a further boost in the relative importance of chemicals, at the expense of metal manufacture. A more detailed sectoral breakdown is given in appendix 2.2, which provides important background information for the detailed industry studies in part 3.

Conclusions

This chapter sets out the methodology underlying benchmark estimates of comparative labour productivity in individual manufacturing industries and the procedures used to obtain figures for aggregate manufacturing. Estimates based on production census data are provided for the US/UK and Germany/UK comparisons at benchmark years covering the period between 1907 to 1987. Allowing for problems of methodology and measurement, estimates for individual industries should be regarded as subject to a margin of error of the order of 10–20 per cent. Britain's better comparative labour productivity performance (i.e. smaller productivity shortfall) in lighter industries accords well with patterns of revealed comparative advantage, as would be expected where labour's share of income is large and there is a unified labour market.

APPENDIX 2.1 COMPARATIVE LABOUR PRODUCTIVITY LEVELS BY INDUSTRY

Table A2.1. *US/UK comparative labour productivity, by industry, 1909/07 to 1967/68 (UK=100)*

	1909/07	1914/12	1925/24	1929/30	1937/35	1947/48	1950	1967/68
Seedcrushing	77		151	131	105			277
Coke	115		306	341	236			
Mineral oil refining			264	346			302	224

Table A2.1. *(cont.)*

	1909/07	1914/12	1925/24	1929/30	1937/35	1947/48	1950	1967/68
General chemicals							372	258
Pharmaceuticals								305
Soap & detergents	221	233	318	326	285	281	249	259
Plastics, synthetics								216
Fertilisers	158	243	203	155				196
Matches					336	248	376	
Chemicals & allied	143		292	315	227		356	281
Iron & steel (general)	283	280	357					259
Blast furnaces			427	480	362	417	408	
Iron & steel smelt/roll				293	197		269	
Tinplate	328							
Iron & steel foundries				270	154		202	
Aluminium								348
Copper	425							245
Lead & zinc	91		254	327				
Metal manufacture	288		371	329	192		274	261
Mech. engineering	203		312	292	268			
Agric. mach. (exc. tractors)							429	
Agric. mach. (inc. tractors)								146
Machine tools							221	162
Electrical mach.							239	255
Radio/electronic comp.								193
Electronic tubes							355	
Broadcast recept.eqt.								288
Radios					347	336	400	
Household appliances							412	239
Electric lamps			587	446	543		356	
Shipbuilding	95	115	164	154			111	185
Motor vehicles	435		720			365	466	438
Motor cars				725	294	284		
Motorcycles				135				
Bicycles				176		180		
Aircraft				315				381
Railway rolling stock			114	173				
Cans & metal boxes					577	496	561	466
Engineering	203		373	333	289		337	294
Man-made fibres								194
Rayon			169	162	185		226	
Spinning								203
Weaving								225
Cotton	151	174	180	194	150	162	249	
Linen			188	202				
Woollen & worsted	112	120	103	131	131		185	208
Jute			200	148		169		
Rope & twine	195	257	205	209		151		188
Hosiery	230	217	186	178	156		187	209

Table A2.1. *(cont.)*

	1909/07	1914/12	1925/24	1929/30	1937/35	1947/48	1950	1967/68
Carpets				223		315		250
Leather							168	208
Outer & underwear							170	
Weatherproof outerwear								204
Men's & boys' outerwear								223
Boots & shoes	170		136	143	141	151	171	173
Textiles & clothing	151		158	169	145		198	225
Grain milling	178		212	206	173	194	183	255
Biscuits				352	345	204		349
Fish curing			46	39	50	95		
Milk & milk products								182
Butter & cheese	196		266	239				
Sugar	110					128	148	169
Beet sugar			108	95	102	97		
Cocoa/sugar confection			307	273				299
Fruit/veg. products								248
Canned fruit & veg.							235	
Margarine			104	145	152	121		405
Manufactured ice	134		263	172	219	75		
Brewing & malting	146	149			201	198	300	294
Spirits	167	173						
Tobacco	108	99	127	134	160		251	371
Food, drink & tobacco	144		209	211	204		215	246
Bricks	217	220	235	213	132	166		169
Glass								218
Glass containers			235	208	264	287	274	
Cement	219	268	241	167	99	115	116	191
Furniture								253
Paper & board	262	222	258	293	247		338	290
Rubber								224
Rubber tyres & tubes			353	337	285	176	241	
Other rubber goods							250	
Linoleum & oilcloth			197	231	170		256	256
Miscellaneous	227		255	252	211		285	276
Total manufacturing	209		274	263	218		273	276

SOURCES
1909/07: Broadberry (1994b).
1914/12, 1925/24 and 1929/30: Output and employment data from the UK *Census of Production* and the US *Census of Manufactures*, compared using physical indicators, as in Rostas (1948a).
1937/35: Rostas (1948a).
1947/48: Frankel (1957).
1950: Paige and Bombach (1959).
1967/68: Smith *et al.* (1982), geometric mean of figures at UK and US prices.

Table A2.2. *Germany/UK comparative labour productivity, by industry, 1907–87 (UK=100)*

	1907	1924	1930	1935	1937	1967/68	1987
Seedcrushing				50			
Coke		124	209	174		102	
Chemicals						120	89
Sulphuric acid		145	252	182			
Soap				110			71
Chemicals & allied				123		124	88
Steelworks				116	103	149	81
Blast furnaces		156	177	148	118		
Iron foundries			124	112	118		
Non-ferrous metals						113	144
Zinc		49	121	85			
Metal manufacture				116		137	96
Mech./elec. engineering			103	112		111	109
Motor vehicles	192	112	187	141		141	111
Engineering				120		117	112
Rayon			135	109			
Cotton spinning		114		100	90	133	133
Cotton weaving				69	52	149	84
Jute			121	116	100	148	
Leather	139		95	99		97	117
Clothing						100	
Boots & shoes			129	121		85	82
Textiles & clothing				97		108	109
Grain milling						65	82
Sugar						50	
Beet sugar	49			33			
Veg./animal fats; marg.						178	195
Margarine				52			96
Brewing & malting	92			62		105	70
Tobacco		27		26		114	83
Food, drink & tobacco				41		94	114
Bricks						182	134
Cement	133	99	109	87		150	81
Paper & board						140	180
Furniture							199
Rubber						94	102
Rubber tyres & tubes				112			
Miscellaneous				102		141	132
Total manufacturing				102		119	113

SOURCES
1907, 1924, 1930, 1935 and 1937: Broadberry and Fremdling (1990).
1967/68: Smith *et al.* (1982), geometric mean of figures at UK and German prices.
1987: O'Mahony (1992a).

CLASSIFICATION

I have largely followed the 1968 British Standard Industrial Classification (SIC), as in Business Statistics Office (1978), *Historical Record of the Census of Production 1907 to 1970* (London: HMSO), although occasionally I have had to break down a Minimum List Heading (MLH) to do justice to the pre-Second World War data. Thus, for example, motor cars and motorcycles, respectively, are sub-categories of motor vehicles. For presentation purposes, I have followed the 1948 SIC convention of placing food, drink and tobacco (order III) after textiles and clothing (orders XIII–XV), since this keeps the lighter industries together. I have also followed the prewar and 1948 SIC conventions of classifying seedcrushing with chemicals rather than food.

BENCHMARK DATES

Benchmark dates refer to the countries in the specific order cited. Hence, for example, the US/UK benchmark for 1909/07 is derived from US data for 1909 and UK data for 1907, while the Germany/UK benchmark for 1967/68 is derived from German data for 1967 and UK data for 1968.

APPENDIX 2.2 EMPLOYMENT AND NET OUTPUT SHARES BY INDUSTRY IN BRITISH MANUFACTURING (%)

Table A2.3. *Employment, by sector, in UK manufacturing, 1907–89 (%)*

	1907	1924	1930	1935	1948	1958	1968	1973	1979	1989
Chemicals	2.6	2.9	2.9	3.2	4.6	5.3	5.2	5.1	5.8	10.9
Coal/petroleum products	0.2	0.6	0.6	0.5	0.5	0.7	0.5	0.5	0.5	0.3
Chemicals & allied	2.8	3.5	3.5	3.7	5.1	6.0	5.7	5.6	6.3	11.2
Metal manufacture	6.9	6.7	6.3	6.5	7.5	7.3	7.0	6.5	6.1	2.8
Mechanical engineering	8.4	7.8	7.6	7.7	11.0	11.8	12.5	11.9	12.8	11.9
Instrument engineering	0.4	0.4	0.7	0.7	1.2	1.3	2.2	2.0	2.2	1.8
Electrical engineering	1.3	2.9	3.9	4.8	7.1	8.4	9.6	10.2	9.7	11.9
Shipbuilding	4.3	4.4	4.1	2.7	4.4	3.5	2.4	2.4	2.2	1.4
Vehicles	6.6	8.4	9.0	6.7	9.0	9.9	10.1	10.4	10.9	9.3
Other metal goods	5.6	5.1	5.5	6.0	6.6	6.8	6.8	7.1	7.1	6.7
Engineering	26.6	29.0	30.8	28.6	39.3	41.7	43.6	44.0	44.9	43.0
Textiles	25.0	22.5	19.2	18.6	12.6	10.8	8.5	7.7	6.5	4.3
Leather & fur	1.2	1.2	1.2	1.2	0.9	0.7	0.6	0.6	0.5	0.4
Clothing & footwear	12.4	10.9	9.9	10.0	7.4	6.8	5.7	5.8	5.4	6.1
Textiles & clothing	38.6	34.6	30.3	29.8	20.9	18.3	14.8	14.1	12.4	10.8
Food, drink & tobacco	8.8	9.5	10.3	11.1	10.0	9.5	10.1	10.5	10.6	12.1

Table A2.3. *(cont.)*

	1907	1924	1930	1935	1948	1958	1968	1973	1979	1989
Bricks/pottery/glass/cement	4.1	4.0	4.4	4.9	4.1	3.9	3.8	3.7	3.6	4.4
Timber & furniture	3.5	3.4	4.3	4.8	3.9	3.2	3.3	3.6	3.6	4.3
Paper, printing & publishing	6.3	6.5	7.3	7.8	6.1	7.0	7.5	7.6	7.7	9.5
Other manufacturing	2.4	2.8	2.8	2.8	3.1	3.1	4.2	4.4	4.8	1.9
Miscellaneous	16.3	16.7	18.8	20.3	17.2	17.2	18.8	19.3	19.7	20.1

Table A2.4. *Net output, by sector, in UK manufacturing, 1907–89 (%)*

	1907	1924	1930	1935	1948	1958	1968	1973	1979	1989
Chemicals	4.5	5.0	5.3	5.9	6.2	8.5	8.7	8.9	9.8	15.4
Coal/petroleum products	0.5	1.1	1.3	1.1	0.8	1.2	1.2	1.6	3.8	1.7
Chemicals & allied	5.0	6.1	6.6	7.0	7.0	9.7	9.9	10.5	13.6	17.1
Metal manufacture	8.4	6.6	5.9	7.0	8.2	8.8	7.0	7.1	5.0	3.7
Mechanical engineering	9.6	7.0	7.3	7.7	10.8	12.3	12.8	11.5	12.6	11.1
Instrument engineering	0.4	0.4	0.7	0.6	1.0	1.2	2.0	1.6	1.8	1.4
Electrical engineering	1.4	2.9	4.3	4.9	6.3	7.8	9.0	8.8	8.8	11.2
Shipbuilding	4.4	3.4	3.8	2.3	3.8	2.9	1.8	1.7	1.6	0.9
Vehicles	5.6	7.7	8.4	6.7	8.3	10.3	10.3	9.8	10.0	10.3
Other metal goods	5.2	4.3	4.6	5.1	6.3	6.3	6.0	6.0	6.1	5.1
Engineering	26.6	25.7	29.1	27.3	36.5	40.8	41.9	39.4	40.9	40.0
Textiles	19.8	18.1	12.4	12.3	11.4	7.7	6.9	6.2	4.4	2.6
Leather & fur	1.2	1.3	1.2	1.2	1.2	0.6	0.5	0.4	0.4	0.3
Clothing & footwear	8.3	7.9	7.0	6.4	5.3	3.9	3.2	3.0	3.0	2.7
Textiles & clothing	29.3	27.3	20.6	19.9	17.9	12.2	10.6	9.6	7.8	5.6
Food, drink & tobacco	14.7	16.2	17.7	17.7	12.9	11.9	12.0	12.9	12.6	12.9
Bricks/pottery/glass/cement	3.5	3.9	4.2	4.8	4.0	3.7	3.8	4.3	4.1	5.4
Timber & furniture	3.1	3.1	3.8	4.2	3.6	2.7	3.0	3.8	3.2	3.2
Paper, printing & publishing	6.8	8.2	9.2	9.3	6.9	7.4	7.8	8.2	8.5	10.8
Other manufacturing	2.6	2.9	2.9	2.8	3.0	2.8	4.0	4.2	4.3	1.3
Miscellaneous	16.0	18.1	20.1	21.1	17.5	16.6	18.6	20.5	20.1	20.7

SOURCES FOR TABLES A2.3 AND A2.4

Business Statistics Office (1978), *Historical Record of the Census of Production 1907 to 1970* (London: HMSO) and *Census of Production*

3 Labour productivity in aggregate manufacturing: Britain, the United States and Germany

Introduction

In chapter 2, we established comparative levels of labour productivity in benchmark years in a number of individual manufacturing industries for Britain, the United States and Germany. We also discussed the aggregation procedures used to establish the aggregate picture for the benchmark years. In this chapter we see how these benchmark estimates can be combined with time series evidence to build up a consistent picture of comparative productivity over time at the level of aggregate manufacturing. These estimates, covering the period from the mid-nineteenth century, build upon work presented originally in Broadberry (1993, 1994a).

The picture that emerges is one of a surprising degree of stationarity in the comparative labour productivity positions of the three countries since the late nineteenth century. The United States has had a large persistent labour productivity lead over the United Kingdom of the order of 2:1 extending back to the mid-nineteenth century, although there have been sustained swings at times, particularly covering major wars. Furthermore, although the size of the US labour productivity lead grew in the period between 1820 and 1850, at no stage was Britain the labour productivity leader in manufacturing. The labour productivity level of Germany has been broadly on a par with Britain since the 1870s, after a period of catching up during the third quarter of the nineteenth century. Again there have been some sustained swings in the Germany/UK labour productivity position, particularly with the growing German productivity lead over the United Kingdom during the 1970s and its subsequent reversal during the 1980s.

Methodology

The basic methodology is to establish comparative US/UK and Germany/UK levels of labour productivity in manufacturing during a year in the middle of the sample period, and then to extrapolate backwards and forwards using time series on labour productivity. In practice, the

34

extrapolation of benchmark comparisons to other years on the basis of time series does not always yield identical results to direct benchmark comparisons for those other years. This is largely because of inaccuracies and inconsistencies in data sources but is also due at least in part to traditional index number problems (Krijnse Locker and Faerber, 1984; Szilagyi, 1984). Thus, for example, it is likely that a Laspeyres quantity index overstates true growth and a Paasche quantity index understates true growth (Wonnacott and Wonnacott, 1990: 669). Hence finally, additional benchmark estimates for other years are used to provide checks on the extrapolations.

Benchmark estimates

The direct benchmark comparisons are reported in parentheses in table 3.1. All comparisons are made on a bilateral basis with the United Kingdom as numeraire country. These benchmark estimates have been discussed in some detail in chapter 2. However, it should be noted that the benchmark comparisons have in some cases been made for slightly different years in the countries being compared, due to the availability of production census material. This means that the original benchmark comparisons must be adjusted to bring them onto a common year basis for table 3.1(a). Thus, for example, the 1907 US/UK benchmark estimate of 201.9 from Broadberry (1994b) is actually based on a comparison of the 1909 US *Census of Manufactures* with the 1907 UK *Census of Production*. The direct comparison for 1909/07 yields a value of 208.6. However, this is too favourable to the United States, since there was positive labour productivity growth in the United States between 1907 and 1909. Reducing US labour productivity back to its 1907 level yields a value for comparative labour productivity in 1907 of 201.9. Similar adjustments have been made to the US/UK benchmarks for 1937 and 1968 and to the Germany/UK benchmark for 1968.

Time series

The benchmark estimates leave too many gaps to analyse long-term comparative productivity performance in detail. Time series on real output and employment in manufacturing are available from the middle of the nineteenth century for all three countries, Britain, the United States and Germany. These can be used to construct time series of labour productivity for each country, so that we can establish movements in comparative labour productivity over time in index number form. These time series of comparative labour productivity can then be linked to benchmark estimates of US/UK and Germany/UK productivity levels to provide a more

Table 3.1. *Manufacturing output per person employed, 1869–1989 and 1819–1907 (UK=100)*

(a) 1869–1989	US/UK		Germany/UK	
1869	203.8			
1871			92.6	
1875			100.0	
1879	187.8			
1889	195.4		94.7	
1899	194.8		99.0	
1907	190.0	(201.9)	106.4	
1913	212.9		119.0	
1920	222.8			
1925	234.2		95.2	
1929	249.9		104.7	
1935	207.8		*102.0	(102.0)
1937	*208.3	(208.3)	99.9	
1950	262.6	(273.4)	96.0	[99.5]
1958	250.0		111.1	
1968	242.6	(272.7)	120.0	(130.4)
1975	207.5	(224.7)	132.9	
1980	192.8		140.2	
1985	182.3		121.5	
1987	188.8	(186.6)	107.8	(112.7)
1989	177.0		105.1	

(b) 1819–1907	US/UK		Germany/UK	
1819/21	148.8			
1839/41	179.4			
1849/51	207.6	[200.3]	87.5	
1859/61	238.5		84.6	
1869/71	192.0		92.6	
1907	*201.9	(201.9)	106.4	

Notes:
* Benchmark year from which the time series are extrapolated. The figures in brackets are actual benchmark comparisons: (.) indicates industry-of-origin benchmarks using physical indicators or factory gate prices; [.] indicates expenditure-based benchmarks using purchasing power parities.
Sources: Benchmark comparisons for US/UK figures are derived from: 1849/51, James and Skinner (1985); 1907, Broadberry (1994b); 1937, Rostas (1948a); 1950, Paige and Bombach (1959); 1968, Smith *et al.* (1982); 1975, van Ark (1990c); 1987, van Ark (1992). Benchmark comparisons for Germany/UK figures are derived from: 1935, Broadberry and Fremdling (1990); 1950, Broadberry (1993); 1968, Smith *et al.* (1982); 1987, O'Mahony (1992a). Time series of output and employment are listed in appendix 3.1.

complete picture of the evolution of comparative productivity levels over time.

In table 3.1(a) the starting point for the extrapolations over the period 1869–1989 is the mid-1930s, or roughly halfway through the sample period. This is preferable to using more recent benchmarks, which would require extrapolations of more than 100 years to obtain estimates for the 1870s. For the extrapolations over the period 1819–1907 in table 3.1(b), I have used the 1907 benchmark for the US/UK, but continued to use the 1935 benchmark for Germany/UK, since this is the earliest available benchmark for this comparison.

The time series are presented in detail in appendix 3.1, together with annual estimates of comparative labour productivity. Here we examine some of the general principles followed. First, I have tried to ensure that the series are collected on the same basis for the different countries. For the post-1950 period, the time series are generally drawn from production census information on net output and employment, with net output in current prices deflated by a price index for manufactures. However, for the pre-1950 period indices of industrial production have been used due to problems with the availability of real net output indices. For all three countries these production indices are based on gross output indicators for individual industries, weighted by net output or employment shares (Fabricant, 1940; Carter *et al.*,1948). Since pre-1950 benchmarks are also based on comparisons of physical indicators there is a consistency between the time series and cross-sectional evidence before as well as after 1950.

A second general principle has been to take both output and employment series from the same source where possible, since we are interested primarily in productivity. This gives a strong presumption in favour of production census sources where possible, since we can then be sure that output and employment refer to the same firms. A third general principle followed has been to try to purge time series for 'industry' of mining, public utilities and construction. This is particularly relevant for Germany, where Hoffmann's (1965) most accessible series refer to industry rather than just manufacturing. All time series for all three countries during the period 1869–1989 refer to manufacturing only. However, for Germany, the earlier data refer to total industry, and must be treated more cautiously.

Boundary changes

There have been a number of boundary changes during the period under consideration, which have to be dealt with in the construction of continuous time series. The most important changes affect Germany. Here, I follow the procedure of Hoffmann (1965: 2) who reports figures for output and employment corresponding to the following territories: 1850–70 the territories of the later German Reich excluding Alsace–Lorraine; 1871–1917 the territories of the German Reich including Alsace–Lorraine; 1918–44 the territories of the German Reich excluding Austria and the Sudetenland, but from 1934 including the Saar; 1945–59 the territories of the German Federal Republic excluding West Berlin and the Saar. Beyond Hoffmann's period, from 1959 to 1989 I work with the official figures of the German Federal Republic including West Berlin and the Saar. Data after 1989 continue to refer to the old German Federal Republic, excluding the new Länder from the former German Democratic Republic. It should be noted that the discontinuities of labour productivity across these major boundary changes are much smaller than the discontinuities of output and employment. Furthermore, it is clear that despite the geographical and political discontinuities, there is a fundamental economic continuity in the German territories considered here, which were perceived as a major force in international trade.

For the United Kingdom, I have simply followed the procedure of Feinstein (1972), who provides estimates including Southern Ireland before 1920 and excluding Southern Ireland after 1920, with an overlap in 1920. In this case, the proportional changes are small for output and employment as well as labour productivity. For the United States, figures before 1960 exclude Alaska and Hawaii, which added less than 0.3 per cent to GDP in 1960. As in the UK case, overlapping estimates were used to adjust the time series for the impact of these geographic changes (Maddison, 1991: 221).

Results

The results are shown in table 3.1, which combines both time series and cross-sectional information. In part (a), the first column reports the level of labour productivity in the United States relative to the United Kingdom, based on extrapolation from the 1937 benchmark estimate. The additional figures in brackets are additional benchmark comparisons carried out by various authors, and can be seen as checks on the plausibility of the time series extrapolations. In general, there is a good measure of agreement between the time series extrapolations and the benchmark estimates. The biggest discrepancy is for 1968, when the time series extrapolation gives US labour productivity at 242.6 per cent of the British level, while the benchmark estimate suggests a value of 272.7. However, by 1987 the discrepancy was tiny, with a time series estimate of 188.8 compared with a benchmark estimate of 186.6. Annual estimates of comparative labour productivity are provided in appendix table A3.1(c).

Part (b) of table 3.1 gives time series extrapolations for the period

1819–1907. Note that the comparisons are for slightly different years, due to data availability. In general, US data was available only for *Census of Manufactures* years (1819, 1839, 1849...), while British data was available only for *Population Census* years (1821, 1841, 1851...). German data is for the years (1851, 1861...). For the Germany/UK case, I continue to base the time series extrapolations on the 1935 benchmark used in part (a), since this is the earliest available benchmark. However, for the US/UK case, I prefer to use the 1907 benchmark for the base, since this is the earliest industry-of-origin study using physical indicators. The benchmark check for 1849/51 is reported in square brackets to indicate that this is based on converting value added at a single purchasing power parity, and should not be treated as reliably as the industry-of-origin benchmarks.

US/UK

Let us now consider closely the results for the US/UK comparison. The first point to note is that the United States already had a labour productivity lead in manufacturing of the order of 2:1 by the middle of the nineteenth century, a point confirmed both by time series extrapolation from the 1930s and by the direct benchmark estimate for 1849/51.

The second point to note is that there has been a considerable degree of persistence in this 2:1 ratio since 1850. Although there have been sustained swings at times, particularly surrounding major wars, US/UK comparative labour productivity in manufacturing over the whole period 1850–1989 is best described as stationary, exhibiting neither upward nor downward trend.

Third, note that one of the largest swings in comparative productivity was across the American Civil War. Between 1859 and 1879 the relative labour productivity position of US manufacturing deteriorated substantially. In fact the fall in the US relative productivity position across the Civil War would be even greater if the Gallman (1960) series for real net output in US manufacturing were used rather than the Frickey (1947) volume index of production, which is more comparable to the Hoffmann (1955) index for the United Kingdom. However, the Gallman series suggests a substantial fall in absolute as well as relative labour productivity in the United States during the Civil War decade, which seems to go too far in revising the Beard–Hacker thesis that the Civil War stimulated industrialisation (Beard and Beard, 1930; Hacker, 1940). Indeed, Cochran (1969) and Engerman (1971), both sympathetic to the revisionist position, cite the Frickey index approvingly.

Fourth, the other major swings in comparative US/UK labour productivity occurred across the two world wars. The peak US lead was in the early 1950s. If we use the direct benchmark estimate from this period, Paige and Bombach (1959) suggest a US lead getting closer to 3:1 than 2:1 in 1950. However, this was followed by substantial British catching up, especially from the 1970s, so that by the end of the 1980s the US lead was back under the 2:1 level.

Fifth, although there was a substantial rise in the US labour productivity lead between about 1820 and 1850, at no stage was Britain the productivity leader in manufacturing. I shall argue in part 2 that this is consistent with the literature emanating from the work of Habakkuk (1962) on the implications of labour scarcity in the New World. However, it should be noted that this conclusion differs from that of Frankel (1957: 28–9) who believed that the United States overtook Britain in terms of manufacturing labour productivity in about 1830. In fact, the difference between Frankel's results and the results of this chapter are easy to explain. Rostas (1948a) extrapolated from his mid-1930s benchmark back to 1907, obtaining a result broadly in line with our benchmark estimate for 1907. Frankel then extrapolated back further simply by making assumptions about productivity growth in Britain and America. However, he made no allowance for the interruption to American productivity growth caused by the Civil War, simply assuming that the rapid American *post-bellum* growth rate had applied throughout the nineteenth century.

Germany/UK

Turning to the Germany/UK comparison, the first point to note is that German manufacturing had already achieved British levels of labour productivity by the end of the second major period of promotional activity (*Gründerperiode*) during the early 1870s. Although there is not enough information to construct a full Germany/UK benchmark comparison for the period before the First World War, the information that is available for selected industries, in appendix table A2.2 (p.000), is consistent with this picture.

Second, as in the US/UK comparison, there has been a considerable degree of persistence in the Germany/UK labour productivity ratio in manufacturing. Although there have been sustained swings, again there has been no clear trend, either upwards or downwards, over the period since the mid-1870s.

Third, the two world wars have again seen major swings in the comparative productivity position of Germany and Britain, but this time with Britain gaining. Clearly, the two world wars had an even more devastating impact on Germany than they did on Britain, but with both countries losing out relative to the United States.

Fourth, the other major swing in comparative productivity occurred over the 1970s and 1980s. Slow productivity growth in Britain during the 1970s led to a substantial German lead by 1980, a lead which was then subsequently almost eliminated by the end of the 1980s with a decade of relatively rapid productivity growth in Britain.

Fifth, although there was a period of catching up by Germany in the third quarter of the nineteenth century, the labour productivity gap between British and German manufacturing at this time was never very large. I would see this as consistent with the view emphasised by Crafts (1985) that Britain's achievement in the nineteenth century was really to have a large rather than an especially productive industrial sector.

Allowing for hours worked

So far, we have worked with labour productivity on a per employee basis. To calculate labour productivity on a per hour basis requires the introduction of another potential source of inaccuracy, and in general I have preferred to use the per employee concept in this study, particularly since there has been little quantitative historical work on hours. Nevertheless, we can establish that with the current state of knowledge the above conclusions about comparative levels of labour productivity in manufacturing would still hold on a per hour basis, since working hours have moved in broadly similar ways in all three countries. Maddison's (1991) figures on average annual hours worked per employee for the whole economy are reported in table 3.2(a). In fact, little is known about hours outside manufacturing for the pre-1950 period, so these figures can be regarded as representative of the manufacturing sector. For the post-1950 period, van Ark's (1993) more detailed figures for manufacturing alone are reported in table 3.2(b). Although the long-run trends are similar in the three countries, there is some evidence of divergence during the 1980s, particularly between Germany and the United States. For 1987, however, this would merely lower the US/UK ratio by about 8 per cent and raise the Germany/UK ratio by a similar amount. Clearly these adjustments are not trivial, but neither do they substantially change the overall picture of the productivity rankings among the three countries.

Conclusions

In this chapter the benchmark estimates of chapter 2 are extended to provide annual estimates of comparative labour productivity in manufacturing for Britain, the United States and Germany. The results show a high degree of stationarity in the US/UK and Germany/UK comparisons,

Table 3.2. *Annual hours worked per person, 1870–1987*

(a) Whole economy	UK	US	Germany
1870	2984	2964	2941
1890	2807	2789	2765
1913	2624	2605	2584
1929	2286	2342	2284
1938	2267	2062	2316
1950	1958	1867	2316
1960	1913	1795	2081
1973	1688	1717	1804
1987	1557	1608	1620
(b) Manufacturing	UK	US	Germany
1950	2017	2033	2331
1960	2045	1916	2102
1973	1849	1905	1839
1987	1763	1909	1630

Sources: Whole economy: Maddison (1991), table C9. Manufacturing: van Ark (1993), appendix tables III.18, III.20, IV.3.

with the United States retaining a roughly 2:1 labour productivity advantage in manufacturing and with Germany and Britain at roughly similar levels.

APPENDIX 3.1 REAL OUTPUT AND EMPLOYMENT IN MANUFACTURING

Table A3.1(a). *Real output and employment in manufacturing, 1869–1989* (*1929=100*)

	UK		US		Germany	
Year	Output	Employment	Output	Employment	Output	Employment
1869	29.3	66.9	7.1	19.9		
1870	31.8	68.8			16.3	
1871	34.6	70.8			18.2	142.1
1872	35.4	71.7			20.9	
1873	36.2	72.1			21.8	
1874	37.0	72.2			22.2	
1875	37.0	72.3			22.0	45.6
1876	36.6	71.8			22.3	
1877	37.4	71.5			22.0	
1878	36.6	70.5			22.7	

Table A3.1(a). *(cont.)*

	UK		US		Germany	
Year	Output	Employment	Output	Employment	Output	Employment
1879	34.5	67.6	10.2	26.6	23.0	
1880	40.1	72.3			22.3	
1881	41.6	74.1			23.4	
1882	44.3	75.9			23.3	50.0
1883	44.6	76.6			25.0	
1884	42.4	73.0			26.1	
1885	40.4	72.9			26.5	52.9
1886	40.1	73.0			27.0	54.5
1887	43.9	75.9			28.6	55.8
1888	46.9	79.0			30.1	57.6
1889	50.3	82.4	18.3	38.3	33.2	60.0
1890	50.7	85.5	19.7	39.9	33.5	62.1
1891	51.2	83.1	20.2	41.1	34.2	61.8
1892	47.9	81.5	21.9	43.6	35.0	61.6
1893	47.8	84.5	19.4	42.1	36.3	61.7
1894	49.4	82.4	18.8	40.0	38.4	62.3
1895	52.5	84.1	22.4	43.6	41.5	64.1
1896	59.7	86.6	20.4	42.7	43.7	67.3
1897	57.3	87.9	22.0	44.2	44.7	69.9
1898	60.6	89.1	25.1	45.4	47.4	72.3
1899	63.0	90.6	27.5	50.8	48.7	74.1
1900	62.3	90.3	27.7	52.8	48.6	75.9
1901	62.1	90.2	30.9	55.5	48.6	74.8
1902	62.3	90.4	35.5	60.4	49.6	74.5
1903	60.8	90.9	35.4	62.7	53.0	76.0
1904	61.2	90.4	34.2	59.1	55.2	78.0
1905	66.5	92.1	29.0	66.1	57.6	80.0
1906	69.6	94.3	41.6	69.6	59.7	82.2
1907	71.5	95.0	42.1	72.8	64.1	83.7
1908	65.4	91.6	33.7	65.2	64.8	82.4
1909	66.2	92.4	43.4	72.7	66.3	82.4
1910	66.9	96.2	45.1	76.0	68.9	84.9
1911	72.6	98.6	42.7	76.0	73.1	87.1
1912	75.6	99.6	51.3	79.4	78.6	89.5
1913	80.5	102.2	53.8	80.2	80.9	90.4
1914	75.0		51.1	77.4		
1915	78.9		59.9	80.9		
1916	73.9		71.2	95.4		
1917	68.4		70.6	102.0		
1918	66.4		69.8	104.0		
1919	74.3		61.0	100.3		
1920	81.7	110.5	66.0	100.1		
1921	63.6	86.9	53.5	77.4		
1922	74.0	90.9	68.1	84.7		

Table A3.1(a). *(cont.)*

	UK		US		Germany	
Year	Output	Employment	Output	Employment	Output	Employment
1923	79.3	93.3	76.9	96.2		
1924	87.3	94.9	73.4	90.2		
1925	90.0	95.5	81.9	92.7	84.7	98.8
1926	87.1	92.8	86.2	94.7	75.9	87.0
1927	96.3	98.7	87.1	93.5	97.3	100.8
1928	96.1	98.6	90.1	93.8	98.4	103.6
1929	100.0	100.0	100.0	100.0	100.0	100.0
1930	95.7	93.0	85.6	89.2	88.4	90.3
1931	89.2	86.8	72.0	75.6	74.0	77.1
1932	89.7	88.1	53.8	63.9	64.5	65.8
1933	96.3	91.4	62.8	68.9	71.0	70.1
1934	105.1	95.6	69.1	79.9	85.6	81.9
1935	114.6	97.9	82.8	85.1	102.3	89.7
1936	125.3	103.3	96.8	92.2	112.9	96.7
1937	132.9	108.5	103.3	101.2	122.3	104.6
1938	129.0	106.9	80.9	87.4	136.3	110.4
1939			102.5	95.5		
1940			118.6	104.3		
1941			157.9	125.7		
1942			197.2	146.1		
1943			238.1	166.3		
1944			232.5	163.1		
1945			196.5	145.5		
1946	135.0		160.6	139.1		
1947	142.8		178.3	145.9		
1948	155.7	127.2	184.2	146.5		
1949	165.7	129.5	173.5	136.1		
1950	177.1	132.8	201.1	143.5	77.8	63.6
1951	184.0	144.5	206.2	151.9	89.7	71.3
1952	183.3	141.6	225.5	156.0	101.5	73.8
1953	201.2	142.9	251.6	166.1	113.2	76.9
1954	222.4	146.0	240.1	156.7	126.7	81.6
1955	234.4	150.5	273.9	163.4	148.3	89.3
1956	237.4	150.5	282.9	166.9	160.0	95.4
1957	242.4	151.4	279.9	166.2	170.9	98.7
1958	252.1	148.1	265.2	155.7	179.9	99.6
1959	270.6	148.4	300.2	161.9	196.9	100.7
1960	296.4	154.3	304.2	162.9	223.2	106.0
1961	301.0	156.0	306.0	158.7	235.9	109.1
1962	306.2	153.8	333.2	162.9	246.3	109.6
1963	321.5	151.4	358.1	164.8	249.5	108.9
1964	350.7	153.5	382.5	167.8	273.5	108.9
1965	360.7	155.0	414.0	175.0	293.7	110.8
1966	367.0	155.0	445.1	184.8	296.5	109.6

Table A3.1(a). *(cont.)*

Year	UK		US		Germany	
	Output	Employment	Output	Employment	Output	Employment
1967	369.4	150.2	460.5	187.7	287.6	103.7
1968	395.1	149.0	488.7	189.7	317.7	104.5
1969	419.3	152.1	503.9	194.7	356.2	108.9
1970	430.3	152.9	478.8	186.7	373.1	111.4
1971	422.8	149.0	485.2	178.4	376.4	110.6
1972	443.5	143.1	527.7	184.9	388.2	108.6
1973	482.4	145.0	551.8	192.8	412.1	109.3
1974	485.8	147.6	516.1	192.8	409.8	106.8
1975	437.5	142.1	454.6	177.8	391.9	100.2
1976	448.6	139.0	502.5	182.2	422.9	98.0
1977	428.7	138.6	541.0	190.3	431.9	98.3
1978	439.0	135.3	545.0	199.2	439.4	98.2
1979	457.1	131.9	574.2	204.4	461.5	99.4
1980	416.9	124.1	520.1	200.6	451.1	100.2
1981	392.6	110.4	514.7	196.9	448.3	98.3
1982	386.0	102.4	494.9	185.5	431.9	95.5
1983	395.4	97.0	524.3	181.8	438.4	92.3
1984	404.7	96.7	570.5	185.8	451.1	91.9
1985	412.2	95.1	577.7	182.6	468.5	93.0
1986	419.7	93.2	611.4	178.5	472.3	94.6
1987	448.8	93.1	670.5	184.1	469.9	94.6
1988	477.9	94.2	694.8	186.0	484.5	94.5
1989	496.2	94.6	687.2	185.0	504.7	95.9

SOURCES FOR TABLE A3.1(a)

1 United Kingdom
A. Output
1869–1950: Feinstein (1972), table 51.
1950–89: Business Statistics Office (various issues), *Census of Production* (London). Census net output deflated by producer price index for manufacturing from Central Statistical Office (various issues), *Annual Abstract of Statistics* (London). For the period 1950–70 interpolated onto an annual basis using the industrial production index from CSO (various issues), *National Income and Expenditure* (London).

B. Employment
1869–1950: Feinstein (1972), tables 59 and 60. An adjustment has been made for the exclusion of Southern Ireland from 1920, using an estimate of employment in manufacturing in the Irish Republic in 1926 from Mitchell (1988: 110). Before 1920, annual estimates are obtained by interpolation using Feinstein's (1972, table 57) series on civil employment.
1950–89: BSO (various issues), *Census of Production* (London). For the period 1950–70, annual estimates are obtained by interpolation using employment data from Feinstein (1972, table 57), Department of Employment (1971), *British Labour Statistics: Historical*

Abstract 1886–1968 (London) and Department of Employment (1976), *British Labour Statistics Yearbook* (London).

2. United States

A. Output

1869–1950: Kendrick (1961), table D–II.

1950–89: Department of Commerce (various issues), *Census of Manufactures* (Washington, DC). Net output deflated by the producer price index for manufacturing from Bureau of Labor Statistics (various issues), *Producer Price Indexes* (Washington, DC).

B. Employment

1869–1950: Kendrick (1961), table D–II.

1950–89: Department of Commerce (various issues), *Annual Survey of Manufactures* (Washington, DC).

3. Germany

A. Output

1869–1950: Hoffmann (1965), table 76, recalculated to exclude construction and gas, water and electricity.

1950–89: Statistisches Bundesamt (1991), *Volkswirtschaftliche Gesamtrechnungen 1950 bis 1990*, Fachserie 18, Reihe S.15 (Wiesbaden).

B. Employment

1869–1950: Hoffmann (1965), table 15, excluding construction and gas, water and electricity.

1950–60: Statistisches Bundesamt (1982), *Lange Reihen zur Wirtschaftsentwicklung* (Wiesbaden).

1960–89: Statistisches Bundesamt (1991), *Volkswirtschaftliche Gesamtrechnungen 1950 bis 1990*, Fachserie 18, Reihe S.15 (Wiesbaden).

Table A3.1(b). *Real output and employment in manufacturing, 1819–1907* *(1907=100)*

UK

Year	Output	Employment	Output per employee
1821	9.18	29.7	30.9
1841	19.0	41.1	46.2
1851	25.8	60.4	42.7
1861	35.1	68.0	51.6
1871	48.4	74.4	65.1
1907	100.0	100.0	100.0

US

Year	Output	Employment	Output per employee
1819			22.8
1839	2.27	5.53	41.1
1849	5.84	13.3	43.9
1859	10.3	16.9	61.0

Table A3.1(b). *(cont.)*

UK

Year	Output	Employment	Output per employee
1869	16.9	27.3	61.9
1907	100.0	100.0	100.0

Germany

Year	Output	Employment	Output per employee
1851	13.5	38.6	35.0
1861	18.1	44.3	40.9
1871	28.4	50.3	56.5
1907	100.0	100.0	100.0

SOURCES FOR TABLE A3.1(b)

1. United Kingdom

A. Output
1821–61: Hoffmann (1955), table 54, recalculated for manufacturing industries only.
1861–1911: Feinstein (1972), table 51.

B. Employment
1821–61: Mitchell (1988: 103–4).
1861–1911: Feinstein (1972), table 60 for population census years, with interpolation to 1907 using Feinstein's (1972, table 57) series on civil employment.

2. United States

A. Output
1839–60: Gallman (1960), table A–1.
1860–9: Frickey (1947), table 6.
1869–1909: Kendrick (1961), table D–II.

B. Employment
1839–1869: Lebergott (1966), table 1.
1869–1909: Kendrick (1961), table D–II.

C. Output per employee
1819–39: Sokoloff (1986), table 13.4.

3. Germany

A. Output
1851–1911: Hoffmann (1965), table 76. For the period after 1870 the index has been recalculated for manufacturing only. Prior to this the total industrial production index is used due to gaps in the individual industry series.

B. Employment
1851–1911: Hoffmann (1965), table 15. For the period after 1870 only manufacturing employment is included. Prior to this total industrial employment is included due to gaps in the individual industry series.

Table A3.1(c). *Comparative labour productivity in manufacturing, 1869–1989 (UK=100)*

Year	US/UK	Germany/UK
1869	203.8	
1870		
1871		92.6
1872		
1873		
1874		
1875		100.0
1876		
1877		
1878		
1879	187.8	
1880		
1881		
1882		83.6
1883		
1884		
1885		94.5
1886		94.6
1887		93.0
1888		92.1
1889	195.4	94.7
1890	200.7	91.9
1891	199.5	94.2
1892	213.6	101.0
1893	203.5	109.0
1894	195.7	107.4
1895	205.5	108.5
1896	181.4	103.3
1897	190.8	102.8
1898	203.3	101.0
1899	194.8	99.0
1900	190.0	97.1
1901	201.9	98.8
1902	213.1	101.1
1903	210.8	109.0
1904	213.4	109.3
1905	204.3	104.4
1906	202.3	103.0
1907	192.0	106.4
1908	180.9	115.3
1909	208.5	117.8
1910	213.2	122.1
1911	190.6	119.3

Table A3.1(c). *(cont.)*

Year	US/UK	Germany/UK
1912	212.8	121.1
1913	212.9	119.0
1914		
1915		
1916		
1917		
1918		
1919		
1920	222.8	
1921	235.9	
1922	246.7	
1923	235.1	
1924	221.0	
1925	234.2	95.2
1926	242.3	97.3
1927	238.4	103.4
1928	246.2	102.0
1929	249.9	104.7
1930	233.0	99.6
1931	231.6	97.8
1932	206.6	100.7
1933	216.2	100.6
1934	196.6	99.6
1935	207.8	102.0
1936	216.4	100.8
1937	208.3	99.9
1938	191.6	107.1
1939		
1940		
1941		
1942		
1943		
1944		
1945		
1946		
1947		
1948	256.6	
1949	249.0	
1950	262.6	96.0
1951	266.3	103.4
1952	278.9	111.2
1953	268.9	109.4
1954	251.5	106.7
1955	268.8	111.5
1956	268.5	111.3

Table A3.1(c). *(cont.)*

Year	US/UK	Germany/UK
1957	262.8	113.2
1958	250.0	111.1
1959	266.9	117.9
1960	243.0	114.7
1961	249.6	117.2
1962	256.7	118.1
1963	255.6	112.9
1964	249.4	115.1
1965	254.0	119.2
1966	254.1	119.6
1967	249.2	118.0
1968	242.6	120.0
1969	234.6	124.2
1970	227.7	124.6
1971	239.5	125.5
1972	230.3	120.8
1973	214.9	118.6
1974	203.2	122.0
1975	207.5	132.9
1976	213.6	140.1
1977	229.6	148.6
1978	210.6	144.2
1979	202.6	140.3
1980	192.8	140.2
1981	183.6	134.1
1982	176.8	125.6
1983	176.8	122.0
1984	183.3	122.7
1985	182.3	121.5
1986	190.1	116.1
1987	188.8	107.8
1988	184.0	105.9
1989	177.0	105.1

4 Extending the picture: manufacturing productivity in other industrialised countries

Introduction

So far, we have established levels and trends of comparative labour productivity in manufacturing for Britain, the United States and Germany. These three countries have accounted for between 40 and 65 per cent of world trade in manufactures over the last 150 years (Broadberry, 1994a). These data are supplemented in this chapter with new estimates for a number of other New World and European countries, thus building up a wider geographical coverage.

The results confirm the picture of a persistent labour productivity lead in the United States rather than convergence to the same labour productivity level by all countries in manufacturing. There is also evidence of convergence to a common level of labour productivity in European manufacturing, although along separate North European and South European paths, with southern countries lagging substantially behind in the first half of the twentieth century. These findings suggest that the extent of industrialisation, and particularly the lack of a large labour force in low productivity agriculture, was of crucial importance for the attainment of high living standards, as measured in national income statistics, a theme which we take up in more detail in chapter 5.

We briefly examine the trends in comparative productivity levels in manufacturing, and compare them with the trends in productivity at the whole economy level. Table 4.1 sets out the whole economy data, based on the latest figures of Maddison (1995), but with some minor adjustments to facilitate comparison with the manufacturing productivity figures. Figures are reported taking the United Kingdom rather than the United States as the numeraire country and are also presented on an output per employee rather than an output per hour worked basis.

Two appendices are provided at the end of the chapter. Appendix 4.1 presents detailed sources for the time series of real output and employment in manufacturing, which are used in the extrapolations. Appendix 4.2 presents sources for the benchmark estimates of comparative levels of labour productivity in manufacturing.

Table 4.1. *Comparative labour productivity for the whole economy,*
1870–1989 (UK GDP per employee=100)

	1870	1913	1929	1938	1950	1973	1989
UK	100	100	100	100	100	100	100
US	86	116	139	131	154	151	132
Canada	61	95	99	86	125	127	119
Australia	126	121	109	111	111	107	102
Germany	60	78	79	82	66	112	116
Netherlands	89	91	113	103	93	124	111
Norway	41	49	62	67	74	90	99
Sweden	46	58	59	69	90	105	96
Denmark	57	76	91	88	94	103	98
France	52	64	75	73	72	117	129
Italy	38	46	51	54	56	92	103
Japan	18	23	33	38	29	85	103

Source: Calculated from Maddison (1995).

Labour productivity in manufacturing

The New World

The figures in table 4.2 suggest a high level of labour productivity relative
to the United Kingdom in US manufacturing throughout the period since
1870, as has already been noted in chapter 3. For the other New World
countries, although there are periods of high productivity relative to the
United Kingdom in manufacturing, the trends are rather different.
Although there does appear to be convergence in North American manufacturing for much of the twentieth century, this follows a dramatic catching up by Canada during the drive to industrialisation in the first decade.
The picture here thus supports Altman's (1987) characterisation of the
period 1900–10 as a significant discontinuity in the Canadian growth
process. However, to really capture the convergence process within North
America it is necessary to consider performance across US states. Barro
and Sala-i-Martin (1991) find convergence across US states, albeit in
overall economic activity rather than in manufacturing alone.

It appears that Australia's early labour productivity lead over Britain has
been lost in the manufacturing sector as well as in the economy as a whole.
The example of Australia is thus useful in placing Britain's relative economic
decline in perspective. The existence of Australian decline relative to Britain
in the manufacturing sector suggests that the national income findings
cannot be seen simply as a result of the dissipation of early resource rents,
but also reflect trends in the productive economy. Long-run trends in the

Table 4.2. *Comparative levels of labour*
productivity in manufacturing: the New World,
1869–1989 (UK=100)

	US	Canada	Australia
1869	203.8		
1870		88.3	
1879	187.8		
1880		80.5	
1889	195.4		
1890		87.8	
1899	194.8		
1900		88.2	
1907	190.0 (201.9)		
1910		153.5	
1913	212.9		138.2
1920	222.8	137.9	139.5
1924		143.1	124.8
1925	234.2	138.1	127.0
1929	249.9	170.5	120.6
1935	207.8	149.9 (133.3)	102.4 (93.1)
1937	*208.3 (208.3)	142.9	100.0
1950	262.6 (273.4)	151.5	95.8
1958	250.0	165.9	*103.1 (103.1)
1968	242.6 (272.7)	162.4	94.2
1975	207.5 (224.7)	163.7	100.6
1980	192.8	153.2	105.3
1985	182.3	*146.6 [146.6]	93.7 [94.9]
1987	188.8 (186.6)	134.2	85.9
1989	177.0	123.4	81.0

Notes:
* Indicates benchmark year from which time series
extrapolations are made.
(.) Industry-of-origin benchmarks, using physical indicators
or factory gate prices.
[.] Expenditure-based benchmarks, using purchasing power
parities.

manufacturing sector of the New World, then, caution against simple claims
of convergence to a common labour productivity level in manufacturing.

Northern and Southern Europe

Tables 4.3 and 4.4 provide data on labour productivity levels relative to the
United Kingdom in the manufacturing sectors of five North European
countries. Twentieth-century data for all five countries suggest that labour

Table 4.3. *Comparative levels of*
labour productivity in manufacturing:
Germany and the Netherlands,
1875–1989 (UK=100)

	Germany	Netherlands
1875	100.0	
1885	94.5	
1889	94.7	
1899	94.7	
1907	106.4	
1913	119.0	
1921		113.6
1924		91.0
1925	95.2	97.3
1929	104.7	101.6
1935	*102.0 (102.0)	125.8
1937	99.9	93.7 (114.5)
1950	96.0 [99.5]	88.2
1958	111.1	94.1 (108.3)
1968	120.0 (130.4)	110.5
1975	132.9	151.5
1980	140.2	163.8
1984	122.7	*152.4 (152.4)
1985	121.5	151.2
1987	107.8 (112.7)	134.6
1989	105.1	127.9

Notes:
* Indicates benchmark year from which time
series extrapolations are made.
(.) Industry-of-origin benchmarks, using
physical indicators or factory gate prices.
[.] Expenditure-based benchmarks, using
purchasing power parities.

productivity in manufacturing was never far below British levels. This
means that the expansion of the industrial sector, and particularly the
reduction in the size of low productivity agriculture, were important factors
in explaining the catching up on Britain which occurred at the whole
economy level. This catching up should not be seen, then, simply as the
result of technology transfer leading to the improvement of productivity
performance within manufacturing.

The figures in table 4.5, however, suggest a somewhat different picture in
Southern Europe, with labour productivity levels in manufacturing substantially lower than in Britain in the pre-Second World War period. The

Table 4.4. *Comparative levels of labour*
productivity in manufacturing: Scandinavia,
1913–1989 (UK=100)

	Norway	Sweden	Denmark
1913	90.4	101.6	
1920	89.1	90.1	
1924	86.7	90.4	
1925	86.7	86.9	
1929	109.0	94.3	114.7
1930	105.0 (106.8)	94.9	119.8
1935	96.4 (96.5)	*97.0 (97.0)	101.6 (96.8)
1937	94.8	96.4	96.4
1950	102.5	118.2	88.3
1958	109.2	116.8	84.0
1968	108.6	130.8	91.4
1975	108.4	138.7	102.1
1980	105.1	136.9	114.9
1984	93.8	130.8	108.5
1985	*91.8 [91.8]	129.6 [124.2]	*102.1 [102.1]
1987	84.7	120.0	93.7
1989	85.4	121.1	93.2

Notes:
* Indicates benchmark year from which time series
extrapolations are made.
(.) Industry-of-origin benchmarks, using physical indicators
or factory gate prices.
[.] Expenditure-based benchmarks, using purchasing power
parities.

figures for the post-1945 period, however, suggest that in France and Italy
convergence to average European productivity levels has been achieved,
both in manufacturing and the whole economy. Northern and Southern
Europe should thus be seen as pursuing two paths to convergence.

Japanese catching up

Table 4.6 shows the remarkable catching up by Japan in manufacturing,
particularly in the post-1945 period. Although Japan has now substantially
overtaken European manufacturers on an output per worker basis and is
continuing to catch up with the United States, it should be noted that on
an output per hour basis German and Japanese manufacturing productivity levels are now broadly similar, as Japanese hours are substantially
longer. In contrast to Northern Europe, where catching up has occurred at

Table 4.5. *Comparative levels of labour
productivity in manufacturing: France
and Italy, 1881–1989 (UK=100)*

	France	Italy
1881		38.3
1896	64.2	
1901		46.0
1907	(64.0)	
1911		58.8
1913	79.2	
1921		59.1
1924	77.5	
1929	82.3	59.2
1935		51.4
1937		51.4
1938	76.3	49.3
1950	83.9	
1951	92.9	68.4
1958	91.0	
1960	91.4	77.1
1968	109.1	95.1
1975	124.0	97.7
1980	138.7	118.3
1984	*120.4 (120.4)	112.7
1985	120.3	*114.0 [114.0]
1987	112.0	111.0
1989	114.5	111.0

Notes:
* Indicates benchmark year from which time
series extrapolations are made.
(.) Industry-of-origin benchmarks, using
physical indicators or factory gate prices.
[.] Expenditure-based benchmarks, using
purchasing power parities.

the whole economy level without substantial catching up in manufacturing,
in Japan the improvement in manufacturing has been much greater than at
the whole economy level.

Conclusions

In chapter 3 we established a number of key findings concerning Britain's
labour productivity performance in manufacturing on the basis of
comparisons with the United States and Germany. Here we extend these
findings on the basis of a larger sample of countries. First, the persistent

Table 4.6. *Comparative levels of labour productivity in manufacturing: Japan, 1907–1989 (UK=100)*

	Japan
1907	20.8
1913	24.4
1920	27.1
1924	25.2
1925	25.2
1929	32.3
1935	38.8 (35.4)
1937	39.4
1950	19.9
1958	35.5
1968	72.7
1975	103.1
1980	134.1
1984	136.4
1985	139.3
1987	137.7
1989	*143.4 (143.4)

Notes:
* Indicates benchmark year from which time series extrapolations are made.
(.) Industry-of-origin benchmarks, using physical indicators or factory gate prices.

and large US labour productivity lead in manufacturing continues to hold, even with the inclusion of Japan in the sample. And second, the finding that British labour productivity performance in manufacturing has been similar to German levels since the late nineteenth century generalises to other North European countries.

APPENDIX 4.1 DATA SOURCES FOR MANUFACTURING SECTOR TIME SERIES

1. United Kingdom
See appendix 3.1.

2. United States
See appendix 3.1.

3. Canada
A. Output
1870–1958: Nominal value added from Urquhart (1965), series Q11. Wholesale price index from Urquhart (1965), series J35, J46.

1958–61: Real GDP at factor cost in manufacturing from Dominion Bureau of Statistics (1963/64), *Canada Year Book* (Ottawa).

1961–90: Real GDP at factor cost in manufacturing from Statistics Canada (1990/91), *Canadian Economic Observer: Historical Statistical Supplement* (Ottawa), table 1.19.

B. Employment

1870–1959: Urquhart (1965), series Q2.

1959–70: Dominion Bureau of Statistics (various issues), *Canada Year Book* (Ottawa).

1970–90: Statistics Canada (1990/91), *Canadian Economic Observer: Historical Statistical Supplement* (Ottawa), table 2.3.

4. Australia

A. Output

1910 to 1948/49: Haig (1975).

1948/49 to 1949/50: Value added deflated by wholesale price index from Commonwealth Bureau of Census and Statistics (1955), *Year Book of the Commonwealth of Australia* (Canberra)

1949/50 to 1962/63: Industrial production index from Commonwealth Bureau of Statistics (various issues), *Year Book Australia* (Canberra).

1962/63 to 1986/87: GDP in manufacturing at constant prices from Norton and Aylmer (1988).

1986/87 to 1989/90: Real GDP in manufacturing from Australian Bureau of Statistics (various issues), *Year Book Australia* (Canberra).

B. Employment

1910/11 to 1960/61: Keating (1973). Based on population census estimates interpolated using industrial census data.

1960/61 to 1966/67: Commonwealth Bureau of Census and Statistics (various issues), *Year Book Australia* (Canberra).

1966–87: Norton and Aylmer (1988), table 4.10c.

1987–9: ABS (various issues), *Year Book Australia* (Canberra).

Where data were collected on a financial year basis (July– June), they have been converted onto a calendar year basis.

5. Germany

See appendix 3.1.

6. Netherlands

A. Output

1921–60: Single-deflated real value added in manufacturing from de Jong (1992).

1960–88: Production index for *nijverheid* from Centraal Bureau voor de Statistiek (1989), *Negentig Jaaren Statistiek in Tijdreeksan* (The Hague).

1988–9: OECD (1991), *National Accounts, Vol.II, Detailed Tables* (Paris).

B. Employment

1921–60: Number of registered workers and salaried employees in the census industries from de Jong (1992).

1960–88: CBS (various issues), *Statistical Yearbook of the Netherlands* (The Hague).

1988–9: OECD (1991), *National Accounts, Vol.II: Detailed Tables* (Paris).

7. Norway

A. Output

1905–50: Paretti and Bloch (1956), annex 3, manufacturing only.

1950–75: Statistisk Sentralbyra (1978), *Historisk Statistikk* (Oslo), tables 136–137.

1975–89: SSB (various issues), *Statistisk Arbok* (Oslo).

B. Employment

1913–30: SSB (various issues), *Norges Industri* (Oslo).

1930–70: Benchmarks from SSB (1978), *Historisk Statistikk*, table 6. Benchmarks for 1930, 1950, 1960 and 1970, interpolated using series on employment in large companies from the same source, tables 132–134.

1979–89: SSB (various issues), *Statistisk Arbok* (Oslo).

8. Sweden

A. Output

1913–70: Statistiska Centralbyran (1975), *Industrieproduktionsindex 1913–1974* (Stockholm).

1970–89: SCB (various issues), *Statistisk Arsbok* (Stockholm).

B. Employment

1913–50: SCB (1960), *Historisk Statistik for Sverige* (Stockholm).

1950–89: SCB (various issues), *Statistisk Arsbok* (Stockholm).

9. Denmark

A. Output

1920–7: Paretti and Bloch (1956), annex 3, manufacturing only.

1927–80: Johansen (1984), tables 3.5(b)–(d).

1980–9: Danmarks Statistik (various issues), *Statistisk Arbog* (Copenhagen).

B. Employment

1929–80: Johansen (1984), tables 3.4(a)–(b).

1980–9: Danmarks Statistik (various issues), *Statistisk Arbog* (Copenhagen).

10. France

A. Output

1896–1949: Production indices from Vincent (1962; 1965), recalculated for manufacturing only using net output weights from Vincent (1962: 927–30).

1949–59: Real value added in manufacturing from INSEE (1979), *Comptes Trimestriels 1949–1959* (Collections de l'inséé C70, Paris).

1959–70: INSEE (1978), *Retrapolation des comptes nationaux dans le nouveau système de compatibilité nationale française, series 1959–1970* (Collections de l'inséé C67–68, Paris).

1970–85: INSEE (1989), *Les Comptes Nationaux Trimestriels: Series longues, 1970–1988 en base 1980* (Inséé Resultats no. 17, Paris).

1985–9: OECD (1991), *National Accounts, Vol.II: Detailed Tables* (Paris).

B. Employment

1896–1949: Employment in manufacturing industries only from Vincent (1965: 87).

1949–59: INSEE (1979), *Comptes Trimestriels 1949–1959* (Collections de l'inséé C70, Paris).

1959–70: INSEE (various issues), *Rapport sur les Comptes de la Nation* (Paris).

1970–85: INSEE (1989), *Les Comptes Nationaux Trimestriels: Series longues, 1970–1988 en base 1980* (Inséé Resultats no. 17, Paris).
1985–9: OECD (1991), *National Accounts, Vol.II: Detailed Tables* (Paris).

11. Italy
A. Output
1861–1960: Real value added from Fua (1965), table 1.
1960–89: Real GDP in manufacturing and mining from OECD (various issues), *National Accounts, Vol.II: Detailed Tables* (Paris).

B. Employment
1881–1961: Benchmarks from Fua (1965). Interpolation 1928–38 using index of blue collar employment in manufacturing and mining from ISTAT (various issues), *Annuario Statistico Italiano* (Rome).
1970–89: OECD (1991), *National Accounts, Vol.II: Detailed Tables* (Paris).

12. Japan
A. Output
1874–1970: Ohkawa and Shinohara (1979), tables A21–A22.
1970–89: Real GDP in manufacturing from Statistics Bureau, Management and Coordination Agency (various issues), *Japan Statistical Yearbook* (Tokyo).

B. Employment
1906–70: Ohkawa and Shinohara (1979), table A54.
1970–89: Employed persons on Labour Force Survey basis from Statistics Bureau, Management and Coordination Agency (various issues), *Japan Statistical Yearbook* (Tokyo).

APPENDIX 4.2 SOURCES FOR BENCHMARK ESTIMATES OF COMPARATIVE PRODUCTIVITY LEVELS

1. US/UK
See notes to table 3.1.

2. Canada/UK
1935: Maddison (1952). Geometric mean of UK and Canadian employment weights.
1985: Output and employment in both countries on a national accounts basis from OECD, *National Accounts, Vol.II: Detailed Tables* (Paris). Purchasing power parity from Eurostat, *Purchasing Power Parities and Gross Domestic Product in Real Terms: Results 1985* (Brussels).

3. Australia/UK
1935: Net output and employment in Australia for 1936/37 from Commonwealth Bureau of Census and Statistics, *Production Bulletin no.31, 1936–37, Part I – Secondary Industries* (Canberra). Net output and employment in the United Kingdom for 1935 from *Census of Production* (London). Unit value ratios are obtained from price and quantity information in the same sources. An adjustment is made using time series listed in appendix 4.1 to bring the benchmark onto a 1935 basis.

1958: Haig (1986), table 20, using census information.

1985: Australian output and employment data on census basis from ABS, *Year Book Australia* (Canberra). British data on net output and employment from Business Statistics Office *Census of Production* (London). Converted at purchasing power parity for 1985 from Eurostat, *Purchasing Power Parities and Gross Domestic Product in Real Terms: Results 1985* (Brussels).

4. Germany/UK
See notes to table 3.1.

5. Netherlands/UK
1937: Rostas (1948a).
1958: Mensink (1966).
1984: van Ark (1990a).

6. Norway/UK
1930: Employment and price and quantity information for Norway from SSB, *Norges Industri 1930* (Oslo). Employment and price and quantity information for the United Kingdom from the 1930 *Census of Production* (London). Comparison based on physical indicators for 24 industries using employment weights, taking the geometric mean of UK and Norwegian weighted results. Employment coverage ratios are 17.6 per cent for the United Kingdom and 21.1 per cent for Norway.

1935: Net output and employment in manufacturing for Norway from SSB (1969), *Historisk Statistikk* (Oslo), table 133. Net output and employment in manufacturing for the United Kingdom from the 1935 *Census of Production* (London). Unit value ratio based on price and quantity information from the same sources.

1985: Value added and employment for Norway from SSB, *Norges Industri, 1985* (Oslo) and for the United Kingdom from BSO, *Report on the Census of Production, Summary Volume* (London). Purchasing power parity from Eurostat, *Purchasing Power Parities and Gross Domestic Product in Real Terms: Results 1985* (Brussels).

7. Sweden/UK
1935: Rostas (1948a).

1985: Value added and employment for Sweden from SCB, *Industri* (Stockholm) and for the United Kingdom from BSO, *Report on the Census of Production, Summary Tables* (London). Purchasing power parity from Eurostat, *Purchasing Power Parities and Gross Domestic Product in Real Terms: Results 1985* (Brussels).

8. Denmark/UK
1935: Employment and price and quantity information for Denmark from Danmarks Statistik, *Produktionsstatistik 1935* (Copenhagen) and for the United Kingdom from the 1935 *Census of Production* (London). Comparison based on physical indicators for 26 industries using employment weights, taking the geometric mean of UK and Danish weighted results. Employment coverage ratios are 21.0 per cent for the United Kingdom and 32.5 per cent for Denmark.

1985: Value added and employment for Denmark from Danmarks Statistik, *Industristatistik* (Copenhagen) and for the United Kingdom from BSO, *Report* on the Census of Production, Summary Tables (London). Purchasing power parity from Eurostat, *Purchasing Power Parities and Gross Domestic Product in Real Terms: Results 1985* (Brussels).

9. France/UK

1907: Dormois (1991).

1984: van Ark (1990b).

10. Italy/UK

1985: Value added and employment data for Italy from ISTAT (1990), *Statistiche Industriali, Anni 1986, 1987* (Rome). Purchasing power parity from Eurostat, *Purchasing Power Parities and Gross Domestic Product in Real Terms: Results 1985* (Brussels).

11. Japan/UK

1935: GDP and employment in manufacturing for Japan from Ohkawa and Shinohara (1979) and for the United Kingdom from Feinstein (1972). Unit value ratio based on price and quantity information from Japan Statistical Association (1986), *Historical Statistics of Japan, Vol.2* (Tokyo) and the 1935 UK *Census of Production,* (London)

1989: Kagomiya (1993).

5   Manufacturing and the whole economy

Introduction

So far, we have concentrated on establishing levels and trends of comparative labour productivity in manufacturing, noting the persistence of a large US manufacturing labour productivity lead over both Britain and Germany, and broadly equal levels of labour productivity in the manufacturing sectors of the latter two economies. However, trends and levels of comparative labour productivity at the whole economy level have been very different. In this chapter we show that these diverse findings are consistent and consider some of the implications for our understanding of the processes of growth and convergence of living standards across nations.

Reconciling the manufacturing and whole economy estimates

The contribution of manufacturing

Care must be exercised in going from estimates of comparative labour productivity performance in manufacturing to comparative labour productivity performance at the whole economy level. The problem arises because of (a) differences between sectors in value added per employee and (b) differences between countries in the structure of employment. It has been noted at least since the writings of Clark (1940) and Kuznets (1946), that value added per employee tends to be substantially higher in the industrial sector than in agriculture and slightly higher again in the service sector. Hence it is theoretically possible for a country with a higher labour productivity in each of the three broad sectors to have lower labour productivity overall because of a greater degree of specialisation in the sectors with lower value added per employee.

In fact, there have been substantial differences in the distribution of the labour force across sectors both between countries and within each country over time. The figures for the United States, Britain and Germany are shown here in table 5.1. A number of features stand out. First, the small proportion of labour in agriculture in Britain before the First World War

63

Table 5.1. *Sectoral shares of employment, 1870–1990 (%)*

A. US	1870	1910	1930	1950	1990
Agriculture	50.0	32.0	20.9	11.0	2.5
Mining	1.5	2.8	2.2	1.5	0.6
Manufacturing	17.3	22.2	21.3	25.0	15.3
Construction	5.8	6.3	5.9	5.5	5.2
Utilities	0.2	0.5	0.8	0.9	0.7
Transport/Commun.	4.6	8.1	8.6	6.0	4.0
Distbn	6.1	9.1	11.7	18.7	22.0
Finance/Services	12.2	17.1	21.4	21.3	40.2
Government	2.3	1.9	7.2	10.1	9.5
Total	100.0	100.0	100.0	100.0	100.0

B. UK	1871	1911	1930	1950	1990
Agriculture	22.2	11.8	7.6	5.1	2.0
Mining	4.0	6.3	5.4	3.7	0.6
Manufacturing	33.5	32.1	31.7	34.9	20.1
Construction	4.7	5.1	5.4	6.3	6.7
Utilities	0.2	0.6	1.2	1.6	1.1
Transport/Commun.	5.4	7.7	8.3	7.9	5.5
Distbn	7.5	12.1	14.3	12.2	19.5
Finance/Services	19.5	20.2	20.9	19.5	37.5
Government	3.0	4.1	5.2	8.8	7.0
Total	100.0	100.0	100.0	100.0	100.0

C. Germany	1875	1913	1935	1950	1990
Agriculture	49.5	34.5	29.9	24.3	3.4
Mining	1.5	2.8	1.7	2.8	0.6
Manufacturing	24.7	29.5	30.0	31.4	31.4
Construction	2.8	5.3	5.9	7.2	6.7
Utilities	0.1	0.3	0.6	0.7	1.0
Transport/Commun.	1.9	3.8	4.8	5.6	5.6
Distbn/Finance	6.0	11.2	13.5	13.2	16.2
Services	10.0	8.3	8.8	7.9	19.9
Government	3.5	4.3	4.8	6.9	15.1
Total	100.0	100.0	100.0	100.0	100.0

Sources: US: Derived from Carson (1949), Lebergott (1966), Department of Commerce, *National Income and Product Accounts of the United States* and *Survey of Current Business.* UK: Derived from Feinstein (1972), CSO, *Annual Abstract of Statistics*, and OECD, *Labour Force Statistics.* Germany: Derived from Hoffmann (1965) and Statistisches Bundesamt, *Volkswirtschaftliche Gesamtrechnungen.*

meant that Britain's employment structure was unusually mature at this time, heavily skewed towards manufacturing and services. This lack of a low productivity agricultural sector is very important in explaining Britain's overall productivity leadership during the nineteenth century, which we have seen was not due to productivity leadership in Britain's manufacturing industry. This view is consistent with much of the recent revisionist work on the nature of the Industrial Revolution in Britain (Crafts, 1985).

Second, note that in 1950 Germany had a higher share of employment in agriculture than Britain had in 1871. The big release of labour from low productivity agriculture in Germany after the Second World War was an important factor in German catching up on Britain at the whole economy level. Note, however, that the release of labour from agriculture has been accompanied by an increase in employment in service sectors rather than in manufacturing. Nevertheless, it should be noted that Germany stands out from the United Kingdom and the United States in the post-Second World War period by maintaining its share of employment in manufacturing and avoiding deindustrialisation.

Third, the rise in importance of service industries is notable in all three countries, particularly during the post-1950 period. The share of agriculture and production industries (mining, manufacturing, construction and utilities) has fallen from 74.8 per cent to 24.3 per cent in the United States, from 64.6 per cent to 30.5 per cent in the United Kingdom and from 78.6 per cent to 43.1 per cent in Germany. This suggests that the problems of output measurement in the service sector have now become of paramount importance for contemporary measurement of international productivity differences. For historians, however, the problems are clearly less severe. As Griliches (1994) notes, the current national accounting framework is really better suited to the measurement of economic activity in the first half of the twentieth century than it is to the second.

US/UK experience

The US/UK experience is summarised in table 5.2, which shows Anglo-American labour productivity differences in manufacturing and the whole economy. The differences are striking. The whole economy evidence suggests that the United States started with lower levels of labour productivity than Britain in 1870, then overtook Britain as the labour productivity leader in the 1890s and continued to forge ahead substantially to the 1950s before Britain began a slow process of catching up, which is still not complete. However, the evidence from manufacturing, as we have seen, suggests that the US labour productivity levels were already about twice the British level in 1870, and that US superiority was still close to this 2:1 level in the

Table 5.2. *Comparative US/UK output per employee in manufacturing and the whole economy, 1870–1989 (UK=100)*

	Manufacturing	Whole economy
1870	192.0	85.9
1913	212.9	115.5
1929	249.9	139.0
1938	191.6	130.5
1950	262.6	153.8
1973	214.9	150.8
1979	202.6	143.0
1989	177.0	131.5

Sources: Derived from Broadberry (1993), Maddison (1995) and OECD, *Labour Force Statistics.*

late 1980s, despite substantial swings in productivity in the intervening years, particularly across the two world wars.

Table 5.2 thus suggests differences in both levels and trends of comparative labour productivity between the manufacturing sector and the whole economy. Dealing first with the issue of different levels, it is clear that British labour productivity performance over the whole period since 1870 has been substantially worse in manufacturing than in the economy as a whole. There have been a number of studies of comparative labour productivity levels by sector for the US/UK comparison in the mid-twentieth century which confirm this finding. In table 5.3, the estimates of Rostas (1948a) for the late 1930s and Paige and Bombach (1959) for 1950 have been reworked on a consistent basis by Broadberry (1997), and suggest that the manufacturing and whole economy estimates in table 5.2 can be reconciled. Britain's comparative labour productivity performance was rather better in agriculture and services than in industrial sectors. However, Britain also gained at the whole economy level from a rather more favourable distribution of employment, especially a smaller agricultural sector and a larger manufacturing sector, as can be seen from table 5.1.

To reconcile the different trends in the manufacturing and whole economy estimates of comparative labour productivity requires either that trends in other sectors offset the trends in manufacturing or that the expansion and contraction in the relative importance of sectors had substantial composition effects on overall labour productivity. In fact, both seem likely.

Table 5.3. *Comparative US/UK*
labour productivity levels, by sector,
1937 and 1950 (UK=100)

	1937	1950
Agriculture	103.3	117.3
Mining & quarrying	232.1	396.9
Manufacturing	208.3	273.4
Construction	107.8	168.6
Utilities	359.3	435.6
Transport/Commun.	283.4	358.9
Distbn	119.8	148.4
Finance & Services	96.1	95.5
Government	100.0	100.0
Whole economy	132.6	162.5

Source: Broadberry (1997), derived from
Rostas (1948a) and Paige and Bombach
(1959).

For the crucial period before the First World War, when the United States overtook Britain at the whole economy level, we can compare growth rates of comparative labour productivity using the data of Matthews *et al.* (1982) and Kendrick (1961). Labour productivity growth was rather more rapid in the United States during the period 1869–1909 than in Britain during the period 1873–1913 in mining, the utilities and transport and communications (Broadberry, 1997). In addition, there was a dramatic drop in the share of the labour force in agriculture in the United States, from half of employment in 1870 to just below one-third of the total in 1910, as can be seen in table 5.1. Given the broadly equal labour productivity in British and American agriculture but the substantially higher American labour productivity in industry, American industrialisation was bound to lead to America forging ahead.

Comparative advantage

When we examined comparative labour productivity performance by industry within the manufacturing sector in chapter 2, we noted that by and large, this was a good guide to comparative advantage. The finding of a rather better British comparative labour productivity performance in agriculture than in manufacturing in table 5.3 may therefore appear puzzling at first sight. How did Britain become the 'workshop of the world' if labour productivity in manufacturing was much higher in America? As Crafts

Table 5.4. *Comparative Germany/UK output per employee in manufacturing and the whole economy, 1870–1989 (UK=100)*

	Manufacturing	Whole economy
1870	92.6	59.6
1913	119.0	78.3
1929	104.7	78.8
1938	107.1	82.6
1950	96.0	65.8
1973	118.6	111.7
1979	140.3	123.9
1989	105.1	115.7

Sources: Derived from Broadberry (1993), Maddison (1995) and OECD, *Labour Force Statistics.*

(1989) notes, it is tempting to ask why Britain did not instead become the 'granary of the world'.

One possible answer to this question might be to draw a distinction between the modernised and unmodernised sectors of manufacturing, as indeed Crafts (1985, 1989) does. Perhaps, it may be argued, Britain was the labour productivity leader in cotton textiles, which so dominated British exports in the nineteenth century. However, as Broadberry (1994b) notes, the crude data on output and employment in the Lancashire and New England cotton industries of the mid-nineteenth century do not offer any support for such a proposition. The answer to the puzzle lies rather in the importance of land as an input in agriculture. Relatively high British labour productivity in agriculture during the nineteenth century is consistent with food being an importable once it is recognised that land was much cheaper in the New World.

Germany/UK experience

The Germany/UK experience is summarised in table 5.4, showing Anglo-German labour productivity differences in manufacturing and the whole economy. As in the US/UK case, there are striking differences between the two series, in terms of both levels and trends. The whole economy evidence suggests that German labour productivity was about 60 per cent of the British level in 1870. This was followed by a steady process of catching up, punctuated by setbacks across the two world wars, so that by the late 1960s Germany had overtaken Britain. Although there was some reversal of this pattern during the 1980s, by the end of that decade Germany still retained a substantial aggregate labour productivity lead over Britain. By contrast, the evidence from manufacturing suggests that German labour productivity levels were already close to British levels in the late nineteenth century. Germany pulled substantially ahead after the Second World War, particularly during the 1970s, but the gap was dramatically narrowed during the 1980s, so that as in the US/UK case, there was little difference in manufacturing between the levels of the 1870s and the 1980s.

Again, as in the US/UK case there is evidence from Anglo-German productivity studies to support the idea that Britain's labour productivity performance has been better in agriculture and services than in manufacturing and other industrial sectors (Smith *et al.*,1982). Also, there is evidence that the different trends in manufacturing and the whole economy can be reconciled, as well as the different levels. For the pre-First World War period, for example, German catching up at the whole economy level can be attributed largely to faster German labour productivity growth in mining, the utilities and transport and communications, with only a small contribution from the sectoral reallocation of labour, as Germany protected her agriculture in contrast to free trade Britain.

Implications for growth and convergence

The findings here have some implications for recent debates on growth and the convergence of productivity and living standards. Before we draw out these implications, however, it will be useful to show very briefly the context of the debates. Data on national income and labour inputs for 16 advanced industrialised countries over the period since 1870 have been collected by Maddison (1964, 1982, 1991,1995). The basic data, some of which we have already seen in a slightly different form in chapter 4, are set out in tables 5.5 and 5.6, which can be used to illustrate the way in which the convergence hypothesis has altered our perceptions of the growth process. From table 5.5, we see that during the period 1950–73 labour productivity growth in the United Kingdom and the United States was relatively slow, while Japan, Germany and a number of other European economies achieved very rapid rates of labour productivity growth. This disparity in economic performance has been widely used to make inferences about the superiority of economic institutions and policy in the more corporatist Japanese and Continental European countries over the more liberal Anglo-Saxon economies (Peaker, 1974; Stafford, 1981; Rowthorn, 1986; Cowling, 1989). However, once we examine levels of labour productivity in table 5.6, this

Table 5.5. *Growth of GDP per hour worked, 1870–1992 (% per annum)*

	1870–1913	1913–1950	1950–1973	1973–1992	1870–1992
Australia	1.1	1.3	2.9	1.8	1.6
Austria	1.7	0.9	5.7	2.4	2.3
Belgium	1.2	1.4	4.4	2.9	2.1
Canada	2.2	2.3	2.9	1.5	2.3
Denmark	1.9	1.5	4.4	1.7	2.2
Finland	1.8	2.1	5.3	2.2	2.6
France	1.7	1.8	5.0	2.7	2.5
Germany	1.8	0.6	5.8	2.7	2.5
Italy	1.6	1.9	5.6	2.4	2.6
Japan	1.9	1.8	7.4	3.1	3.1
Netherlands	1.3	1.3	4.7	2.2	2.1
Norway	1.6	2.4	4.1	3.2	2.6
Sweden	1.7	2.7	4.1	1.3	2.4
Switzerland	1.4	2.7	3.2	1.7	2.2
UK	1.2	1.8	3.1	2.2	1.8
US	1.9	2.4	2.7	1.1	2.1

Source: Derived from Maddison (1995: 249).

Table 5.6. *Comparative levels of labour productivity, 1870–1992 (US GDP per hour worked=100)*

	1870	1913	1950	1973	1992
Australia	147	103	69	72	78
Austria	62	70	48	70	98
Belgium	94	61	42	64	86
Canada	71	82	77	81	87
Denmark	67	66	46	68	75
Finland	37	35	32	57	70
France	60	56	45	76	102
Germany	70	68	35	71	95
Italy	46	41	34	66	85
Japan	20	20	16	48	69
Netherlands	103	78	51	81	99
Norway	48	43	43	60	88
Sweden	54	50	56	77	79
Switzerland	77	63	69	78	87
UK	115	86	62	68	82
US	100	100	100	100	100

Source: Maddison (1995: 47).

conclusion is seen to be much less secure. The rapid postwar growth in Japan and Europe was from a much lower base and can be seen largely as catch up growth.

In fact, the idea that economic backwardness may lead to a spurt of catch up growth is not new in economic history, going back at least to Veblen's (1915) study of Imperial Germany and Gerschrenkon's (1962) analysis of Continental European and especially Russian industrialisation. However, the idea received a considerable boost with the development of the Maddison data set and two important papers by Abramovitz (1979, 1986). A paper by Baumol (1986) then sparked off a huge debate in economics, spreading out to consider many more countries during the period since 1960, utilising the data set of Summers and Heston (1984, 1991).

Here, we restrict our attention to the advanced industrialised countries, where it is widely accepted that convergence of labour productivity and living standards has occurred at the whole economy level. The findings reported in chapter 4 suggest that this convergence of labour productivity at the whole economy level has not been matched by convergence of labour productivity in manufacturing to anything like the same extent. In particular, there has been a large and persistent North American labour productivity lead in manufacturing. This suggests that we cannot see convergence at the whole economy level simply in terms of technology transfer in manufacturing, as is often assumed in the literature (Cornwall, 1977; Gomulka, 1971). It also calls into question accounts of overall relative economic decline in Britain from the late nineteenth century or in the United States from the late 1960s that are concerned solely with technology in manufacturing (Elbaum and Lazonick, 1986; Lazonick, 1990).

Indeed, it may be that persistent productivity differences at the sectoral level are part of the process of convergence at the overall level. With specialisation in the world economy, we may expect to see adjustment through expansion or contraction of sectors as well as through changing comparative productivity levels. It is clear from table 5.1 that changes in the relative sizes of traded goods sectors in the different countries have played a part in the convergence process. This suggests that openness to international competition and other open economy forces such as migration and capital flows may have just as important a part to play in convergence as technology transfer in manufacturing, as emphasised in recent work by Williamson (1995) and O'Rourke et al. (1996).

Underlying the convergence debate is a conflict over the vision of the growth process. The standard neoclassical growth model predicts convergence of productivity and living standards (Lucas, 1988). Rejection of convergence thus implies a move away from the model which has dominated economists' thinking about growth in recent decades. Rather than seeing growth as given by exogenous technical progress and population growth, and independent of savings and investment as in the standard neoclassical model, in the more recent literature the rate of growth has been endogenised and can be influenced by the accumulation strategy of individuals and governments. This growth literature has placed a new emphasis on the accumulation of human capital (Lucas, 1988, 1993; Romer, 1990). Learning effects and externalities mean that there is no guarantee of convergence in a world of competitive economies since social and private returns often differ. In models with more than one sector, specialisation according to comparative advantage can have persistent growth effects (Lucas, 1988; Young, 1991; Grossman and Helpman, 1991).

The historical approach taken in this book suggests a number of points about the debate over exogenous versus endogenous growth models. First, although a number of economists have rallied to the defence of the standard neoclassical model, it is doubtful that many economic historians will want to continue to subscribe to a model in which the rate of growth is exogenous (Mankiw *et al.*,1992). Indeed, in many ways, much of economic history can be seen as endogenising economic growth. Thus Chandler (1990), for example, clearly sees growth as the result of a three-pronged investment in production, marketing and management, while Habakkuk (1962) stresses the role of resources in technical choice. It is hoped that the historical model of growth used in this book will go some way towards integrating the historical and economic approaches to growth.

Second, it should be noted that the new endogenous growth models have been rather more successful in explaining differences in growth rates between countries than in explaining changes in the rate of growth within a particular country (Easterly *et al.*, 1993; Crafts, 1995). In the current state of knowledge, there must still be a role for exogenous factors. The comparative perspective may thus be seen as one way of screening out these exogenous factors, allowing us to concentrate on the systematic economic mechanisms underlying the growth process. However, it should be noted that the comparative perspective does not give a complete picture of the growth process. As Supple (1994: 442) notes, despite the concern at British relative decline since the Second World War, productivity has grown at a faster rate than in earlier periods, suggesting improved performance in an absolute sense. Accordingly, in part 3 of the book, we shall examine growth rates of output and productivity in individual industries in addition to comparative levels of productivity to provide a more balanced assessment of industrial performance.

Third, understanding the growth process requires going beyond a single sector aggregate growth model. Even if a large labour productivity gap exists at the whole economy level, we have seen that this does not mean that a similar gap exists in all sectors. Furthermore, and contrary to the spirit of all the aggregate models, endogenous or exogenous, there is no unique optimal technology, suitable in all countries. Rather, as we shall see in part 2, technological change is a path dependent process, responding to demand conditions, resource endowments and previous accumulations of reproducible factors.

Conclusions

In this chapter, comparative productivity performance in manufacturing is contrasted with performance at the whole economy level. Whereas the United States overtook Britain during the 1890s at the whole economy level, in manufacturing US labour productivity was already twice the British level by the mid-nineteenth century. And although German labour productivity in manufacturing was already as high as in Britain by the late nineteenth century, it was only during the 1960s that Germany overtook Britain in terms of GDP per employee. These findings are reconciled through (a) offsetting trends in non-manufacturing sectors and (b) changes in the structure of economic activity. The early maturity of Britain's economic structure was of particular importance; Britain owed its relatively high overall living standards before the Second World War to the absence of a large agricultural sector with low labour productivity. The findings here suggest that convergence at the whole economy level cannot be seen simply as a result of technology transfer in manufacturing. Indeed, persistent productivity gaps at the sectoral level with adjustment through the relative size of sectors may be a part of the aggregate convergence process.

Part 2

Explaining comparative productivity performance

6 Technology

Introduction

We now turn in part 2 to explanation of the comparative labour productivity performance in manufacturing that has been established in part 1 of the book. In particular, the persistence of a large labour productivity lead in the United States needs to be explained. In this chapter a general framework is provided, in which productivity differences between countries can persist as a result of technical choice and factor accumulation around those technical choices, despite all countries having access to the same technology. Here I draw on a number of historical models of technology and growth which are surveyed below, before deriving a model of technical choice based on Broadberry (1994a).

Historical models of technology and growth

The survey offered here aims to highlight the key themes of the model developed below, rather than to provide a comprehensive literature survey. The starting point is the Rothbarth–Habakkuk thesis, which traces the origin of transatlantic technological differences to land and resource abundance in the New World. Given complementarity between natural resources and machinery, a more machine-intensive technology developed in America. This had implications for the labour process, a theme taken up in the work of Piore and Sabel (1984) and others. American manufacturing substituted resource-using machinery for skilled labour, which was in short supply in the New World. In Europe, however, skilled labour was abundant and resources scarce, so that European technology remained skilled labour-intensive. These effects were reinforced on the demand side by homogeneous demand patterns in America, permitting a greater degree of standardisation, and hence further economisation of skilled shopfloor labour. These developments, however, required the three-pronged investment in production, management and marketing emphasised by Chandler (1990). However, whereas Chandler sees a unique best technology and assesses British and German industry according to how quickly they adopted American methods, I follow the business strategy literature in noting that competitive advantage requires developing distinctive capabilities rather than slavishly copying. Technical change within each country is therefore best seen as a path dependent process, with all countries able to draw on a common pool of knowledge but developing distinctive capabilities and adapting innovations to local circumstances. Finally, some common trends in the development of technology in all countries are noted.

The Rothbarth–Habakkuk thesis

The central problem suggested by the empirical findings reported in part 1 is to explain the persistence of a large labour productivity lead in US manufacturing. Here we turn to the literature concerned with Anglo-American productivity differences in the nineteenth century, which relates the higher labour productivity in America to the greater abundance of land. Although Habakkuk (1962) concentrated on the implications of land abundance for technical choice in the early nineteenth century, it is clear that Rothbarth (1946) intended to use the idea to explain higher labour productivity in the United States during the twentieth century as well.

The simplest version of the Rothbarth–Habakkuk thesis, with land abundance leading to greater capital intensity and hence greater labour productivity in American manufacturing clearly has some logical and empirical difficulties. As Temin (1966a, 1971) points out, in a standard two-good, three-factor neoclassical model it is not obvious that land abundance leads to greater capital intensity in manufacturing. In fact, what Temin calls the 'Basic Theorem' requires some very restrictive assumptions about the production functions in agriculture and manufacturing. Assume two sectors, agriculture and manufacturing and three factors, capital, labour and land. Temin (1971) argues that the Basic Theorem holds only under the following assumptions:

A. *Only land and labour are used to produce agricultural goods.*
B. *Only labour and capital are used to produce manufactured goods.*

Comparing two economies with different land endowments at a point in time is likened to increasing the land endowment in a single country. Since land is used only in agriculture, it can increase only agricultural output. However, this can occur only through drawing labour away from manufacturing into agriculture. Since capital can be used only in manufacturing, this raises the capital intensity of manufacturing production. Suppose we assume more realistically, however, that capital is also used in agriculture, and a section of manufacturing is engaged in processing agricultural commodities:

C. *All three factors (land, labour and capital) are used to produce agricultural goods.*
D. *Manufactured goods are produced using labour, capital and agricultural goods.*

Now an increase in land increases the production of agricultural goods, and the increased output of agricultural goods in turn tends to increase the output of manufactured goods. However, offsetting this increase in manufactured output, the extra agricultural output also requires extra capital and labour inputs, which must be drawn from the manufacturing sector. It is not possible to say whether the net effect is to increase or decrease capital intensity in manufacturing, since both factors are drawn to agriculture. In contrast to the labour scarcity in manufacturing suggested by assumptions A and B, assumptions C and D lead to a 'dual scarcity' of both capital and labour.

One way in which the dual scarcity result can be turned back into a labour scarcity result is to assume complementarity between material inputs (agricultural output) and capital in manufacturing (Ames and Rosenberg, 1968). This ensures that an increase in land draws more labour than capital from manufacturing to agriculture, thus raising capital intensity in manufacturing. Ames and Rosenberg particularly stressed the resource-using bias of some of the key machines in the 'American system of manufactures'. Thus, for example, there is general agreement that American woodworking machinery was very wasteful of wood, which was in abundant supply in America. However, such machinery could not be widely used in Britain where the price of wood was much higher.

This still leaves an empirical problem, however, that the most widely accepted historical sources on the British and American capital stocks during the nineteenth century, calculated to be consistent with later 'official' capital stock estimates, do not appear to support the notion of greater capital intensity in the United States (Field, 1985). Recent research by Maddison (1993) attempts to overturn this finding by calculating new estimates of capital stocks in Britain and America using the same asset life assumptions in both countries. The problem with the official data is that despite relatively low levels of investment by international standards, Britain has a relatively large capital stock because assets are assumed to last a longer time in Britain. Accepting the official estimates of investment but assuming the same asset lives in the two countries therefore lowers British capital relative to American capital stocks. However, there is a problem in that for some assets, especially buildings, the historical estimates with official assumptions were based directly on stock estimates rather than the accumulation of investments.

Even if we accept the standard sources, however, James and Skinner (1985) suggest that a distinction should be made between the skilled and unskilled manufacturing sectors, with greater US capital intensity only in the former. The distinction is based on the skill of the workers; only in the skilled manufacturing sector were there sufficient incentives for US firms to substitute capital and cheap natural resources for skilled labour. Furthermore, as Field (1985) points out, it is important to distinguish between machinery and capital. Even if total fixed capital per worker was greater in nineteenth-century Britain, it is still possible that machinery per worker in manufacturing was greater in the United States, due to the importance of structures (55–60 per cent of the US capital stock), inventories (10–20 per cent) and consumer durables (7–15 per cent).

Labour processes

James and Skinner's emphasis on the role of the skilled worker is important, providing a link to another literature on labour processes, which also sees a large difference between American and European production methods (Piore and Sabel, 1984; Lazonick, 1990; Tolliday and Zeitlin, 1991). In the labour process literature, the key distinction is between standardised mass production, associated with American methods, and flexible production, associated with European methods. For our purposes, there are two important differences between the two methods of production. First, and most obviously, there is the difference between the standardised output of mass production methods aimed at homogeneous market demands, and the customised output of flexible production methods, tailored to individual differentiated demands. But second, there is the difference in the labour processes, with mass production methods dependent on relatively unskilled labourers using special purpose machines, and flexible production methods dependent on skilled shopfloor workers using general purpose machines.

It should be noted that the distinction is not between large-scale production in factories and small-scale production in workshops. Flexible production methods can be applied in the largest factories. It is the size of individual batches rather than overall output that is important. It is these two key features of customised output and skilled shopfloor labour that allow us to trace a common thread from the British craft-based flexible production methods of the nineteenth century to the modern German flexible production methods of the period since the late 1960s.

Chandler's 'scale and scope'

Some features of the labour process literature do square with the historical model of growth suggested by Chandler (1990). Chandler sees American success in manufacturing between the late nineteenth century and the mid-twentieth century as the result of investment in production, marketing and management. This three-pronged investment strategy allowed firms to reap economies of scale and scope in production. Investment in marketing can be seen as helping with the standardisation of demand, while investment in management can be seen as a necessary corollary of the deskilling of the shopfloor labour process. Unskilled workers required strict supervision to secure the rapid throughput to justify the investment in the special purpose machinery used in the production process. Flexible production methods did not require such strict managerial control, since control of large elements of the production process remained in the hands of the skilled craft workers. Hence in a Chandlerian framework we should expect to see less emphasis on investment in managerial hierarchies in European firms in the early twentieth century.

Chandler assesses British and German performance in the first half of the twentieth century on how closely they conform to the American model. On average, German firms are seen as conforming more closely to the American ideal than British firms, but in each country successful companies are seen as having made the three-pronged investments in production, marketing and management.

The findings of part 1 of this book immediately raise some doubts about the Chandler framework. Despite the claim of a greater closeness of German business organisation to the American model than the British model, in terms of productivity outcomes, German manufacturing has been much closer to the British than the American level (Chandler, 1990: 393). Furthermore, as noted in Broadberry and Crafts (1992), developments in the post-Second World War period cast serious doubt on the proposition that success required copying the American model. The British seem to have copied American organisational forms more closely than the Germans but nevertheless been less successful. Thus, for example, it is striking that by 1970 72 per cent of the top 100 British companies had adopted the multi-divisional form, much praised by Chandler, whereas the corresponding figure for Germany was only 40 per cent (Channon, 1973: 67; Dyas and Thanheiser, 1976: 29). Similarly, as the mergers advocated by Chandler's analysis of interwar Britain occurred during the 1950s and 1960s, the results were disappointing, to say the least (Cowling *et al.*, 1980; Meeks, 1977).

Competitive advantage and comparative advantage

A clear problem with the Chandler view is that it fails to take adequate account of the different circumstances in the three countries. British and

German firms could not succeed by simply copying their American counterparts. Firms need to develop strategies that build on their strengths, or competitive advantages. This is a point which is emphasised in the extensive literature on business strategy (Porter, 1990; Kay, 1993). It has also been argued forcefully in a historical context by Hannah (1995).

Kay (1993: 372) defines competitive advantage as the ability of a firm to add more value than another firm in the same market. He sees competitive advantage as related to distinctive capabilities, which cannot be easily replicated. The idea is related to the efficient markets hypothesis, which states that in a competitive market there are no bargains, because prices fully reflect any available information (Fama, 1970). As Kay (1993: 63) puts it,

The advice, 'Buy Glaxo shares because Glaxo is a well-managed company with outstanding products', is worthless, even if it is a type of advice that is often given, because these facts about Glaxo are well known and fully incorporated in the value of its securities.

Similarly, business opportunities which are available to everyone cannot be profitable for everyone. Before entering a market, an individual company must ask itself if it can do better than other potential entrants. A company may be able to benefit from its organisational knowledge (or 'architecture'), from its reputation, from an innovation, or from a strategic asset such as a statutory monopoly. Within this framework, then, it is hopeless to try to simply copy rivals, as suggested by the Chandler approach. A firm must develop a strategy to transform its distinctive capabilities into a competitive advantage.

When moving from the level of the firm to the level of the economy, although a country may be expected to concentrate on its strengths much as a firm would, economists have been reluctant to use the term 'competitive advantage', preferring to stick with the older term 'comparative advantage' (Krugman, 1994). This largely reflects the fact that when we examine international trade we move away from a zero sum game. Whereas an individual firm may wish to wipe out a competitor and supply the whole market, this reasoning cannot apply to a whole economy. Indeed, trade can only occur if both countries have something to offer. Hence trade can still occur if one country has an 'absolute advantage' in all products, with the low productivity country specialising in the products in which its productivity inferiority is relatively small.

Path dependence

The models discussed so far tend to emphasise the origin rather than the persistence of transatlantic differences in factor proportions. To understand persistence, we need to introduce the idea of path dependence. This is most easily done through David's (1985) famous example of the QWERTY keyboard. The basic question that David raises is why we continue to operate computers with a keyboard where the home keys spell QWERTYUIOP? This is a problem because there are more efficient alternatives. For example, the Maltron has a home row with 91 per cent of the most frequently used letters in English compared with only 51 per cent on the QWERTY. This means that you have to make your hands jump upwards or sideways 256 more times than with the Maltron arrangement.

The reason that the QWERTY arrangement came about is that in the late nineteenth century there was a serious problem with typebar clashes in the early typewriters. Since the paper carriage was not visible to the typist, there were serious consequences to a typebar clash, which resulted in a string of repeated letters. It turned out that the QWERTY arrangement minimised these typebar clashes. Hence the QWERTY keyboard gained an early advantage over rival arrangements. However, eventually the typebar clash problem was solved and other keyboard arrangements were tried. But by this stage it was too late. Having gained an early lead, QWERTY became the universal standard and drove out all other arrangements. QWERTY became 'locked-in' as the dominant keyboard.

David sees this 'lock-in' as occurring due to technical inter-relatedness, economies of scale and quasi-irreversibility of investment. Technical inter-relatedness arose from the fact that typewriters were only one element of a system, involving typists and organisations for training typists as well as the hardware itself. As more and more people used the QWERTY arrangement, so it became more difficult for a potential typist to justify learning another arrangement or for an employer to justify buying a different typewriter. Conventional economies of scale could be exploited by private business colleges teaching touch-typing, so that the pioneers in this field exercised considerable leverage. Quasi-irreversibility of investment refers to the fact that it is very difficult to unlearn a particular keyboard arrangement, making change a costly process.

This idea of technological lock-in is very powerful. We do not need to look to customary behaviour by non-rational individuals who have been socialised into maintaining an antiquated technology, or a conspiracy among the members of a keyboard oligopoly, as the bitter inventor of the Dvorak keyboard believed.

In the QWERTY example, the same standard has come to dominate on both sides of the Atlantic. However, there are well known examples where this is not the case. Thus in railway gauge, although a single standard came to dominate in each country, there was no standardisation between countries. Similarly with which side of the road to drive on. National technological systems within manufacturing can be seen as developing in a similar fashion, with path dependence leading to technological lock-in within each country, but without international standardisation.

Technological trends

In much of what follows we shall be concentrating on differences in the technology used in different countries. However, it is also clear that technology in all countries has changed in similar ways over time, and here we provide a brief overview of these changes. Nelson and Wright (1992) argue for a transition from a largely empirically-based technology in the nineteenth century to a more codified science-based technology by the second half of the twentieth century.

Although some features of the earlier technologies were described in writing, they needed large amounts of learning by doing to bring under control, and technical progress was local and incremental, building from and improving on prevailing practice (Nelson and Wright, 1992: 1935). Sustained technological advance involved many interacting people and firms in a process described by Allen (1983) as 'collective invention'. The twentieth century, by contrast, has seen the evolution of more science-based technologies, increasingly requiring trained scientists and engineers. Progress in these technologies has occurred increasingly through organised research and development; the skills and experience needed to advance a modern technology now include much more than can be acquired simply by working with that technology and learning from experience (Nelson and Wright, 1992: 1950).

Despite these common trends affecting the development of technology in all countries, important differences have remained. The idea of 'national innovation systems' is sometimes used to describe these differences (Nelson, 1993). This concept, which clearly draws on the idea noted above that successful innovation requires building upon distinctive characteristics that are not easily replicable by competitors, will be explored more fully in chapter 8.

A model of technical choice and productivity

Competition between technologies

In this section a simple model of technical choice is described, drawing on the historical models of growth surveyed above. As in the Rothbarth–Habakkuk thesis, at any point in time technical choice is determined by relative factor endowments. Resource endowments and demand

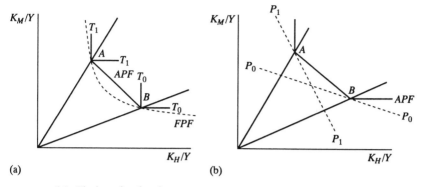

6.1 Choice of technology
(a) The APF frontier and the FPF
(b) The role of factor prices

conditions play an important role in explaining the early adoption of a more machine- intensive technology in American manufacturing (for standardised mass production) and a more skilled labour-intensive technology in Britain and Germany (for flexible production).

However, subsequently accumulation occurs around the technique adopted. Thus we find the patterns of accumulation associated with Chandler's (1990) analysis, with American human capital accumulation concentrated in management, but British and German human capital accumulation oriented more towards shopfloor labour. The two technologies can coexist, given different conditions on the two sides of the Atlantic, so long as innovation in one technique brings forth a response in the other, through imitation or adaptation. It should be noted that simple copying is not an adequate response.

A technological advantage will generally be short-lived, as an innovation in one technique brings forth imitation in the other. However, large technological shifts or market changes can cause problems because of the investment in the specific skills needed to reap the economies of scale and scope in any particular technique. Such changes can undermine the value of specific human capital, which can cause serious adjustment problems.

Endowments, factor prices and technical choice

The choice of technology in this model can be characterised as one of substitution between fixed capital in the form of machinery and human capital in the form of skilled labour, as in figure 6.1, which is adapted from David (1975). In figure 6.1(a) there are two available technologies which differ in the proportions of machine capital (K_M) and human capital (K_H). Once the

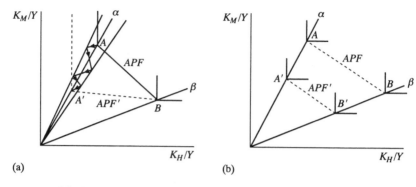

6.2 Technical progress
(a) Localised technical change
(b) Competition between technologies

technique has been chosen, substitution possibilities are very limited, so that to all intents and purposes fixed coefficient technology can be assumed. The convex combination of these alternative techniques determines the available process frontier (*APF*), since firms could in principle use a combination of both processes. If a further set of latent techniques is assumed, spanning the range of factor proportions, then joining up the points of minimum input combinations a continuous, differentiable isoquant of the fundamental production function (*FPF*) is obtained.

In figure 6.1(b) relative factor prices are added in. If, as in Britain, skilled labour is relatively cheap, the relevant factor price line is P_0 and firms produce at *B*. On the other hand, if skilled labour is relatively expensive as in America, the factor price line is P_1 and firms produce at *A*. Although British and American firms produce with different techniques, they have access to a common technology in the form of the fundamental production function.

Technical progress and factor proportions

David (1975) goes on to explain how the initial choice of technique led to differential rates of technical progress in Britain and America, although the possibility of imitation allows for catch up growth. David's model of endogenous localised technical change draws on the work of Atkinson and Stiglitz (1969). This can be seen as a form of trial and error process, or what Mokyr (1990) has called 'micro inventions'. American firms, having settled at point *A* in figure 6.2(a), attempt to reduce inputs and thus move towards the origin around the process ray α. The 'elastic barriers' surrounding the process ray can be seen as representing non-convexities in micro-

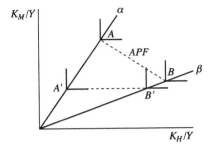

6.3 β-technology redundant

engineering designs. David (1975: 81) gives an example of a batch brewing process. If you try to reduce capital costs by drastically increasing the size of the vessel (costs rise in proportion to surface area and hence the square of the radius, while volume rises in proportion to the cube of the radius) this is likely to cause problems for the cooling system and raise unit cooling costs. Hence it is likely that small local changes will be introduced which do not drastically alter factor proportions, i.e. technical progress is locally neutral. Technical progress is path dependent and where you end up depends on where you start from (David, 1985; Arthur, 1989). In figure 6.2(a), technical progress shifts the available process frontier from *APF* to APF′ as technical progress occurs as a stochastic process between the elastic barriers around the α-ray.

Figure 6.2(b) illustrates competition between the two technologies. As technical progress occurs in America along the α-ray, the changes can be adapted to British conditions and imitation occurs along the β-ray. British firms, faced with relatively cheap skilled labour will continue to produce using the (evolving) British technology, while American firms, faced with relatively expensive skilled labour, will continue to produce using the (evolving) American technology.

Adjustment problems

Consider the situation in figure 6.3, however. Technical progress in America has been so rapid from *A* to *A*' along the α–ray that the new available process frontier makes the American technology superior at all relative factor prices. At this point, competition should force the British firms to abandon the British technology. It might be thought, then, that what Mokyr (1990) calls 'macro inventions' would provide an opportunity to break free from path dependence. Note, however, that even if the old technology is abandoned, it will not simply lead to the British firms adopting the American technology. Rather, they will be forced to search for a new technique on a different part of the fundamental production function. If the search is successful, British firms will end up using a technique which continues to be more skilled labour-intensive and less machine-intensive than the American technique. In fact, though, the owners of the specific human capital (and indeed the physical capital) embodied in the old technique may attempt to frustrate the workings of competition and continue to produce with the outmoded methods. Hence the degree of competition in product and factor markets may play an important role in the adjustment process.

Note, however, that technological dynamism does not have to originate in the country with the higher labour productivity. Equally, innovation in the less machine-intensive country could begin to undermine the viability of the more machine-intensive technology and force imitative responses. Indeed, this seems to have occurred from the late 1960s, with what is widely perceived as a shift of technological leadership to flexible production methods associated with Germany and Japan, as the cost of information processing declined dramatically (Broadberry, 1994a). Given the dramatic fall in the cost of computation, production can be geared cheaply to individual demands by skilled workers using computer aided design, numerically controlled machine tools and robots (Edquist and Jacobsson, 1988; Milgrom and Roberts, 1990). These methods can be linked to the earlier British craft production methods through their emphasis on the role of the skilled labourer on the shopfloor as well as through the production of customised output. Note also that British technological leadership during much of the nineteenth century was not accompanied by labour productivity leadership.

Within this framework, then, long-run productivity ratios are determined by choice of technique, determined in turn by resource and factor endowments and demand conditions. Any divergence from long-run ratios should be followed by catch up as imitation and switching of technologies occurs. However, there is no reason to believe that countries will converge on the same level of labour productivity unless their endowments and demand conditions are similar. Furthermore, given that accumulation takes place around specific techniques, it is highly unlikely that factor endowments will converge.

Overview and concluding comments

The model set out in this chapter provides an explanation for the large and persistent transatlantic labour productivity gap in manufacturing. The origins of the gap lie in the abundance of land and resources in America compared with Europe. During the period of British technological leadership during much of the nineteenth century, technology transfer from Britain to America required adaptation to local circumstances, economising on scarce skilled labour but utilising abundant natural resources. This led to the development of a distinctive American machine-intensive and resource-using technology that economised on skilled shopfloor labour. This 'American system of manufactures' could not simply be copied in Britain or Germany because of different resource and factor endowments. As the American system developed into mass production during the twentieth century, it required Chandler's (1990) three-pronged investment in production, management and marketing. During the period of American technological leadership during much of the twentieth century, successful technical development in Britain and Germany required adapting American methods to local circumstances, making use of abundant skilled shopfloor labour and customising output to meet heterogeneous demands. British and German 'flexible production' technology thus developed in different ways to American 'mass production' technology, despite the fact that all countries had access to the same common pool of knowledge.

Since technical change is a path dependent process and success requires the development of distinctive capabilities, there are clearly problems when a 'macro invention' in one country undermines the viability of a technology in another country. Slavish copying is unlikely to be a viable response, given different local circumstances. One tempting alternative for firms under threat is to lobby the government for protection or subsidies. However, once cut off from the stimulus of international competition, there is a danger that firms will allow technology to stagnate and fall behind international rivals. Britain after the Second World War appears to offer examples of both types of defensive response; attempts to copy American methods in British circumstances were notoriously unsuccessful, while protection and subsidies allowed many inefficient British firms to survive. The neglect of shopfloor skills during the period of Americanisation left Britain in a poor position to take advantage of the rejuvenation of flexible production techniques from the late 1960s, while the change of government policy after 1979, with a renewed emphasis on market forces, led to a painful period of adjustment for British manufacturing.

7   Economic geography: markets and natural resources

Introduction

The historical growth model of chapter 6 has pointed to differences between Europe and America in the areas of resource endowments and demand conditions as important factors explaining technical choice on both sides of the Atlantic. These differences have been highlighted in a number of empirical studies of comparative productivity in manufacturing during the nineteenth and twentieth centuries, including Habakkuk (1962), Ames and Rosenberg (1968), Rostas (1948a), Melman (1956), Frankel (1957) and Wright (1990). Demand factors are considered below, while in the following section the role of resources is examined. As in recent theoretical work on international trade, economic geography is seen to matter (Krugman, 1991).

Demand

Market size and standardisation

An important factor explaining the adoption of machine-intensive production methods in the United States is the nature of demand. Rostas (1948a), Frankel (1957) and more recently Chandler (1990) emphasise the importance of a large homogeneous American home market in permitting economies of scale through the adoption of mass production methods. It should be noted that this is not simply a matter of the size of the home market. For although the population of the United States has been substantially greater than in all individual European countries in the twentieth century, this was not the case for much of the nineteenth century. Data from Maddison (1991) in table 7.1 suggest that the US population level overtook the British level only during the 1850s, and pulled decisively ahead of the German level as late as the 1870s.

A further problem with the simple market size argument is that in most industries output was spread over a number of firms. As Rostas (1948a) points out, the British market was generally large enough to support a firm

90

Table 7.1. *Population, 1820–1989 (000)*

	UK	US	Germany
1820	21,240	9,618	24,905
1830	23,935	12,901	28,045
1840	26,758	17,120	31,126
1850	27,418	23,261	33,746
1860	28,840	31,513	36,049
1870	31,393	39,905	39,231
1880	34,623	50,262	45,095
1890	37,485	63,056	49,241
1900	41,155	76,094	56,046
1910	44,916	92,407	64,568
1920	43,718	106,466	60,894
1930	45,866	123,188	65,084
1940	48,226	132,122	69,838
1950	50,363	152,271	49,983
1960	52,373	180,671	55,433
1970	55,632	205,052	61,566
1980	56,314	227,757	61,566
1989	57,236	248,777	61,990

Notes: UK: excludes Southern Ireland from
1920 onwards. Germany: includes
Alsace–Lorraine after 1870; refers to the 1937
territory of the Reich from 1920, including the
Saar, which was not returned to Germany until
1935; refers to the territory of the Federal
Republic from 1950, including the Saar, which
was not returned until 1959, and West Berlin.
Source: Maddison (1991), tables B1–B4.

operating at the output level of the largest American firm in the same industry. And if plant size is measured in terms of number of employees, British
plants were generally larger than their American counterparts in the mid-
twentieth century. This suggests that the issue is standardisation of demand
rather than market size *per se.*

Chandler (1990) emphasises the importance of investment in marketing
in conjunction with the investments in production and management to
attain economies of scale and scope. However, Frankel (1957), while
acknowledging the benefits of standardised demand, accepts the possibility that greater inequality in the distribution of income and wealth and
greater class distinctions in Britain may have made standardisation more
difficult to attain. It is difficult to verify this argument quantitatively

because of great uncertainty about the degree of inequality within each country. Indeed, the two major modern researchers who have tried to establish the degree of inequality in both Britain and the United States during the nineteenth and twentieth centuries have studiously avoided making comparative statements. Indeed, they have disagreed very fundamentally about inequality trends in both countries. Whereas Soltow (1968,1969, 1990) is sceptical of any change in the degree of inequality in either country before the twentieth century, Williamson (1985, 1991) sees a substantial increase in inequality during the process of industrialisation, followed by a narrowing of the dispersion, as hypothesised by Kuznets (1955). The lack of agreement on the most fundamental trends within each country and the large array of Gini coefficients, Pareto constants and income shares means that it is difficult to make any reliable international comparisons of the degree of income inequality.

Most authors have nevertheless accepted a role for demand factors in the greater extent of standardisation in America. For at least some products the lack of a standardised mass market in Britain should be seen as a serious constraint rather than as a failure of advertising policy. In guns, which played an important role in the development of the American system of manufactures, it is clear that there could be no private market in Britain for cheap standardised products (Hounshell, 1984). The British market was for luxury, sporting guns, in contrast to the American market for a cheap gun, available to all. As Rothbarth (1946: 386) writes,

The ease with which the US industry has been able to install mass production methods is probably due as much to the structure of the buying public as to anything else; for the US public is very ready to buy standard articles which are not differentiated by marked individual features. In the United Kingdom, on the other hand, there remains an aristocracy and a middle class impregnated with aristocratic ideas, who reject mass produced articles and insist on articles with individual character.

Nevertheless, as Hounshell (1984) notes, there were limits to the willingness of even the American public to accept standardised products, and attempts to standardise furniture were met with consumer resistance.

In motor vehicles, the demand constraint in Britain during the first half of the twentieth century arose from the fact that *per capita* incomes were too low to support a mass market, as a number of authors have noted (Bowden, 1991; Tolliday, 1987b). This argument can also be applied to other consumer durables. It may be, then, that demand constraints at the beginning of the mass production era should be seen as arising more from social and institutional differences and low *per capita* incomes than from income inequality.

The lack of standardisation in Britain was reinforced by a greater

reliance on foreign trade, and in particular by an increasing concentration
on Empire markets, particularly in the face of rising protection in the
United States and Continental Europe. The role of this concentration on
Empire markets will be assessed in some detail below.

Whatever its origins, there is little doubt that a greater degree of
standardisation has been a factor in higher American labour productivity
over a long period. As Frankel (1957: 77) notes, there were already many
references to standardisation in the 1855 *Report of the Committee on the
Machinery of the United States*, reprinted in Rosenberg (1969). Thus, for
example, in the manufacture of locks at Messrs Davenport and Mallory's
Works in New Haven it was noted that

the same system of machinery is applied to every particular part; and all the locks
of each description produced are identical, and their parts can be interchanged.
(Rosenberg, 1969: 104)

On the general approach to woodworking in the districts visited, it was
noted that

the determination to use labour-saving machinery has divided the class of work
usually carried on by carpenters and the other wood trades into special manufactures, where only one kind of article is produced, but in numbers or quantity almost
in many cases incredible. (Rosenberg, 1969: 167)

During the First World War, the Board of Trade Engineering Trades
Committee contrasted the variety of British output with the standardisa-
tion in the United States (cited in Committee on Industry and Trade, Part
IV, *Survey of the Metal Industries*, London: HMSO, 1928: 146). Witnesses
before the Balfour Committee in the late 1920s noted that product
differentiation was often actively encouraged rather than simply tolerated.
Thus, for example, a representative of the Agricultural Engineers'
Association notes that

British manufacturers had carefully studied the home market and ... had even produced appliances to suit the peculiar and possibly eccentric requirements of farmers
in the different parts of the country who have differing ideas as to the characteristics
of the implements required. (*Survey of the Metal Industries*: 162)

Further evidence is available for the late 1940s and early 1950s through
the reports of the Anglo-American Council on Productivity (AACP), set
up as part of the postwar Labour government's productivity drive. As
Hutton (1953: 96–101) notes, most of the productivity reports saw the
'three Ss' of Simplification, Standardisation and Specialisation as important factors in the attainment of high labour productivity in the United
States. Although simplification and standardisation have come to be used
interchangeably, the AACP Report on *Simplification in British Industry*

(1950) maintained a distinction between a reduction in the number of varieties produced (simplification) and the use of common parts in different final products (standardisation). However, although most industry reports saw greater standardisation in America as a source of higher labour productivity, there were some doubts voiced about the possibility of the adoption of such methods in Britain, given different demand patterns. Thus, for example, the AACP Report on *Metalworking Machine Tools* (1953: 53) includes a statement by a number of team members who doubted the practicality of the adoption of American methods.

Rostas (1948a) sought to go further than listing the greater extent of standardisation in the United States, and attempted to provide some estimates of the impact on labour requirements in one or two cases. Thus, for example, he notes that in the US Jantzen knitting mills an operator turned out an average of 45 seams instead of the former 9 after the mills switched over to the production of swimming suits of one quality instead of a variety of knitted goods (Rostas, 1948a: 63). In Britain, Rostas notes, Cadbury reduced the number of lines and packings from 237 in 1939 to 29 in 1942 with a 40 per cent reduction in labour requirements per ton (Rostas, 1948a: 63).

For the early 1970s, a study by Pratten (1976) found that longer production runs could account for a good proportion of the labour productivity differences within international companies. Thus, for example, in a sample of companies that produced in both Britain and the United States in 1971–2, labour productivity was on average 50 per cent higher in US plants. Of this, 20.5 percentage points could be explained by longer production runs. More recently still, Mason and Finegold (1995) have continued to find large transatlantic differences in batch sizes in mechanical engineering.

Spheres of influence

The large homogeneous American market came to be served largely by American manufacturers behind high tariff barriers during the first half of the nineteenth century (Taussig, 1892). However, it is equally clear that from the late nineteenth century British manufacturers came to view the British Empire as their natural market, while German manufacturers came to view Continental European markets as their natural domain (Schlote, 1952; Hoffman, 1933).

Already before the First World War, the division of the world into spheres of influence by the three major manufacturing countries of Britain, Germany and the United States to avoid head-to-head competition was apparent in a number of industries. A survey of many of the pre-

1914 international combines is given in Plummer (1951: 4–10). The chemical industry was one of the most prone to international combination, with formal agreements in alkalis and explosives. As Reader (1970: 60) puts it,

In deciding how to share markets, the principle generally followed in each group, was that the British member ... should have the markets of Great Britain and the British Empire; the European member or members, Europe. Markets elsewhere in the world were a matter for negotiation. The United States, the richest, stood alone by reason of the formidable nature of the natives. Latin America, where both British and European connections were strong, was apt to be looked upon by American companies, particularly in the explosives trade, as being covered by a businessman's version of the Monroe Doctrine ... For the purposes of market-sharing the Russian Empire was generally taken as a province of Europe and the Chinese as a dependency of the British.

The upshot of these trends was a clear move towards concentration by British producers on Empire markets from the late nineteenth century. Furthermore, as Schlote's (1952) data in part (a) of table 7.2 make clear, this was a new departure, since there was no clear upward trend in the Empire share of British exports between 1830 and 1870. The trend towards concentration on Empire markets, particularly the Dominions of Australia, New Zealand, the Union of South Africa, Canada and Newfoundland, accelerated in the interwar period. The upheaval in the British trade data caused by the independence of the Irish Free State does not affect these trends, since the share can be calculated on both the old and the new basis in parts (a) and (b) of table 7.2, respectively. Continuing to the present in part (b) of table 7.2, the share of British exports to the original six members of the EEC as well as the share to 'British countries' can be seen. Clearly the rise to dominance of Empire markets (peaking at 55 per cent in 1951) was the other side of a serious decline in the importance of Continental European markets during the interwar and transwar periods. Imperial Preference was clearly no small sideshow for the British economy in the twentieth century. Indeed, as Drummond (1974: 426) notes, Imperial economic matters took up more Cabinet time than any other aspect of economic affairs between the wars. As late as 1970, more British exports were going to 'British countries' than to the EEC. Since Britain joined the EEC in 1973, however, trade with 'British countries' (including the Republic of South Africa and the Irish Republic) has dramatically declined in importance.

It might be thought that Britain's entry into the EEC in 1973 would have put Britain on an equal footing with the United States by giving access to a large free market. However, it is clear that European industry has not yet regrouped on a continent-wide basis. As Krugman (1991) notes, there are

Table 7.2. *British export markets, 1830–1990*

(a) British Empire share of British exports of home products (%)

1830	26.1
1840	32.3
1850	27.2
1860	32.1
1870	26.0
1880	33.7
1890	33.1
1900	32.4
1913	37.2
1925	39.6
1929	41.5
1931	38.8
1932	41.1
1933	41.2
1934	44.0

Note: Old area of trade statistics after 1925 (i.e. United Kingdom of Great Britain and Ireland).
Source: Schlote (1952), table 22.

(b) Shares of British exports to 'British countries' and EEC6 (%)

	British countries	EEC6
1907	32.2	24.8
1912	36.0	22.7
1924	42.1	18.7
1930	43.5	18.3
1935	48.0	14.7
1948	52.7	9.8
1951	55.0	10.4
1954	53.0	13.0
1958	49.3	13.1
1963	37.5	20.3
1968	31.2	19.3
1970	25.1	21.7
1980	20.1	34.6
1990	16.7	41.3

Note: 'British countries' includes the Irish Free State/Republic and the Republic of South Africa, as well as the Commonwealth.
Source: HM Customs and Excise (various issues), *Annual Statement of the Trade of the United Kingdom* (London: HMSO).

still four large centres of car production in Europe, based in Germany, France, Italy and Britain, compared with one in the United States, based in the Mid-West. This pattern persists in most industries, with national governments reluctant to see major national producers exit.

It is frequently argued that the concentration by British producers on Empire markets for much of the twentieth century should be seen as a sign of failure, retreating into 'soft' markets to avoid competition (Hobsbawm, 1968; Mathias, 1969; Kirby, 1981; Lazonick, 1986). However, an obvious question arises: did British manufacturers have any alternative? Faced with protection in the American and European markets, was not concentration on Empire markets a rational alternative? With hindsight we can see that after the Second World War the Dominions stagnated and Europe became a rapidly growing market so that the lack of an adequate marketing network in Europe proved a major drawback. But is it unreasonable for businessmen at the time to have expected the opposite?

Once it is accepted that British firms actively pursued an Empire oriented strategy, it becomes much easier to understand other business decisions, in particular with respect to technology. Clearly Empire markets lacked the homogeneity of the US market; but even European markets, so important for German industry, must have seemed relatively homogeneous compared with the diversity of conditions between the important imperial markets of India, Australia, South Africa and Canada, scattered across different continents. The conclusion of a number of the AACP reports from the early 1950s that the standardisation of American demand was an important factor in higher American productivity, but could not be so easily adopted in Britain begins to look more like rational decision making than unreasonable conservatism in this light.

The interaction between demand conditions and technology has recently been explored in some detail for the iron and steel industry during the period 1870–1914, building on the work of Temin (1966b), who argued that British producers did as well as could have been expected given their exclusion from the rapidly growing protected markets of Germany and America. Tolliday (1991) relates the much higher productivity in the United States compared with Britain to the much greater degree of specialisation and standardisation, which was in turn related to demand patterns. Furthermore, he notes that 'German practice was closer to the British, and there was a large gap between European and American practice' (Tolliday, 1991: 54). Nevertheless, Wengenroth (1994) and Fremdling (1991) note how different demand patterns led to technological differences between Britain and Germany, with British output more strongly geared towards open hearth steel for ship-plate and tinplate rather than Bessemer steel which was the staple German product.

Growth of demand and investment

Frankel (1957) also points to the advantages for the United States of the rapid growth of output as population expanded more rapidly than in Britain. The greater investment opportunities at a time of rapid technical progress gave the United States an advantage in adoption of the latest production methods. These effects would have been amplified to the extent that asset lives were shorter in the United States (Frankel, 1957: 90). In a more stable economy like Britain, however, new techniques could only be adopted as replacements for existing ones, and unless the prospective cost savings were great enough, replacement could occur only as old plant and equipment wore out (Frankel, 1957: 92).

Frankel (1957: 99) also draws attention to the possibility of adverse technological 'lock-in' effects through early industrialisation. With slow growing demand, and only piecemeal investments, the existing capital stock may constrain the adoption of new technology. The classic example used by Frankel to support this argument is the continued use of small freight wagons on the British railway system, which Veblen (1915: 126) famously referred to as 'silly bobtailed carriages'. Frankel argues that Britain was locked-in to this system because the terminal facilities, tracks, shunting facilities and all the ways and means of handling freight were already adapted to the bobtailed car.

Natural resources

Resource endowments

Some of the key dimensions of the differences in resource endowments between Britain and the United States in the mid-twentieth century are given in table 7.3, taken from Frankel (1957: 31). Figures are available for *per capita* outputs and reserves of the basic metals and fuels and supplies of land. Reserves and output at this time were vastly superior in the United States in all but two categories. In coal, however, the higher British output largely reflected the greater abundance of alternative fuels in the United States, and furthermore reserves were greater in the United States. And in tin, both countries imported most of their needs, so the slightly higher British output was of little significance.

Direct effects

Frankel (1957: 33–4) notes that the abundance of resources in the United States had direct effects in the processing industries. Thus, taking some

Table 7.3. *Output and reserves of selected raw materials in the mid-twentieth century*

	Output *per capita*		Reserves *per capita*	
	US	UK	US	UK
Bauxite (tonnes)	0.011		0.33	
Coal (tonnes)	29.26	45.37	13,480	3,430
Copper (pounds)	12.3		218.25	
Iron (tonnes)	0.40	0.09	169.35	18.29
Lead (pounds)	4.54	0.29	110	
Natural gas (000 m³)	1.58		36.47	
Petroleum (tonnes)	2.12		25.04	
Timber (hectares)			1.36	0.03
(m³)	1.85	0.06		
Tin (pounds)		0.05		
Zinc (pounds)	7.27	0.13	112	
Land (hectares)			12.85	1.20
Arable (hectares)			3.02	0.36
Pasture (hectares)			4.40	0.60
Other (hectares)			5.43	0.24

Notes:
Output data are for 1953, reserves for various years 1944–53. For copper, iron ore, lead, tin and zinc, the data refer to metal content.
Source: Frankel (1957: 31).

examples from the 1950s, based on the reports of the AACP, he attributes part of the higher American labour productivity in steel making to the lower phosphorous and sulphur content of American iron, access to cheap bentonite and high quality silica sands which facilitated the use of labour saving techniques, as well as the benefits of cheap and abundant fuels (AACP, *Steel Founding*, 1949). In food processing, Frankel (1957: 34) saw the wide range and volume of fruit and vegetables available to American processors as contributing to the greater scale of operations and intensity of mechanisation (AACP, *Food Canning*, 1950). In the manufacture of paper and paperboard containers, and in the packaging process itself, Frankel (1957: 33) saw American manufacturers as benefiting from the abundant supplies of good quality paper and board (AACP, *Packaging*, 1950).

An alternative way of demonstrating the importance of abundant resources for American production is to examine the data on international trade. In table 7.4, taken from Wright (1990), the relative resource intensity of US manufactured exports over the period 1879–1940 is shown. The

Table 7.4. *Non-renewable natural resource coefficients in American manufactured goods, 1879–1940 (1947 coefficients)*

(a) Direct use	1879	1899	1909	1914	1928	1940
Exports	0.0742	0.0677	0.0918	0.0988	0.0998	0.0564
Imports	0.0131	0.0194	0.0170	0.0133	0.0290	0.0369
Exports/Imports	5.66	3.49	5.40	7.43	3.44	1.53
(b) Direct and indirect use	1879	1899	1909	1914	1928	1940
Exports	0.1107	0.1239	0.1647	0.1800	0.1635	0.1240
Imports	0.0565	0.0747	0.0766	0.0749	0.0934	0.1127
Exports/Imports	1.96	1.66	2.15	2.40	1.75	1.10

Source: Wright (1990: 657).

coefficients for each industry are taken from the input–output table for 1947, and an average figure obtained for total manufacturing. Changes in the average figure over time therefore reflect changes in the composition of trade, since the same input–output coefficients are used in all years. Two alternative measures can be obtained, the first based only on direct use of resources, but the second based on the more inclusive direct and indirect use of resources. The latter measure takes account of the resource intensity of intermediate inputs used in the production of final output. Thus, for example, machinery appears more resource-intensive if account is taken of the resources used in the production of the steel used as an intermediate input.

Table 7.4 suggests that US exports had a higher natural resource content than imports over the whole period, whether or not account is taken of indirect use. Furthermore, Wright notes that the ratio was growing over the period to 1914, when the United States was rapidly gaining world market share. He thus sees resource abundance as one of the key sources of American comparative advantage at this time. Wright also sees this advantage as being eroded during the interwar period, although exports remained more resource-intensive than imports in 1940. Although the role of resources as the third factor in addition to capital and labour has increasingly been supplanted by human capital to a large extent in postwar work on trade flows, international economists have continued to see a role for resources in determining trade flows for resource-based 'Ricardo goods' (Stern and Maskus, 1981).

Indirect effects

Rostas (1948a), Melman (1956), Frankel (1957) and Franko (1976) all emphasise the role of resource endowments in determining the amount of

Table 7.5. *Hourly costs of labour and electricity in manufacturing, 1924–48*

(a) UK

	(1) Hourly labour cost (pence)	(2) kWh cost (pence)	(3)=(1)/(2) Labour/electricity cost ratio
1924	12.80	1.14	11.2
1930	12.58	0.82	15.3
1935	12.24	0.69	17.7
1938	13.00	0.64	20.3
1948	30.70	0.91	33.7

(b) US

	(1) Hourly labour cost (pence)	(2) kWh cost (pence)	(3)=(1)/(2) Labour/electricity cost ratio
1924	54.7	1.40	39.1
1930	55.2	1.30	42.5
1935	55.0	1.20	45.8
1938	62.7	1.10	57.0
1948	135.0	0.93	145.2

(c) Comparative ratios of labour/electricity costs (UK=100)

	US/UK	Germany/UK
1924	349.1	
1930	277.8	
1935	258.8	
1938	280.8	93.6
1948	430.9	

Source: Melman (1956: 206, 213).

machinery used and hence the level of labour productivity. Melman (1956) makes explicit the link between relative prices and factor proportions, calculating the relative cost of an hour of labour and a kilowatt hour (kWh) of electricity. He finds this ratio to be substantially higher in the United States, i.e. labour is much more expensive than electricity in the United States, giving an incentive to use more electrically driven machinery. Figures are given here in table 7.5 for *Census of Production* years between 1924 and 1948. The ratio between US and UK relative labour/electricity costs varied between 258.8 and 430.9, i.e. labour was between 2½ and 4⅓ times as expensive in the United States. Similar calculations for Germany and France also suggest much more expensive labour in the United States during the first half of the twentieth century (Melman, 1956: 213).

Changes since the Second World War

Nelson and Wright (1992) suggest that the American resource endowments have lost much of their economic significance in the period since the Second World War, for two reasons. First, they argue that there have been major resource discoveries in other countries so that the US superiority is no longer so apparent and second, they argue that transport improvements and declining trade barriers have unified world resource markets so that cheap resources are available to all. These arguments undoubtedly have some force, but resource differences should not be discounted entirely for the postwar period.

The increasing integration of world markets would be expected to have reduced the dispersion of relative resource costs during the postwar period. Nevertheless, repeating Melman's (1956) calculations for the 1980s, electricity still remains substantially cheaper in the United States than in the United Kingdom. For 1988, the ratio between US and UK relative labour/electricity costs is 178.9 (International Energy Agency, *Energy Prices and Taxes*, Paris: OECD, 1992). Furthermore, the International Energy Agency data allow us to see that labour/fuel cost ratios are also higher in the United States for other fuels. Frankel (1957) also draws attention to the US advantage in resources besides energy, while Franko (1976) and Davidson (1976) provide a generalisation of Melman's labour/energy cost calculations for other materials including lumber, cement, steel, aluminium, glass, rubber and water as well as oil and coal.

Conclusions

In this chapter we have examined the role of demand factors and resource differences in the transatlantic labour productivity gap. Dealing first with demand, a large homogeneous home market has undoubtedly been of benefit to the United States in allowing a high degree of standardisation. However, it should be noted that from the late nineteenth century to the middle of the twentieth century, the American advantage was consolidated through the division of the world into separate spheres of influence. The increasing dependence of British firms on heterogeneous and geographically dispersed Empire markets did little to facilitate standardisation and created problems of adjustment after the Second World War as the world economy became more integrated. The contrast between rapid growth of population and hence demand in America and slow growth in Britain can also be seen as creating problems of technological lock-in for Britain. The much greater resource endowments of the United States conferred substantial benefits. As well as direct benefits in the processing industries, there were indirect benefits in all industries through the cheaper relative price of energy, creating incentives to adopt machine-intensive methods. Although energy remains relatively cheap in America, the American resource advantage has been reduced since the Second World War with resource discoveries elsewhere and the increased integration of the world economy. Thus, to understand the continued differences of technology on both sides of the Atlantic, we need to consider the accumulation of factor inputs, to which we now turn.

8 Accumulation of physical and human capital

Introduction

The analysis so far suggests that endowments and demand conditions dictate a more machine-intensive technology in the United States, leading to higher labour productivity than in Europe. It might be expected, then, that an approach relating comparative labour productivity to comparative fixed capital per worker via a conventional production function would be successful in explaining international differences in labour productivity. However, this chapter shows that in practice differences in total factor productivity (TFP), incorporating fixed capital as well as labour inputs, are almost as large as differences in labour productivity. Although there are a number of measurement and conceptual problems, which make it likely that the role of physical capital is understated in the traditional growth accounting or levels accounting approach, it is also necessary to look more closely at the accumulation of human capital.

Here, it is important to distinguish between the different types of human capital needed to operate mass production and flexible production systems, since the standard data on years of schooling suggest little difference between the major industrialised countries (Maddison, 1987, table A12). Even if we accept that there are problems of international comparability with the schooling data, there must still be doubts about the precise links between general schooling and the jobs actually performed by the majority of workers in manufacturing (Howell and Wolff, 1992). Hence it is important to look at human capital accumulation that is more directly relevant to the skills actually used in the manufacturing sector. In this chapter, we therefore examine human capital accumulation in three areas, dealing with shopfloor skills, managerial capabilities and research capabilities. This section builds on the work of Broadberry and Wagner (1996).

Before looking at the evidence in detail, it will be helpful to set out the main arguments in relation to the model developed in chapter 6. First, American methods were more intensive in the use of resources and machinery, which substituted for relatively scarce skilled labour on the shopfloor. Second, however, this did not initially imply higher total fixed capital per worker in the United States because machinery was only a small part of total fixed capital. Third, American methods increasingly required high levels of human capital accumulation above the shopfloor level, in managerial and research capabilities. Fourth, after the Second World War British manufacturing pursued a relatively unsuccessful policy of Americanisation, which led to a neglect of human capital accumulation on the shopfloor and left Britain in a weak position to gain from the rejuvenation of flexible production techniques during the 1970s and 1980s.

Accumulation of physical capital

Much of the literature on Anglo-American comparisons has suggested that at least part of the difference in labour productivity levels between the two countries has been due to the use of more capital per worker in the United States (Habakkuk, 1962; Rostas, 1948a; Frankel, 1957; Davies and Caves, 1987). Hence it is of some interest to calculate comparative levels of TFP as well as labour productivity.

Comparative TFP levels for two countries can be calculated as the geometric weighted average of comparative capital productivity and comparative labour productivity, using the shares of capital and labour in net output as weights. An alternative way of expressing this is to see comparative TFP as the ratio between comparative output and comparative total factor input (TFI):

$$\frac{TFP^*}{TFP} = \frac{Y^*/Y}{TFI^*/TFI} = \frac{Y^*/Y}{(K^*/K)^\alpha (L^*/L)^{1-\alpha}} \tag{8.1}$$

where γ is output, L is employment and K the capital stock. Variables relating to the United States are indicated by an asterisk. The share of wages in net output $(1-\alpha)$ is 0.77, the geometric mean of US and UK weights for 1975, from van Ark (1990c).

The benchmark level of US/UK comparative TFP can be established for 1975 using data from van Ark (1990c). Post-1950 gross capital stock series for manufacturing are available from the US and UK National Accounts. Gross capital stock series before 1950 were taken from Feinstein (1972, 1988) for Britain and Kendrick (1961) for the United States. The results using the official estimates of the capital stock are shown in part (a) of table 8.1. Although the effect of allowing for capital is not very large, from 1889 onwards the TFP results are more favourable to the United Kingdom than the labour productivity results. Prior to that date, however, capital per worker was higher in Britain, which means that the TFP results are even more favourable to America. Repeating the TFP calculations for the Germany/UK comparison in table 8.2, again if the official capital stock

Table 8.1. *Comparative US/UK levels of output per worker and capital per worker, in manufacturing, 1869–1987 (UK=100)*

(a) Official capital stock data			
	Y/L	K/L	TFP
1869	203.8	93.7	204.9
1879	187.8	91.8	189.7
1889	195.5	159.0	174.0
1899	194.8	188.2	166.8
1909	208.5	183.0	179.7
1919	206.9	178.1	179.5
1929	249.9	173.1	218.2
1937	208.3	151.2	187.7
1950	262.6	155.2	235.1
1958	250.0	165.1	220.7
1968	242.7	133.1	225.1
1975	207.5	142.1	189.2
1980	192.9	120.7	183.0
1984	183.3	110.5	177.5
1987	188.8	109.9	183.1

(b) Standardised capital stock data			
	Y/L	K/L	TFP
1950	262.6	235.6	203.0
1958	250.0	253.1	189.2
1968	242.7	182.4	202.6
1975	207.5	194.5	169.9
1980	192.9	168.4	164.9
1984	183.3	157.5	160.0
1987	188.8	160.0	164.0

Sources: For the basic series, see appendix tables A8.1 and A3.1. The standardised capital stock estimates are from O'Mahony (1996).

estimates are used in part (a), then capital plays only a minor role in explaining labour productivity differences.

The conventional 'levels accounting' approach based on the Solow (1957) 'growth accounting' model fails for a number of reasons. The first problem concerns the measurement of the capital stock from data on investment. The perpetual inventory method calculates the capital stock by cumulating investments and allowing for retirements. However, since there are large differences in the asset lives assumed in different countries, with slender evidence to justify them, peculiar results emerge. For example, the

Table 8.2. *Comparative Germany/UK levels of output per worker and capital per worker, in manufacturing, 1875–1987 (UK=100)*

(a) Official capital stock data

	Y/L	K/L	TFP
1875	100.0	60.4	116.4
1889	94.7	71.2	104.9
1899	99.0	97.6	99.8
1909	117.7	98.0	118.5
1913	119.0	105.3	117.2
1925	95.2	61.0	110.5
1929	104.7	67.1	118.0
1937	99.9	73.2	109.8
1950	96.0	77.8	103.6
1958	111.1	71.5	122.8
1968	120.0	95.3	121.8
1975	132.9	107.2	130.2
1980	140.2	92.7	143.5
1984	122.7	81.2	130.7
1987	107.8	76.4	116.9

(b) Standardised capital stock data

	Y/L	K/L	TFP
1950	96.0	116.0	91.8
1958	111.1	120.9	104.9
1968	120.0	155.2	105.1
1975	132.9	174.7	112.4
1980	140.2	157.6	122.3
1984	122.7	142.9	110.3
1987	107.8	137.5	98.0

Sources: For the basic series, see appendix tables A8.1 and A3.1. The standardised capital stock estimates are from O'Mahony (1996).

United Kingdom is shown by the official capital stock estimates to have higher capital per worker than Germany, despite investing less over long periods of time (O'Mahony, 1996). To counter this, it is possible to provide alternative estimates, using standardised asset lives. Capital stock estimates standardised on US asset lives are presented in tables 8.1(b) and 8.2(b) for the post-Second World War period. Standardised capital stock data are taken from O'Mahony (1996), using common asset life assumptions of 31 years for structures and 17 years for equipment. These assumptions lead to the conclusion that capital per worker was substantially greater in the

United States during the postwar period, so that the Anglo-American TFP gap was substantially narrower than the labour productivity gap. Similarly, the standardised capital stock data go some way towards reducing the labour productivity gap between Britain and Germany during the postwar period.

However, for the pre-Second World War period, this procedure runs into difficulties because the historical capital stock estimates of Feinstein (1972), Kendrick (1961) and Hoffmann (1965) for the United Kingdom, the United States and Germany respectively are derived at least in part from stock data. Indeed, Giffen's (1889) study based on stock data did suggest that capital per worker was greater in the United Kingdom than in the United States, as indicated by the official figures for 1869 and 1879 in table 8.1. This clearly presents a problem for the conventional levels accounting approach because higher labour productivity in the United States cannot be explained by higher capital intensity in the United States. Although Maddison (1993) has provided some estimates of standardised capital stocks back to the nineteenth century at the whole economy level, which suggest greater capital intensity in the United States, it is not clear that these estimates overcome the problem that the original estimates were based at least in part on direct stock estimates, derived from insurance and tax data. Furthermore, Maddison's standardised data are not available for manufacturing.

The second problem concerns the relationship between capital and machinery. For economists often have in mind machinery when they write about capital as a determinant of labour productivity. Yet, as Field (1985) notes, machinery has historically been a relatively small proportion of the capital stock, which has been dominated by structures. It is possible that during the nineteenth century US manufacturing was more machine-intensive despite UK manufacturing being more capital-intensive, although Field (1985) appears not to believe so.

For the first half of the twentieth century, indeed, there is evidence of a strong link between machine intensity and labour productivity for manufacturing as a whole. For the pre-Second World War period, the evidence from table 8.3 suggests that US horse-power per worker was about twice the British level, while in Germany and France, horse-power per worker was of the same order of magnitude as in Britain. These ratios are roughly the same as the labour productivity ratios.

The strong link between machinery and labour productivity suggested by the above data for the pre-Second World War period is given further support for the post-Second World War period by De Long and Summers (1991), who note a strong relationship between productivity growth and equipment investment, thus avoiding the calculation of capital stocks with

Table 8.3. *Comparative output per worker and horse-power per worker, in manufacturing, 1906–39 (UK=100)*

Country	Year	Output per worker	Horse-power per worker
US/UK	1909/07	208.5	212.8
	1929/30		195.6
	1939/30		255.8
	1937	208.3	
Germany/UK	1933/30		107.6
	1935	102.0	
France/UK	1906/07	65.0	77.1

Sources: US/UK: UK, *Census of Production* (1907); US, *Census of Manufactures* (1909); Rostas (1948a).
Germany/UK: Melman (1956); Broadberry and Fremdling(1990).
France/UK: Dormois (1991).

doubtful asset life assumptions. These results are confirmed by De Long (1992) for the period 1870–1980.

The figures in table 8.3 suggest the possibility of a unit coefficient on machine capital, which would be consistent with a model of endogenous growth along the lines suggested by Romer (1986). However, the evidence of Rostas (1948a) suggests the need for caution here. In the cross-sectional sample assembled by Rostas for the United States and the United Kingdom in the mid-1930s, the relationship is not so simple. Out of a sample of 28 industries, he found only six cases where there was a proportional relationship between comparative horse-power per worker and comparative output per worker. In 14 industries, the United States employed disproportionately more horsepower per worker to achieve higher output per worker, while in eight industries the United States productivity advantage was greater than the horse-power per worker advantage.

Whilst there must inevitably be qualifications about the use of horse-power per worker as a measure of machine intensity, the relationship between horse-power per worker and output per worker identified by writers such as Rostas (1948a) and Melman (1956) is suggestive of a higher coefficient on machine capital than that commonly used in conventional TFP studies. This brings us to the third problem with the levels accounting approach, which assigns a low coefficient to capital, based on capital's share of income (usually between a quarter and a third). This means that huge differences in capital per worker are needed to explain even relatively small differences in labour productivity. Going to the other extreme and using a unit coefficient on comparative capital per worker in tables 8.1 and 8.2

Table 8.4. *Apprentices in prewar British engineering, 1914–50 (%)*

	Apprentices	Employment	Apprentice share of employment
1914	44,917	297,680	15.1
1921	55,852	390,175	14.3
1928	38,899	416,710	9.3
1933	24,658	299,219	8.2
1938	52,840	608,897	8.7
1950	64,818	1,480,201	4.4

Notes: Blue collar male employment from EEF data adjusted to allow for female and white collar workers using information from Wigham (1973: 303–4) and the *Census of Production.*
Sources: Engineering Employers' Federation, 'Number of Workpeople Employed'; 'Total Number of Men, Apprentices and Boys and Youths Employed' (EEF MSS.237/13/3/1–56).

would go a long way towards explaining comparative output per worker, especially using standardised capital in the post-Second World War period. Although this would be in the spirit of Romer's (1986) early work stressing external economies from capital accumulation, a more promising approach is surely to broaden out our conception of capital to include human capital, as in much of the later new growth literature (Lucas, 1988; Romer, 1990).

Accumulation of human capital

Technical choice affects the accumulation of human capital as well as fixed capital. Here, it is important to distinguish between the different types of human capital needed to operate mass production and flexible production systems, since (a) the standard data on years of schooling suggest little difference between the major industrialised countries (Maddison, 1987, table A12) and (b) the links between general schooling and the jobs performed by the majority of workers in manufacturing are unlikely to be particularly close (Howell and Wolff, 1992).

Shopfloor labour

For Britain it is possible to estimate apprentices as a share of employment in engineering, broadly defined (including shipbuilding) back to 1914. The data are presented in table 8.4. Figures on the numbers of apprentices and male blue collar employees are available in the Engineering Employers'

Table 8.5. *Apprentices in postwar Britain, 1964–89*

	Manufacturing	Engineering
A. Apprentices (000)		
1964	240.4	152.5
1966	243.7	170.4
1970	218.6	151.2
1980	149.5	101.3
1989	53.6	34.1
B. Employment (000)		
1964	8067.9	3461.1
1966	8158.0	3550.8
1970	8033.0	3539.2
1980	6519.4	3026.5
1989	4953.1	2130.3
C. Apprentices as a share of employment (%)		
1964	2.98	4.41
1966	2.99	4.80
1970	2.72	4.27
1980	2.29	3.35
1989	1.08	1.60

Sources:
Apprentices: Gospel (1995).
Employment: Business Statistics Office (1978), *Historical Record of the Census of Production, 1907 to 1970* (London). Adjustment from census years to benchmark years using employment from Department of Employment and Productivity (1971), *British Labour Statistics Historical Abstract, 1886–1968* (London); Business Monitor (various issues), *Report of the Census of Production; Summary Tables* (London).

Federation (EEF) archive held in the Modern Records Centre at the University of Warwick. The employment data can be adjusted to allow for female employment using data from Wigham (1973: 303–4) and to allow for white collar employment using *Census of Production* data. The data show a decline in apprenticeship as a proportion of the labour force in engineering during the 1920s from about 15 per cent to a little under 10 per cent, and a further decline across the Second World War to a little less than 5 per cent.

The data in table 8.5 take up the story from the 1960s. A further decline in apprenticeship occurred in British engineering from the late 1960s, and has continued steadily to the present. Data here are taken from Gospel (1995) and rely on figures collected by the Department of Employment

(DE). Data are also available for total manufacturing and follow a similar downward trend but starting from a lower level. It should be noted that the DE data tend to understate the role of training in Britain, since they rely on employer reporting and adopt a stricter definition of apprenticeship than is the case in Germany. Thus, for example, trainee technicians are included in the German but excluded from the British data.

For Germany the share of apprentices in employment can be tracked from the end of the nineteenth century using industrial census data. Table 8.6 presents prewar data on apprentices and total employment for the whole economy, manufacturing, and metals and engineering, the latter category corresponding broadly to the British engineering sector of table 8.4, since vertical integration of firms and craft organisation of labour makes it very difficult to separate out engineering from metal production. The proportion of engineering employees in apprenticeships was stable before the Second World War. However, this is consistent with a sharp rise in the absolute number of apprentices during the 1930s which is interpreted by Gillingham (1986) as part of a 'deproletarianisation' of German society in the Third Reich. Table 8.7 takes the story into the postwar period. Comparing the German with the British data, there is a clear difference in trends. Whereas in Britain there has been a sharp decline in apprenticeship since the Second World War, in Germany there has been no clear downward trend. Indeed, although there was a small drop in apprentices as a share of employment in the engineering and manufacturing sectors, the ratio rose in the economy as a whole. Germany has retained a commitment to apprenticeships which has evaporated in postwar Britain.

Judgements concerning levels are always more hazardous than judgements about trends. Nevertheless, taken at face value, the apprenticeship data indicate a greater commitment to shopfloor training in Britain before the First World War, and only a small German advantage in the interwar period. In fact, this would not be too far out of line with the existing literature (Zeitlin, 1994). Indeed, there is much favourable comment on the skills of the British labour force in the late nineteenth and early twentieth centuries. Fremdling (1986) notes the extent to which British workers were sought after by Continental iron and steel producers, while Pollard and Robertson (1979) argue that Britain's success in the shipbuilding industry was based on the skill of the British workforce which allowed firms to economise on fixed capital. Harley (1974) stresses the influence of the large stock of skilled labour on the choice of technique in Edwardian Britain.

However, it may be argued that the above figures give too favourable a view of British training. First it should be noted that well into the post-Second World War period, British apprenticeships typically lasted five years in contrast to the three years more usual in Germany. A broadly equal

Table 8.6. *Prewar German apprenticeship data, 1895–1940*

	Metals and engineering	Manufacturing	Whole economy
A. Apprentices			
1895	158,477	519,616	701,033
1907	214,128	560,163	809,286
1925	346,441	796,999	986,567
1933	199,588	564,416	880,407
1940	483,885	740,042	1,443,447
B. Employment (000)			
1895	1,189	6,472	23,405
1907	1,994	8,459	28,166
1925	2,858	9,972	31,033
1933	1,637	7,075	26,687
1939	4,544	12,681	39,680
C. Apprentices as a share of employment (%)			
1895	13.3	8.0	3.0
1907	10.7	6.6	2.9
1925	12.1	8.0	3.2
1933	12.2	8.0	3.3
1939/40	10.6	5.8	3.6

Sources:
Apprentices:
1895: Berufs- und Gewerbezählung vom 14.Juni 1895. Gewerbestatistik für das Reich im Ganzen, *Statistik des Deutschen Reichs,* Neue Folge, Band 113 (Berlin, 1898).
1907: Berufs- und Betriebszählung vom 12 Juni 1907. Gewerbliche Betriebsstatistik, *Statistik des Deutschen Reichs,* Band 213 (Berlin, 1910).
1925: Volks- Berufs- und Betriebszählung vom 16. Juni 1925, Gewerbliche Betriebszählung. Die Gewerblichen Betriebe und Unternehmungen im Deutschen Reich, Teil III, Die Technischen Betriebseinheiten im Deutschen Reiche (Berlin, 1929).
1933: Volks- Berufs- und Betriebszählung vom 1933. Das Personal der gewerblichen Niederlassungen nach der Stellung im Betrieb und die Verwendung von Kraftsmaschinen (Berlin, 1935).
1940: *Statistisches Handbuch von Deutschland, 1928–1944* (Länderrat des Amerikanischen Besatzungsgebiets, München, 1949).
Employment: Hoffman (1965).

proportion of the labour force being trained in both countries thus resulted in a larger stock of skilled workers in Germany. Against this, however, it might be argued that the British workers were more highly trained.

A second and related reason for believing the figures to be too kind to Britain might be that they take no account of the quality of the training received. However, studies from the 1950s and 1960s do not suggest that Britain was seriously out of step with Europe at this time (Williams, 1957,

Table 8.7. *Postwar German apprenticeship data, 1950–88*

	Metals and engineering	Whole Manufacturing	economy
A. Apprentices			
1950	203,571	304,728	1,023,786
1960	339,713	553,890	1,426,389
1970	289,158	447,342	1,277,864
1980	363,245	611,734	1,674,064
1988	374,038	621,094	1,765,652
B. Employment (000)			
1950	2,553	6,576	22,074
1960	4,739	10,016	26,247
1970	5,393	10,181	26,668
1980	5,095	9,017	27,059
1988	5,004	8,409	27,366
C. Apprentices as a share of employment (%)			
1950	8.0	4.6	4.6
1960	7.2	5.5	5.4
1970	5.4	4.4	4.8
1980	7.1	6.8	6.2
1988	7.5	7.4	6.5

Sources:
Apprentices:
Statistik der BRD 45 'Die nichtlandwirtschaftlichen Arbeitsstätten' 13.9 1950 Heft 1;
Fachserie C Unternehmen und Arbeitsstätten Arbeitsstättenzählung, 6. Juni 61 Heft 2;
Arbeits und Sozialstatistik Hauptergebnisse 92/91/89/87/81; Unternehmen und
Arbeitsstätten Fachserie 2 Heft 1.
Employment:
Statistisches Jahrbuch 1954 (Erwerbstätige 1950); Fachserie C Unternehmen und
Arbeitsstätten Arbeitsstättenzählung 6. Juni 61 Heft 2; Arbeits und Sozialstatistik
Hauptergebnisse 92; Zahlen für ausgewählte Wirtschaftsgruppen aus *Statistisches Jahrbuch*
1992.

1963; Liepmann, 1960; Organisation for European Economic Cooperation, *Vocational Training in the Footwear Industry*, Paris, 1960). This ties in
with the findings of later research for the 1980s, which suggest that Britain's
skills gap has more to do with the quantity rather than the quality of
trained workers (NIESR, 1991). It is true that there are comments about
the lack of flexibility exhibited by British craft workers, but it might be
argued that this has more to do with the enforcement of strict lines of
demarcation by craft unions than with the quality of training.

A third issue concerns the level of general education of British workers
before training, a factor which again features in recent discussions of train-

Table 8.8. *Proportions of the manufacturing workforce with certified qualifications in Britain and Germany, 1978/79 and 1989 (%)*

	1978/79	1989
A. Britain		
Upper level	4.7	7.9
Intermediate level	24.4	35.2
No qualifications	71.0	56.8
B. Germany		
Upper level	3.6	6.6
Intermediate level	60.9	67.0
No qualifications	35.5	26.4

Source: O'Mahony and Wagner (1994).

ing (NIESR, 1991). However, for the prewar period, recent work has tended to argue that Anglo-German differences were much exaggerated in the early literature since the German centralised state-run system was being compared with the much harder to document British decentralised system, which actually underwent major reforms (Pollard, 1989; Sanderson, 1988).

Alternatively, it might be thought that the above figures give too gloomy a view of British training by concentrating only on apprenticeships and neglecting other forms of training for shopfloor workers. In particular, it may be thought important to consider alternative ways of obtaining intermediate level skills, since apprenticeships have traditionally been associated with old-style craft unionism, which has been under severe attack since the late 1970s. Recent figures from the *Labour Force Survey* suggest that the decline in apprenticeships in manufacturing has been offset by a rise in City and Guilds and other similar level qualifications, so that the stock of workers with intermediate level qualifications has risen slightly between 1979 and 1989. In fact, the proportion of workers with intermediate qualifications has risen by rather more, since the reduction of employment in manufacturing during the 1980s took the form of shedding unskilled labour. However, this still leaves the stock of skilled workers in Britain far below German levels (O'Mahony and Wagner, 1994). The stock data for the manufacturing workforces in Britain and Germany from the late 1970s are given in table 8.8. This confirms the bleak picture of the shopfloor skills of British workers that was built up through the 1980s by researchers at the National Institute of Economic and Social Research (NIESR, 1991). However, it also suggests that during the 1980s British manufacturing has begun to reverse the postwar trend towards greater use

Table 8.9. *Prewar US apprenticeship data,*
1880–1940

	Manufacturing and mechanical
A. Apprentices	
1880	44,170
1900	81,603
1920	140,400
1930	89,982
1940	84,080
B. Employment (000)	
1880	4,060
1900	7,729
1920	12,595
1930	12,612
1940	13,195
C. Apprentices as a share of employment (%)	
1880	1.1
1900	1.1
1920	1.1
1930	0.7
1940	0.6

Sources:
Apprentices: Bolino (1989); US Bureau of the Census.
Employment: US Department of Commerce (1960),
Historical Statistics of the United States: Colonial
Times to 1957 (Washington, DC).

of American methods, and is returning to a more skilled labour-intensive strategy.

For the United States, the quantitative picture is rather more difficult to establish beyond the widespread agreement that apprenticeship had virtually died out by the turn of the century as a significant form of training for industrial workers (Elbaum, 1989). This is what would be expected given the rise of mass production in the United States. As Hounshell (1984: 6) notes, Henry Ford believed that 'In mass production there are no fitters'. A reduction in the demand for skilled labour would seem to be a useful additional explanation for the decline of apprenticeship in addition to the problems with the enforcement of bonds which Elbaum stresses. The US apprenticeship data in tables 8.9 and 8.10 are patchy. For the prewar period, the Bureau of the Census data have been collected together by Bolino (1989). These figures cover largely the manufacturing and construction

Table 8.10. *Postwar US apprenticeship data, 1952–91*

	Metal working	Whole economy
A. Apprentices		
1952	14,645	172,477
1960	24,898	172,161
1970	57,406	269,626
1975		265,000
1991	57,573	255,455
B. Employment (000)		
1952	7,026	58,918
1960	7,246	65,778
1970	7,157	78,678
1975		85,846
1991	8,303	116,877
C. Apprentices as a share of employment (%)		
1952	0.21	0.29
1960	0.34	0.26
1970	0.80	0.34
1975		0.31
1991	0.69	0.22

Sources:
Apprentices: Bolino (1989); US Department of Labor.
Employment: US Department of Commerce (various issues),
Annual Survey of Manufactures (Washington, DC); US
Department of Commerce (various issues), *Statistical Abstract of
the United States* (Washington, DC).

sectors, although for some years a small number of apprentices in transport
and mining are included. Attempts to disaggregate the figures are unreli-
able, but it seems likely from the evidence of later years that construction
accounts for a high proportion of these apprentices. These low figures
should thus be seen as 'upper bound' estimates for engineering, particularly
since it is likely that a number of machine minders have been included due
to ambiguity in the wording of the Census questions. For the postwar
period, data from the Department of Labor are again collected together by
Bolino (1989), allowing us to distinguish metal working from the whole
economy estimates. Again, the share of apprentices in employment is rather
small, even in metal working.

The available figures, then, suggest that training of shopfloor workers has
been much more important in Britain and Germany compared with the
United States throughout the twentieth century. They also suggest that the
post-1945 period has seen a serious decline in apprenticeship in Britain,

Table 8.11. *Educational qualifications of British managers, 1951–89*

A. *Top managers*

Date	Sample size	% managers graduates	% graduates science & eng.
1951	1,173	36	42
1954	455	30	
1970	Boards of 200 cos	52	
1974	199	46	
1975	90	57	21
1976	1145	27	
1979	Top 50 chairmen	62	
1989	Top 50 chairmen	72	

Sources: Copeman (1955); Acton Society Trust (1956); Heller (1970); Stanworth and Giddens (1974); Fidler (1981); Melrose-Woodman (1978); Hannah (1990).

B. *All managers*

Date	Sample size	% managers graduates	% graduates science & eng.
1954	3,327	19	73
1954–5	646	26	63
1964	818	35	80
1976	4,525	28	57
1980	1,058	33	56
1986	2,757	69	

Sources: Acton Society Trust (1956); Clements (1958); Clark (1966); Melrose-Woodman (1978); Poole *et al.* (1981); Peppercorn and Skoulding (1987).

while in Germany there has been a consolidation of the industrial apprenticeship system. Recent *Labour Force Survey* data, however, suggest that there has been a revival in intermediate level qualifications in Britain during the 1980s, suggesting a return to a more skilled labour-intensive strategy in British manufacturing.

Managerial capabilities

Although data exist on the educational qualifications of American managers in the late 1920s, comparable British and German data are available only from the early 1950s. These figures, presented in tables 8.11–8.13, provide quite a range of estimates for the proportion of managers with degrees,

Table 8.12. *Educational qualifications of German managers, 1954–93*

A. *Top managers*

Date	Sample size	% managers graduates	% graduates science & eng.
1954	6,578	31	37
1964	318	89	57
1967	217	76	46*
1970	538	58	61
1981	695	67	
1985	759	69	38*
1986	346	61	
1993	765	72	43

Notes: * Engineering only.
Sources: Hartmann (1959); Zapf (1965); Brinkmann (1967); Pross and Bötticher (1971); Kienbaum Vergütungsberatung, *Gehalts-Struktur-Untersuchung '81*, Gummersbach; Kienbaum Vergütungsberatung, *Gehalts-Struktur-Untersuchung '85*, Gummersbach; Wuppermann (1989); Kienbaum Vergütungsberatung, *Gehalts-Struktur-Untersuchung '93*, Gummersbach.

B. *All managers*

Date	Sample size	% managers graduates	% graduates science & eng.
1964	21,707	27	36
1965	31,427	32	
1967	14,221	58	28
1981	6,670	52	
1985	5,622	58	68*
1993	4,326	59	31*

Notes: * Engineering only.
Sources: Hartmann and Wienold (1967); Kruk (1967); Brinkmann (1967); Kienbaum Vergütungsberatung(1981); Kienbaum Vergütungsberatung (1985); Kienbaum Vergütungsberatung (1993).

largely because of variation in the level of management surveyed (Melrose-Woodman, 1978; Lawrence, 1980; Evers and von Landsberg, 1982; Granick, 1972). They do nevertheless appear to confirm the existence of rather different human capital strategies in Europe and America. The proportion of graduates among British and German top management in the

Table 8.13. *Educational qualifications of American managers, 1928–86*

A. Top managers

Date	Sample size	% managers graduates	% attended college
1928	7,371	32	45
1950		62	
1952	8,300	57	76
1964		74	
1986		85	

Sources: Taussig and Jocelyn (1932); Newcomer (1955); Warner and Abegglen (1955); Newcomer (1965); Handy *et al.* (1988).

early 1950s was at about the level of American business leaders in the late 1920s, with Britain and Germany lagging equally behind America. By the 1970s and 1980s, the proportion of top managers with degrees had risen in both Britain and Germany, although still remaining below the very high American levels.

The figures in tables 8.11 and 8.12 may seem surprising at first sight in the light of the extensive literature on the lack of qualifications in British management (Keeble, 1992; Coleman, 1973; Gourvish, 1987; Handy *et al.,* 1988). Clearly, although some studies show a much lower proportion of graduates in British management, on the whole the impression is of similar proportions in Britain and Germany, especially if allowance is made for the different levels of management being sampled. Indeed, if membership of professional institutions is taken into account, Britain has a small advantage over Germany in higher level qualifications, as has been pointed out by researchers at the NIESR (Prais, 1993).

The importance of membership of professional institutions as a share of higher level qualifications in British manufacturing has declined sharply during the 1980s according to the *Labour Force Survey*, accounting for 15.3 per cent in 1990, down from 41.4 per cent in 1979. This suggests that many managers now obtain a degree before taking their professional examinations. Furthermore, the fact that this is a relatively recent phenomenon suggests a way of reconciling Prais' (1993) finding of no shortfall of higher level qualifications in Britain during the 1970s with the traditional emphasis in the management literature on the poor educational background of British managers, with the latter literature concentrating on degrees and ignoring the professional qualifications.

Sometimes this downplaying of the positive role of professional qualifications in British management is taken one step further, with the claim that a preponderance of accountants has had significant negative effects, causing an excessive concentration on short-term financial goals (Handy *et al.*,1988). Although the extent of the differences between Britain and Germany is sometimes exaggerated by not comparing like with like, it does seem to be the case that there are substantially more qualified accountants in Britain, where accountancy is seen as an established route into management (Handy *et al.*, 1988). In 1992, there was a total of about 195,000 accountants in Britain compared with 62,000 in Germany. This reliance on large numbers of accountants in Britain appears to have long historical roots (Edwards, 1989; Jones, 1981). Recent research by Matthews (1993) suggests that accountants already played a significant role in management of the quoted company sector before the First World War.

The emphasis on accountancy in British management is usually contrasted with the emphasis on technology in German companies. However, it should be borne in mind that many British accountants have a background in science and engineering. Analysis of the 1992/3 entry to the Institute of Chartered Accountants in England and Wales reveals that of 4,070 entrants, 3,714 were graduates, of whom 1,091 had degrees in engineering, science or mathematics. Furthermore, the data in tables 8.11 and 8.12 suggest a high proportion of managers with degrees in science and engineering in both Britain and Germany. This finding is consistent with the work of Prais (1993), although he stresses the greater emphasis on pure science than on engineering in Britain. As Lawrence (1980) notes, science and engineering in Germany means mainly engineers with a few pure scientists. Thus, for example, in table 8.12, Hartmann's (1959) figure of 37 per cent for the proportion of graduates in science and engineering is made up of 36 per cent in engineering and 1 per cent in science. This discussion of the role of scientists and engineers leads on naturally to a consideration of research skills.

R&D

Tables 8.14–8.16 assemble data on the scale of research in Britain, Germany and the United States. Tables 8.14 and 8.15 show the level of spending on R&D and the employment of researchers in Britain, the United States and Germany between 1933 and 1989, drawing on studies by Mowery (1986), Freeman (1962) and Sanderson (1972) for the period before the availability of official statistics. Figures relate as closely as possible to total R&D in manufacturing, whether carried out by private firms, public corporations or industrial research associations, and whether financed by private or public funds. Although there are obvious problems of comparability, most

Table 8.14. *R&D expenditures in manufacturing, 1934–89*

A. Britain

	(£m)	(£m)	(£m)	(%) R&D	(%) R&D
	R&D	Net output	Value added	Net output	Value added
1934	5.15	1,204		0.43	
1938	6.65	1,559		0.43	
1959	273.8	7,848		3.49	
1964	476.3	10,820		4.40	
1968	629.5	18,531		3.40	
1975	1,293.4	36,948	32,390	3.50	3.99
1983	3,869.9	80,804	65,753	4.79	5.88
1989	6,450.5	135,207	108,291	4.77	5.96

B. US

	($m)	($m)	($m)	(%) R&D	(%) R&D
	R&D	Net output	Value added	Net output	Value added
1937	247	25,174		0.98	
1959	9,400	161,536		5.82	
1981	49,904	837,507	649,631	5.96	7.68
1987	85,427	1,165,747	862,331	7.33	9.91

C. Germany

	(m DM)	(m DM)	(%) R&D
	R&D	Value added	Value added
1950	215	37,290	0.58
1959	1,413	100,660	1.40
1964	3,289	167,520	1.96
1969	7,079	229,590	3.08
1975	13,664	352,540	3.88
1983	29,733	519,420	5.72
1989	48,224	697,810	6.91

Sources:
Britain:
R&D: 1934 from Mowery(1986); 1938 from Sanderson (1972); 1959 from Freeman (1962); 1964–89 from Business Monitor (various issues), *Industrial Research and Development Expenditure and Employment* (London).
Net Output and Value Added: Business Statistics Office (1978), *Historical Record of the Census of Production, 1907 to 1970* (London), with adjustments from census years to benchmark years using GDP in manufacturing from Feinstein (1972); Business Monitor (various issues), *Report of the Census of Production; Summary Tables* (London).

historians agree that the British research effort was substantially smaller than the American effort before the Second World War and into the 1950s, and this is indeed borne out by the figures in tables 8.14 and 8.15. Equally clearly, there was a large increase in resources devoted to R&D in both countries after the Second World War, although the increase is probably overstated because of the failure of the prewar statistics to adequately capture some of the research effort (Nelson and Wright, 1992: 1952).

The position of Britain compared with other European countries, however, is much less clear for the prewar period, because there are no national data. However, research by Erker (1990) and Edgerton and Horrocks (1994) suggests that British firms did not generally lag behind European competitors in the employment of research staff in the interwar period. The data on companies in table 8.16 are taken from Edgerton and Horrocks (1994), and there are doubts about comparability between companies and over time. Nevertheless they do appear to reflect the generally larger American research effort, with Du Pont employing more researchers than ICI and GE employing more than GEC.

The exception to the large American lead in R&D appears to be chemicals, where Germany established an early strong position. In table 8.16 this is reflected by the figures for IG Farben, which dominates both Du Pont and ICI. However, amongst the electrical producers, the British firms employed more research staff then the German firms. Edgerton and Horrocks note further that it has never been suggested that France, Italy or Japan did more R&D than Britain during the interwar period. The above figures cast serious doubt on the claims of many writers that British industry has performed badly because of a deep-rooted bias against science and technology which permeates British society (Landes, 1969; Wiener, 1981).

Turning to the postwar period, the British research effort continues to lag behind the American effort as measured by the ratio of R&D expenditure

Sources: (cont)
US:
R&D: 1937 from Mowery (1986); 1959 from Freeman (1962); 1981–7 from OECD (1991), *Basic Science and Technology Statistics* (Paris).
Net Output and Value Added: Department of Commerce (various issues), *Census of Manufactures* (Washington, DC); OECD (1993), *National Accounts: Detailed Tables, Vol. II* (Paris).
Germany:
R&D: SV-Gemeinnützige Gesellschaft für Wissenschaftsstatistik mbH (1966), *Wissenschaftsausgaben der Wirtschaft: Ergebnisse der Registrierungen des Stifterverbandes 1948–1963* (Essen); SV-Gemeinnützige Gesellschaft für Wissenschaftsstatistik mbH (various issues), *Forschung und Entwicklung in der Wirtschaft* (Essen).
Value Added: Statistisches Bundesamt (1991), *Volkswirtschaftliche Gesamtrechnungen 1950 bis 1990*, Fachserie 18, Reihe S.15 (Wiesbaden).

Table 8.15. *Employment of researchers in manufacturing, 1933–89*

A. Britain

	Researchers	(000) Employment	(%) Researchers / Employment
1933	1,724	5,260	0.032
1935	2,575	5,634	0.046
1938	4,505	6,148	0.073
1945–6	5,200	7,080	0.073
1959	44,300	7,955	0.57
1968	216,000	8,033	2.69
1975	181,000	7,467	2.42
1983	186,000	5,079	3.66
1989	176,000	4,953	3.55

B. US

	Researchers	(000) Employment	(%) Researchers / Employment
1933	10,900	6,558	0.17
1940	28,000	9,527	0.29
1946	45,900	14,294	0.32
1959	219,100	16,662	1.31

C. Germany

	Researchers	(000) Employment	(%) Researchers / Employment
1964	127,765	9,885	1.29
1969	167,752	9,883	1.70
1975	175,326	9,097	1.92
1989	285,966	8,696	3.29

Sources:
Britain:
Researchers: 1933 to 1945–6 from Mowery (1986); 1959 from Freeman (1962); 1968–89 from Business Monitor (various issues), *Industrial Research and Development Expenditure and Employment* (London).
Employment: Business Statistics Office (1978), *Historical Record of the Census of Production, 1907 to 1970* (London). Adjustment from census years to benchmark years using employment in manufacturing from Feinstein (1972); Business Monitor (various issues), *Report of the Census of Production; Summary Tables* (London).

Table 8.16. *Employment of qualified researchers in companies, 1928–38*

	1928	1930	1933	1935	1938
IG Farben	1,050	1,100	1,000	1,020	1,150
Du Pont		687	725	847	979
ICI				464	510
GE	223	202			
GEC		125		175	
Metropolitan–Vickers		73		87	117
BTH		73		104	
Philips	48	72			
Siemens	92	68			
AEG	30		60		

Source: Edgerton and Horrocks (1994, table 6).

to net output in manufacturing. Converting to a value added basis for comparison with Germany (by subtracting non-industrial services from net output), we see that the US research effort has remained strong into the 1980s, with the ratio of R&D expenditure to value added substantially greater than in Germany or Britain.

It should be noted, however, that the German research effort looks rather better if we consider R&D expenditures as a proportion of GDP, since manufacturing accounts for a much larger share of output and employment in Germany than in Britain or the United States. Indeed, for 1989, figures from OECD, *Main Technology Indicators*, give R&D to GDP ratios of 2.88 for Germany compared with 2.82 for the United States and 2.25 for Britain. To the extent that the large German research effort has been successful in expanding the manufacturing sector, then, expressing R&D as a share of value added in manufacturing gives a misleading impression.

It is also usual to point out that in Britain and the United States a large share of R&D is in defence-related areas. In 1981, for example, defence budget R&D accounted for 54 per cent of government financed R&D in the

Sources: (cont.)
US:
Researchers: 1933–46 from Mowery (1986); 1959 from Freeman (1962).
Employment: Department of Commerce (various issues), *Census of Manufactures* (Washington, DC).
Germany:
Researchers: SV-Gemeinnützige Gesellschaft für Wissenschaftsstatistik mbH (various issues), *Forschung und Entwicklung in der Wirtschaft* (Essen).
Employment: Statistisches Bundesamt (1991), *Volkswirtschaftliche Gesamtrechnungen 1950 bis 1990*, Fachserie 18, Reihe S.15 (Wiesbaden).

United States and 49 per cent in the United Kingdom, compared with just 9 per cent in Germany (Ergas, 1987: 54). In a sophisticated generalisation of this observation, Ergas (1987) draws a distinction between 'mission oriented' and 'diffusion oriented' approaches to technology policy. In mission oriented countries like Britain and the United States, technology policy is geared towards radical innovations aimed at clearly set out goals of national importance. By contrast, in diffusion oriented countries like Germany, technology policy is aimed at the provision of innovation-related public goods, to help diffuse technological capabilities throughout industry. A similar distinction is made by Soskice (1993).

Ergas (1987) sees the appropriate technology policy as intimately bound up with overall production strategy, with R&D forming one part of the 'national innovation system' (Nelson, 1993). Ergas sees the United States as pursuing a mission oriented technology policy which fits in with an overall production strategy based on 'technology shifting', or concentrating on the emergence phase of new technologies. By contrast, Ergas sees Germany as following a diffusion oriented technology policy based on 'technology deepening', or the improvement of existing technologies. It should be noted that Ergas sees the German system of vocational training as a good example of an innovation-related public good. The United Kingdom is seen as caught somewhere between the United States and Germany. Too little benefit has been reaped from a mission oriented technology policy because of insufficient interaction between private and public researchers, which has meant relatively few spin-offs for the rest of the economy. The rest of the economy has therefore been forced to fight for competitiveness through technology deepening, but without the scale of resources devoted to the problem in Germany.

Conclusions

We have seen in chapter 7 that American demand conditions and resource endowments led to the development of a more machine-intensive technology. However, this did not initially lead to higher total fixed capital per employee in the United States, as machinery was only a small part of total fixed capital. Hence conventional 'levels accounting' calculations using total fixed capital suggest comparative levels of TFP of the same order of magnitude as comparative levels of labour productivity. However, there seems to be a closer link between horse-power per worker and output per worker during the first half of the twentieth century. Furthermore, capital would play a larger role in explaining labour productivity differences if the coefficient on capital were not restricted to capital's share in income, or if asset lives were standardised across countries.

However, a more promising line of inquiry is to examine the role of differences in human capital accumulation. Whereas American mass production methods economised on skilled shopfloor labour, they increasingly relied on high levels of human capital accumulation above shopfloor level, developing managerial and research capabilities. British and German flexible production methods, by contrast, relied on skilled shopfloor workers, trained under an apprenticeship system. However, whereas German manufacturing retained a commitment to apprenticeships after the Second World War, British manufacturing moved increasingly towards American methods and allowed shopfloor skills to decline. This had unfortunate consequences for Britain when technological leadership returned to flexible production methods from the late 1960s, as the information revolution made cheap customised production with skilled workers possible.

APPENDIX 8.1 CAPITAL STOCK IN MANUFACTURING

Table A8.1. *Gross reproducible capital stock in manufacturing at constant replacement cost, 1869–1987 (1929=100)*

Year	UK	US	Germany
1869	27.0	4.4	
1875	32.2		18.4
1879	36.3	7.6	
1882	38.4		22.2
1889	41.2	17.6	31.9
1899	48.1	29.3	57.2
1909	65.4	54.4	85.1
1913	72.6		100.8
1919	91.0	92.9	
1925	97.7		91.8
1929	100.0	100.0	100.0
1937	104.8	85.4	110.2
1950	140.8	136.5	78.2
1958	184.4	185.0	132.2
1968	268.2	262.8	267.1
1975	322.5	344.9	374.6
1980	368.5	415.7	411.3
1984	376.5	461.9	433.3
1987	384.8	483.0	445.7

SOURCES FOR TABLE A8.1
1. UK
1869–1920: Feinstein (1988), table XI.
1920–50: Feinstein (1972), table 45.
1950–87: Central Statistical Office (various issues),

Sources for table A8.1 (cont.)
National Income and Expenditure (London).

2. *US*
1869–1950: Kendrick (1961), table D–I.
1950–82: Department of Commerce (various issues),
National Income and Product Accounts (Washington).
1982–7: Department of Commerce, *Survey of Current
Business* (Washington).

3. *Germany*
1875–1959: Hoffmann (1965), table 39.
1959–87: Statistisches Bundesamt (1991),
Volkswirtschaftliche Gesamtrechnungen 1950–1990,
Fachserie 18, Reihe S.15 (Wiesbaden).

9 Competition and adjustment

Introduction

In chapter 6 it was noted when considering the competition between mass production and flexible production systems that there could be problems of adjustment if one system pulled sufficiently far ahead of the other. In a stochastic world, a process of trial and error may lead to improvements in one technology that cannot be incorporated in the lagging technology. If market forces were allowed to operate freely, this would result in the elimination of the inferior technique. However, the owners of the specific physical and human capital embodied in the inferior technique may resist this, and the outcome may depend on bargaining power in product and labour markets. Protection and cartelisation may be seen by firms as ways of obtaining product market power, enabling them to resist unfavourable technological change. Similarly, trade unions may be able to use monopoly power in the labour market to block unwelcome changes in work practices. Furthermore, the operation of capital markets may have important implications for the removal of underperforming management.

It should be noted, however, that this does not amount to a general presumption that high levels of concentration, protection or unionisation must always be associated with poor performance. Rather, it is a more limited argument that market power may hinder adjustment in difficult circumstances. Competition is not an accumulation strategy in itself, but it may make the transition from an unsuccessful to a successful strategy easier to achieve.

Successful productivity performance necessarily builds upon previous investment in human and physical capital. If the specific investments have not been made in one country, then no amount of liberalisation can lead to a better productivity performance than in countries with higher levels of human and physical capital. Thus we should not expect to see a simple correlation between the degree of competition and productivity performance at a point in time. Furthermore, it is likely that the dynamic interactions will also be complex. In the short run, it may be that output can be maintained and productivity raised by preventing the operation of competitive forces. Since productivity usually declines in slumps as capacity utilisation falls and fixed factors become proportionally more important, the use of anti-competitive devices such as tariffs may offer gains in the short run. However, the gains from short-run increasing returns may be offset in the long run as pressures on firms to improve performance are reduced.

It may even be the case that through manipulation of incentives, governments can encourage accumulation in the medium run. However, there are still dangers in the long run from over-riding market mechanisms. If the world changes, the shielding of the economy from market forces may make the necessary adjustments harder to achieve. Recent work on the 'Scandinavian model' may be interpreted in this light. Although Eichengreen (1996) argues that the institutions established as part of the 'postwar settlement' were initially conducive to accumulation, Henrekson *et al.* (1996) note that in the long run the same institutions came to hinder growth by reducing pressures to adjust.

This analysis suggests that we need to review the extent of competition in product and factor markets before considering the role of competition in the adjustment of accumulation strategy. We shall see that for much of the twentieth century, British adjustment has been hampered by too little competition, contrary to the claims of Elbaum and Lazonick (1986: 15) that

Britain was impeded from making a successful transition to mass production and corporate organisation in the twentieth century by an inflexible nineteenth century institutional legacy of atomistic economic organisation.

Competition in product markets

There is no simple agreed measure of the degree of competition in product markets. Hence we need to consider a range of indicators, including concentration, plant size, cartels and collusion, protection and the degree of openness.

Concentration

The most readily available evidence on concentration that is not beset with definitional problems is the share of the largest 100 corporations in manufacturing net output. Table 9.1 provides a comparison of this aggregate concentration index for the United Kingdom and United States over the period since 1909. The level of aggregate concentration in the United Kingdom started the period below that of the United States, but caught up after a rapid rise in the 1920s. After falling back slightly during the 1930s

Table 9.1. *Shares of the largest 100 firms in manufacturing net output, 1909–89 (%)*

	UK	US
1909	16	22
1924	22	
1929		25
1935	24	26
1947		23
1949	22	
1953	27	
1954		30
1958	32	30
1963	37	33
1967		33
1968	41	
1970	41	33
1975	42	
1977	41	33
1982	41	33
1984	39	
1989	38	

Sources: Prais (1976: 4, 213); UK *Census of Production*; US *Census of Manufactures*.

and 1940s, a further rise put the level of overall concentration in the United Kingdom above the US level by the end of the 1950s. Aggregate concentration in the United Kingdom increased further during the 1960s but stabilised during the 1970s and began to fall back during the 1980s. In the United States, the share of the 100 largest firms remained stable from the early 1960s at a level below that of the United Kingdom. The share of giant firms, or the aggregate 100-firm concentration ratio, then, does not suggest the persistence of atomistic competition in Britain. However, there are doubts about the ability of such a broad measure to capture the market power of firms.

The industrial concentration index measures the proportion of output or employment in an industry accounted for by a small number of leading firms, and is therefore in principle a better guide to the market power enjoyed by firms. However, there are serious problems in deriving consistent measures of industrial concentration over time within a single country and even more serious problems in making reliable international comparisons.

Dealing first with the difficulties encountered in charting changes in

Table 9.2. *Trends in UK concentration at industry level, 1935–89*

	CE3 (n=42)	CE5 (n=79)	CE5 (n=93)	CE5 (n=107)
1935	26.3			
1951	29.3			
1958	32.4	36.9		
1963	37.4	41.6		
1968	41.0	45.6		
1970	41.2		44.8	
1975			45.5	
1979			45.6	
1980				44.0
1985				40.4
1989				39.1

Notes: Unweighted average employment concentration ratios, where *n* is the number of 3-digit industries.
Sources: Clarke (1993: 122, 124); Hart and Clarke (1980: 27).

industrial concentration within a single country, problems arise with changes in industrial classification and the availability of different concentration ratios. Thus, for example, the large changes in the British industrial classification system introduced in 1980 create problems of comparability over this divide, while earlier changes affect the number of industries that can be included in intertemporal comparisons, as can be seen in table 9.2. Similarly, early British studies tended to focus on the 3-firm employment concentration ratio, while later British studies have tended to focus on 5-firm concentration ratios, which are available for sales and value added as well as employment. Nevertheless, the trends in British industrial concentration suggested by table 9.2 are widely accepted; a modest rise between 1935 and 1958, an acceleration in the rate of increase between 1958 and 1968 and a period of stability during the 1970s. Finally, the 1980s saw a sharp fall in industrial concentration (Clarke, 1993).

The available figures for trends in industrial concentration over time in the United States are given in table 9.3. In contrast to the United Kingdom, they show a high degree of stability between 1947 and 1970.

International comparisons of industrial concentration are even more difficult. The major problem is caused by differences in classification; clearly, the more narrowly industries are defined, the more likely it is that high rates of concentration will be found. Since most comparisons work with a larger number of industries in the United States, it is likely that there is an upward bias in US concentration. Another problem arises from the

Table 9.3. *Trends in US concentration at industry level, 1947–70*

	CS4 (n=166)
1947	40.9
1954	40.6
1958	40.3
1963	41.3
1967	41.4
1970	42.7

Notes: Unweighted average shipment concentration ratios, where n is the number of 4-digit industries.
Source: Mueller and Hamm (1974: 512).

fact that most comparisons have had to make do with 3-firm or 5-firm concentration ratios for the United Kingdom but 4-firm concentration ratios for the United States. In addition, employment concentration ratios were usually available for the United Kingdom but shipment concentration ratios for the United States. Nevertheless attempts have been made to compare the United Kingdom and the United States in the interwar and early postwar periods. As might be expected from the statistical problems outlined above, the results of these studies are not unambiguous.

For 1935, both Florence (1953) and Rosenbluth (1955) are agreed that concentration was probably higher in the United Kingdom, although Florence is more tentative about this conclusion. Florence simply notes that the average 3-firm employment concentration ratio in Britain was the same as the average 4-firm concentration ratio in the United States. Rosenbluth, however, adjusts the American data onto a 3-firm basis, using regression analysis for a sample of industries where both 3-firm and 4-firm ratios were available, and concludes more strongly that concentration was higher in the United Kingdom.

For the early postwar period, Pashigian (1968) again finds the average 3-firm concentration ratio in the United Kingdom equal to the average 4-firm concentration ratio in the United States, suggesting higher concentration in the United Kingdom. However, his results are based on the 1951 employment concentration ratio for the United Kingdom and the 1954 shipments concentration ratio for the United States. By contrast, Shepherd (1961) applies the Rosenbluth correction factor to the US 4-firm employment ratio for 1951 and finds higher concentration in the United States. Given the trends in concentration in the two countries, this result would be difficult to

Table 9.4. *Sales and employment shares of the largest 100 German firms in manufacturing and mining, 1968–89 (%)*

	Sales	Employment
1968	31.5	25.4
1970	32.3	27.3
1975	35.6	28.9
1977	36.2	29.2
1982	39.2	30.4
1989	36.4	28.5

Sources: Statistisches Bundesamt (1985), *Konzentrationsstatistische Daten für den Bergbau und das Verarbeitende Gewerbe, 1954 bis 1982,* Fachserie 4, Reihe S.9 (Wiesbaden); Statistisches Bundesamt (various issues), *Konzentrationsstatistische Daten für den Bergbau und das Verarbeitende Gewerbe sowie das Baugewerbe,* Fachserie 4, Reihe 4.2.3 (Wiesbaden).

reconcile with the Florence/Rosenbluth results for the 1930s. Hence it is reassuring to find that Sawyer (1971) confirms the higher level of concentration in the United Kingdom for 1958, with the gap widening somewhat to 1963. This does seem to be consistent with the known trends in the two countries. The data on industrial concentration, like the data on the share of giant firms, then, do not support the idea of the persistence of atomistic competition in Britain. If anything, the data point the other way, to greater levels of concentration in Britain.

Comparisons between Britain and Germany are more limited. Data in table 9.4 on the sales and employment shares of the 100 largest firms in Germany are not directly comparable to the British and American figures in table 9.1 because of the inclusion of mining as well as manufacturing and the fact that the British and American data refer to net output. Nevertheless, it would be difficult to use this data to argue for substantially lower concentration in Britain then in Germany in the 1960s or 1970s. This would also be suggested by the results of George and Ward (1975), shown in table 9.5; they found substantially higher concentration in Britain during the early 1960s, using the 4-firm employment concentration ratio. Again, then, there is no suggestion of a lower level of concentration in Britain.

Some authors suggest that industrial concentration ratios should be adjusted to take account of foreign trade, since some domestic production is exported and part of the domestic market is supplied by imports (Utton, 1982; Clarke, 1993). Hence the concentration of domestic production over-

Table 9.5. *Average 4-firm employment concentration ratios in the United Kingdom and West Germany, 1963*

Industry group	UK	West Germany
A ($n=11$)	62	28
B ($n=10$)	39	24
C ($n=10$)	22	16
D ($n=10$)	13	12
Weighted average ($n=41$)	30	19

Notes: The 41 industries are arranged in descending order of their concentration ratio in the United Kingdom and divided into groups of 10 or 11.
Source: George and Ward (1975: 17).

states the market power of domestic producers in their home markets. Although differences in the classification systems for domestic production and foreign trade make it difficult to calculate trade adjusted concentration ratios, there seems little doubt that growing openness among the major industrialised countries will have weakened the market power of firms in their home markets during the 1970s and 1980s. This has been demonstrated for the United Kingdom by Utton (1982) and Clarke (1993) using adjusted concentration ratios, and by Shepherd (1982) for the United States using more informal methods. This raises the issue of protection, which will be considered in more detail below. Protection can be seen as an important method of limiting competition and has varied enormously between countries and over time.

Plant size

An alternative way of evaluating the claim of writers like Elbaum and Lazonick (1986) and Chandler (1980) that atomistic structures persisted in Britain is to examine the data on plant size, which avoids many of the problems of comparability encountered with the concentration data. Data on median plant sizes are calculated by Prais (1981) for the period 1925–73, and are shown here in table 9.6, distinguishing between light and heavy industries.

For all manufacturing, median plant size was similar in Britain and the United States during the interwar period, but expanded much more rapidly in postwar Britain, so that by the 1970s, median plant size was higher in Britain than the United States. The biggest rise in median plant size was in Germany, although plant size remained higher in Britain than in Germany

Table 9.6. *Median plant sizes in light and heavy industries, 1925–39 to 1970–3 (number of employees)*

	Britain	Germany	US
A. All manufacturing			
1925–39	300	140	330
1958–61	470	350	390
1970–3	440	410	380
B. Light industries			
1925–39	200	70	230
1958–61	220	120	190
1970–3	240	140	210
C. Heavy industries			
1925–39	630	750	920
1958–61	1,140	1,140	1,100
1970–3	820	1,080	810

Notes: The years compared are dependent on when censuses were held. For Britain they are 1935, 1958 and 1973; for Germany they are 1925, 1961 and 1970; for the United States they are 1939, 1958 and 1972.
Source: Prais (1981: 27).

throughout the period. These trends seem to mirror the patterns identified in the measures of concentration discussed above.

Further insights can be gleaned by distinguishing between light and heavy industries in panels B and C of table 9.6. In heavy industry, median plant size during the interwar period was substantially smaller in Britain than in the United States, and German median plant size was also a little higher than in Britain. This would suggest that Elbaum and Lazonick (1986) pay too much attention to a small number of unrepresentative industries. However, even here, note that by the 1950s the British shortfall had been eliminated. In light industry, it is clearly Germany that stands out, with substantially smaller median plant size than in Britain or the United States. The plant size data, then, like the concentration data, do not support the idea of a persistent atomistic structure in Britain.

Cartels and collusion

Although there has been an upward trend in concentration during the twentieth century in all three countries, it seems likely that there has been an offsetting decline in the importance of cartels and collusion among firms, at least since the Second World War. Thus we need to look briefly at trends and international differences in cartelisation and anti-trust policy. The enforcement of a strict anti-trust policy began in the United States with the Sherman Act of 1890 and the Clayton and Federal Trade Commission Acts of 1914 (Neale, 1960). Although American anti-trust policy has surely remained more vigorous than in other countries, it remains true that the policy was relaxed somewhat during the Great Depression of the 1930s. Indeed, the National Industrial Recovery Act of 1933, with its concept of 'fair competition', encouraged collusion among firms to raise prices before it was struck down by the Supreme Court in 1935 (Hawley, 1966; Kaysen and Turner, 1959).

Although the post-Second World War period has seen the adoption and gradual strengthening of an anti-trust stance in Britain, governments during the interwar period generally tolerated and even encouraged collusion among firms (Yamey, 1966). In Germany, the tendency towards cartelisation was even stronger than in Britain before the Second World War, but as in Britain, the postwar period has seen the emergence of an anti-trust policy stance, albeit not as strongly as in the United States (Audretsch, 1989).

It would clearly be difficult to capture the extent of collusion and its variation over time and between countries in a simple quantitative measure. Nevertheless, it will be helpful to consider the studies which have attempted to address the issue of the scale of collusion across the manufacturing sector as a whole. For Britain, there are a number of surveys outlining the growth of collusion in the 1920s and 1930s. Books by Rees (1922), Levy (1927) and Lucas (1937) discuss the main examples of collusive behaviour, industry by industry, although no overall quantitative evaluation is attempted. Mercer (1989) attempts an estimate of the proportion of gross output covered by cartel agreements in the factory trades defined by the 1935 *Census of Production*, arriving at a figure of 29.4 per cent. Gribbin (1978) argues that by the 1950s up to 60 per cent of manufactured output may have been produced in cartels, with Trade Associations having grown from about 500 in 1919 to 2,500 by 1943. Only with the Restrictive Practices Act of 1956 did serious legislative action attack cartels. The early work of the Monopolies Commission was highly critical of cartel activities and ultimately only 10 of the 2,430 agreements registered under the Restrictive Practices Act were successfully defended as being in the public interest.

In Germany, there has been a long history of legalised cartels (Audretsch, 1989). Wagenführ (1931) estimated that there were 300 cartels in German manufacturing at the turn of the century, rising to 1,000 by 1922 and 2,500 by 1925. Although there has been a clear change of policy since the Second World War, with the prohibition of monopoly and collusive agreements imposed by the Allies giving way to the Laws against Restraints of

Competition (*Gesetz gegen Wettbewerbsbeschränkungen* or GWB) in 1957, the German position has remained rather more discretionary than in the United States or Britain (Berghahn, 1986; Owen Smith, 1994). Indeed, sections 2–8 of the GWB provide for explicit exemptions permitting legalised cartels. The number of legalised cartels has risen from 217 in 1973 to 321 in 1986 (Audretsch, 1989).

For the United States, the most comprehensive study is by Shepherd (1982) who assigns industries to one of four categories: pure monopoly, dominant firm, tight oligopoly and effectively competitive. Shepherd finds an increase in the proportion of the economy that is effectively competitive from 52.4 per cent in 1939 to 76.7 per cent by 1982, as a result of anti-trust actions, deregulation and increased import competition. In manufacturing the proportion that is effectively competitive had risen from 51.5 per cent in 1939 to 69.0 per cent by 1982, largely as a result of anti-trust actions and increased import competition, with deregulation playing only a minor role in manufacturing. The role of import competition in addition to anti-trust action and deregulation in Shepherd's study leads naturally to a consideration of the issues concerning openness to international trade.

Protection and the degree of openness

In an open economy context, domestic rivals may not be the only source of competition, so the role of protection also needs to be considered. The most widely used measure of protection is the ratio of customs duties to imports. Although in theory this may fail to capture the effect of tariffs set so high as to discourage all imports, in practice it has served as a reasonably good indicator of the general level of protection (Capie, 1994; Lindert, 1991). Furthermore, it has the advantage of being widely available on a comparable basis over long periods of time.

For the United States, data on customs duties as a proportion of the value of total imports and also as a proportion of the value of dutiable imports are presented in table 9.7. Although the ratio of duties to dutiable imports is somewhat higher, as would be expected, it is also clear that the two series follow similar trends. A declining level of protection in the first half of the nineteenth century was sharply reversed during the Civil War, and although there was a further downward drift in the level of protection during the period 1870–1913, protection remained high by international standards before the First World War. The United States remained protectionist between the wars, with the Fordney–McCumber and Smoot–Hawley tariffs of 1922 and 1930, respectively, before becoming increasingly liberal under the GATT system during the post-Second World War period.

Table 9.7. *Tariff rates in the United States, 1821–1989 (%)*

	Ratio of duties to total imports	Ratio of duties to dutiable imports
1821	43.2	45.0
1830	57.3	61.7
1840	17.6	34.4
1850	24.5	27.1
1860	15.7	19.7
1870	44.9	47.1
1880	29.1	43.5
1890	29.6	44.6
1900	27.6	49.5
1910	21.1	41.6
1913	17.7	40.1
1920	6.4	16.4
1929	13.5	40.1
1935	17.5	42.9
1938	15.5	39.3
1940	12.5	35.6
1945	9.3	28.2
1950	6.0	13.1
1960	7.4	12.2
1970	6.5	10.0
1980	3.1	5.7
1989	3.4	5.2

Sources: US Department of Commerce, Bureau of the Census (1975), *Historical Statistics of the United States: Colonial Times to 1970, Part 2* (Washington, DC); US Department of Commerce (various issues), *Statistical Abstract of the United States* (Washington, DC).

British data on the ratio of duties to total imports are given in table 9.8. The trend towards free trade in the nineteenth century is clearly visible. Equally clear is the retreat from free trade in the interwar period, culminating in the General Tariff of 1932. Perhaps more surprising at first sight is the high level of protection in the post-Second World War period. This seems to be the result of regional trade groupings in the postwar period. While Britain remained outside the EEC, trade with member countries was growing strongly, while trade within EFTA stagnated. And although Britain joined the EEC in 1973, trade with non-member countries, subject to the common external tariff, remained important.

German data on the ratio of customs duties to total imports are given in table 9.9 for the period after the formation of the German Reich. Although there is a small increase during the 1880s, the degree of protection is much

Table 9.8. *Tariff rates in the United Kingdom,*
1820–1980 (%)

	Ratio of duties to total imports
1820	24.0
1830	34.3
1840	25.4
1850	21.7
1860	11.6
1870	7.1
1880	4.7
1890	4.8
1900	4.6
1910	4.5
1913	4.4
1920	7.7
1929	9.7
1935	24.5
1938	24.1
1940	22.7
1945	38.2
1950	31.2
1960	30.2
1970	34.3
1980	12.7

Notes: From 1965 separate data for customs duties not
available; customs and excise duties have been adjusted in
line with the 1965 ratio for later years.
Source: Mitchell (1988: 451–4, 581–6).

closer to the British than the American level. Alternative data on the
unweighted average level of duties confirm that the scale of the retreat from
free trade in Continental Europe towards the end of the nineteenth century
should not be exaggerated (Liepmann, 1938). Thus, for example, Capie
(1983: 26) reports an average *ad valorem* rate of duty of 8.6 per cent for
Germany in 1910. The rise of protection in Germany between the wars, particularly with the growth of bilateralism under the Third Reich, is clearly
visible in table 9.9. Equally clear is the firm embrace of a liberal trading
policy after the Second World War. Given the strong trading links with
other European countries, European integration via the EEC has resulted
in very low ratios of customs duties to imports in Germany. However, Weiss
(1988) offers a qualification to this view, noting the growth of subsidies to
a number of German industries, thus to some extent undermining the

Table 9.9. *Tariff rates in Germany, 1880–1989 (%)*

	Ratio of duties to total imports
1880	5.8
1890	8.8
1900	8.1
1910	7.4
1913	6.3
1925	4.8
1929	8.2
1935	30.1
1938	33.4
1948	31.3
1950	5.4
1960	6.5
1970	2.6
1980	1.3
1989	1.3

Sources: Customs duties and imports from Mitchell (1980) to 1975, updated from Statistisches Bundesamt (various issues), *Statistisches Jahrbuch für die Bundesrepublik Deutschland* (Wiesbaden).

liberal trade regime. This would be consistent with the analysis of Giersch *et al.* (1992), who argue that the free market shock therapy of the early postwar period gave way to a more managed social market economy, resulting in a 'fading miracle'.

Thus whilst Britain was clearly the most free trade oriented country during the late nineteenth century, this has not been the case during the twentieth century. Although the abandonment of free trade was a long and painful process, Britain has clearly not been in the vanguard of the moves towards freer trade in the second half of the twentieth century. Slowness in moving from a system of Imperial Preference to membership of the EEC meant that customs duties remained high relative to imports well into the 1970s.

The figures on customs duties as a proportion of import values in tables 9.7–9.9 refer to all traded goods. Since some duties are raised for revenue purposes rather than for protection, and since some dutiable items are used as inputs, these figures can be misleading as a guide to the extent of protection offered to manufacturing. This has led some writers to consider also the concept of effective protection. This takes account of the tariff on inputs as well as outputs and expresses such a net tariff as a proportion of value added per unit of output, and is thus particularly useful for evaluating the overall impact of protection on particular sectors of the economy. Hawke (1975) notes that legislative increases in tariffs in the late nineteenth century were not as protective of American industry as some-times believed because of offsetting effects from higher prices for inputs and a growing share of value added in gross output. Capie (1983) finds that the British construction and shipbuilding industries had negative protection during the 1930s, while iron and steel had only a low rate of effective protection. Irwin (1993) has recently taken Nye (1991) to task for concluding that Britain was more protectionist than France during much of the late nineteenth century on the basis of customs duties as a propor-tion of import values without taking account, for example, of the impor-tance of tariffs on tropical products not domestically produced. Similarly, for the post-1945 period, Lindert (1991) notes that the exclusion of duties on oil makes a big difference to the ratio of duties to imports in non-oil-producing countries.

Given the objections to the standard measures of protection, it is usual also to consider the shares of imports and exports in GDP as indicators of the openness of an economy to competition from overseas (Capie, 1994). Trade ratios can be calculated both for goods and for goods and services, although only the former are available for Germany before 1950. For the United Kingdom, the figures in table 9.10 show a period of increasing open-ness as protection declined before the First World War, while trade ratios declined during the protectionist interwar period. The early post-Second World War period, although relatively open compared to the interwar period did not match the degree of openness seen before the First World War. Only during the 1980s have trade ratios come near to regaining the high levels of the pre-1913 years.

The US trade ratios in table 9.11 suggest that international transactions were much less significant for American than for British firms. The US economy remained relatively self-sufficient until the 1970s, when trade ratios doubled. But even then, US trade ratios remained relatively low com-pared with European nations. The German data in table 9.12 suggest that the exposure of German firms to competition from overseas has varied enormously, although we do need to bear in mind the extensive boundary changes that have occurred. German trade ratios for goods were somewhat lower than in Britain before the First World War, but became higher during the 1970s. The collapse of German trade ratios during the highly protec-tionist 1930s is particularly striking.

Another form of product market openness that is sometimes considered in the literature is multi-national production, which might be expected to play an important role in technology transfer (Teichova *et al.*, 1986; Jeremy,

Table 9.10. *UK trade ratios, 1870–1989 (% of GDP))*

	Imports		Exports	
	Goods	Goods & services	Goods	Goods & services
1870	24.9	27.1	22.0	29.1
1880	28.4	30.8	21.8	29.0
1890	26.6	28.8	22.9	29.8
1900	24.9	27.4	18.3	23.9
1910	28.3	30.6	24.0	30.9
1913	28.6	30.9	25.3	32.4
1920	30.3	34.0	27.8	35.6
1925	26.0	29.2	20.3	24.9
1929	23.6	26.8	18.1	23.2
1935	15.3	18.0	11.5	14.6
1938	15.2	18.0	10.1	13.6
1940	13.3	20.6	5.3	8.0
1945	7.1	17.3	4.6	8.1
1950	17.9	23.8	17.5	23.2
1960	16.3	21.4	14.7	19.9
1970	15.7	21.4	15.7	22.2
1980	19.8	24.9	20.3	27.0
1989	22.6	27.7	17.9	23.5

Sources: Feinstein (1972,tables 3 and 15); CSO (1994) *Economic Trends Annual Supplement* (London),tables 1.3 and 1.17.

1992). In fact, consideration of this issue will be left for the section on capital markets below.

Competition in labour markets

Labour force unionisation

Strong labour market interest groups may act as barriers to change (Olson, 1982). Hence it will be useful to review the quantitative evidence on the extent of unionisation. Again, however, a simple relationship between levels of unionisation and economic performance should not be expected. Rather, high levels of unionisation may be expected to cause difficulties in periods when rapid adjustments are necessary.

The British data in table 9.13 suggest growing trade unionism from the 1890s to the First World War, with a strong surge across the war. This was followed by a period of decline during the depression and industrial strife of the 1920s and early 1930s, and a revival in the late 1930s. A further surge

Table 9.11. *US trade ratios, 1870–1988 (% of GDP)*

	Imports		Exports	
	Goods	Goods & services	Goods	Goods & services
1870	5.7	6.2	5.6	6.0
1880	6.3	6.8	8.4	8.7
1890	6.5	7.2	6.9	7.2
1900	4.6	5.6	8.7	8.8
1910	4.6	5.5	5.7	5.8
1913	4.6	5.6	6.6	6.8
1920	5.9	7.0	9.3	10.6
1925	4.6	5.4	5.4	5.8
1929	4.4	5.4	5.1	5.7
1935	3.5	4.1	3.3	3.9
1938	2.6	3.3	3.8	4.5
1940	2.7	3.4	4.1	4.8
1945	2.5	3.5	2.5	3.1
1950	3.2	4.0	3.6	4.3
1960	3.0	4.4	4.0	4.9
1970	4.0	5.5	4.4	5.6
1980	9.2	10.9	8.3	10.3
1988	9.2	11.3	6.6	9.1

Notes: Imports and exports of certain goods, primarily military equipment purchased and sold by the Federal Government are included in services.
Sources: 1870–1929: Trade data from US Department of Commerce (1975), *Historical Statistics of the United States: Colonial Times to 1970* (Washington, DC), series U2–U4 and U9–U11; GDP from Kendrick (1961) and Balke and Gordon (1989); 1929–58: Trade and GDP data from US Department of Commerce (1993), *National Income and Product Accounts of the United States, Vol.1, 1929–58, Vol.2, 1959–88* (Washington, DC),tables 1.1 and 4.1.

in union growth across the Second World War was followed by continued growth to 1980. However, the 1980s saw a serious decline in the proportion of the labour force unionised. These trends at the whole economy level are mirrored in the manufacturing sector, where the level of unionisation has generally been somewhat higher.

The US data in table 9.14 suggest similar trends to those in Britain, but with a generally lower level of unionisation. However, it should be noted that the level of unionisation in the American manufacturing sector rose to levels comparable with British manufacturing in the early post-Second World War period. Hence the contrasts between Britain and the United States should not be overdrawn if we are considering manufacturing in the postwar period.

Table 9.12. *German trade ratios, 1880–1988 (% of GDP)*

	Imports		Exports	
	Goods	Goods & services	Goods	Goods & services
1880	16.6		17.3	
1890	17.5		14.1	
1900	17.8		14.2	
1910	19.5		16.3	
1913	20.5		19.3	
1925	18.5		13.8	
1929	16.9		17.0	
1935	5.8		5.9	
1938	5.6		5.4	
1950	11.7	12.7	11.9	15.1
1960	13.2	17.4	16.1	20.0
1970	15.0	20.5	18.2	22.6
1980	21.9	28.6	22.9	28.5
1988	21.2	28.6	27.4	35.0

Sources: 1880–1950: Hoffmann (1965,tables 125, 127 and 248); 1950–89: Statistisches Bundesamt (1991), *Volkswirtschaftliche Gesamtrechnungen, Revidierte Ergebnisse 1950 bis 1990*, Fachserie 18, Reihe S.15 (Wiesbaden),tables 2.2.1, 2.2.12 and 2.2.13.

Table 9.13. *Rates of labour force unionisation in the United Kingdom, 1892–1990 (%)*

	Whole economy	Manufacturing
1892	9.4	13.0
1901	10.8	13.7
1911	15.4	18.6
1921	33.0	48.5
1926	25.6	34.2
1929	23.2	29.4
1935	21.7	26.6
1938	25.7	31.1
1950	39.3	47.0
1960	39.1	45.6
1970	44.2	55.8
1980	48.3	
1985	39.0	
1990	35.0	

Sources: Union membership data from Bain and Price (1980) and CSO (various issues), *Annual Abstract of Statistics* (London); Labour force data from Feinstein (1972) and *Annual Abstract of Statistics.*

Table 9.14. *Rates of labour force unionisation in the United States, 1897–1989 (%)*

	Whole economy	Manufacturing
1897	1.8	4.3
1900	3.2	5.3
1910	5.9	8.6
1920	11.5	18.1
1930	7.0	8.4
1935	8.2	10.5
1940	14.2	23.6
1947	23.6	39.7
1953	24.8	42.0
1960	23.2	52.1
1970	25.1	47.8
1980	21.2	
1989	14.2	23.6

Sources: Union membership data from Bain and Price (1980) and US Department of Commerce (1975), *Historical Statistics of the United States: Colonial Times to 1970* (Washington, DC); Labour Force Data from Kendrick (1961) and US Department of Commerce (various issues), *Statistical Abstract of the United States* (Washington, DC).

Unionisation rates are unavailable for the German manufacturing sector, due to the way that the unions are grouped. Nevertheless, the whole economy data in table 9.15 suggest rather different levels and trends in Germany compared with Britain. A continuously rising trend to 1930 was followed by a period when unions were proscribed under the Third Reich. Although German levels of unionisation generally remained below British levels, by the early 1930s German levels were higher. During the post-Second World War period unionisation increased to 1980, but has subsequently fallen back, although not as rapidly as in Britain or the United States.

Varieties of unionism

It has been argued so far that high levels of union density may cause problems in periods of adjustment. However, even this may be too simple. Delving more closely into the Olson (1982) framework suggests a more complex link between high levels of union density and barriers to change.

Table 9.15. *Rate of labour force
unionisation in Germany, 1891–1989 (%)*

	Whole economy
1891	1.5
1900	3.3
1910	10.8
1913	12.7
1925	20.3
1930	24.1
1950	26.8
1960	28.5
1970	29.7
1980	33.1
1989	31.8

Notes: Unions were proscribed during the Third
Reich.
Sources: Union members from Bain and Price
(1980) and Statistisches Bundesamt (various issues),
*Statistisches Jahrbuch für die Bundesrepublik
Deutschland* (Wiesbaden). Labour force from
Hoffmann (1965) and *Statistisches Jahrbuch.*

Consider the incentives facing an interest group that is being called upon
to accept painful changes that will increase the size of the cake to be divided
among all members of society (say a trade union resisting technical
progress which will raise productivity but result in the redundancy of some
members). A preferable strategy might be to resist the changes and press
instead for a larger share of the existing cake (say by securing tariff protection or subsidies). From the point of view of the interest group, the advantage of the latter, redistributive strategy is that its members reap all of the
benefits of its actions. Accepting the change yields benefits which cannot be
appropriated by the interest group, which nevertheless has to bear the costs.

Notice, however, that the interest group can gain from the redistributive
strategy only if it is not too big. In the limit, an interest group that encom-
passes all members of society has nobody to redistribute from. Hence a
country with a high level of union density, but strong control exercised by
an encompassing central organisation may be just as capable of avoiding
distributional struggles as a country with a highly fragmented labour
market structure. The problems may be expected to be most severe in a
country with high levels of union density but a highly fragmented structure.
In this view, the greater cohesion of industry unions in Germany is seen as

preferable to the fragmented craft structure of British unions (Calmfors and Driffill, 1988; Batstone, 1986; Bean and Crafts, 1996).

Competition in capital markets

Industrial finance and corporate control

There is a long-standing debate on the implications of international differences in financial institutions for comparative performance in manufacturing. Writers hostile to competitive market forces tend to look favourably on the German system of industrial finance, which is seen as providing long-term finance to industry through universal banks. By contrast, British and American industry is seen as being dependent on finance from institutions much more interested in short-term returns (Elbaum and Lazonick, 1986; Kennedy, 1987). In fact, the position is complex, with institutions evolving in the unique circumstances faced in each country. Inevitably, each system has its strengths and weaknesses (Mayer, 1993). Thus rather than arguing for the superiority of the competitive system in all circumstances, I would seek only to make the weaker claim that a system which allows competition is likely to facilitate adjustment in difficult times.

Industrialisation in Britain and America is usually seen as having been financed largely from retained earnings and private wealth. This is in contrast to the situation in Germany, where a more active role was taken by banks providing long-term finance. But whereas banks played an active role in the American merger boom of the late nineteenth century, British banks at this time became increasingly risk-averse in their attitudes towards industrial loans, with the liquidity crisis of 1878 being singled out for particular attention (Collins, 1991; Best and Humphries, 1986). Nevertheless, as Collins (1991: 42) points out, the consequent stability of the British financial system brought advantages. Furthermore, these advantages became more evident during the interwar period, when Britain avoided the bank failures of the American and German systems. Indeed, the American response was to legislate the separation of commercial and investment banking in the Glass–Steagall Act of 1933.

The development of the hostile take-over bid in the Anglo-American system during the 1950s is often seen as hindering the development of an effective accumulation strategy, based on long-term commitments. However, as Mayer (1993) points out, the German 'insider' system, with large equity stakes held by other firms as well as by banks, finds it difficult to restructure in the face of large external shocks, without the anonymity of the market.

International mobility of capital

Another aspect of competition in capital markets concerns the degree of international mobility of capital. Here we concentrate on the implications of direct overseas investment, as opposed to portfolio investment, since the former is often seen as an important means by which the diffusion of innovations in technology and organisation takes place (Teichova *et al.,*1986; Casson, 1983; Jones, 1986; Stopford and Turner, 1985). This can occur both through the exposure of investing companies to the global economic environment and through the competitive effects on companies in recipient countries.

Dunning (1983) charts the scale of multi-national enterprise over the twentieth century, breaking down the stock of accumulated foreign direct investments by both country of origin and by recipient country or area. The most striking finding is the importance of the United Kingdom and the United States as sources of overseas investment. In 1914, British-based multi-nationals accounted for 45.5 per cent of the stock of accumulated foreign direct investment, while the United States accounted for another 18.5 per cent. By 1978, the United States and United Kingdom accounted for 41.4 per cent and 12.9 per cent respectively. Turning to the breakdown by recipient countries, the share going to developing countries has declined from roughly two-thirds before the Second World War to roughly one-third since. Whereas before the Second World War the United States attracted the largest share of investments going to the developed countries, since 1950 Western Europe has been a more important recipient, with the United Kingdom in particular attracting a large share of American overseas investment. The importance of Australasia and South Africa until the 1970s reflects the Imperial bias in British overseas investments. During the 1980s the United Kingdom has become an important recipient of growing Japanese overseas investments (Stopford and Turner, 1985).

German participation in foreign direct investment has been much more limited. Although in 1914 Germany accounted for 10.5 per cent of the stock of accumulated foreign direct investment, this had fallen to 1.3 per cent in 1938 and 1.2 per cent in 1960 following wartime expropriations and interwar dislocations. By 1978, Germany's share had risen to 7.3 per cent. On the recipient side, Dunning does not provide separate figures for Germany, but it is clear from the evidence of Feldman (1989) that Germany was not a major recipient of foreign direct investment, at least before the Second World War.

There seems little doubt, then, that when product market competition weakened in the mid-twentieth century through protection and cartelisation, British industry nevertheless remained in touch with international competitors through multi-national enterprise. If the British overseas investments in the Empire did little to sharpen the competitive instincts of British industry, the presence in Britain of American and German multi-nationals must have provided a competitive stimulus (Jones, 1988; Dunning, 1958). Similarly, the presence of Japanese multi-nationals in Britain during the 1980s is often seen as important in improving the performance of indigenous producers (Oliver and Wilkinson, 1988).

Adjustment of accumulation strategy and the role of competition

The various dimensions of competition considered above can now be brought together to see how they impact on the adjustment of accumulation strategy, which I would see as the fundamental determinant of manufacturing performance. Competition should not be treated as a fundamental strategy in its own right. This means that in the short run, at least, a country with a successful accumulation strategy but a low degree of competition may perform better than a country which has a high degree of competition but a poor accumulation strategy. Furthermore, this 'short run' may last for substantial periods of calendar time. In the long run, however, I would make the weaker claim that competition provides the best way of ensuring that the accumulation strategy adjusts successfully. This general framework will now be applied briefly to a number of historical episodes.

British adjustment to industrialisation abroad, 1870–1914

There is a vast literature on the adjustment of British industry to industrialisation in other countries, particularly the United States and Germany, during the late Victorian and early Edwardian periods. Clearly some loss of market share by British manufacturers was inevitable as other countries industrialised, but many authors have gone further than this and seen the beginnings of entrepreneurial failure (Landes, 1969; Aldcroft, 1964; Elbaum and Lazonick, 1986).

Within the above framework, I would see this overseas industrialisation as presenting a challenge to British industry, requiring an adjustment of accumulation strategy. Markets needed to be secured and technology adapted in the light of innovations abroad. To what extent was Britain successful in meeting this challenge? McCloskey and Sandberg (1971) concentrate on the issue of technology, pointing out that it is necessary to show substantial forgone profits arising from a decision not to switch to the new technology before entrepreneurial failure can be asserted. Furthermore, they point out that in a competitive environment with free entry, the neglect of profitable opportunities by incumbent firms will lead to their replacement by more dynamic rivals. The one well documented case of failure in the sense of forgone profit opportunities concerns the lag in the adoption of the Solvay process in soda making (Lindert and Trace, 1971). And yet this case merely serves to underline the general validity of the McCloskey–Sandberg view, because the failure occurred in an industry that operated as a cartel protected by barriers to entry. In industries that operated under competitive conditions, technical choice was generally seen to be consistent with profit-maximising behaviour (Sandberg, 1974; McCloskey, 1973).

Turning to the issue of markets, there has been much retrospective criticism of the concentration on the old staple industries of iron and steel, cotton, shipbuilding and coal, which Richardson (1965) regards as 'overcommitment'. As McCloskey (1981: 120–1) points out, however, it is difficult to make this judgement without the benefits of hindsight. It was surely not clear to Victorian businessmen that specialisation in a global system would be undermined by a world war and the rise of the highly protectionist interwar economy. Similarly, there has been much retrospective criticism of the growing concentration on Empire markets from the late nineteenth century, as we have already seen in chapter 7. Again, however, it is not clear that this was a bad strategy viewed without the benefit of hindsight.

British and German adjustment to the Second Industrial Revolution, 1914–1950

The interwar period is often characterised as a period of 'rationalisation' in both Britain and Germany, in response to the innovations of the 'Second Industrial Revolution' in the United States, although clearly there were many other shocks that called for adjustment, not the least of which were two world wars and a major world slump. American firms are seen by Chandler (1977; 1990) as having developed around the turn of the century a three-pronged investment strategy based on fixed capital, management and marketing, which amounted to a distinctive American form of 'competitive managerial capitalism'. Although Hounshell (1984) sees this mass production system as evolving from the earlier 'American system of manufactures', we need to bear in mind that the First World War provided an element of discontinuity at a critical time. This is important because, as we have seen, adjustment was occurring before 1914, with British and German flexible production methods developing in parallel with the emerging American mass production methods.

The issue of rationalisation in interwar Britain is often cast in terms of the persistence of an atomistic market structure (Elbaum and Lazonick, 1986). Yet, as we have seen, there is very little evidence to support this interpretation. In terms of concentration, median plant size, collusion, protection, openness, unionisation, etc. the interwar period must be viewed as a time when the operation of competitive market forces was seriously curtailed. Broadberry and Crafts (1990a, 1990b, 1992) see this suspension of competitive forces as underpinned by government policy. Governments were worried about the unemployment consequences of the negative demand shocks hitting the British economy from abroad. Given the downward nominal rigidity of wages, an apparently attractive option was to promote measures such as cartelisation and protection which raised prices, but without setting off an inflationary spiral.

Seen in this light, British policy in the 1930s makes a great deal of sense. The world downturn from 1929 had the potential to raise real wages and unemployment in the short run due to nominal wage rigidity, and in the long run to raise the natural rate of unemployment by raising the real value of unemployment benefits set in nominal terms, and through the reaction of wage and price setters to the fall in real import prices (Dimsdale *et al.*, 1989). In the event, the worst effects of the world depression were avoided in Britain through exchange rate depreciation following Britain's early departure from the Gold Standard in September 1931, which alleviated the downward pressure on prices. Recent research on government sources suggests that this was all part of a conscious and coherent strategy to offset the impact of the world depression, with the possibility of an inflationary spiral and collapse of confidence in sterling protected against by the maintenance of a balanced budget and the General Tariff (Howson, 1975; Peden, 1985; Booth, 1987).

Although the short-run labour productivity position improved compared with the United States in the early 1930s, this was largely the result of greater capacity utilisation in Britain. In the long run, painful rationalisation had been avoided, and the consequences for comparative productivity performance were detrimental (Broadberry and Crafts, 1990b).

German rationalisation during the interwar period is usually seen as largely unsuccessful, although there is some disagreement over the reasons for this (James, 1986: 146–9). Whereas early writers such as Röpke (1931) see rationalisation leading to a misallocation of resources through overinvestment, later scholars such as Balderston (1983) point out that Weimar profit and investment levels were in fact unusually low. James sees rather a sectoral maldistribution of investment, leading to overcapacity in some basic heavy industries like steel and chemicals and in textiles. The persistence of overcapacity resulted from the fact that the industry cartels acted as agents of the large trusts (James, 1986: 156). Market signals were distorted and hence effective rationalisation could be avoided.

The generally low level of investment in Weimar Germany is linked by Borchardt (1979) to the distributional struggles following the First World War. With real wage growth running ahead of labour productivity growth, profitability and investment were reduced. This can be seen as one way in which labour market imperfections hampered adjustment. A similar argument can be made for labour market imperfections slowing down adjustment in interwar Britain (Broadberry and Ritschl, 1994, 1995).

British adjustment to the end of Empire, 1950–1970

The concentration on Empire markets and the system of Imperial Preference can be seen as a rational response to the rise of protection and dislocation in Europe during the first half of the twentieth century. It nevertheless left an unfortunate legacy for the period following the Second World War, when Europe became a major growth market and Commonwealth countries grew relatively slowly. Clearly a major reorientation of export markets was needed, but this was hampered by the anti-competitive culture of much of British industry at this time. After decades of avoiding head-to-head competition with producers from other industrialised countries through international cartels, British firms were reluctant to break with the old market-sharing arrangements. Hence an opportunity to enter European markets before continental producers recovered was missed (Jones and Marriott, 1970: 174).

It may be argued that restrictions on capital mobility further exacerbated the problems of adjustment. Given the strict controls on foreign exchange, it was difficult for manufacturers of durable goods to set up adequate marketing and servicing networks abroad. And yet some writers argue that it was in precisely these areas that British failures were most glaring (Williams et al., 1983, 1987). Prevarication over EEC entry further hampered British companies in raising European market share, by limiting access to markets (Foreman-Peck, 1991).

American adjustment to flexible production, 1970–90

Since the late 1960s American manufacturing has faced a challenge to its technological leadership. As well as the threat from a resurgent Germany, US manufacturing has been challenged by the rise of Japan (Baily and Chakrabarti, 1988; Dertouzos et al., 1989). The modern flexible production technology is intensive in the use of skilled shopfloor labour, which presents a challenge to American manufacturers with their emphasis on standardised mass production with unskilled shopfloor labour. The key factor explaining the change in technological leadership is the decline in the cost

of computation (Milgrom and Roberts, 1990). Given the dramatic reduction in the cost of information processing, production can be geared
cheaply to individual demands by skilled workers using computer aided
design, numerically controlled machine tools and robots (Edquist and
Jacobsson, 1988).

As yet, it seems that the change in technological leadership has not been
matched by a change in productivity leadership, at least for manufacturing
as a whole. Furthermore, estimates by van Ark and Pilat (1993) suggest that
labour productivity remains higher in the United States than in Germany in
all branches of manufacturing. However, although Japanese labour productivity remains substantially lower than in the United States for manufacturing as a whole, in two sectors (machinery and transport equipment
and rubber and plastic products) Japan now has higher labour productivity.

At this stage it is too early to do more than make a provisional judgement about the adjustment of American manufacturing to the challenge of
flexible production. Nevertheless, there are signs that where US firms have
been forced to face up to global competition, the response has been positive. McKinsey Global Institute (1993) argue that persistent poor productivity performance tends to be associated with the avoidance of global
competition.

Conclusions

As we have seen in chapters 6–8, success in manufacturing depends ultimately on a basic strategy of accumulation. Without an accumulation of
physical and human capital around specific techniques, there are limits to
what can be expected from a policy of liberalisation. Hence we should not
expect to find a simple correlation at a point in time between the degree of
competition in one country (compared with other countries) and comparative productivity performance. However, there do seem to be dangers in
the long run if a country insulates itself from competitive pressures. If the
world changes radically, an economy shielded from market forces may find
it very difficult to adjust. The British economy during much of the twentieth century provides a clear illustration of these dangers. Although
Imperial Preference coupled with interventionist industrial policies
appeared to work in the interwar period, insulating the British economy
from the worst of the Great Depression, they created serious problems of
adjustment during the post-Second World War period, the legacy of which
had still not been completely overcome by the end of the 1980s.

Part 3

Reassessing the performance of British industry

10 The rise of competition from abroad, 1850–1914

Introduction

On average, over the period 1850–1914, labour productivity in British man-ufacturing was only about half the American level, but on a par with the German level. This reflects the differences in demand conditions and resource endowments examined in chapter 7 and the accumulation strategy appropriate to those conditions, examined in chapter 8. Hence these per-sistent labour productivity differences should not be seen as evidence of entrepreneurial failure or technological backwardness. By and large, tech-nical choice was rational, given the environment faced by British firms. As writers like McCloskey and Sandberg (1971) argue, in most industries com-petitive forces acted as a spur to efficiency, with existing rivals or new entrants ready to take up opportunities neglected by incumbent producers. The barriers to adjustment examined in chapter 9 remained relatively weak in most industries during this period.

Aggregates, however, can conceal a great deal, and the disaggregated evi-dence shows a high degree of variation in the comparative productivity per-formance of individual industries, as we saw in chapter 2. There were three broad types of industry where Britain did relatively well, i.e. where the Anglo-American labour productivity gap was below the roughly 2:1 for manufacturing as a whole. The first type of industry in which Britain achieved high productivity levels was where craft-based flexible production techniques remained competitive despite the adoption of high throughput mass production methods in the United States. Britain clearly did well in textiles, with labour productivity not far below American levels. As a result, with substantially lower wages, Britain was able to dominate world markets. Despite the use of high throughput methods in America, such as ring spinning and the automatic loom in cotton, British firms continued to make improvements through trial and error and raised productivity sufficiently to remain competitive. British production in small-scale verti-cally specialised firms was efficient, leading to high labour productivity through Marshall's acclaimed external economies of scale. Clearly, however, it was highly dependent on a liberal trading environment. If there

157

was any ominous trend for Lancashire before 1914 it was the growing threat of protection.

The second type of industry where Britain continued to achieve productivity levels not dissimilar to American levels was where mass production techniques proved difficult to apply, so that flexible production methods continued to be used on both sides of the Atlantic. This gave Britain an advantage because of the supply of skilled labour. The clearest example of this type of industry was shipbuilding where, much as in textiles, a large number of small British firms utilised a skilled craft labour force to attain external economies of scale. British production methods were more labour-intensive even than in other European countries, which helped British firms to survive in cyclical downturns by reducing fixed overheads. Clearly there were other parts of the engineering sector where mass production methods had still not been widely applied before 1914, but there are data problems in attaining reliable comparative productivity estimates, largely because the British *Census of Production* tended to report quantities of engineering goods only in tons.

The third type of industry where Britain attained high levels of productivity was where demand factors allowed the early adoption of high throughput techniques in Britain. Examples here include seedcrushing, coke, sugar refining and tobacco before cigarettes became important. In these relatively homogeneous products, there was no substantial Anglo-American labour productivity gap before the First World War. Furthermore, although information on German productivity levels at this time is patchy, it is possible to infer from the qualitative literature together with quantitative information from the interwar period that Britain was a long way ahead of Germany in the application of high throughput methods in the food, drink and tobacco industries. This should come as no surprise given the much greater degree of urbanisation in Britain. It is worth emphasising the good performance of the British food, drink and tobacco sector, since it is often left out of consideration when evaluating manufacturing performance.

The poor British performers tended to be industries where high throughput techniques had been successfully developed in the United States, but where demand conditions or resource and factor endowments simply prevented the adoption of such techniques in Britain. The most easily established example of this is motor vehicles, where there was simply no mass market in Britain. Other cases are more difficult to establish quantitatively before the First World War because of the availability mainly of tonnage data in the British *Census of Production.*

Before 1914, then, the British economy was adjusting satisfactorily to the rise of competition from abroad. By and large, operating in competitive

Table 10.1. *World production of sulphuric acid,*
1867–1913 (000 tons of 100% acid)

	1867	1878	1900	1913
UK	155	600	1,000	1,082
Germany	75	112	950	1,686
US	40	180	940	2,250
World total	500	1,300	4,200	8,300

Source: Svennilson (1954: 286).

conditions, British firms made rational technical choices. The one established case of failure, the lag in the adoption of the Solvay process in soda making, merely serves to underline this conclusion, because here the industry operated as a cartel.

Chemicals

Britain began to lose market share in chemicals during the late nineteenth century, in the face of German and American competition. Sulphuric acid production is sometimes used as a crude indicator of the development of the chemical industry during the nineteenth century, and the figures in table 10.1 suggest a sharply declining share of world production for Britain and a rising share for Germany and the United States. To some extent this was inevitable, since Britain could not hope to retain her dominant position of the mid-nineteenth century as other countries industrialised. However, there is a widespread perception of poor performance and technological lag in the British chemical industry, which is largely explained by the well documented persistence of the Leblanc process for soda ash production long after the demonstrable superiority of the Solvay process and the failure of British companies to compete with Germany in synthetic dyestuffs (Clapham, 1938: 171–4; Richardson, 1968: 280; Musson, 1978: 222). However, as the figures on shares in world production in table 10.2 make clear, Britain still held a dominant position in soda ash in the early twentieth century, and the United States also lost out to Germany in dyestuffs. If we add in to the picture soap, explosives and other chemical industries, a more balanced assessment is possible.

Technological lag in alkali production

Britain's strong position in alkali production in the nineteenth century reflected a comparative advantage based on mineral deposits (Clapham,

Table 10.2. *Shares in world production of chemical products, 1913 (%)*

	UK	Germany	US
All chemicals	11.0	24.0	34.0
Sulphuric acid	13.0	20.3	27.1
Soda ash	50.0	19.1	7.1
Superphosphates	7.0	15.9	27.6
Chemical nitrogen	11.7	15.5	4.7
Synthetic dyestuffs	3.1	85.1	1.9

Notes: Soda ash figures relate to 1904. Output measured in tons, except for All chemicals, where output measured in values.
Sources: Derived from Svennilson (1954: 165, 287–90); Richardson (1968: 278).

Table 10.3. *Estimated production costs of Solvay and Leblanc processes, 1872 (per ton)*

	Leblanc			Solvay		
	£	*s.*	*d.*	£	*s.*	*d.*
Mond, 1872a	9	1	0	7	4	8
Mond, 1872b	9	7	0	6	17	11
Brunner, 1872	9	7	6	7	8	3

Source: Warren (1980: 104).

1938: 172, 174). However, the slowness of British alkali producers to switch to the Solvay process threatened that position towards the end of the century. As the figures in table 10.3 suggest, the ability of the Solvay process to produce soda ash of higher purity at lower cost was already apparent by the 1870s from work at Brunner Mond. However, as Lindert and Trace (1971) note, the picture was complicated by the fact that the Leblanc process could produce caustic soda more cheaply, and also allowed the production of bleach and other by-products. Allowing for these complications, Lindert and Trace attempt a quantification of the costs to the economy of the prolonged retention of the Leblanc capacity.

The most obvious gain from switching to the Solvay process is from the reduction in average costs on the output previously being produced by the Leblanc process. In figure 10.1 this is given by the area $ABCD$, given by the Leblanc output (λQ_0) multiplied by the long-run average cost difference

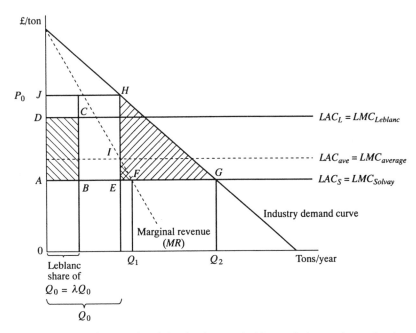

10.1 Private and social gains from switching to Solvay soda production
Lindert and Trace (1971: 254).

between the two techniques ($LAC_L - LAC_S$). Initial profit-maximising output (Q_0) is derived from the intersection of the marginal revenue curve (MR) with the long-run marginal cost curve for the average technology (LMC_{ave}), a weighted average of the long-run marginal cost curves for the Solvay and Leblanc processes, with weights given by the shares of the two processes in output. Given constant long-run marginal costs, average cost curves are also horizontal. The share of the Leblanc producers in output (λ) is fixed by the cartel governing the industry, and the initial price (P_0) is read off the industry demand curve.

However, there are further gains because the elimination of the Leblanc producers means that the long-run average cost curve for the industry is given by the long-run average cost curve for Solvay producers. If the industry remains cartelised, output rises to Q_1, given by the intersection of the marginal revenue curve with long-run marginal costs for the Solvay process ($MR = LMC_S$). There is a small social gain given by the excess of marginal revenue over long-run marginal costs on the increased output, represented by the triangle EFI. However, if the cartel is broken, output rises to the competitive level Q_2 and there is a gain in consumer surplus of EGH.

The annual gains over the period 1894–1914 from the switch to Solvay

Table 10.4. *Approximate private and social gains from switching to Solvay soda production, 1894–9 and 1900–14 (£000 p.a.)*

	1894–9	1900–14
Private gains from cost reduction	110	170
Social gains with collusion	50	40
Social gains with competition	330	590
Total gains with collusion	160	210
Total gains with competition	440	760

Source: Lindert and Trace (1971: 262).

production, with a sub-division to allow for renegotiation of prices, are given in table 10.4. Lindert and Trace see no substantial forgone profits from the retention of the Leblanc capacity before 1886 because of high royalty payments. Brunner Mond produced under licence from 1872 to 1886 when the patent ran out, making a royalty payment of 8 shillings per ton, but this agreement stipulated that no other British licence would be granted for less than £1 per ton (Lindert and Trace, 1971: 253). However, they argue that there was little excuse for not making the switch in 1890 when most of the remaining Leblanc producers merged to form the United Alkali Company. So long as the cartel remained effective, gains were of the order of £200,000 per annum. Discounted back to 1890 at a discount rate of 3 per cent, this yields a capitalised value of about £2.5 million. Even this figure is seen as too large by Sandberg (1971) who notes that Lindert and Trace failed to take account of the fact that Leblanc producers had already paid for their capital, whereas they had to invest in new capital when switching to the Solvay process. Hence the relevant comparison is between variable costs for the Leblanc process and total costs for the Solvay process. Allowing for this delays the optimal switching point to 1897 and reduces the capitalised gains to £1.9 million at a 3 per cent discount rate and just £0.9 million at 6 per cent. Against a GDP figure of £1,300 million for 1890, this does not look particularly large for one of the most glaring failures of the pre-1914 period. At a discount rate of 8 per cent the gains fall to zero.

Perhaps the most significant point about this failure is that it occurred in an industry subject to a collusive agreement. If Brunner Mond had chosen to operate in a more aggressively competitive fashion, they could have forced the United Alkali Company to adjust or exit. Hence this example of failure is an exception rather than the rule. It does not invalidate McCloskey and Sandberg's (1971) general claim that competition could be relied upon to prevent persistent failure in most sectors of the late Victorian and Edwardian British economy.

Failure in synthetic dyes

Another aspect of the British chemical industry before 1914 that has received much attention is the failure to establish a significant synthetic dye industry based on coal-tar. The success of the Germans in dominating world production of dyestuffs is seen as all the more remarkable since Britain possessed a large textile industry (the main potential customers) and because the first synthetic aniline dye was produced in Britain in 1856 by William Henry Perkin, then a 17-year-old student trying to make the drug quinine from aniline (Bronowski, 1966: 104).

The simplest interpretation of the rise to dominance of the German dyestuffs manufacturers is to see it as a result of the greater pool of scientific resources that they could call upon because of government support for science and technical training (Wrigley, 1986). This would confirm the views of those who stress the importance of external effects in the growth process. However, as Lindert and Trace (1971: 266) point out, we also need to take account of the effects of British patent law, which until 1907 allowed patentees to leave their patents unworked in Britain without requiring them to grant licences. There are also allegations of anti-competitive practices by German firms, including dumping of alizarin dyes when British production started in 1883.

Soap, explosives and other chemical industries: some British success stories?

Clapham (1938: 174) and Richardson (1968: 280–1) balanced their accounts of the problems in alkali and dyestuffs with more favourable assessments of other branches of the British chemical industry, including soap and explosives. In soap, Britain's healthy balance of trade surplus was improving as exports grew rapidly in the first decade of the twentieth century, based on the aggressive marketing strategy of Lever Brothers, Crosfields and Gossage (Wilson, 1954, vol.I; Musson, 1965). In explosives, Nobel's Ardeer factory in Ayrshire was the world's largest in this field (Richardson, 1968: 280).

Although Musson (1978: 222) acknowledges the dangers of drawing an over-pessimistic conclusion on the basis of soda ash and dyes, he is nevertheless critical of the soap and explosives branches for relying on foreign scientific and technical expertise (Musson, 1978: 220–1). This is rather difficult to understand, given the widespread criticism that British

Table 10.5. *Comparative labour productivity in chemicals, 1909/07 and 1914/12 (UK=100)*

US/UK	1909/07	1914/12
Seedcrushing	77	
Coke	115	
Soap & detergents	221	· 233
Fertilisers	158	243

Notes: US/UK figures based on output per operative.
Source: Appendix table A2.1.

Table 10.6. *British imports and exports of selected chemical products, 1907 (£000)*

	Imports	Exports
Coal-tar dyes	1,705	
Coke and manufactured fuel	20	1,948
Fertilisers	2,736	4,003
Soap	632	1,458
Seed oil	1,107	3,111
Soda ash	2	462
Alkalis	127	1,889

Source: HM Customs and Excise, *Annual Statement of the Trade of the United Kingdom, 1907* (London: HMSO).

discoveries were being more effectively exploited abroad. Musson does not see it as a weakness of the German dyestuffs producers that they were reliant on Perkin's discovery imported from Britain. A British producer like Lever Brothers exploiting German discoveries more effectively through better organisation and marketing should be seen as an unqualified British success.

In contrast to the bias of the literature towards the poor British performers, the US/UK comparative labour productivity figures for 1909/07 in table 10.5 include a number of good British performers, particularly in seedcrushing, where again Lever Brothers were involved (Wilson, 1954, vol.I: 57–8). Data from the *Annual Statement of Trade* for 1907 suggest that the export earnings in these sectors swamped the £1.7 million cost of the imported coal-tar dyes. In table 10.6 we see substantial export surpluses in coke and manufactured fuel, soap, fertilisers and seed oil. Even in soda ash and alkalis in general, Britain had a substantial balance of trade surplus.

Conclusions

The chemical industry, then, reflects the importance of many of the factors highlighted in chapters 6–9, although experience is varied. The importance of resources and demand can be seen, for example, in the location of a cluster of chemical companies around the salt fields of Cheshire, with the alkali producers meeting the demands of the soap and glass manufacturers. And yet we see in the case of coal-tar dyes that the existence of ample raw material deposits and a ready customer in the Lancashire textile industry did not prevent the British dyestuffs industry from being wiped out by German competitors pursuing a determined strategy based on the accumulation of human capital. The importance of previously accumulated fixed capital is also seen in the case of the retention of the Leblanc plant. However, in this case the most important factor explaining the persistence of failure was the lack of competition in the industry. In other branches of the chemical industry openness, at least to German and Swiss scientists, allowed Britain to benefit from the externalities provided by the German and Swiss systems of scientific education.

Metals

Iron and steel

Britain's dominance of world iron and steel production was increasingly challenged by Germany and the United States in the last quarter of the nineteenth century, as the figures in table 10.7 make clear. In pig iron, Britain's share of world production fell from 50.3 per cent in 1870 to 13.2 per cent in 1913. Over the same period, Germany's share rose from 10.5 per cent to 21.2 per cent while the US share increased dramatically from 14.1 per cent to 39.8 per cent. In steel, Britain's share fell from 43.1 per cent to 10.2 per cent, while Germany's share remained stable and the US share again increased dramatically. Nevertheless, output continued to rise in Britain, with steel registering an average annual growth rate of 8.6 per cent over the period 1870–1913. Furthermore, as the export figures in table 10.8 show, British exports continued to grow and remained higher than German exports until the very end of the period, while American exports remained lower throughout the period. The growing import penetration in Britain reflects the commitment to free trade, in contrast to the protectionist policies pursued in Germany and the United States.

Many authors have used these figures to support allegations of entrepreneurial failure (Burnham and Hoskins, 1943; Burn, 1940; Levine, 1967; Landes, 1969). However, others have explained these trends largely in terms

Table 10.7. *Production of iron and steel, 1870–1913 (m tons)*

A. Pig iron	UK	Germany	US	World
1870	5.96	1.24	1.67	11.84
1880	7.75	2.43	3.84	18.16
1890	7.90	4.03	9.20	26.75
1900	8.96	7.43	13.79	39.81
1910	10.01	12.89	27.30	64.76
1913	10.26	16.49	30.97	77.90
B. Steel production	UK	Germany	US	World
1870	0.22	0.13	0.04	0.51
1880	1.29	0.69	1.25	4.18
1890	3.58	2.10	4.28	12.28
1900	4.90	6.36	10.19	27.83
1910	6.37	12.89	23.09	59.33
1913	7.66	17.32	31.30	75.15

Source: Burnham and Hoskins (1943: 272–4).

Table 10.8. *Exports and imports of iron and steel, 1870–1913 (000 tons)*

A. Exports	UK	Germany	US
1870	2,715		
1880	3,793	772	174
1890	4,001	943	50
1900	3,447	1,525	1,154
1910	4,588	4,797	1,536
1913	4,934	6,401	2,907
B. Imports	UK	Germany	US
1870	156	700	
1880	348	400	
1890	386	950	665
1900	800	923	210
1910	1,367	215	510
1913	2,231	300	253

Source: Burnham and Hoskins (1943: 30, 276–9).

Table 10.9. *Average annual per capita consumption of pig iron, 1876–80 to 1911–12 (cwt)*

	UK	Germany	US
1876–80	3.2	1.0	0.9
1881–5	3.8	1.5	1.6
1886–90	3.6	1.8	2.1
1891–5	3.3	2.0	2.5
1896–1900	3.9	2.8	2.9
1904–8	3.8	3.7	5.0
1911–12	3.6	4.7	5.7

Source: Payne (1968: 78).

of the inevitable consequences of economic maturity in Britain coupled with tariff protection in the rapidly developing German and American markets (Temin, 1966b; Tolliday, 1991; Wengenroth, 1994). Figures on average annual *per capita* consumption of pig iron in table 10.9 show stagnation in Britain but rapid growth in Germany and the United States. Growth in *per capita* consumption of steel was also much more rapid in Germany and the United States (Payne, 1968: 78). Hindered by tariff barriers in the United States and major continental European markets, British exporters were forced to fight for markets in the Empire and overseas. They continued to supply the bulk of the import requirements of Empire countries, but in other countries were overtaken by the Germans and seriously challenged by the Americans and Belgians (Payne, 1968: 84–6).

Although the slow growth of demand may be expected to have caused some technological lag because less investment implies an older capital stock, proponents of entrepreneurial failure have frequently seized upon technological differences as evidence of conservative tendencies among British entrepreneurs. These allegations of entrepreneurial failure usually focus on two related issues, the slow adoption of the basic process of steel making and the neglect of phosphoric ores in Lincolnshire and Northamptonshire (Burn, 1940: 169–82; Burnham and Hoskins, 1943: 120, 177–85). However, when the decisions are examined in detail, it is difficult to find evidence of substantial forgone profit opportunities.

To put the technological differences between Britain and her major competitors into perspective, we need to note the suitability of different types of steel for different uses. Bessemer steel, produced by blowing oxygen through molten pig iron to reduce the carbon content, was used mainly for rails, while open hearth (Siemens–Martin) steel, produced in a regenerative furnace and allowing more sampling during the conversion process, was

Table 10.10. *Proportion of steel produced by open hearth process, 1875–1913 (%)*

	UK	Germany	US
1875	12.5		
1880	19.3	4.9	8.1
1890	43.6	17.4	12.0
1900	64.3	32.2	33.4
1910	72.1	37.3	63.2
1913	79.2	40.2	69.0

Sources: Burnham and Hoskins (1943: 183); Hogan (1971: 413).

more suitable for plates and custom work in general (Harley, 1974: 400; Landes,1969: 255–62). As Tolliday (1991: 27–8) notes, this had important consequences for the proportions of the different types of steel produced in different countries. Britain was particularly dominant in shipbuilding, the major user of plates, while 76 per cent of the British railway network was complete by 1880, compared with 53 per cent in Germany and 36 per cent in the United States. Thus the figures in table 10.10 show a much earlier dominance of open hearth steel in Britain.

The concentration on open hearth steel in Britain helps to explain the slow diffusion of the basic process, which allowed the use of cheaper phosphoric ores by including a lining of a chemically basic material, limestone, in the furnace walls to remove the embrittling acid phosphorous (Landes, 1969: 258). The innovation was originally applied to the Bessemer converter by Sidney Thomas in 1878, but was soon applied to the open hearth process. However, open hearth steel production in Britain remained predominantly acid until after 1900, despite a rapid switch to the basic process among German and American open hearth producers (Tolliday, 1991: 32–3). The idea that this delay in the adoption of the basic open hearth process can be explained by conservatism is undermined by the rapidity of the shift when it did occur after 1900. McCloskey (1973: 71) explains this through the introduction of the Talbot tilting furnace in 1900. This allowed the easy removal of slag, the accumulation of which was particularly great in the basic process. The alternative way of dealing with slag accumulation was to charge the furnace with a high proportion of scrap iron, with fewer impurities. However, although this was possible in Germany and America because of the ready availability of basic Bessemer scrap, the dominance of the open hearth process in Britain meant that scrap prices were relatively high (McCloskey, 1973: 72; Tolliday, 1991: 42). Hence the Talbot tilting

Table 10.11. *Comparative labour productivity in metal manufacture, 1909/07 and 1914/12 (UK=100)*

US/UK	1909/07	1914/12
Iron & steel	283	280
Tinplate	328	
Copper	425	
Lead & zinc	91	

Notes: US/UK figures based on output per operative.
Source: Appendix table A2.1.

furnace was much more rapidly adopted in Britain than in Germany or America.

The concentration on the open hearth process and the problem of slag accumulation go some way towards explaining the neglect of the Lincolnshire and Northamptonshire phosphoric ores, at least before 1900. However, this is not a complete explanation since, in theory at least, Britain could have sought an export market for basic Bessemer steel by exploiting these cheap domestic ores (Tolliday 1991: 31). Indeed, this is the basis of Burn's (1940) indictment of British steel producers. However, Wengenroth (1994: 263) argues that there were important technical problems which needed to be solved before the East Midlands ores could be used to make basic steel, and solutions were found by research scientists only after the First World War. In the meantime, East Midlands ores had to be mixed with other ores or used to make foundry iron only (Tolliday, 1991: 37). McCloskey's (1973: 57–67) suggestion that the Midlands ores were neglected because any gain in lower ore prices would have been offset by the transport costs incurred in shipping the Lincolnshire pig iron to Cleveland for conversion into basic steel is dismissed by both Tolliday (1991: 36) and Wengenroth (1994: 253), since Burn had clearly envisaged integrated iron and steel production in the East Midlands, as occurred at Corby in the 1930s.

If the revisionists are correct, then the substantial American labour productivity lead in iron and steel apparent in comparisons based on production census material for 1909/07 in table 10.11 should be explicable largely in terms of differences in resource and factor inputs. In fact McCloskey (1973: 114–24) claims that there was little difference in total factor productivity (TFP) levels between Britain and America at this time. His calculations are based on the cost dual of the production-based approach to the calculation of TFP. TFP growth is usually calculated from quantity data as the growth of output relative to the growth of

Table 10.12. *Comparative US/UK TFP in*
rolled iron and steel, 1909/07 (UK=100)

	A*/A
Heavy plates	98.8
Rails	108.4
Bars, rods, etc.	107.5
Structural shapes	106.6
Black plates and sheets	98.5

Source: Calculated from McCloskey (1973: 122–3).

inputs, weighted by their shares in costs. In the case of two inputs, capital
(K) and labour (L):

$$A*/A = \frac{Q*/Q}{(K*/K)^{S_K} (L*/L)^{S_L}} \qquad (10.1)$$

where A is total factor productivity, Q is output and S_K and S_L are the cost
shares of the capital and labour inputs, respectively. When comparing
changes over time, an asterisk indicates the level of a variable relative to the
base period, although in cross-sectional international comparisons it
denotes the level of a variable relative to the base country.

In competitive conditions, TFP can also be measured as the fall in the
final output price relative to the change in input prices, again weighted by
cost shares:

$$A*/A = \frac{(P_K*/P_K)^{S_K} (P_L*/P_L)^{S_L}}{P*/P} \qquad (10.2)$$

where P, P_K and P_L are the prices of output, capital and labour respectively.
In the case of steel products considered by McCloskey, the key inputs are
pig iron and labour. Given knowledge of the prices of these key inputs,
output prices and cost shares from McCloskey (1973: 122), TFP can be calculated on a comparative US/UK basis for the five products in table 10.12.
A figure above 100 implies higher TFP in America. There is higher
American TFP in only three of the five products, and in general the
differences are small, certainly when compared with the labour productivity differences.

These calculations have been criticised by Allen (1979), who argues that
they rely heavily on the assumption of a competitive industry. If the mark-

Table 10.13. *Real costs in the Cleveland and American pig iron industries, 1883–1913 (1913=100)*

	Cleveland	America
1883	105	184
1885	96	161
1890	108	121
1895	70	137
1900	120	123
1905	104	127
1910	99	107
1913	100	100

Source: Jones (1933: 278, 296).

up of prices over costs was not constrained by competition and varied across countries and over time, the level or movement of output prices relative to input prices could not be taken as an indicator of efficiency. However, Allen's contention that British firms were less profitable than their American or German counterparts and lowered prices by reducing mark-ups rather than improving efficiency has not been backed up by hard evidence on profits. Indeed, Wengenroth (1994: 265) is highly critical of Allen's calculations which fail to distinguish adequately between the different varieties of output produced and the varieties of inputs required to produce them.

In addition to comparative levels of TFP at a point in time, trends in TFP in the British and American pig iron industries can be established. Jones (1933) calculated indices of real cost, the exact inverse of the price-based TFP measure given in (10.2), for the Cleveland and American pig iron producers. His figures are given in table 10.13, where a fall in real cost is equivalent to an increase in TFP. The real cost indices exhibit a high degree of volatility over the cycle, but the conclusion seems to be that there was little improvement in efficiency in either country after 1890.

However, the data in table 10.14 suggest that labour productivity continued to rise in the British iron and steel industry as a whole until the turn of the century. Here, the output index combines the pig iron and steel series using value added weights and making an allowance for rolling and special steels (Lewis, 1978: 252). Employment figures from Phelps-Brown and Handfield-Jones (1952) are based on Census material on occupations and industries.

Table 10.14. *Labour productivity in the British iron and steel industry, 1861–1911*

	Output (1911=100)	Employment (000)	Output per employee (1911=100)
1861	21.5	149.9	44.6
1871	39.4	216.4	56.6
1881	57.3	239.7	74.3
1891	63.5	242.5	81.4
1901	85.4	264.6	100.4
1911	100.0	311.0	100.0

Sources: Lewis (1978: 248–50); Phelps-Brown and Handfield-Jones (1952: 298).

Table 10.15. *British production and exports of tinplate, 1805–1912 (000 tons)*

	Production	Exports
1805	4	2
1837	18	9
1850	37	25
1865	84	63
1868	107	88
1872	143	118
1878	199	155
1880	302	218
1886	426	335
1891	586	448
1896	450	267
1900	500	273
1905	668	354
1912	848	481

Source: Minchinton (1957: 27–9, 74, 80).

Tinplate

The British tinplate industry grew rapidly during the nineteenth century, exporting the bulk of its output, as can be seen from the data in table 10.15. This rapid growth was based on satisfying a rising demand for kettles, pans, cans, etc. In the United States, by far the largest export market, tinplate was also used for roofing, and there was a rising demand based on food canning and petrol cans (Musson, 1978: 177).

Table 10.16. *Geographical distribution of British tinplate exports, 1891–1913 (000 tons)*

	1891	1898	1913
Total	448.4	250.9	494.5
US	325.1	65.3	21.5
France		11.3	21.3
Germany		12.5	34.7
Holland		10.0	43.0
Canada	16.1	20.9	12.3
Norway			25.2
Italy			20.4
Bengal			28.1
Straits			16.7
China			15.6
Japan			28.2
Russia	22.7	28.0	9.9
Portugal			14.8

Source: Minchinton (1957: 80).

However, the British tinplate industry suffered a major setback in 1891 with the imposition of the McKinley tariff, which largely shut Britain out from her major export market (Minchinton, 1957: 65). In fact, though, the industry recovered remarkably after a difficult period during the 1890s, returning to strong growth of exports and production after 1900. As can be seen in table 10.16, the heavy dependence on the US market was overcome, so that by 1913 British exports were widely distributed across the world's major markets. This suggests an effective marketing campaign in tinplate to set against the allegations of poor marketing in other sectors of industry.

British production occurred mainly in small-scale firms specialised in tinplate production, using labour-intensive craft-based flexible production methods. John (1950: 59) suggests that skilled workers made up 25 per cent of total employment in the tinplate industry as a whole, rising to 30–40 per cent in the larger integrated concerns. Nevertheless, the linking of steel and tinplate interests as in Richard Thomas & Co. and Baldwin's remained the exception rather than the rule. However, the fact that the American industry needed strong tariff protection suggests that the small-scale labour-intensive British flexible production techniques were well suited to British conditions. Hence, as in the iron and steel industry, the substantially higher labour productivity of the American tinplate industry in 1909/07, seen in table 10.11, should not be seen as indicating greater overall efficiency.

Table 10.17. *Mining and refining of non-ferrous metals in Britain, 1850–1913 (000 tons)*

| A. Mineral content of non-ferrous metals mined | | |
Copper	Lead	Zinc
1850		64.5	
1854	19.9	64.0	
1860	16.0	63.3	4.4
1870	7.2	73.4	3.9
1880	3.7	56.9	7.2
1890	0.9	33.6	8.6
1900	0.8	24.4	9.1
1910	0.4	21.5	4.2
1913	0.4	18.1	5.8

| B. Output of refined non-ferrous metals | | |
Copper	Lead	Zinc
1850	23.8	65.6	
1854	23.1	64.8	
1860	29.7	63.8	
1870	34.2	82.1	15.8
1880	59.9	66.8	22.1
1890	88.0	47.7	29.1
1900	78.4	35.0	29.8
1910	69.9	29.2	62.1
1913	51.8	30.1	65.2

Source: Mitchell (1988: 308, 310).

Non-ferrous metals

The fate of the British non-ferrous metals industry appears to be closely linked to natural resources. Table 10.17 shows the exhaustion of British ores from the mid-nineteenth century in copper and lead, while British supplies of zinc ores were never large. The output of refined lead began to fall during the 1870s and remained on a downward trend until the First World War. The output of refined copper, however, continued to rise on the basis of imported ores until the 1890s, when it became possible to use much lower grade ores. At this point, the economics of location changed. While high grade ores were being used, 2 tons of coal were required to smelt a ton of ore and it paid to locate near a coalfield (Newell, 1990: 75). However, when it became possible to smelt low grade ores, the ore:coal ratio rose considerably and it paid to locate near ore fields. Hence the utilisation of the low grade American porphyry ores saw comparative advantage shift decisively to the United States. Indeed, the most successful German company in non-ferrous metals, Metallgesellschaft, made larger investments in smelting and refining in America than in Europe (Chandler, 1990: 126). This exploitation of low grade ores led to an increase in the scale of operations in America, with the development of vertically integrated mining and refining corporations such as Anaconda (Schmitz, 1986). The large US/UK labour productivity gap in copper for 1909/07, seen in table 10.11, undoubtedly reflects these developments. However, the position in lead and zinc suggests that there were no substantial economies of scale being reaped by the United States in these industries.

Conclusions

The experience of the metal industries illustrates a number of the themes highlighted in chapters 6–9. The importance of demand factors can be seen in the neglect of the basic process in the British steel industry, since in Britain there was relatively heavy demand for acid open hearth steel, especially from shipbuilders. The decline of the non-ferrous metal smelting and refining industries in Britain in line with non-ferrous metal mining suggests an important role for resource endowments in determining industry location. The tinplate industry illustrates the viability of the British flexible production strategy, with small-scale British firms continuing to win export markets on the basis of craft-based skilled labour.

Engineering

Shipbuilding

Shipbuilding provides an interesting contrast to the industries studied so far because in the second half of the nineteenth century Britain came to dominate world markets, largely at the expense of American producers. British shipping and shipbuilding benefited from the disruption caused by the American Civil War, but as Pollard and Robertson (1979: 11) note, the underlying forces explaining the shift in comparative advantage were the rise of iron and steam, bringing about a shift from wooden sailing ships to iron steamships. Prior to this, Britain lacked a ready supply of the essential raw material for shipbuilding. Shipbuilding output and employment grew rapidly, as can be seen from table 10.18. Gross tonnage is the total volume of a ship in cubic feet divided by 100, while net tonnage makes a deduction from gross tonnage to allow for space not available for carrying cargo (Lorenz, 1991a: 143). The figures in table 10.19 show that by the early 1890s Britain accounted for more than 80 per cent of world output, and despite

Table 10.18. *Output and employment in the British merchant shipbuilding industry, 1861–1911*

	Net tonnage (000)	Gross tonnage (000)	Employment (000)	Net tons per employee
1861	208		60.6	3.43
1865	448		71.8	6.24
1871	391		76.4	5.12
1877	451		85.5	5.27
1881	609	1000	90.4	6.73
1886	332	474	121.8	2.73
1891	809	1268	118.0	6.86
1898	871	1367	169.1	5.15
1901	983	1524	171.8	5.72
1907	1038	1608	184.6	5.62
1911	1111	1804	195.1	5.69

Source: Pollard and Robertson (1979: 34, 250–2).

Table 10.19. *World merchant shipbuilding output, 1892–1911 (000 gross tons)*

	UK	Germany	US	World
1892	1110	65	63	1358
1898	1368	153	173	1893
1901	1525	218	433	2618
1907	1608	275	475	2778
1911	1804	256	172	2650

Source: Pollard and Robertson (1979: 249).

the build-up of German, American, French and Dutch capacity behind protective barriers, Britain's share remained over 60 per cent before the First World War. Lorenz (1991b: 914) quotes an estimate from the 5 February 1926 edition of the *Glasgow Herald* that Britain controlled 80 per cent of the export market in 1913.

Pollard and Robertson (1979: 7) argue that Britain's craft-based flexible production system was important in explaining the success of British ship-builders. In a highly cyclical industry, it was important to be able to economise on fixed capital, which was a serious burden during downturns. This could be done by substituting skilled labour for machinery. Britain's large stock of skilled craft workers thus gave British shipbuilders an advan-

Table 10.20. *The proportion of skilled labour in British shipyards,*
1892–1913 (%)

	Eight English yards 1892	Six Scottish yards 1892	Scotland 1911	North East Coast 1913
Skilled woodworkers and 'amphibians'	58	66	21	47
Skilled metal and engine workers	46	13		
Unskilled	29	22	18	25
Miscellaneous	13	12	15	15

Notes: 'Amphibians' are tradesmen who work both in shipyards and on land, including plumbers, painters, etc. 'Miscellaneous' includes apprentices.
Source: Pollard and Robertson (1979: 153).

tage over their American and European rivals. The high proportion of skilled workers in British shipyards can be seen in table 10.20. Given the highly cyclical nature of the industry, many of these skilled workers were 'amphibians', working as painters, plumbers, carpenters, metalworkers, etc. on land as well as in shipyards. Given the general thrust of the literature on the inadequacies of the British craft-based production system in the late nineteenth century, shipbuilding serves as a useful counter-example. Furthermore, it reinforces the message of McCloskey and Sandberg (1971) that the latest technology is not always the most efficient; some of the latest technological developments were more quickly adopted in less successful American and German shipyards than in Britain (Musson, 1978: 198).

There was, however, one cloud on the horizon arising from Britain's craft-based production system, and that concerned the frequency of demarcation disputes between the many trades represented by their craft unions. On the Tyne, for example, there was an average of one major strike per month over demarcation issues during the period 1890–3 (Pollard and Robertson, 1979: 167). Pollard and Robertson (1979: 169) claim that demarcation disputes should not be seen as more than a minor annoyance at this time, arguing that they did not significantly retard technical change or the rate of growth of the industry. Nevertheless, it is striking that the output and employment figures in table 10.18 show labour productivity reaching a peak in 1891 and stagnating thereafter.

The comparative labour productivity position in shipbuilding before the First World War can be seen in table 10.21. The two observations for

Table 10.21. *Comparative labour productivity in engineering, 1909/07 and 1914/12 (UK=100)*

US/UK	1909/07	1914/12
Mechanical engineering	203	
Shipbuilding	95	115
Motor vehicles	435	
Germany/UK	1907	
Motor vehicles	192	

Notes: US/UK figures based on output per operative; Germany/UK figures based on output per employee.
Source: Appendix tables A2.1, A2.2.

1909/07 and 1914/12 suggest that British shipbuilding labour productivity was about the same as in America. This in turn suggests that Britain's dominance of world markets meant that the labour intensity of British production methods was offset by economies of specialisation, with each yard concentrating on a narrow range of vessels (Pollard and Robertson, 1979: 84). The British shipbuilding industry at this time is surely an excellent example of Marshall's (1920: 223–7) idea of external economies of scale, with a large number of specialised producers highly localised in the North East on the Tyne, Wear and Tees and in Scotland on the Clyde. However, the absence of a labour productivity gap also reflects the fact that mass production methods had not yet been applied successfully to shipbuilding; this did not really occur until the widespread application of prefabrication and welding techniques to tanker production after the Second World War (Lorenz and Wilkinson, 1986: 118).

Vertical linkages between British shipbuilders and shipping lines were strong, which helped to smooth out the effects of cyclical demand patterns; strong shipping lines with financial reserves could afford to order during slumps, and this helped to maintain capacity utilisation at shipyards as well as guaranteeing repeat orders and facilitating standardisation of designs. Vertical linkages between shipbuilders and marine engineers also became increasingly important as steam replaced sail (Pollard and Robertson, 1979: 89–96). This suggests that industrial organisation did not act as a constraint on entrepreneurial behaviour. In shipbuilding, at least, this aspect of Elbaum and Lazonick's (1986) work cannot be accepted.

Table 10.22. *Labour productivity in British engineering industries,*
1861–1911

	Output (1911=100)	Employment (000)	Output per employee (1911=100)
1861	22.9		
1871	37.2		
1881	50.4	423.4	91.3
1891	58.9	519.3	87.0
1901	81.4	680.2	91.8
1911	100.0	766.9	100.0

Sources: Lewis (1978: 248–50); Phelps-Brown and Handfield-Jones (1952: 298).

Mechanical and electrical engineering

Mechanical and electrical engineering are usually seen as performing badly in late Victorian and Edwardian Britain, with the former slow to adapt to the rise of American mass production techniques and the latter slow to develop at all. Nevertheless, output growth was faster than for manufacturing as a whole. The Lewis (1978) output index in table 10.22 is calculated from data on consumption of iron and steel by the engineering sector. This is calculated as pig iron and steel output *minus* the pig iron used in making steel, *minus* iron and steel use in shipbuilding and railmaking and *minus* net exports of unfabricated iron and steel (Lewis, 1978: 253). Two adjustments are then made to allow for stock changes and a rising trend in the value added per ton of metal fabricated. Average annual output growth in engineering over the period 1870–1913 was 3.0 per cent, compared with 2.2 per cent in total manufacturing. Comparable data on employment are difficult to obtain, but using the Phelps-Brown and Handfield-Jones (1952) estimates from 1881 suggests a recovery of labour productivity growth in the first decade of the twentieth century after stagnation during the 1890s.

The performance of the British mechanical engineering industry cannot be seen as uniformly poor (Saul, 1968). Indeed, the export figures in table 10.23 suggest specialisation according to comparative advantage. Britain retained a commanding export position in textile machinery, and a small lead in prime movers and boilers. German exports were ahead in machine tools, sewing machines and locomotives, while American exports were ahead in agricultural machinery. Britain's competitive position appears reasonably secure in all branches except machine tools and agricultural machinery.

To what extent, then, does it make sense to see British producers as losing

Table 10.23. *Exports of mechanical engineering products, 1913 (£m)*

	UK	Germany	US
Agricultural machinery	3.0	2.5	6.7
Boilers	1.8	0.8	
Prime movers	5.2	4.7	1.9[a]
Machine tools	1.0	4.0	2.9
Locomotives (rail & road)	3.4	3.9	1.2
Sewing machines	2.4	2.8	2.4
Textile machinery	8.3	2.8	0.3
Miscellaneous	9.7	15.7	14.2
Total	34.8	37.2	29.6

Note: a Combined figure for prime movers and boilers.
Source: Saul (1968: 227).

ground to the rise of American mass production technology in this sector? First, as Floud (1974, 1976) notes, American exports of machinery to Britain did not become significant until the 1890s, and British producers then responded by adopting or adapting American methods. This is consistent with the McCloskey and Sandberg (1971) hypothesis of rational behaviour, with new techniques only being used when they become profitable. It is also consistent with the findings of Hounshell (1984), who argues that the breakthrough to genuine interchangeable mass production in American engineering was delayed until the very late nineteenth century. Thus, for example, parts of Singer sewing machines were hand fitted together by skilled fitters as late as 1883 (Hounshell, 1984: 6). Second, the large stock of skilled engineering workers in Britain made the continued use of craft-based flexible production methods profitable, even when mass production methods were profitable in America. As Harley (1974: 406) notes, British textile machinery builders were slow to adopt American production techniques, yet were unquestionably the world's major suppliers. It seems that American firms were unable to match with machinery the skill and accuracy of the British fitters. These differences in choice of technique help to explain the comparative advantages noted above, with the British concentrating on heavy machinery, where building to custom was the norm, and the advantages of a skilled labour force were correspondingly greatest. The differences in choice of technique can also be seen in the comparative labour productivity position for mechanical engineering in table 10.21, with American producers achieving a roughly 2:1 labour productivity lead over the skilled labour-intensive British producers.

Table 10.24. *British trade in electrical goods, 1913 (£m)*

A. *Imports*

	Total	From Germany
Electrical machinery	1346	721
Electric cables	513	362
Electric lamps	479	352

B. *Exports*

	Total	To British possessions
Electrical machinery	2364	1103
Electric cables	3605	1514
Electric lamps	283	162

Source: Byatt (1968: 259–61).

The major criticism of the British electrical engineering industry seems to be that it was highly dependent on American and German multi-national enterprise (Byatt, 1968: 273). Yet in my view, this is not a valid criticism. Rather, I would see the entry of American and German firms as securing the viability of production in Britain. As Byatt (1968: 273) also notes, without the entry of foreign producers, the adoption of electrical methods in Britain may have been further delayed.

The figures in table 10.24 show that in electrical machinery and electric cables British exports exceeded imports by a substantial margin, although there was a small trade deficit in electric lamps. This is again suggestive of specialisation according to comparative advantage. The strong German position in electrical engineering is apparent from the high proportion of British imports supplied, while the British dependence on Empire markets is equally clear from the export figures.

Motor vehicles

Figures on output levels of the 10 leading British and American motor vehicle producers in 1913, shown in table 10.25, suggest very different production strategies on the two sides of the Atlantic, with a much larger scale of operations in the United States. Even Ford, in its British factory at Trafford Park produced only 6,139 vehicles in 1913 (Saul, 1962: 25). This conforms to the pattern of multi-national experience noted by Foreman-Peck (1982) for the 1920s, with American producers forced to adapt

Table 10.25. *Output levels of the 10 leading American and British vehicle producers, 1913*

American	Output	British	Output
Ford	202,667	Wolseley	3,000
Willys–Overland	37,442	Humber	2,500
Studebaker	31,994	Sunbeam	1,700
Buick	26,666	Rover	1,600
Cadillac	17,284	Austin	1,500
Maxwell	17,000	Singer	1,350
Hupmobile	12,543	Arrol–Johnston	1,150
Reo	7,647	Belsize	1,000
Oakland	7,030	Daimler	1,000
Hudson	6,401	Star	1,000

Source: Lewchuk (1987: 117).

American production techniques to the different demand conditions and factor supplies of Europe.

Comparative labour productivity levels in motor vehicles for the US/UK and Germany/UK cases can be seen in table 10.21. The large American labour productivity lead suggests economies of scale in the large, homogeneous US market, and a rather more labour-intensive production process in Britain. Lewchuk (1987: 119) notes that vehicle production was much more of a complete manufacturing operation in Britain than in America, where production tended to consist of assembling bought-out components. The origin of these different production strategies is traced back to the abundance of skilled workers in Britain experienced in the operation of metal working machines and to difficulties experienced by American producers in raising sufficient capital to buy the metal working machines (Lewchuk, 1986: 138). However, the German labour productivity lead over Britain seen in table 10.21 suggests that even if the American lead could not have been completely eliminated, it could at least have been substantially reduced. Lewchuk's (1987: 66–77) analysis, which stresses difficulties over the wage–effort bargain in the British vehicle industry, may be of some relevance here. Lewchuk sees the development of craft control of the production process as important in limiting the effort of workers, but allowing the continued profitability of companies through the operation of a piece-rate wage payment system. This analysis will be discussed in more detail when considering the interwar period.

Conclusions

In shipbuilding we see the importance of resources, with the switch from wood to iron and from sail to steam leading to a shift of comparative

Table 10.26. *British cotton consumption and exports, 1850–1913*

	Cotton consumption (m lb)	Cotton yarn exports (m lb)	Cotton piece goods exports (m lin. yd)
1850	588	131.4	1385.2
1860	1084	197.3	2776.2
1870	1075	186.1	3267.0
1880	1361	215.6	4494.6
1890	1664	258.3	5125.0
1900	1737	158.3	5031.7
1910	1632	191.7	6017.6
1913	2178	210.1	7075.3

Source: Robson (1957: 332–3).

advantage from America to Britain. The large number of British ship-building firms clustered around a small number of locations are suggestive of Marshallian external economies of scale. In shipbuilding and in other engineering industries where mass production methods had not yet been successfully applied, British craft-based flexible production methods continued to be highly successful. In other industries, such as motor vehicles, demand factors were important in limiting the adoption of standardised mass production methods in Britain despite their success in the United States. The problem of inflexible craft unions impeding technical change was just becoming visible, especially in the growth of demarcation disputes in shipbuilding. Although this was of relatively minor significance at this stage, it became a major problem in later years.

Textiles and clothing

Cotton: the stubborn English mule

The British cotton industry continued to expand output and exports during the period 1850–1913, as can be seen from the figures in table 10.26. Indeed, Britain retained a large share of world spinning and weaving capacity right up to the First World War (Clapham, 1938: 175–6). Cotton textiles accounted for about half the value of British exports in 1830 and still accounted for about a quarter in 1913 (Sandberg, 1974: 6). At the time, criticism of the industry was restricted to social matters, such as the treatment of women and children, the length of the working day and sanitary conditions, since economic performance was generally seen as good (Sandberg, 1974: 7).

However, after the collapse of the Lancashire cotton industry between the wars, economists and historians began to look back for signs of weakness in the pre-1914 period. Writers such as Jones (1933: 117–18) and Clapham (1938: 176–7) pointed to the delay in Lancashire in switching from mule spinning to ring spinning and from the powerloom to the automatic loom in weaving, despite the widespread adoption in the United States and other countries of the ring spindle and the automatic loom.

The technological decisions to retain the mule and the powerloom are examined by Sandberg (1969, 1974), who argues that they were rational given the conditions faced by British producers. The ring spindle could be operated by largely female unskilled labour, while the mule required the strength and skill of largely male operatives. Thus the ring spindle saved on labour costs. This saving on labour costs had to be balanced against higher raw cotton costs, because the ring frame put extra strain on the cotton. For a coarse yarn of a low 'count' (the number of 840 yard 'hanks' per pound of cotton yarn), cheap short staple cotton could bear the extra strain of the ring spindle, so that there were no significant extra material costs to set against the labour cost savings. However, for the finer high counts, the ring required a more expensive long staple cotton, which significantly raised material costs (Sandberg, 1981: 115). There were additional differences in capital and power costs, but these were relatively unimportant.

Sandberg found that in the United States the labour saving was greater than the extra raw cotton cost on all counts except the very finest, above 100. In Britain, however, where there was an abundant supply of skilled mule spinners so that wages were lower and the labour cost savings were correspondingly smaller, the mule was superior on counts above about 40. On counts below about 40, however, where short staple cotton could be used so that there were no substantial extra raw cotton costs, the ring was superior. There was a small difference depending on whether warp or weft yarn was being spun, since different grades of raw cotton were required and because with ring weft yarn there was an additional transport cost arising from the need to ship yarn to specialised weaving mills on heavy wooden bobbins rather than in packages made up only of yarn. This meant that rings were preferable on counts a little below 40 for warp yarns, but for weft yarns rings were preferable even for counts in the low 40s. Sandberg argued that when installing new spindles, British and American mill owners acted rationally; Americans installed mainly rings, except in a few plants specialising in very high counts, while British entrepreneurs installed mainly mules, except in plants specialising in sub-40 counts. Furthermore, when contemplating scrapping existing mules and moving to rings, the retention of mules was rational so long as the variable costs of mule spinning were less than the total costs of ring spinning, since the capital cost of the mules was a sunk cost. The situation in Germany and France was similar to that

Table 10.27. *Spinning spindles installed, 1913 (m)*

	Total	Mule	Ring	% of ring
UK	55.7	45.3	10.4	18.7
US	31.5	4.1	27.4	87.0
Germany	11.2	5.1	6.1	54.5
France	7.4	4.0	3.4	45.9
Italy	4.6	1.1	3.5	76.1
Austria–Hungary	4.9	2.5	2.4	49.0
Russia	9.2	3.8	5.4	58.7
India	6.1	1.7	4.4	72.1
Japan	2.3	0.1	2.2	95.7
Other countries	10.6	3.6	7.0	65.4
World	143.5	71.3	72.2	50.3

Sources: Tyson (1968: 121; Robson, 1957: 355).

in Britain, and in both countries a substantial number of spindles in 1913 were still mules, as can be seen in table 10.27.

Sandberg provides similar calculations to show that the choice of the powerloom over the automatic loom was also rational in the conditions faced by Lancashire weavers before the First World War. The automatic loom, which automatically stopped for breakages and automatically rethreaded the shuttle, saved on labour costs since each worker could tend more looms, but raised capital costs since the looms were more expensive. Hence the technical choice hinged on the relative costs of labour and capital. In Britain, cheap labour meant that the extra cost of the automatic loom could not generally be justified.

The precise details of Sandberg's cost calculations have been the subject of a long-running and sometimes acrimonious debate since Lazonick (1981a) suggested a number of corrections. The details need not concern us, since at no point has Sandberg's fundamental contention that British mill owners acted as rational cost minimisers been challenged. However, whereas Sandberg emphasised labour cost differences as the key factor explaining the slower diffusion of ring spinning in Britain, Lazonick (1981a) argues for a number of 'institutional constraints'. The most important of these was the vertical specialisation of spinning and weaving in Britain, compared to the existence of larger vertically integrated concerns in the United States. This is seen as important because of a complementarity between the ring spindle and the automatic loom, introducing a potential coordination problem. The industrial relations system and the location of the most important cotton market in Liverpool are also seen as giving rise to institutional constraints. Since the mule spinners' wage lists did not specify normal standards of breakages arising from the use of inferior cotton, mill owners could take advantage of the proximity of the Liverpool cotton market to mix different grades of cotton and pass on the burden of extra breakages to the workers (Lazonick, 1981b: 504–5; Lazonick and Mass, 1984: 16).

Lazonick's (1981a: 104–7) analysis appears at first sight to offer a distinction between British mill owners successfully optimising within given constraints but still performing badly because they passively accepted constraints which they should have overcome. However, as Saxonhouse and Wright (1984: 519) point out, the suggestion that the decline of the British industry between the wars could have been avoided if the British industry had invested in rings rather than mules before 1914 is belied by the fact that the New England cotton industry with its ring spinning and vertically integrated mills suffered an even more catastrophic decline than Lancashire. Furthermore, the American cotton industry, whose technology and structure Lazonick urges upon pre-1914 Lancashire, was never competitive on world markets for any sustained period (Saxonhouse and Wright, 1987: 92). Higher labour productivity was always more than offset by higher wages or other costs. Furthermore, once the huge differences in wage costs between countries are noted, the interesting issue becomes not how choice of technique led to the demise of the British cotton industry, but rather how Britain managed to hang onto such a large share of the world market for so long given the much lower wages in countries like Japan, India and China (Clark, 1987: 144). From this product cycle perspective, where industries locate in high wage economies during their early stages but migrate to low wage economies as the technology is standardised and simplified, the retention of a comparative advantage in cotton textiles into the early twentieth century attests to the success of Lancashire's cotton entrepreneurs, not their failure (albeit only in a Schumpeterian sense of failing to relax constraints) as Lazonick would have it.

The calculation of productivity growth in the cotton industry has also been dogged by controversy. Jones' (1933) real cost index for the Lancashire cotton industry is shown here in table 10.28 together with real costs in the Massachusetts cotton industry. The lack of a downward trend in real costs implies that there was no improvement in efficiency in the Lancashire cotton industry from the 1880s. It should be noted that although Sandberg (1974: 94) repeats Jones' (1933: 117) statement about a fall in efficiency (rise in real costs) between 1900 and 1910, this is true only of the 10-year moving average series, and the unadjusted series actually shows a slight fall in real costs between these two years. In Massachusetts, although the fall in real costs slowed down from the 1880s, stagnation of efficiency did not set in until the turn of the century.

Table 10.28. *Real costs in the British and American cotton industries, 1850–1913 (1913=100)*

	Lancashire	Massachusetts
1850	113	178
1860	121	195
1870	103	152
1880	95	141
1890	98	109
1900	94	105
1910	93	93
1913	100	100

Source: Jones (1933: 274, 289).

However, Sandberg argues that there are a number of biases in Jones' calculations for Lancashire. The most important problem is the incorrect splicing of two cotton cloth price series in 1899. The problem arose because the earlier series was based on 1845 weights, and behaved strangely around the turn of the century. Sandberg (1974: 102) obtains the later series back to 1898 and splices at this earlier date, which makes quite a difference since the old set of prices rose by 11 per cent between 1898 and 1899 while the new set of prices remained constant. Correcting for this and several other minor biases results in a fall in real costs of 11–12 per cent between 1885 and 1914 (Sandberg, 1974: 108).

Sandberg's real cost or TFP calculations have in turn been criticised by Lazonick and Mass (1984) for failing to take account of an alleged deterioration in the quality of the raw cotton input. However, they do not provide any direct evidence of quality deterioration and hence are unable to provide any new estimates of TFP growth, the calculation of which they anyway think relies on untenable distributional assumptions (Lazonick and Mass, 1984: 33).

Lazonick and Mass (1984: 20–32) are also critical of Sandberg's (1974: 96) use of the Phelps-Brown and Handfield-Jones (1952) index of labour productivity to show that there was no 'climacteric' after 1885, as had been suggested by the Jones' real cost index. They attach great significance to the use of employment data from the *Factory Inspectors' Reports* (Lazonick and Mass, 1984: 20). In fact, however, this makes little difference; combining their employment series with their preferred output series from Jones (1933) yields the labour productivity series shown in table 10.29. Jones' measure of output differs from the raw cotton consumption series in table

Table 10.29. *Labour productivity in the British cotton industry, 1870–1913 (1913=100)*

	Output	Employment	Labour productivity
1870	47.9	69.9	68.5
1874	56.4	72.3	78.0
1878	51.4	73.5	69.9
1885	60.2	77.6	77.6
1890	74.8	80.3	93.2
1895	74.4	84.6	87.9
1896	74.8	84.4	88.6
1898	78.8	82.9	95.1
1901	76.6	82.8	92.5
1904	73.3	82.6	88.7
1907	90.7	91.0	99.7
1911	90.7	96.1	94.4
1912	99.4	97.2	102.3
1913	100.0	100.0	100.0

Sources: Output from Jones (1933: 275–6); Employment from Lazonick and Mass (1984: 40).

10.26 by attempting to measure output in the spinning and weaving sections separately, although in practice the two series move closely together. Labour productivity grew at an annual rate of 0.88 per cent over the whole period 1870–1913, and slightly faster at 0.91 per cent per annum over the later period 1885–1913.

The claim by Lazonick and Mass (1984: 21) that labour productivity growth was only 0.50 per cent per annum between 1885 and 1913 against 0.91 per cent over the whole period 1870–1913 seems to be due largely to the use of a three-year moving average for output, which has the effect of raising trend output for 1885 relative to 1870 and 1913. Whilst it is clear that cyclical fluctuations affect labour productivity, the procedure used by Lazonick and Mass would be difficult to defend. First, a three-year span is inappropriate for smoothing what is generally seen as a 9–10-year cycle. Indeed, Jones (1933: 275–6) provided a 10-year moving average of output. But secondly, it is surely inappropriate to smooth output without smoothing employment. Sandberg (1974: 96) reported a smoothed series where the filter had been applied to annual data on labour productivity. Without the three-year moving average adjustment, the labour productivity series in table 10.29 shows merely cyclical fluctuations around a stable, rising trend.

The US/UK comparative labour productivity position in cotton textiles for 1909/07 and 1914/12, shown in table 10.30, is consistent with the view

Table 10.30. *Comparative labour productivity in textiles and clothing, 1909/07 and 1914/12 (UK=100)*

US/UK	1909/07	1914/12
Cotton	151	174
Woollen & worsted	112	120
Rope & twine	195	257
Hosiery	230	217
Boots & shoes	170	

Germany/UK	1907	
Leather	139	

Notes: US/UK figures based on output per operative; Germany/UK figures based on output per employee.
Source: Appendix tables A2.1, A2.2

that this was one of Britain's better performing industries. As in ship-building, then, the labour intensity of British production methods was to some extent offset by the economies of specialisation made possible by Britain's dominant position in world markets. Indeed, the Lancashire cotton industry is perhaps the best known example of Marshall's (1920) external economies of scale.

Woollen and worsted

The British woollen and worsted industry has generally been seen as per-forming relatively well in the pre-First World War period. The data on wool consumption in table 10.31 have been calculated from separate figures for retained imports and retained domestic clip, and continue to show growth in output to 1914. Furthermore, it is clear from the export data in table 10.32 that Britain continued to dominate world markets. Indeed, Britain's share of world exports rose from 37 per cent in 1880–4 to 46 per cent in 1909–13 (Jenkins and Malin, 1990: 67). As in so many other industries, expansion into Europe and the United States was prevented by tariffs, and Britain became increasingly dependent on Empire markets (Sigsworth and Blackman, 1968: 156).

Despite the generally good performance of British woollen and worsted exports, there was nevertheless a period of setback during the 1890s before the recovery after 1900. However, it is important to distinguish between

Table 10.31. *Output and employment in the British woollen industry, 1861–1911*

	Wool consumption (m lb)	Employment (000)	Labour productivity (1911 = 100)
1861	222.1	235	39.0
1871	328.1	263	51.5
1881	309.4	252	50.8
1891	467.1	275	70.2
1901	516.0	235	90.6
1911	600.6	248	100.0

Sources: Mitchell (1988: 336, 340–1); Jenkins and Ponting (1982: 89).

Table 10.32. *Wool textile exports, 1880–4 to 1909–13 (£m)*

Annual averages	UK	Germany	France	US
1880–4	18.5	11.3	14.7	
1885–9	20.1	11.7	13.9	0.03
1890–4	17.4	10.9	12.3	0.04
1895–9	16.5	10.5	11.0	0.11
1900–4	15.8	11.5	8.7	0.13
1905–8	20.4	13.5	8.6	0.10
1909–13	24.6	12.8	8.2	0.17

Source: Jenkins and Malin (1990: 67).

trends in the woollen and worsted branches of the industry. As the figures in table 10.33 suggest, the overall decline masks stagnation followed by recovery in woollen cloth, but sustained decline in worsted cloth. The weaker position in worsted reflects a shift in fashions towards French cloth woven from mule-spun yarn and away from Bradford cloth woven from frame-spun yarn, reinforced by French superiority in design and dyeing (Sigsworth and Blackman, 1968: 143–5). However, this did not prevent a greater overall decline in French woollen and worsted exports. Although there were recurrent fears that Germany would take away British export markets, German gains remained relatively modest (Jenkins and Malin, 1990: 70).

Jenkins and Malin (1990) attribute Britain's improving competitive position in woollen cloth to economies of raw material use, particularly the increasing use of recovered wool (mungo and shoddy). The proportion of mungo and shoddy rose from 26 per cent in 1870–4 to 35 per cent in

Table 10.33. *British exports of woollen and worsted cloth, 1890–4 to 1910–13*

Annual averages	Woollen cloth		Worsted cloth	
	m yd	£m	m yd	£m
1890–4	50.2	5.5	140.0	8.6
1895–9	53.1	5.6	125.7	7.6
1900–4	52.1	6.0	101.8	6.3
1905–9	78.3	9.8	92.8	6.7
1910–13	99.9	13.5	77.1	7.0

Source: Jenkins and Malin (1990: 70).

1910–14 (Jenkins and Ponting, 1982: 204). However, despite the derogatory meaning which the word 'shoddy' has acquired, Jenkins and Malin (1990: 75) are careful not to jump to the conclusion that this necessarily meant a reduction in quality; indeed, better qualities of shoddy could be preferred to the lower grades of new wool.

Employment in the woollen and worsted industries remained stable at about a quarter of a million during the second half of the nineteenth century, as the figures in table 10.31 show. Hence labour productivity continued to grow in line with output through to the First World War. As in cotton, Britain's comparative labour productivity position in woollen and worsted was relatively favourable. The US/UK position in 1909/07 and 1914/12 is shown in table 10.30. Here again, the large share of the world market obtained by British producers enabled them to reap economies of specialisation. The West Riding of Yorkshire was the world's largest producer and exporter of wool textiles, while other areas hung on to their specialisms: the West Country in superfine broadcloths, Kidderminster in carpets, Witney in blankets, Leicester in hosiery yarns and the Scottish border counties in tweeds (Musson, 1978: 209). Again, it is easy to see Marshall's (1920) external economies of scale at work.

Boots and shoes and leather

In the boot and shoe industry, British producers successfully fought back against a substantial rise in import penetration, largely from the United States during the 1890s. The figures in table 10.34 show that between 1900 and 1914 imports fell and there was a surge in exports, especially after 1910.

The successful British fight-back is attributed by Church (1968) to a process of concentration and mechanisation of production. Rather than substituting

Table 10.34. *British trade in leather*
boots and shoes, 1885–1914 (doz.pairs)

	Imports	Exports
1885	102,782	560,309
1890	99,613	695,802
1895	132,058	674,620
1900	233,668	630,244
1905	214,639	774,061
1910	168,236	1,086,638
1914	170,522	1,432,297

Source: Church (1968: 224).

cheap unskilled for skilled labour, mechanisation was accompanied by the continued employment of skilled labour. This transition to mechanised craft production was thus encouraged by the National Union of Boot and Shoe Operatives, although disputes over the division of the fruits of new machinery continued as in many other industries (Head, 1968: 175–6, 178–80).

Again as in many other industries, the growth of British exports was very much oriented towards the Empire, with the settler colonies of Australia and South Africa being of most importance (Head, 1968: 159). The figures in table 10.30 suggest a relatively good British labour productivity performance in boots and shoes compared with the United States before the First World War.

In the leather industry, which provided the primary material for boots and shoes, British performance was weak. There was a big surge in imports from the 1870s and exports remained stagnant (Church, 1971: 552). One problem was that South America became a major source of supply for hides, which favoured the United States over both Britain and Germany on transport cost grounds (Church, 1971: 555). However, German leather manufacturers made a better response to American competition than British producers, especially in the production of lighter leathers. Here, German producers were quicker in the adoption of new chrome tanning techniques, drawing on German strengths in industrial chemistry (Church, 1971: 561–2). Figures in table 10.30 suggest an Anglo-German labour productivity gap of the order of 40 per cent in the leather industry in 1907.

Hosiery and clothing

The second half of the nineteenth century saw the gradual mechanisation and concentration in factory production of the hosiery and clothing trades

(Musson, 1978: 212–14; 228–31). Nevertheless, in hosiery, factories tended to remain dispersed in the traditional hand-frame knitting villages and small towns of the East Midlands rather than becoming concentrated in the commercial centres of Nottingham and Leicester. Here, they could rely upon a good supply of cheap female labour (Wells, 1972: 160; Musson, 1978: 213). In clothing, out-working remained common and independent master tailors and dress makers continued to cater for the better off (Wray, 1957: 16–19; Musson, 1978: 231). Hence British labour productivity continued to lag behind levels achieved by American producers using more mechanised methods to supply a market more prepared to accept standardised, ready-made clothing. The more than 2:1 Anglo-American labour productivity gap in hosiery in 1909/07 is shown in table 10.30.

Conclusions

In the textile trades, Britain attained labour productivity levels not too far short of American levels, but without adopting high throughput American production methods. These industries are the classic cases of Marshallian external economies of scale. In cotton textiles, for example, a large number of vertically separated spinning and weaving firms clustered in different parts of Lancashire were able to hold their own against the vertically integrated American mills. Furthermore, technology developed in parallel on both sides of the Atlantic, with British producers continuing to use the mule and the powerloom despite the dominance of the ring frame and the automatic loom in the United States. Similar British success stories can be seen in the Yorkshire woollen and worsted industry, the Belfast linen industry and the Dundee jute industry. In the clothing trades, however, British labour productivity lagged further behind American levels as demand patterns limited the extent of standardisation and mechanisation in Britain.

Food, drink and tobacco

The 1907 *Census of Production* records the fact that food, drink and tobacco accounted for 17.8 per cent of net output in manufacturing and had a net output per employee of £193.0 against an average for manufacturing as a whole of £97.6. Despite this, the food, drink and tobacco industries have rarely been cited in the debate over British relative economic performance (Landes, 1969; Levine, 1967; Elbaum and Lazonick, 1986). This neglect helps to reinforce the view of poor British performance, since these industries have undoubtedly been some of Britain's most progressive. Although Chandler (1990) has recently acknowledged the success of these industries in Britain, his favourable comments are countered by the suggestion that it would have been better if more of the large industrial firms had been concentrated in the 'new, technologically advanced, growth industries' producing industrial rather than consumer goods (Chandler, 1990: 239–40).

The strong labour productivity performance of the British food, drink and tobacco sector in the second half of the nineteenth century and the first half of the twentieth century reinforces the view that demand matters as well as supply. Britain was a highly industrialised and urbanised country with an extensive transport network, and the major food, drink and tobacco firms grew by successfully developing a strategy of branding, packaging and advertising to serve those markets, accompanied by a revolution in retailing (Jefferys, 1954; Mathias, 1967). This was all very much along classic Chandlerian lines.

Brewing

Brewing already occurred on a large scale in Britain, with steam powered machinery, during the late eighteenth and early nineteenth centuries (Mathias, 1959). However, a sizeable share of total output continued to be made by 'private' brewers (for example colleges, hospitals, or gentlemen brewing in country houses for consumption on the estate), by publicans brewing beer for sale on their own premises and by licensed victuallers. Gourvish and Wilson (1994: 69) estimate the proportion of output accounted for by 'common brewers' in England and Wales as only 54 per cent in 1832, but rising to 95 per cent by 1900. Thus the nineteenth century saw a growing concentration of production in larger-scale breweries. Trends were even more favourable for the common brewers as consumption *per capita* rose between the 1850s and the 1870s, as can be seen from the data in table 10.35. Social historians usually relate this increase in *per capita* consumption of beer to rising working class living standards and urbanisation, in a period during which the licensing laws were relaxed (Gourvish and Wilson 1994: 27–37).

From the late 1870s, *per capita* beer consumption began to fall as leisure opportunities for the working class expanded, the temperance movement became more influential and the licensing laws were tightened (Gourvish and Wilson, 1994: 37–40). Faced with a declining demand and restrictions on the number of outlets, brewers began a scramble for tied houses (Vaizey, 1960: 7). To finance the acquisition of property on a large scale, the brewers turned to the capital markets, and the £6 million Guinness public issue of 1885 was followed by a boom in brewery issues which lasted to the turn of the century (Watson, 1990; Vaizey, 1960: 8–12). As Watson (1990) notes, then, there is little evidence to suggest that the brewing industry was ham-

Table 10.35. *Brewing output, consumption and employment in Great Britain, 1851–1911*

	Output (000 st.bl)	Consumption *per capita* (gal)	Employment (000)	Labour productivity (1911=100)
1851	15,552	29.7		
1861	18,087	30.3	32.742	72.6
1871	24,815	36.5	38.674	84.2
1881	26,315	33.1	36.091	95.8
1891	29,652	34.0	38.392	101.4
1901	32,907	33.5	40.908	105.7
1911	30,938	28.4	40.623	100.0

Notes: Output figures before 1900 are in standard barrels, while figures for 1900–13 are in bulk barrels. However, it is unlikely that bulk barrels greatly exceeded standard barrels before 1900 as the standard gravity of 1055° was near the average. Gourvish and Wilson's consumption figures are for England and Wales only, although no account is taken of the small but increasingly negative net trade balance in beer with Scotland and Ireland.
Sources: Wilson (1940: 369–70); Gourvish and Wilson (1994: 600–2); Phelps-Brown and Handfield-Jones (1952: 298).

pered by lack of finance, as has been alleged in other manufacturing industries (Kennedy, 1987).

Drawing parallels with other industries, Sigsworth (1965) suggested that the British brewing industry was scientifically backward, with the post-Pasteurian revolution in brewing chemistry having little influence on brewing practice. More recently, however, Gourvish and Wilson (1994: 58–63) have suggested that this is misleading, arguing that brewers kept abreast of scientific developments through membership of the Institute of Brewing and reading the brewing journals, and were prepared to consult a laboratory if things went wrong. Sigsworth seems to have been misled by the fact that since beer is in the end a matter of taste, a combination of science and empiricism was inevitable. Gourvish and Wilson (1994: 63) conclude that 'most brewers turned out better beers in 1900 than they had fifty years earlier. In this, science played a large part.'

Employment in brewing grew more slowly than output to the turn of the century, allowing a steady rise in labour productivity, shown here in table 10.35. However, as output fell after 1900, labour productivity declined slightly. The comparative labour productivity position in brewing nevertheless still shows the British industry in relatively favourable light before

Table 10.36. *Comparative labour*
productivity in food, drink and tobacco,
1909/07 and 1914/12 (UK=100)

US/UK	1909/07	1914/12
Grain milling	178	
Butter & cheese	196	
Sugar	110	
Manufactured ice	134	
Brewing & malting	146	149
Spirits	167	173
Tobacco	108	99
Germany/UK	1907	
Beet sugar	49	
Brewing & malting	92	

Notes: US/UK figures based on output per
operative; Germany/UK figures based on output per
employee.
Source: Appendix tables A2.1, A2.2

1914. The figures in table 10.36 show that the labour productivity gap with
the United States in this industry was well below the average for manufacturing, while British labour productivity was higher than in Germany. What
are the implications of the successful performance of the British brewing
industry for the debate over entrepreneurial performance? First, demand
matters; when the market existed, British entrepreneurs could respond
vigorously. Second, in these circumstances, obtaining finance was not a
problem, even in a manufacturing industry. And third, British industry was
capable of applying science to improve its product.

Spirits

Output of spirits in the United Kingdom, shown in table 10.37, rose during
the second half of the nineteenth century, but without an increase in *per
capita* consumption. After 1900, a sharp fall in *per capita* consumption led
to a fall in production, although the industry found some respite in rising
exports.

Despite the stagnant *per capita* consumption, a number of Scotch whisky
companies increased sales in the English market during the second half of
the nineteenth century with the introduction of blends, allowing the more
easily produced grain whiskies to be mixed with the more restricted malt

Table 10.37. *Production and consumption of*
spirits in the United Kingdom, 1850–1913

	Production (000 proof gal)	Consumption *per capita* (proof gal)
1850	25,845	1.04
1860	28,316	0.93
1870	27,679	1.01
1880	37,412	1.07
1890	40,969	1.02
1900	59,246	1.12
1910	43,831	0.65
1913	46,693	0.70

Source: Wilson (1940: 332–3, 337–9).

whiskies (Fraser, 1981: 211). The 'Big Five' of Haig, Dewar, Buchanan, Walker and Mackie, were particularly successful in the London market with standardised blends from the 1880s, using sophisticated advertising campaigns (Daiches, 1976: 78).

The decline in the demand for spirits after 1900 was part of a general trend away from alcohol as leisure opportunities widened and the temperance movement gained influence. Consumption of spirits was also hit by rising excise duties. The response of the industry was a mixture of combination and seeking new markets (Weir, 1989: 379). Exports rose from 5.7 million proof gallons (m.p.g.) in 1900 to 10.1 m.p.g. by 1913 (Wilson, 1940: 353). The industry became dominated by amalgamations; the Distillers Company Limited absorbed Haig upon its foundation in 1877, Buchanan–Dewar (which combined in 1915) and Walker in 1925 and Mackie in 1927 (Daiches, 1976: 87–106). These were large companies, with Distillers featuring in Hannah's (1983: 188) list of the top 50 manufacturing companies of 1905 by capitalisation.

The comparative labour productivity position of the British spirits industry remained relatively favourable, as the figures in table 10.36 show. The productivity gap with the United States remained well below the average before the First World War. Clearly, the large British firms were able to benefit from economies of scale.

Tobacco

According to Alford's (1973) estimates, shown here in table 10.38, domestic sales of tobacco grew at an average annual rate of 1.9 per cent during the

Table 10.38. *British domestic sales and exports of manufactured tobacco, 1871–1913 (m lb)*

	Sales	Exports
1871	54.9	0.6
1880	63.5	0.3
1890	72.0	1.2
1900	91.7	5.5
1910	98.0	20.5
1913	104.1	33.0

Sources: Alford (1973: 461, 463, 476); HM Customs and Excise (1913), *Annual Statement of the Trade of the United Kingdom* (London: HMSO).

period 1870–1913. Although exports grew more rapidly as cigarettes became more important after 1900, overall output growth remained modest. Nevertheless the period saw the emergence of national producers, breaking out of an earlier regional structure which had been preserved by transport difficulties, close knowledge of local markets and excise regulations giving local monopolies to enumerated ports (Alford, 1973: 77).

Branding, packaging and advertising played an important part in the emergence of W.D. & H.O. Wills as the leading tobacco manufacturer in Britain by the 1880s, although at this stage the firm was merely *primus inter pares*, with a market share of about 5 per cent (Alford, 1973: 136). In 1883, however, Wills obtained a UK monopoly of the Bonsack cigarette making machine. The industry was now developing in two parts, with intense competition in loose tobacco but an oligopolistic structure in cigarettes, where Wills had a technical lead. Wills' share of the domestic market rose to 10.9 per cent by 1900 and their share of exports rose to 47.3 per cent (Alford, 1973: 221–2). However, Wills were faced with a serious competitive threat in 1901 when the American Tobacco Company entered the British market by purchasing Ogden's of Liverpool. Wills led the British response to form an amalgamation of the major producers, to be known as the Imperial Tobacco Company (of Great Britain and Ireland) Limited. After a short competitive struggle involving price cuts, attempts to tie retailers and a threat by Imperial to enter the American market, a deal was struck whereby the American Tobacco Company sold Ogden's to Imperial and Imperial agreed to stay out of the American market. In addition, the British American Tobacco Company was formed to trade in the rest of the world, two-thirds owned by American Tobacco and one-third by Imperial (Alford, 1973: 269).

Table 10.39. *Output in British food processing industries, 1850–1913 (1913=100)*

	Grain milling	Sugar	Confectionery
1850	59.2	28.4	5.9
1860	50.0	40.9	6.2
1870	64.7	59.6	11.8
1880	68.2	80.0	20.3
1890	72.4	72.2	38.9
1900	71.6	62.1	72.8
1910	99.1	82.6	102.9
1913	100.0	100.0	100.0

Source: Hoffmann (1955, table 54B).

The comparative labour productivity figures in table 10.36 suggest that there was no substantial difference between British and American tobacco manufacturers at this time. American producers possessed no advantages of technology or scale in this industry before the First World War.

Grain milling

The output of the grain milling industry, shown in table 10.39, is measured by Hoffmann (1955: 270) from the input of wheat, estimated from home grown wheat *plus* net imports. Although no allowance is made for changes in stores, this is unlikely to seriously distort the long-run trend. The growth of the industry was hit from the 1870s to the turn of the century by growing imports of flour (Burnett, 1945: 51). From the turn of the century, however, flour imports declined as large-scale mills at port sites came to dominate the British industry and became competitive with the best Continental millers. Figures from the *Annual Statement of Trade* show imports of wheatmeal and flour rising from 4.8 million hundredweight (cwt) in 1870 to 21.5 million cwt by 1900, before falling back to 12.0 million cwt by 1913.

The growth of these large-scale mills at port sites, owned by large firms such as Joseph Rank and Spillers, reflected the fact that during the second half of the nineteenth century Britain had become increasingly dependent on imported wheat from the New World, allowing her own indigenous grain production to contract. It also reflected the growing replacement of traditional windmills using circular grinding stones by roller mills using steam power (Musson, 1978: 234). Some smaller inland mills persisted, but, as Clapham (1938: 185–6) notes, '[if] a firm controlled both an inland and a tide-water mill, the second was sure to be the more important'. Perren

(1990) notes that the ability of the grain millers to transform their industry from an atomistic to a concentrated structure as grain supply conditions changed casts doubt on the Elbaum and Lazonick (1986) claim that Britain's export industries were constrained by their atomistic structure.

The US/UK comparative labour productivity position in grain milling for 1909/07 is shown in table 10.36 The British performance was better than average, but the persistence of production at the small-scale rural mills lowered the overall labour productivity performance of the industry.

Sugar refining

Output trends in sugar refining, shown in table 10.39, clearly reflect trade policy. Hoffmann's (1955) index is based on net imports of raw sugar, which diverged sharply from total net imports of sugar in the second half of the nineteenth century due to cheap imports of refined beet sugar from Europe, subsidised by bounties (Chalmin, 1990: 25–38). Hence the British sugar refining industry suffered a major setback during the 1880s and 1890s, before the Brussels Convention of 1902 led to the abolition of the bounties (Chalmin, 1990: 39–40). From 1902 to 1913 British refined sugar output recovered dramatically.

Against this generally unpromising background of free trade allowing in subsidised foreign beet sugar, two British companies enjoyed considerable success. Both companies developed sugar refining interests from other trades, and both successfully used branding and packaging (Hugill, 1978: 35–56). Henry Tate & Sons moved into sugar refining from a Liverpool grocery business, and marketed sugar cubes to replace the traditional sugar loaves that had to be broken by retailers into smaller pieces with a hammer (Watson, 1973: 15; Chalmin, 1990: 75–6). Abram Lyle & Sons developed sugar refining interests from a family shipping business based in Greenock, and successfully marketed Golden Syrup, a high quality product based on sugar and molasses, to complement its range of classical sugars at competitive prices (Chalmin, 1990: 101).

Comparative labour productivity figures in sugar are available for the US/UK in 1909/07 and for Germany/UK in 1907 in table 10.36. In this industry, labour productivity in Britain was close to US levels, and substantially higher than in Germany.

Confectionery

Hoffmann's (1955) index of output in the confectionery industry, shown in table 10.39, is based on the consumption of cocoa beans, the most important raw material. Although cocoa had first been introduced in the seventeenth century, demand had been relatively stagnant until the 1860s (Fraser, 1981: 171). From 1860 to 1913 demand took off, with an average annual growth rate of 5.4 per cent, after the introduction by Cadbury Brothers of a 'pure' cocoa based on a new process for extracting fats (or cocoa butter) from the cocoa. Previously, only a very adulterated cocoa had been available, with starch added to counter the fats. The new process had been discovered by a Dutchman, C.J. van Houten in 1828, but was only introduced in Britain by Cadburys in 1866 (Williams, 1931: 39). Three Quaker firms, Cadburys, Frys and Rowntrees grew to become the market leaders, with large-scale factories (Fraser, 1981: 172). However, many smaller-scale firms continued to supply market niches. Although there are no comparative productivity figures for this industry before the First World War, the large productivity gap in the 1920s suggests that the productivity performance of the industry as a whole was dominated by the persistence of the small-scale producers.

Dairy produce

The growing demand for dairy produce was largely supplied by imports. Hence despite rising consumption, output of cheese in England fell from 1.5 million cwt in 1860 to 0.5 million cwt in 1910, while output of butter fell from 0.5 to 0.2 million cwt over the same period (Taylor, 1976: 590–1). The English dairy industry concentrated on the liquid milk market, where it had a locational advantage in supplying a fresh product. Liquid milk sales rose from 150 million to 600 million gallons between 1860 and 1910 (Taylor, 1976: 591).

The figures on US/UK comparative labour productivity in butter and cheese for 1909/07 are shown in table 10.36. The larger British cheese and butter making factories had been closed in the face of rising imports during the late nineteenth century, leaving only a number of small-scale producers (Fraser, 1981: 155). American labour productivity was a little less than twice the British level.

British butter was also facing stiff competition from margarine, a nutrient fat made originally from beef tallow and skimmed milk (Fraser, 1981: 158). The market was dominated by the Dutch producers, van den Berghs and Jurgens, although they increasingly manufactured in Britain. Lever Brothers did not enter the margarine market until the war years, utilising an alternative process for hardening vegetable oils (Wilson, 1954, vol.I: 227).

Conclusions

The food, drink and tobacco sector is often neglected when discussing the performance of British manufacturing. This is unfortunate, because it has

Table 10.40. *Output of paper and board in Britain and America, 1849–1914 (000 tons)*

	UK	US
1849	62	
1859	100	113
1869	146	345
1879	233	404
1889	379	835
1899	680	1,936
1904	823	2,774
1907	900	
1909	949	3,765
1913	1,166	
1914	1,202	4,705

Notes: US data converted from short tons to long tons. UK data converted from index number form to tonnage using output data from the 1907 *Census of Production*.
Sources: Hoffmann (1955, table 54); Frickey (1947: 16).

been one of Britain's most successful sectors. Before the First World War, British producers developed a strategy of branding, packaging and advertising to serve the relatively homogeneous demands of a highly industrialised and urbanised society with an extensive transport network. In a number of industries, high throughput techniques were applied as extensively in Britain as in the United States, resulting in similar levels of labour productivity.

Miscellaneous industries

Paper

Paper output expanded rapidly in Britain during the second half of the nineteenth century. However, the figures in table 10.40 show that growth was more rapid in the United States. Britain's loss of export market share, shown in table 10.41, reflects a shift in comparative advantage occurring during the late nineteenth century as wood pulp replaced rags as the primary raw material in paper making (Clapham, 1938: 192). Indeed, the other established European paper producers, Germany, France and Austria–Hungary also suffered, with the major gainers being the timber-producing countries of Scandinavia and North America (Magee, 1994: 106–7).

Table 10.41. *National shares of world paper exports, 1888–1912 (%)*

	UK	Germany	France	Austria–Hungary	Sweden	Norway	US
1888	17.8	27.8	16.8	10.3	1.4	0.5	2.2
1892	14.3	26.2	20.5	9.6	2.5	1.3	2.6
1896	12.5	25.7	16.6	8.1	2.9	2.9	4.3
1900	10.1	22.7	13.3	8.8	4.2	2.9	7.9
1904	10.5	19.4	14.5	8.3	6.3	3.1	8.8
1908	9.7	20.6	14.3	7.2	6.7	3.9	7.1
1912	11.0	20.2	17.3	5.1	6.9	4.2	6.8

Notes: Figures are based on export values for the 11 major paper producing countries.
Source: Magee (1994: 107).

Magee (1994) examines in some detail the performance of the British paper industry in comparison with its American competitor over the period 1861–1913, paying particular attention to the choice of production process. He notes that as a shortage of rags appeared in the second half of the nineteenth century, British paper makers and paper machinery makers invested a lot of effort in the development of rag substitutes. At this stage it was unclear whether the future lay with wood pulp or esparto. Indeed, at this stage, mechanically ground wood pulp could only produce low quality paper, unacceptable to the markets served by British paper makers. Hence the share of esparto rose rapidly in Britain between 1861 and 1877. As the wood pulp technology improved with the emergence of the sulphate and sulphite process, however, wood pulp began to replace esparto as a substitute for rag between 1877 and 1889. At this stage, although wood pulp could make paper of a similar quality to esparto, rag remained the preferred material when available. Finally, with further improvements to the chemical processes, wood pulp became the preferred material after 1899 (Magee, 1994: 177–84).

Magee's (1994) work is particularly valuable because he goes beyond the McCloskey–Sandberg (1971) methodology of showing that technical choice was rational at a point in time, and examines the research and patenting activity of British paper makers. This can be seen as a practical response to the worry of writers like Elbaum and Lazonick (1986: 2) that the static neoclassical framework does not take account of attempts by entrepreneurs to alter the constraints that they faced.

Magee (1994: 215) notes that when it was clear that wood pulp was the dominant technology, technological leadership in paper making passed from Britain to the United States. He also shows that this occurred without

Table 10.42. *Comparative labour*
productivity in miscellaneous industries,
1909/07 and 1914/12 (UK=100)

US/UK	1909/07	1914/12
Bricks	217	220
Cement	219	268
Paper & board	262	222
Germany/UK	1907	
Cement	133	

Notes: US/UK figures based on output per
operative; Germany/UK figures based on output per
employee.
Source: Appendix tables A2.1, A2.2.

a change in labour productivity leadership, as suggested more generally by Broadberry (1994a). Magee finds comparative US/UK labour productivity in the paper industry remaining of the order of 2:1 throughout the period 1861–1913, broadly consistent with the figures for the end of the period reported here in table 10.42. For the period of American technological leadership, Magee (1994: 377–8) becomes critical of British paper makers, describing their disinclination to invest in new ideas and strategies to the same extent as their American counterparts as 'incipient conservatism'. However, it may equally be seen as a realistic assessment of a shift in comparative advantage which made such investments distinctly less attractive in Britain once wood pulp had become dominant. This view is reinforced by Magee's (1994: 374–5) examination of the unfavourable market environment faced by British producers in the face of widespread protection overseas and dumping by German producers in the open British market.

Cement and bricks

The output of building materials before the First World War can only be proxied by activity in the construction sector. The Lewis index, in table 10.43, combines information on urban and rural houses built, house repair, commercial property built, commercial repair and other construction represented by railway building and local authority loan expenditure (Lewis, 1978: 254). The index displays large cyclical swings, which had important implications for productivity in the construction sector. The

Table 10.43. *British output of building materials, 1852–1913 (1913=100)*

	Lewis Index
1852	46.3
1860	47.2
1870	61.4
1880	76.6
1890	82.6
1900	125.4
1910	92.8
1913	100.0

Notes: Proxy measure based on activity in the construction sector.
Source: Lewis (1978: 248–50).

evidence in appendix table A2.1 suggests that these cyclical swings in construction also had implications for comparative labour productivity in the building materials industries. Thus, when the American construction industry was booming but the British construction industry was in a slump, there was a large labour productivity gap in America's favour, but when the British construction industry was booming and the American construction industry was in a slump, the labour productivity gap was largely eliminated in cement and bricks. Thomas (1973: 175) sees the British building cycle as falling from a peak in 1899 to a trough in 1912 while the American cycle rose from a trough in 1900 to a peak in 1909. The roughly 2:1 Anglo-American labour productivity gaps in cement and bricks in 1909/07 and 1914/12, seen in table 10.42, can thus be at least partly explained by the different phases of the cycle in the two countries.

In brick making, Bowley (1960: 79) sees the entry of new firms during upturns as important in bringing about the diffusion of innovations during the second half of the nineteenth century, as minimum efficient scale remained small in this industry. Apart from the introduction of the semi-dry pressed brick, of which the Fletton was the most successful, innovation after 1860 consisted largely of small improvements of processes invented earlier and not requiring a substantial increase in scale (Bowley, 1960: 66–8). Hence cyclical fluctuations in labour productivity in brickmaking can be seen as resulting at least in part from changes in the proportion of firms using the latest techniques.

In cement, however, the picture is more complex, with varying levels of capacity utilisation amongst incumbent oligopolistic producers playing an important role in the cyclical fluctuations of labour productivity (Rostas, 1948a: 113). During the second half of the nineteenth century, Portland cement, which was both strong and hydraulic (water-resisting), replaced other forms of cement (Cook, 1958a: 22). The cement industry thus became increasingly localised on the Thames and Medway Estuaries, where there was an unrivalled supply of the key raw materials, good facilities for inland and coastal water transport and proximity to the important London market (Bowley, 1960: 89). Improvements in grinding and burning, the latter culminating in the introduction of the rotary kiln, raised the minimum efficient scale and led to an increase in the concentration of ownership and production (Cook, 1958a: 23–5). Concentration dramatically increased in 1900 with the formation of the Associated Portland Cement Manufacturers (APCM), an amalgamation of most of the existing Thames and Medway producers, which aimed to raise prices within limits set by import competition (Bowley, 1960: 89–90). However, without control over entry, the amalgamation could not hope to achieve its aims. As predicted by the McCloskey and Sandberg (1971) approach, the restrictive behaviour of the cartel created profit opportunities for new entrants, and the market share of APCM fell from over a half in 1900 to just over a third by 1907 (Cook, 1958a: 41). Hence the diffusion of innovations through entry has some role to play in productivity fluctuations in cement as well as in brick making.

Glass

The British glass industry faced two waves of intense foreign competition during the nineteenth century. The first surge in imports came primarily from Belgium after the abolition of glass duties in 1845 and tariffs in 1858. The second period of intense competition came during the 1890s as the American market was effectively closed to European exporters by the McKinley and Dingly tariffs (Cook, 1958b: 282; Barker, 1968: 320). This deterioration of the trade balance in glass during the 1890s is clearly visible in table 10.44. As Barker (1968: 308) notes, however, the picture was not one of 'unrelieved gloom'. Although the flint glass and tableware section of the industry largely buckled under the weight of Belgian competition, there was something of a revival in the other two major branches of bottle and jar making and flat glass. Thus the trade balance in glass improved rapidly after 1900.

In bottle making there was substantial patenting activity during the second half of the nineteenth century as producers searched for a mechanical bottle maker. However, early designs were not competitive with skilled glass blowers and machinery was not widely adopted until after 1900. By

Table 10.44. *British trade in glass, 1875–9 to 1910–14 (£m)*

	Imports	Exports & re-exports	Trade deficit
1875–9	1,823	1,035	788
1880–4	1,670	1,203	467
1885–9	1,707	1,200	507
1890–4	2,389	983	1,406
1895–9	2,944	943	2,001
1900–4	3,507	1,138	2,369
1905–9	3,053	1,392	1,661
1910–14	2,989	1,759	1,230

Source: Barker (1968: 308).

this stage, technological leadership had passed to the United States and it was the American Owens machinery that was used (Barker, 1968: 311–14).

In flat glass, the British industry came to be dominated by Chances of Smethwick and Pilkingtons of St Helens as other producers succumbed to foreign competition in the face of rapidly changing technology (Cook, 1958b: 287–8). Pilkingtons used their strength in window glass to help them survive the intense competition of the 1890s in plate glass and thus to remain on the technological frontier across a range of products (Barker, 1977a: 145). As Barker (1968: 324) notes,

The important thing was to have a good intelligence service and to be sure to obtain a licence for a successful process as soon as it became a paying proposition. This the British glass manufacturers seem to have been notably successful in doing at this time.

The British glass industry, then, seems to fit perfectly the McCloskey and Sandberg (1971) criteria for rational entrepreneurial behaviour.

Rubber

The rubber industry received a boost with the discovery and development of the sulphur-heat vulcanisation process by the American Charles Goodyear and the British Thomas Hancock between 1839 and 1843 (Woodruff, 1955: 376–7; Donnithorne, 1958: 17). The way was then open for the growing use of rubber in mechanical devices, footwear and clothing (Woodruff, 1958: 68). This growth in output is reflected in the data on consumption of crude rubber in table 10.45. There was a further demand side boost for rubber after the rediscovery of the pneumatic tyre in 1888 by J.B. Dunlop (McMillan, 1989: 1). Growth was also affected on the supply

Table 10.45. *British consumption of crude rubber,*
1850–1913 (cwt)

	Imports	Re-exports	Consumption
1850	7,617	1,048	6,569
1860	43,039	12,895	30,144
1870	152,118	50,737	101,381
1880	169,587	76,732	92,855
1890	264,008	142,524	121,484
1900	513,286	293,624	219,662
1910	876,969	467,872	409,097
1913	1,405,749	900,240	505,509

Sources: Woodruff (1958: 46); HM Customs and Excise
(1913) *Annual Statement of the Trade of the United*
Kingdom (London: HMSO).

side by the availability of crude rubber, which came largely from the
Amazon Valley. Large fluctuations in the price and quality of supplies led
American producers to develop the use of reclaimed rubber, and British
producers to transplant rubber seeds from the Amazon Valley to colonies
in the Far East, to secure alternative supplies (Woodruff, 1955: 378–9).

In both Britain and America the nineteenth century saw a process of
mergers leading to a highly concentrated structure in rubber manufacturing. Although the process began later in Britain, Dunlop was in a dominant
position by the First World War. Woodruff (1955: 380) suggests that labour
productivity, as measured by crude rubber consumption per wage earner,
was broadly similar in Britain and America before the First World War, but
with a small US advantage from the 1870s. His graph shows a substantial
labour productivity gap opening up only after the First World War.

Conclusions

The industries grouped together in the 'miscellaneous' sector illustrate a
number of themes highlighted in chapters 6–9. The paper industry is
perhaps the best documented example of the parallel development of technology on the two sides of the Atlantic, with resources playing an important part. Once it was clear that wood pulp rather than esparto would
replace rag as the key raw material, technological leadership passed from
Britain to the United States. However, evidence on patenting activity suggests that British firms not only made rational technical choices at any
given point in time, but also made substantial investments to alter the
technological constraints that they faced. The example of the glass indus-

try also suggests rational technical choice, with British firms importing technology from abroad under licence as soon as it became profitable to do so. The rubber and building materials industries suggest an important role for demand factors, with American labour productivity in rubber pulling decisively ahead only with the dramatic growth of the demand for rubber tyres after the First World War, and cement and bricks showing strong cyclical fluctuations in comparative labour productivity in line with fluctuations in the construction industry.

Conclusions

The picture of the British manufacturing sector that emerges from this chapter is one of rational adaptation to the rise of competition from abroad. In general, the continued use of flexible production techniques in Britain despite the emergence of mass production technology in the United States was not irrational conservatism, but rather profit maximisation under different demand conditions and with different resource and factor endowments. Facing heterogeneous demand patterns, expensive natural resources and large stocks of skilled shopfloor workers, most British producers could not have profitably adopted American mass production techniques. Most industries were characterised by a high degree of competition, which acted as a spur to efficiency, with existing rivals or new entrants ready to take up opportunities neglected by incumbent producers.

11   War and depression, 1914–1950

Introduction

The years between 1914 and 1950 were highly disturbed, covering two world wars and a world slump of unprecedented severity. Over the period as a whole, Britain's manufacturing labour productivity position relative to the United States deteriorated somewhat, but there was no deterioration relative to Germany. In both Britain and Germany, attempts to adjust accumulation strategy in the light of the American innovations of the Second Industrial Revolution did not close the productivity gap during this turbulent period. Although it is possible to see demand conditions, resource and factor endowments and the disturbed nature of the economic environment as preventing a full elimination of the productivity gap, I would also argue that lack of competition weakened the pressure on firms to adjust. The barriers to adjustment, which remained relatively weak before the First World War, were considerably strengthened after 1914.

As the world economy became increasingly protectionist, British exporters became increasingly dependent on Empire markets. Although this had short-run advantages, helping to maintain output and employment during the 1930s, I would see it as having adverse long-run consequences. Direct competition with the United States and Germany was avoided, and marketing was oriented towards remote areas that would not be natural British markets as the world economy re-integrated after the Second World War. On the domestic front, cartelisation and collusion became commonplace to avoid cut-throat price competition during the Depression of the 1930s. As this collusion became institutionalised through the rapid growth of trade associations, more problems of adjustment were stored up for the future.

As in the pre-First World War period, there was a wide range of productivity performance in interwar Britain. In general, there was a high degree of continuity with the prewar comparative productivity position, with British performance better in the lighter textiles and clothing and food, drink and tobacco sectors, and particularly lagging in the heavier metals and engineering sectors.

One distinction that is commonly made in the literature is between new and old industries. However, the figures on comparative labour productivity levels tend to support those who are sceptical of the value of such a distinction (Dowie, 1969; Alford, 1972; von Tunzelmann, 1982). Although in some new industries such as rayon or fertilisers, British labour productivity was not far below American levels, in others such as radios, electric lamps, motor vehicles or aircraft, the Anglo-American labour productivity gap was very large. Similarly, although in some old industries, such as blast furnaces, there was a large Anglo-American labour productivity gap, in others, such as cotton or shipbuilding, British labour productivity was not far below American levels.

Clearly these figures on productivity levels need to be supplemented with information on trends in output and employment for a full evaluation of performance. Thus, for example, it would be wrong to conclude that the British cotton industry was successful in interwar Britain because of the small productivity gap, without taking account of the fall in output and employment. The point is rather that the contraction of the industry occurred in such a way as to maintain Britain's relative productivity position before the Second World War. It was only moving across the Second World War that the external economies of scale disappeared and Britain's comparative productivity position in cotton moved close to that for manufacturing as a whole.

In shipbuilding, Britain also retained a strong comparative productivity position through to the late 1940s, although in this case it is possible to detect capacity utilisation effects during the 1920s, when an Anglo-American labour productivity gap of about 50 percentage points opened up. The reason for the strong British productivity showing in shipbuilding into the 1940s was that mass production techniques had still not been widely applied in this industry.

In the new industries, cartels were strong in electrical goods, helping to shore up inefficient producers. In motor vehicles, craft-based flexible production techniques continued to be used in Britain. Although Lewchuk (1987) probably underestimates the effect of demand differences on technology, his focus on industrial relations systems serves to underline the fact that issues of craft control versus managerial control could surface just as easily in new industries as in old industries.

Perhaps the most important message to take away from the Anglo-German comparisons is that Britain did not lag behind Germany in manufacturing productivity as a whole before the Second World War. Although Germany had higher labour productivity in some heavy industries, such as blast furnaces or sulphuric acid, this was offset by a British productivity lead in other industries such as cotton weaving, beet sugar, brewing or

Table 11.1. *Output, employment and capital in the British chemical industry, 1907–51 (1924=100)*

	Output	Employment	Capital	Labour productivity	TFP
1907	79.0	77.4		102.1	
1913	90.0				
1924	100.0	100.0	100.0	100.0	100.0
1929	112.2	109.6	112.0	102.4	101.6
1930	106.6	104.1	112.0	102.4	100.0
1935	133.9	107.8	116.0	124.2	121.3
1937	148.7	119.6	124.0	124.3	122.9
1948	232.9	202.3	128.0	115.1	130.5
1951	313.9	220.9	159.5	142.1	155.9

Sources: Output: Lomax (1959: 192); Employment: 1907–24: *Historical Record of the Census of Production*, 13; 1924–51: Feinstein (1972: T130); Capital: Feinstein (1972: T101).

tobacco. Britain and Germany were much more evenly matched before the Second World War than a reader of Chandler (1990) would expect.

Chemicals

Output, employment and capital stock trends for chemicals and allied products are shown in table 11.1. Although output received a boost during both world wars the effect was much greater across the Second World War. The small fall in output per employee across the First World War is largely explained by the sharp fall in the length of the standard working week during 1919–20 from 54 to 47 hours (Dowie, 1975; Broadberry, 1986, 1990). On a per hour worked basis, labour productivity also rose between 1907 and 1924 (Lomax, 1959: 203). The trend in total factor productivity (TFP) was similar to the trend in labour productivity. TFP growth in chemicals over the period 1924–37 was 1.6 per cent per annum, somewhat lower than in manufacturing as a whole, where TFP growth was 2.5 per cent per annum. Hence, as Dowie (1969: 70) notes, growth in the new industries such as chemicals owed as much to growth of factor inputs as to growth of TFP.

The First World War and its aftermath: the formation of ICI

As was noted in chapter 10, before 1914 German chemical producers had become heavily dominant in a number of products, including dyes and associated products of the fine chemical industry, based on organic (carbon-based) chemistry. This proved highly embarrassing with the outbreak of war, and agreements between British and German chemical companies had to be severed, while the government had to set up investments in branches of the industry where Britain had been weak. In particular, there were embarrassing shortages of dyes for military uniforms and drugs to treat the wounded (Reader, 1979: 156). The war years saw a profitable expansion of explosives production at Nobels, diversification out of ammonia soda at Brunner Mond and the establishment of a fledgling dyestuffs industry in the government promoted British Dyes (Reader, 1970: 258–314).

Nevertheless, the postwar viability of the British chemical industry was threatened by the resurgence of competition from Germany. To protect the government sponsored British Dyestuffs Corporation, formed in 1919 from a merger of British Dyes with Levinstein, the other significant British producer, the 1921 Dyestuffs (Import Regulation) Act allowed the purchase of foreign dyes only if there was no domestically produced equivalent or if the price was significantly (initially more than three times, but later reduced to 1.75 times) higher. (Reader, 1979: 164). The Act was to remain in force for 10 years, justified on the basis of an infant industry argument, although in practice it was extended into the 1930s. In 1918, worried at the prospect of lack of demand after the war, Nobels brought about a merger of British explosives interests in Explosives Trades Ltd, which quickly reverted to using the more diplomatic Nobels name. Nobels also pursued a strategy of diversification to maintain postwar profitability.

Nevertheless, the British industry still felt threatened by the creation of the giant *Interessengemeinschaft Farbenindustrie Aktiengesellschaft* (IG) in 1925. This full merger of the major German chemical firms built upon a looser form of association going back to 1916, the *IG der deutschen Teerfarbenfabriken AG*. Harry McGowan, Nobel's Chairman and Managing Director, sought a merger of the major British companies, which ultimately led to the formation of Imperial Chemical Industries Ltd (ICI) in 1926. However, this came about only after Alfred Mond, Chairman of Brunner Mond, had explored the possibility of an international alliance, including the IG, in which he was prepared to allow the Germans access to the British dyestuffs market. This would undoubtedly have been fatal for the British Dyestuffs Corporation, but the Germans held out for tough terms and no agreement was reached (Reader, 1970: 451–66).

ICI brought together four companies, two strong and two weak. The stronger companies were Nobels and Brunner Mond, while the British Dyestuffs Corporation and United Alkali Producers were weak. Nobels were dominant in explosives and had diversified on a small scale into products based on similar technology (cellulose), such as leathercloth and paints. However, their diversification programme was centred on the vehicle industry, which they saw as having strong growth potential. Investments were made in component suppliers such as Lucas and Dunlop, and a large shareholding was taken in General Motors (Reader, 1979: 160–1). Brunner Mond had moved away from its reliance on ammonia soda during the war, taking a keen interest in the Haber–Bosch process for synthesising ammonia, which had been working in Germany from 1913. The process involved combining one molecule of nitrogen (N_2) with three molecules of hydrogen (3 H_2) to form two molecules of ammonia (2 NH_3) (Bronowski, 1966: 90). The difficulties lay in getting the process working on a large scale under the very exacting conditions of heat and high pressure. However, Brunner Mond saw a chance to catch up on the Germans at the end of the war by sending a team to the Oppau plant of BASF, which was under Allied control. Despite non-cooperation by the German staff and the removal of the report from a locked railway wagon under armed guard (by cutting through the floor!), the industrial spies managed to learn the secrets and transfer them back to Britain (Reader, 1970: 354–5). The main peacetime use of this technology was the production of nitrogenous fertiliser, mainly ammonia sulphate. However, there were also some similarities with the techniques needed to produce oil-from-coal, which involved combining hydrogen with carbon under high pressure and temperature (Reader, 1975: 162).

Turning to the weaker members of the merger, the British Dyestuffs Corporation pinned its hopes on R&D. Although this was to pay dividends in the future, at the time of the merger the company was in a weak position, able to survive only through protection. The United Alkali Company was technically moribund, a hangover from the days of the Leblanc process of alkali production (Reader, 1979: 167).

The name of the new company was of some significance, since the aim was to dominate the supply of chemicals to the Empire and to participate in international market-sharing arrangements. The close relationship between Nobels and the American company Du Pont was carried over to ICI, and with the onset of the world slump in 1929 agreement was reached with the IG. This led to the establishment of a Nitrogen Cartel in fertilisers, a Hydrogenation Cartel in oil-from-coal and a Dyestuffs Cartel (Reader, 1979: 173).

ICI's first major investment decision was the construction of a large plant at Billingham for the production of fertiliser. By the time of its completion in the early 1930s, this investment amounted to about £20 million, against a total capital employed in ICI of £73 million in 1927 (Reader, 1979: 170). This investment turned out disastrously since demand had been seriously over-estimated, and world supply of nitrogenous fertilisers seriously under-estimated. The world slump from 1929 brought home the scale of the failure, and resulted in capital write-offs, wage cuts and sackings for the first time in a company that prided itself on good industrial relations (Reader, 1979: 171).

An attempt was made to salvage something from the expensive failure at Billingham by switching some of the idle plant to the production of oil-from-coal. However, at oil prices ruling in the 1930s this required protection against cheap imported oil. ICI could argue that the scheme would provide employment in the badly depressed North East and also stimulate the coal industry. The 1935 British Hydrocarbon Oils Protection Act gave ICI a fiscal protection of 8*d*. per gallon for 4½ years (Reader, 1979: 172). Cheap oil in the postwar period would ensure that this was also a wasted investment.

ICI were rather more successful in the synthesis of new organic compounds, arising out of research first set in train at British Dyestuffs Corporation. New possibilities were beginning to open up with the development of new fibres and plastics. However, these activities remained underdeveloped before the war partly as a result of resources being diverted to Billingham, but also partly as a result of ICI's collusive approach to business. Because they were concerned not to offend major customers or suppliers, ICI kept out of any line of business that might be seen as competing directly. Thus, for example, to avoid giving offence to Courtaulds, an important customer for caustic soda, ICI kept out of rayon and cellophane (Reader, 1979: 174).

The cartel system came under increasing strain after 1939. As with the First World War, there were problems of entanglements with German companies. However, the mortal blow to the cartel system was dealt by an antitrust offensive in the United States, culminating in a general case against ICI and Du Pont launched by the American authorities in 1944 (Reader, 1975: 428). The Second World War also saw a substantial increase in output, with the expansion of munitions production and involvement in complex scientific projects such as the development of the atomic bomb, code named the innocuous sounding 'Tube Alloys' (Reader, 1975: 259–94).

To what extent should ICI be seen as having successfully emulated American organisational methods? And hence to what extent does ICI represent a model that, if it had been more widely followed in Britain, would have resulted in much greater industrial success? Chandler (1990: 358) is in little doubt, noting that ICI

was the first merger in Britain to consolidate major sectors of a basic industry in the American manner. Indeed, it provides one of the very few examples of systematically planned, large-scale, organization building in British industry before World War II comparable to that carried out in the United States and Germany in the early twentieth century. Such organization building permitted a sizable part of the British industrial chemical industry to compete effectively at home and abroad.

Table 11.2. *Comparative labour productivity in chemicals, 1925/24 to 1947/48 (UK=100)*

US/UK	1925/24	1929/30	1937/35	1947/48
Seedcrushing	151	131	105	
Coke	306	341	236	
Mineral oil refining	264	346		302
Soap & detergents	318	326	285	281
Fertilisers	203	155		
Matches			336	248
Germany/UK	1924	1930	1935	
Seedcrushing			50	
Coke	124	209	174	
Sulphuric acid	145	252	182	
Soap			110	

Notes: US/UK figures based on output per operative; Germany/UK figures based on output per employee.
Source: Appendix tables A2.1, A2.2.

At the least, there must be doubts about this. A significant proportion of the firm's capital was wasted in expensive projects at Billingham, which deprived the research teams in new organic fields of badly needed funds. Furthermore, these activities were further hindered by the collusive approach to business which, far from ensuring that ICI was able to 'compete effectively at home and abroad', was designed with precisely the opposite intention of avoiding competition wherever possible. The adoption of a multi-divisional structure looks like a small gain to set against these drawbacks in the way business was conducted once competition had been suppressed.

There are no comparative labour productivity data during the interwar period for many of the branches of the chemical industry dominated by ICI. Nevertheless US/UK figures for fertilisers and Germany/UK figures for sulphuric acid are available in table 11.2. Although there was a large German productivity lead in sulphuric acid in 1924, 1930 and 1935, the American lead in fertilisers was relatively small in 1925/24 and 1929/30. This is consistent with Reader's (1979: 170) judgement that the problem in fertilisers was that Brunner Mond's commercial planning did not match their technical skills. However, it might also be seen as testimony to the success of the industrial espionage at Oppau. Also, it should be borne in mind that ammonia sulphate accounted for only about half of fertiliser production, the bulk of the rest being superphosphates, made from phosphate

Table 11.3. *Shares in world production of chemicals, 1913–51 (%)*

A. Total chemicals	1913	1927	1935	1938	1951	
UK	11.0	10.2	9.3	8.6	8.8	
Germany	24.0	16.0	17.7	21.9	5.8	
US	34.0	42.0	32.3	29.7	43.2	
B. Sulphuric acid	1913	1925	1929	1936–8	1948	1950
UK	13.0	7.7	7.3	6.1	6.7	6.6
Germany	20.3	10.2	13.0	11.4	3.3	5.2
US	27.1	38.7	36.8	28.8	45.2	42.7
C. Soda ash	1904	1929	1935	1938	1948	1950
UK	50.0		14.5	11.9	14.3	14.9
Germany	19.1	12.0	12.7	15.7	4.5	8.4
US	7.1	46.9	39.8	39.5	49.4	39.1
D Synthetic dyestuffs	1913	1924	1927	1938	1948	1950
UK	3.1	11.6	9.8	9.5	19.3	16.2
Germany	85.1	43.9	40.8	25.9	5.9	10.8
US	1.9	18.9	23.4	16.8	37.4	33.1
E. Superphosphates	1913	1926	1928	1938	1948	1950
UK	7.0	2.7	2.4	2.6	4.7	4.1
Germany	15.9	5.2	5.4	7.3	2.1	2.5
US	27.6	25.7	27.8	21.2	35.4	31.9
F. Chemical nitrogen	1913	1926–8	1936–7	1949	1950	
UK	11.7	6.1	5.7	8.6	7.7	
Germany	15.5	42.9	26.6	9.1	10.5	
US	4.7	10.1	12.9	29.2	28.1	

Note: Post-Second World War figures for Germany refer to West Germany only, except for superphosphates.
Source: Svennilson (1954: 165, 287–90).

rock treated with sulphuric acid (Bronowski, 1966: 160; Keatley, 1976: 17). The world market share data in table 11.3 illustrate the importance of the two world wars, with the United States the principal beneficiary in both cases. Britain's position remained strongest in soda ash during the interwar period. However, there is much less evidence of national specialisation between the wars than during the pre-1914 period; evidently, comparative advantage was one of the casualties of the First World War.

Table 11.4. *Labour productivity in the British*
soap industry, 1907–51

	Output (000 tons)	Operatives producing main products	Output per operative (tons)
1907	372.0	10,932	34.0
1912	429.1	12,417	34.6
1924	470.9	15,256	30.9
1930	454.1	13,106	34.6
1935	498.7	12,513	39.9
1937	561.1	13,652	41.6
1948	548.8	12,141	45.2
1951	682.8	12,442	54.9

Source: Census of Production.

Soap and seedcrushing: the formation of Unilever

In chapter 10 the success of Lever Brothers in the branding and packaging of soap from the late nineteenth century was noted. However, an attempt by Lever to monopolise the British soap trade was foiled in 1906 by a press campaign led by the *Daily Mail*. The proprietor, Lord Northcliffe, claimed to be protecting the public interest, but no doubt the threatened loss of advertising revenue from one of the most advertising-intensive industries weighed heavily on his mind (Edwards, 1962: 162). Lever nevertheless gradually bought up competitors and by 1920 controlled all the leading soap manufacturers apart from the Cooperative Wholesale Society (CWS) (Corlett, 1958: 50).

There seems little doubt that Lever attempted to exploit his quasi-monopoly position, maintaining prices above competitive levels in the aftermath of the First World War (Edwards, 1958: 174). However, Lever's high prices resulted in increasing market share for CWS and new entry, most notably by the British Oil and Cake Mills Ltd with their 'New Pin' brand and the American Palmolive Company with its green toilet soap. However, the labour productivity data in table 11.4 show little evidence of effective rationalisation before the 1930s. After a fall in output per worker during 1919–20, when the standard working week was cut from 54 to 47 hours, labour productivity was still only back to prewar levels in 1930. Furthermore, the comparative labour productivity data in table 11.2 suggest a widening Anglo-American productivity gap during the 1920s.

Chandler (1990: 382) sees the merger of Lever Brothers with the Dutch firm Margarine Unie to form Unilever in 1929 as a necessary condition for the effective rationalisation of the Lever soap interests. However, it is equally possible to see the entry of the American giant Procter & Gamble into the British market through the purchase of Thomas Hedley & Sons in 1930 as the essential catalyst of change (Wilson, 1954, vol.II: 344). Indeed, if our interest is primarily in the industry rather than the firm, it is surely the new competition that is the more significant. For if Unilever had failed to rationalise, their market share would surely have fallen further and the improvement in aggregate productivity performance would have been located largely in other firms.

Analysts of the British soap industry have failed to uncover any significant technological lag in the first half of the twentieth century, either in products or processes (Corlett, 1958; Edwards, 1962). Indeed, Corlett (1958: 39–45) sees much similarity of trends in Britain and the United States. In both countries, *per capita* consumption of soap products was similar, soap powders and flakes gained at the expense of hard soap during the 1930s, and synthetic detergents began to appear. Rather than eliminating a technological lag, then, the rationalisation drive of the 1930s was based on concentrating production in fewer plants and reducing the number of varieties (Wilson, 1954, vol.II: 345–7). The labour productivity gap with the United States was reduced during the 1930s, and British labour productivity was almost on a par with German levels in 1935, as the figures in table 11.2 show.

Although Lever Brothers, like many other British companies, had tended to concentrate on Empire markets, the merger with Margarine Unie ensured that the company also took a strong interest in European markets (Fieldhouse, 1978). Although this created problems with exchange control in the 1930s and war disruption and destruction in the 1940s, it was to prove an immense benefit in the postwar world (Reader, 1960: 47–9).

Lever Brothers had expanded into seedcrushing in 1896 as part of a strategy to secure their supply of oils (Wilson, 1954, vol.I: 57–8). However, they remained small players in this industry until the merger with British Oil and Cake Mills in 1925 and the formation of Unilever in 1929, the latter bringing Jurgens' seedcrushing capacity (Edwards, 1958: 181; Wilson, 1954, vol.II: 239). The data in table 11.5 suggest that in seedcrushing, as in soap, labour productivity fell across the First World War and improved only slowly during the 1920s, before growing rapidly during the 1930s. The improvement during the 1930s was largely the result of a vigorous rationalisation programme conducted by Herbert Davis, closing uneconomic mills in Liverpool and Hull (Wilson, 1954, vol.II: 339). Turning to the comparative labour productivity data in table 11.2, it can be seen that the productivity gap that had opened up with America after the First World War had been all but eliminated by the late 1930s. Furthermore, the data also suggest a substantial British labour productivity lead over Germany in seedcrushing.

Table 11.5. *Labour productivity in the British*
seedcrushing industry, 1907–51

	Output (000 tons)	Operatives producing main products	Output per operative (tons)
1907	1,371.0	6,794	201.8
1924	1,961.4	11,081	166.4
1930	1,605.0	9,065	177.1
1935	2,283.3	10,200	223.9
1937	2,498.9	10,390	240.5
1948	2,361.8	7,585	311.4
1951	2,599.2	7,493	346.9

Source: Census of Production.

Oil refining

Oil is seen by Chandler (1990: 298) as a rare example of successful British enterprise during the first half of the twentieth century, through the activities of the Anglo-Persian Oil Company (APOC), which became the Anglo-Iranian Oil Company in 1935 and then British Petroleum in 1954. The APOC and Royal Dutch-Shell, the latter 40 per cent British owned, successfully broke into the world oil oligopoly between the wars, forming two of the 'Seven Sisters', together with the Gulf Oil Corporation, the Texas Company (later Texaco), the Standard Oil Company of New Jersey (later Exxon), the Standard Oil Company of New York (later Mobil) and the Standard Oil Company of California (later Chevron) (Bamberg, 1994: 2).

However, the British oil companies at this time are of limited interest in a study of manufacturing because refining activities in the United Kingdom were very limited. Charles Greenway, the early architect of the APOC's development, as managing director from 1910 and chairman from 1914, determined to build a vertically integrated enterprise involved in exploration, extraction, shipping, refining and marketing (Ferrier, 1982: 160). From 1927, when Greenway was succeeded as chairman by John Cadnam, the APOC moved away from a strategy of self-sufficiency and pursued a more collusive policy. This resulted in the Achnacarry Agreement signed in 1928 between the big three oil companies, Standard Oil of New Jersey, Royal Dutch-Shell and the APOC (Bamberg, 1994: 107). This became known as the 'As is' agreement, by which the three companies agreed to accept existing market shares, stabilise prices and cooperate in the use of existing resources. This was bolstered by agreements covering the other major oil companies, including the Memorandum for European Markets of 1930 and a Draft Memorandum of Principles in 1934 covering all countries except the United States, where it was illegal (Bamberg, 1994: 109–15; Chandler, 1990: 302).

In petroleum refining, however, production in the United Kingdom was relatively unimportant. The APOC's main refinery was at Abadan in Iran and the British refineries at Llandarcy in South Wales (imaginatively named after the founder of the APOC, William Knox D'Arcy) and Grangemouth in Scotland had much smaller throughputs (Ferrier, 1982: 673–4). Figures from the 1924 British *Census of Production* and the 1925 American *Census of Manufactures* show British refinery output at 12.3 million barrels compared with 269.3 million barrels in the United States. The much larger scale of operations in the United States seems to have resulted in substantially higher labour productivity, with the figures in table 11.2 showing the American lead rising above 3:1 by the end of the 1920s. Although technological leadership in crude oil production and new refining methods rested with the Americans, there is no suggestion in the literature of any substantial British technological lag in this industry (Ferrier, 1982: 397–460; Bamberg, 1994: 189–205). The company's first research laboratory was set up at Sunbury in 1917 under A.E. Dunstan, head of the chemical department at the East Ham Technical College (Ferrier, 1982: 279).

Other chemicals: pharmaceuticals and matches

The British pharmaceutical industry received a boost from the First World War, when German supplies were cut off. However, as Robson (1988) notes, the impact of the war should not be exaggerated. First, the German superiority did not extend to all areas and was most noticeable in synthetic drugs; second, German drugs continued to find their way into Britain via neutral countries; third, the scale of R&D remained relatively small during the interwar period.

The Second World War provided a more lasting stimulus to the British pharmaceutical industry. In 1941 the five major British pharmaceutical companies formed a cooperative body, the Therapeutic Research Corporation (TRC). The five original companies, Burroughs Wellcome, Glaxo, May & Baker, Boots and British Drug Houses, were joined in 1942 by the Pharmaceuticals Division of ICI (Davenport-Hines and Slinn, 1992: 138). Wartime achievements included the production of penicillin in collaboration with American companies, building on the work of Florey and Chain, who discovered the therapeutic possibilities of Fleming's original discovery. This was the 'hinge of fortune' that turned Glaxo from a supplier of dried milk with pharmaceutical interests into a major pharmaceuticals company (Davenport-Hines and Slinn, 1992: 141–9).

Labour productivity performance in the British match industry was comparatively poor during the first half of the twentieth century, as can be seen from table 11.2. This is almost certainly due to the dominant position held by Bryant and May, together with an international agreement with the Swedish Match Company, the principal overseas supplier (Fitzgerald, 1927: 152–4; Levy, 1927: 274). Monopoly power allowed the continuation of production at the many plants grouped under common ownership, without effective rationalisation.

Conclusions

A key feature of the British economy between the wars was the strengthening of the trend towards increased dependence on Empire markets. This was reflected in the chemicals sector by the choice of name for the newly merged British champion, ICI or Imperial Chemical Industries. Another trend was the growing importance of R&D; in some important areas, such as pharmaceuticals, investments were made between the wars which would bear fruit in the decades to come. The cases of ICI and Unilever suggest that misleading conclusions can be drawn by paying too much attention to organisational structures and insufficient attention to firm conduct in the sphere of competition. Chandler (1990) sees ICI as having successfully emulated American organisational methods, enabling a sizeable part of the British chemical industry to compete effectively at home and abroad. In fact, however, the mergers leading to the formation of ICI and the collusive approach to business adopted by the new company were designed to suppress competition at home and abroad. In this anti-competitive environment, much of ICI's capital was wasted in expensive fertiliser and oil-from-coal projects at Billingham, and research in new organic fields was hindered. Chandler (1990) also sees the formation of Unilever as a necessary prerequisite for the rationalisation of the Lever soap interests during the 1930s. However, it is doubtful whether such rationalisation would have occurred without the entry into the British market of the American firm Procter & Gamble.

Metals

Iron and steel

Output, employment and capital trends in the British iron and steel industry are shown in table 11.6. Output remained below the 1913 level until the mid-1930s, although this was followed by a period of rapid expansion due to rearmament, war production and reconstruction. Output per worker in iron and steel grew by 2.2 per cent per annum during the period 1924–37,

Table 11.6. *Output, employment and capital in the British iron and steel industry, 1907–51 (1924=100)*

	Output	Employment	Capital	Labour productivity	TFP
1907	91.3	92.8		98.4	
1913	105.5				
1924	100.0	100.0	100.0	100.0	100.0
1929	104.3	99.4	100.0	104.9	104.7
1930	93.0	85.6	100.0	108.6	103.3
1935	116.4	91.7	102.6	126.9	122.4
1937	146.9	109.7	107.9	133.9	134.6
1948	167.4	120.6	98.0	138.8	148.3
1951	189.2	123.9	112.1	152.7	157.7

Sources: Output: Lomax (1959: 192); Employment: 1907–24: *Historical Record of the Census of Production*, 23; 1924–51: Feinstein (1972: T130); Capital: Feinstein (1972: T101).

Table 11.7. *Production of iron and steel, 1913 to 1949–50 (m tons)*

A. Pig iron and ferro alloys				
	UK	Germany	US	World
1913	10.4	12.3	31.5	79.0
1927–8	7.1	14.3	38.0	87.7
1936–7	8.2	15.6	34.6	98.1
1949–50	9.7	10.3	54.6	124.0

B. Steel ingots and castings				
	UK	Germany	US	World
1913	7.8	14.3	31.8	76.3
1927–8	8.9	17.4	49.0	105.8
1936–7	12.6	19.5	50.0	130.0
1949–50	16.2	13.3	79.2	174.8

Source: Svennilson (1954: 134).

just below the average for manufacturing of 2.4 per cent per annum. Similarly, TFP growth in iron and steel of 2.3 per cent per annum was slightly below the average for manufacturing of 2.5 per cent during the period 1924–37. Output, labour productivity and TFP all grew more slowly during the transwar period 1937–51.

It is useful to break down the output data into the separate categories of pig iron and ferro alloys and steel ingots and castings, as in table 11.7, which

Table 11.8. *Average annual output per blast furnace, 1913–50 (000 tons)*

	UK	Germany	Saar	France	Belgium	Luxembourg
1913	31	59	53	47	46	59
1925	42	97	63	57	64	69
1929	49	134	79	66	71	82
1935	66	144	89	71	81	93
1937	69	147	97	78	82	103
1950	98	132	102	83	94	110

Source: Svennilson (1954: 265).

also places the British performance in its international perspective. The stagnation of overall output in Britain during the 1920s masks a fall in pig iron production and growth in steel output. Although there was a world-wide decline in the relative importance of pig iron due to a reduction in foundry demand and the increased use of scrap in the steel making process, the absolute fall in pig iron output was unique to Britain, which had retained a large export trade in pig iron before the First World War (Svennilson 1954: 121). This adversely affected the rate of modernisation in the blast furnace section of the industry, as can be seen in table 11.8. Average annual output per blast furnace in Britain lagged behind all other continental countries until the post-Second World War period.

Nevertheless, the production data in table 11.7 suggest that the British steel industry held its own against Germany. This is confirmed by the trade data in table 11.9, which show an export performance by Britain on a par with Germany and the United States in the interwar period. The other striking feature of the trade data is the serious decline in exports during the 1930s, shared by all countries. Britain, which maintained an open market during the 1920s abandoned free trade in steel during the 1930s, leading to a drastic curtailment of imports. This move to protection was accompanied by a policy of Imperial Preference, which helped to maintain exports. Hence British iron and steel exports remained highly dependent on Empire markets (Svennilson, 1954: 272).

The stagnation of demand before the rearmament boom of the 1930s meant that there was substantial excess capacity in the British iron and steel industry for much of the interwar period. Hence this period is often characterised as one of attempted rationalisation, with the aim of concentrating production in the most efficient units. However, the term 'rationalisation' is also usually taken to imply a more general process of modernisation in response to developments in the United States, and can be taken to apply to Germany as well as to Britain. In the context of the

Table 11.9. *Trade in semi-finished and finished steel, 1913–50 (000 tons)*

A. Exports	UK	Germany	US
1913	2,790	4,115	2,159
1924	2,602	1,434	1,395
1929	2,935	4,631	2,162
1935	1,702	1,997	788
1938	1,334	1,821	1,482
1950	2,233	1,574	2,417

B. Imports	UK	US
1913	1,595	113
1924	1,687	219
1929	2,189	344
1935	938	152
1938	807	135
1950	444	884

Source: Svennilson (1954: 268).

steel industry this largely meant gradual improvements to the great steel making innovations from the pre-1914 period, involving larger units, more mechanisation and process control (Svennilson, 1954: 131). Perhaps the most obvious technological lag in the European steel industry was in the appearance of the continuous strip mill, which first appeared in the United States in 1924. By 1939 there were 28 strip mills in the United States with an aggregate capacity of 12.5 million tons. In Britain the first continuous strip mill was introduced in 1938 and the second in 1940, while in Continental Europe there was a single mill in Germany which began operation in 1937 (Svennilson, 1954: 132–3).

Tolliday (1987a) provides a detailed account of the failure of the rationalisation movement in the interwar steel industry, stressing the interaction between interest groups. This can be interpreted as consistent with Olson's (1982) framework, with fragmented interest groups blocking socially desirable changes, although Tolliday (1987a: 348) is careful to note that American-style mass production was not the only option facing the British steel industry, which might alternatively have pursued skilled specialisation. Furthermore, Tolliday (1987a: 159) notes that the British steel industry, despite muddling along, still did as well as its European rivals.

As well as examining interactions among steel firms, Tolliday (1987a) looks at the role played by banks and the state in the rationalisation movement. Business strategy is examined in the context of heavy steel making on the North East Coast, heavy steel making in Scotland and steel and tinplate in South Wales. On the North East Coast, rationalisation would have required amalgamation among the two major firms of Dorman Long and South Durham & Cargo Fleet, but this was prevented by failure to agree terms that would satisfy all the major stakeholders, including customers and banks as well as shareholders and managers (Tolliday, 1986: 85–8). In Scotland, although amalgamation was finally achieved in 1936 under Colvilles, Tolliday (1986: 88–91) sees it as occurring too late and achieving little effective rationalisation, again because of opposition from vested interests. Tolliday probably overstates his case here, since, as Payne (1979: 221–2) points out, labour productivity increased substantially at Colvilles during the 1930s. In South Wales, Richard Thomas pursued a strategy of buying up rivals to obtain a monopoly of tinplate production and attempted a move into continuous strip production of sheet steel. Although a strip mill was opened in 1938, Tolliday (1987a: 154) argues that it was 'spoiled' by the intervention of rival firms, bankers and the government. Again, Tolliday is probably too critical here since, as was noted above, the lag in continuous strip production was equally long in Continental Europe.

Banks were important players in the rationalisation process because of the high level of indebtedness of many steel firms. This was in turn largely the result of overdrafts given freely during the postwar boom of 1919–20, with slack provisions for repayment (Tolliday, 1987a: 177). After the collapse of the boom, many steel firms became dependent on the goodwill of their bankers. Although the banks were thus in a position to force through reorganisation, in general they failed to do this since they lacked expert knowledge and feared that if they obtained a reputation for interfering in business decisions, their more profitable industrial clients would switch banks (Tolliday, 1987a: 179). The Bank of England became involved in rationalisation schemes partly as a result of its continued commercial operations, but also partly as a result of concerns about the threat to financial stability caused by the high level of indebtedness of the old staple industries. However, Tolliday (1986: 96) notes that the Bank was unable to play an exceptional role since it was neither prepared to risk its own capital nor to countenance the introduction of government money. Hence the Bank became just one more interest group in the process and subject to manipulation by other interests. Thus, for example, when the Bank gave financial assistance to the Richard Thomas strip mill scheme in 1938, it acquired control, which was exercised through the British Iron and Steel Federation (BISF). However, board members from other companies who were brought in with a view to a grand merger scheme in fact took the opportunity to stifle a competitor and there was a period of vicious boardroom infighting (Tolliday, 1987a: 252).

Table 11.10. *Comparative labour productivity in metal manufacturing,*
1925/24 to 1947/48 (UK=100)

US/UK	1925/24	1929/30	1937/35	1947/48
Iron & steel (general)	357			
Blast furnaces	427	480	362	417
Iron & steel smelt/roll		293	197	
Iron & steel foundries		270	154	
Lead & zinc		254	327	
Germany/UK	1924	1930	1935	1937
Steelworks			116	103
Blast furnaces	156	177	148	118
Iron foundries		124	112	118
Zinc	49	121	85	

Notes: US/UK figures based on output per operative; Germany/UK figures based on output per employee.
Source: Appendix tables A2.1, A2.2.

The other major interest group involved in the rationalisation process was the State, which acquired new power and responsibility over the steel industry with the General Tariff of 1932. The Bank of England had feared that protection would reduce the pressure for rationalisation, and these fears seem to be borne out (Tolliday, 1987a: 204). The Import Duties Advisory Committee (IDAC) was lobbied by the BISF, which thus acted more or less as a state sponsored cartel. Freed from competition, the BISF became an organisation geared to defending the existing interests of its members rather than promoting change in the industry. This organisational inertia continued across the Second World War, which stimulated closer cooperation between the BISF and the government (Tolliday, 1986: 103).

The comparative labour productivity position of the British iron and steel industry during the interwar period can be seen in table 11.10 for both the US/UK and Germany/UK cases. The general picture is of a growing American labour productivity lead during the 1920s, with some narrowing of the gap during the 1930s. However, the improvement of Britain's performance during the 1930s owed as much to the severity of the Depression in America as to the rationalisation of production in Britain. Furthermore, the gap remained substantial, especially in blast furnaces where, as we have seen, excess capacity was greatest. The labour productivity performance of the German iron and steel industry was a little better than its British rival, but the general impression is one of both Britain and Germany lagging a

Table 11.11. *Output, employment and capital in the British non-ferrous metal industry, 1907–51 (1924=100)*

	Output	Employment	Capital	Labour productivity	TFP
1907	69.1				
1913	78.3				
1924	100.0	100.0	100.0	100.0	100.0
1929	117.8	105.5	102.0	111.7	117.1
1930	111.6	97.5	104.1	114.5	112.0
1935	148.7	105.7	112.2	140.7	138.1
1937	185.8	135.2	122.4	137.4	141.8
1948	297.7	219.6		135.6	
1951	345.3	225.3		153.3	

Sources: Output: Lomax (1959: 192); Employment: 1924–37: Chapman (1953: 98); 1937–51: *Historical Record of the Census of Production*, 25; Capital: Feinstein (1965: 119).

long way behind the United States. The Anglo-German comparison also reveals a pattern of a substantially worse British performance in blast furnaces, although the position was much improved by 1937.

Non-ferrous metals

There were three periods of rapid growth in the British non-ferrous metal industry, across the First World War, during the 1930s and across the Second World War. The data in table 11.11 permit an assessment of labour productivity and TFP growth over the period 1924–37. Labour productivity growth, at 2.4 per cent per annum was the same as in manufacturing as a whole, while TFP growth at 2.7 per cent per annum was a little above the average for manufacturing of 2.5 per cent per annum. The fall in the rate of labour productivity growth to 0.8 per cent per annum over the period 1937–51 suggests that diminishing returns were beginning to set in.

Britain had been highly dependent on imports of zinc from Germany and Belgium before 1914, and the outbreak of the First World War created a supply problem which was met initially by increased imports from America (Cocks and Walters, 1968: 21). In the longer run, however, British and Australian zinc interests came up with an 'Imperial Scheme' to erect smelters in Britain and Australia to supply the Empire (Cocks and Walters, 1968: 25). The National Smelting Co. was set up in 1917 to establish a zinc works at Avonmouth with the help of a government loan of £500,000. In fact, there was little activity at first, and in 1922 a question was asked in the House of Commons about who got away with the 'boodle'? (Cocks and

Walters, 1968: 32). The falling price of zinc during the 1920s led to a process of concentration, resulting ultimately in the emergence of the Imperial Smelting Corporation as the sole British producer. The Imperial Smelting Corporation was formed in 1929 as a result of a reorganisation of the National Smelting Co., and by 1933 had acquired all four other British zinc smelters (Cocks and Walter, 1968: 67). Although protection was granted under the General Tariff, duties remained low until May 1939 (Cocks and Walters, 1968: 75).

Comparative labour productivity data in table 11.10 suggest a substantial productivity gap in zinc (and lead) between Britain and the United States during the 1920s, but a much more modest gap between Britain and Germany, with the latter gap being eliminated during the 1930s. The US labour productivity lead reflected a technological lead, culminating in the development of the vertical retort process by the New Jersey Zinc Co. This was a large-scale, high throughput, continuous process compared with horizontal distillation. Although Imperial Smelting acquired a licence to use the vertical retort process, there were operational difficulties and the company continued to rely on horizontal distillation furnaces for the bulk of its output during the 1930s (Cocks and Walter, 1968: 90).

In contrast to zinc, where ores continued to be imported for smelting, the British lead industry came to rely increasingly on imports in semi-manufactured form (Musson, 1978: 307). The First World War led to a rise in profits for British lead producers, but there was no increase in output due to the fall in demand for lead sheet and pipe with the slump in house building (Rowe, 1983: 279). The war encouraged mergers since lead supply was brought under the control of the Ministry of Munitions and a strong producers' organisation was needed for bargaining. An initially informal arrangement led to the formation of Associated Lead Manufacturers Limited (ALM) in 1919, but this quickly collapsed due to financial problems. In 1924 the dormant ALM was resurrected and over the next five years took over the other major British lead producers, also integrating forward into paint manufacture in 1930 (Rowe, 1983: 285–308). From the late 1920s ALM entered into international cartel agreements, and from 1932 there was a 20 per cent tariff on white lead, the principal lead product traded internationally (Rowe, 1983: 321–4).

Rowe (1983: 332) argues that ALM remained backward in engineering technology throughout the interwar period. Attempts to rationalise the production of white lead ran up against customer resistance, as many painters and white lead grinders continued to demand white lead produced by the stack process rather than the newer chamber process because of its 'fuller body' (Rowe, 1983: 334). Nevertheless, it seems unlikely that all the problems lay on the demand side. The old company structures remained relatively unchanged despite the mergers, and sales unification, although discussed in 1939, was postponed until 1949 because of the war (Rowe, 1983: 340–3). R&D, however, was centralised, with the establishment of a laboratory at Perivale, Middlesex in 1933. Furthermore, ALM entered into an agreement on the exchange of information with the National Lead Co. of America, which resulted in a flow of information chiefly to Britain, apart from in the area of red lead production, where Britain had a technological lead (Rowe, 1983: 333, 346–7).

Conclusions

The British iron and steel industry faced excess capacity after the First World War and lagged behind the United States in terms of technological developments such as the continuous strip mill. Although the very wide Anglo-American productivity gap of the 1920s narrowed somewhat during the 1930s, this was largely due to the cyclical effects of the devastating depression in the United States. Attempts at rationalisation in Britain are shown by Tolliday (1987a) to have foundered because of the failure to come up with plans acceptable to all the major interests involved, including the firms, their banks and the State. Nevertheless, the British industry appears to have held its own against Germany in terms of labour productivity. The collapse of the liberal trading system had important consequences for non-ferrous metal manufacture in Britain. Largely for strategic reasons, the industry received a substantial boost during the period 1914–50, after a long period of decline.

Engineering

Motor vehicles

Output, factor inputs and productivity all grew rapidly in the British vehicle industry during the interwar period. The data in table 11.12 show output growth of 6.1 per cent per annum over the years 1924–37, with inputs of employment and capital growing at 2.8 per cent and 2.9 per cent per annum respectively to yield both labour productivity and TFP growth rates of 3.3 per cent per annum. The vehicle industry overall was massively dominated by the motor and cycle trade, but also included aircraft and railway rolling stock. Motor vehicles, particularly passenger cars, will be examined here, leaving aircraft for a separate section.

Production of passenger cars in Britain, Germany and the United States is shown in table 11.13. The dramatically higher level of output in the United States reflects the much higher level of car ownership, which is

Table 11.12. *Output, employment and capital in the British vehicle industry,*
1907–51 (1924=100)

	Output	Employment	Capital	Labour productivity	TFP
1907	35.1	70.1		50.1	
1913	43.3				
1924	100.0	100.0	100.0	100.0	100.0
1929	133.4	117.4	100.0	113.6	119.6
1930	127.8	116.1	109.1	110.1	112.3
1935	166.6	125.0	127.3	133.3	132.5
1937	221.2	144.3	145.5	153.3	152.9
1948	279.9	211.2	387.9	132.5	109.1
1951	348.2	229.7	427.8	151.6	124.2

Sources: Output: Lomax (1959: 192); Employment: 1907–24 and 1937–51: *Historical Record*
of the Census of Production, 37; 1924–37: Chapman (1953: 98); Capital: Feinstein (1972:
T101).

Table 11.13. *Production of passenger*
cars, 1924–50 (000)

	UK	Germany	US
1924	117	36	3,186
1929	182	117	4,587
1930	170	61	2,785
1935	312	201	3,252
1937	390	264	3,916
1948	335	30	3,909
1950	522	216	6,666

Note: Post-Second World War figures for
Germany refer to West Germany only.
Source: Svennilson (1954: 149)

shown in table 11.14. Even after adjusting for geographical differences (by
dividing the cars per head indicator by geographic area) to obtain an indicator of motorisation, it is clear that demand conditions were very different
on the two sides of the Atlantic (Svennilson, 1954: 148).

Lewchuk (1986, 1987) nevertheless stresses supply side factors in the persistence of British craft-based flexible production methods during the interwar period, despite the development of mass production methods by Ford
in the United States during the first two decades of the twentieth century.

Table 11.14. *Passenger cars per 000
inhabitants and motorisation
indicator, 1922–50*

A. Passenger cars per 000 inhabitants		
	UK	Germany	US
1922	7.4	1.3	84.9
1926	16.9	3.4	163.7
1930	24.5	7.8	186.7
1935	33.0	12.7	176.8
1938	38.7	20.7	193.9
1950	46.2	12.6	260.7

B. Motorisation indicator		
	UK	Germany	US
1922	9.2	1.5	31.6
1926	23.0	4.0	63.4
1930	33.4	9.1	74.0
1935	45.2	15.2	71.3
1938	54.6	25.1	78.9
1950	66.6	17.5	114.7

Note: Post-Second World War figures for
Germany refer to West Germany only.
Source: Svennilson (1954: 280).

The Fordist strategy used high throughput, capital-intensive, flow production technology, with rigid hierarchical control by management and
payment on fixed day rates. This resulted in high levels of labour productivity compared with the British strategy, which relied on low levels of capital
intensity, low levels of machine integration along flow principles, craft
labour control over the production process and payment by piece rates
(Lewchuk, 1986: 136).

Lewchuk (1986: 138–42) traces the origins of the differences between
British and American systems of production in the interwar period back to
the early development of car production in the two countries. American car
production began as an assembly operation, with most components bought
in from outside, due to difficulties in raising capital. In Britain, however, car
production grew largely out of bicycle manufacture and was organised on
similar principles. Skilled craft workers were widely used to make components which were then assembled at the same site. These workers brought
with them experience of unionism and labour independence, which was
strengthened during the First World War with the shop stewards' move-

Buyers of labour time
estimated payoffs

Sellers of labour time
estimated payoffs

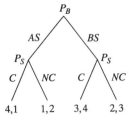

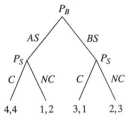

AS = American system
C = Cooperative workforce
P_B = Buyers move

BS = British system
NC = Non-cooperative workforce
P_S = Sellers move

11.1 Game-theoretic representation of technological choice in the interwar British vehicle industry
Lewchuk (1987: 224).

ment. In the British system, then, the pace of work was largely determined by the workers. Profitability was ensured by the payment of piece rates, which meant that managers continued to retain control over the wage–effort bargain. Since lost output meant lost pay, the workers had an incentive to perform tasks such as parts delivery, machine maintenance and quality control, which were seen as the responsibility of management in the American system.

Lewchuk (1987: 221–5) argues that British car producers should have switched to American technology during the 1920s, but failed to do so as a result of non-cooperative interaction with the unions. The argument is set out in game-theoretic terms in figure 11.1. Managers, or buyers of labour time have to make the first move (P_B) in a two-stage game, facing a choice between adopting the British system (*BS*) or the American system (*AS*). The choice they make depends on how they expect workers to behave. At the second stage of the game, when the technology has been installed, workers can be either cooperative (*C*) or non-cooperative (*NC*). The payoffs give the buyers' payoff first and the sellers' payoff second. The highest payoff is 4 and the lowest is 1. Thus, for example, if managers invest in the American system and workers cooperate, the (4,1) payoff estimated by managers indicates that managers see this as yielding the highest possible payoff for managers but the lowest possible payoff for workers.

Lewchuk assumes that managers and workers agree on how managers rank different strategy pairs, so that in both diagrams the buyers' rankings are the same: the American system with cooperation is best while the American system with non-cooperation is worst. Non-cooperation under the American system is worst because firms are then stuck with a lot of capital which cannot be used efficiently. Cooperation under the British system is not as good as cooperation under the American system, but it is better than non-cooperation under the British system. Finally, non-cooperation under the British system is not as bad as non-cooperation under the American system because under the British system the reduction in output caused by the non-cooperation results in lower wages and thus profitability can be retained.

The disagreement and mistrust between managers and workers is evident in how buyers and sellers estimate the preference ranking of sellers. Looking first at the estimates of managers, they believe that if the American system is introduced workers will not be prepared to accept the intensity of work and driving supervision needed to make it profitable. Hence they believe that workers really rank cooperation under the British system highest and cooperation under the American system lowest. Turning to the estimates of workers, however, we see that they most prefer cooperation under the American system. Furthermore, they least prefer cooperation under the British system because of a long-standing distrust of managers, fearing a cut in piece rates in response to any cooperative increase in productivity.

Under these conditions, it is clear that rational decision makers end up with non-cooperation under the British system. To see why, consider the managers' strategy, using the left-hand side of figure 11.1. If they choose the American system, they could end up with their worst outcome if labour does not cooperate, so risk-averse managers will choose the British system. But then at the second stage of the game, using the right-hand side of figure 11.1, given that managers have chosen the British system, it is rational for workers to be non-cooperative. For workers fear that if they cooperate, managers will cut piece rates. Mistrust between managers and workers results in a sub-optimal outcome.

Lewchuk's model places industrial relations at the centre of the story, and his description of the mistrust between management and unions rings true of much of British engineering. Nevertheless, it is not clear that the Fordist mass production strategy was realistically available to British car producers between the wars. We have already seen the gulf between levels of car ownership in Britain and America, which suggests that there simply was no mass market for cars in Britain at this time. Work by Tolliday (1987b) and Bowden (1991) emphasises the role of demand factors in determining the business strategy of interwar British vehicle producers. Given the lack of a mass market, British concentration on customised production, using skilled labour can be seen at least to some extent as a positive strategy, and not just something imposed on managers by non-cooperative unions. The

Table 11.15. *British car imports and exports, 1924–37 (%)*

	Imports as a share of domestic sales	Exports as a share of total sales	Empire share of exports
1924	15.4	10.7	86.6
1929	12.8	18.7	89.9
1937	5.8	20.6	87.2

Source: Miller and Church (1979: 187, 195).

well known persistence of a large number of models in the British car industry, despite the growing concentration of ownership, can also be understood in this light (Musson, 1978: 348).

Trade data in table 11.15 indicate a decline in import penetration during the 1920s as well as the 1930s. The car industry was protected by the McKenna Duties, introduced as an emergency wartime measure in 1915 to raise revenue and save shipping space, but retained after the war apart from a brief period during the 1924 Labour government. Foreman-Peck (1979) argues that the McKenna duties substantially raised domestic output and lowered domestic prices by enabling domestic producers to reap economies of scale, although this study ignores any interaction between levels of protection in Britain and overseas. To the extent that granting overseas producers freer access to British markets might have led to reciprocal access for British firms to overseas markets, protection could be seen as damaging. In this connection, the importance of Imperial Preference for the rising share of output exported can be seen in the high proportion of exports to Empire markets.

Given the different demand conditions on the two sides of the Atlantic, which affected the extent to which standardised mass production methods could be used, the large US/UK labour productivity gap in motor vehicles between the wars, shown in table 11.16 is not surprising. However, the Germany/UK data suggest that not all of this gap can be explained by demand factors. The supply factors stressed by Lewchuk also played some role.

Aircraft

The British aircraft industry is often characterised as backward during the interwar period, and this state of affairs is usually blamed on government policy (Fearon, 1974, 1979; Barnett, 1986). Fearon (1974: 251) argues that government demand was biased towards military aircraft, and that a policy of encouraging competition between design teams prevented the emergence

Table 11.16. *Comparative labour productivity in engineering, 1925/24 to 1947/48 (UK=100)*

US/UK	1925/24	1929/30	1937/35	1947/48
Mech. engineering	312	292	268	
Radios			347	336
Electric lamps	587	446	543	
Shipbuilding	164	154		
Motor vehicles	720			
Motor cars		725	294	284
Motorcycles		135		
Bicycles		176		180
Aircraft		315		
Railway rolling stock	114	173		
Metal boxes			577	496
Germany/UK	1924	1930	1935	
Mech./elec. eng.		103	112	
Motor vehicles	112	187	141	

Notes: US/UK figures based on output per operative; Germany/UK figures based on output per employee.
Source: Appendix tables A2.1, A2.2.

of a small number of strong companies. He argues further that civil demand was distorted towards flying boats by Imperial needs (Fearon, 1974: 251).

This view has been challenged by Robertson (1975) and Edgerton (1991), who argue that British backwardness has been much exaggerated. Edgerton (1991: 19) argues that Fearon is comparing the British aircraft industry with 'an idealised model of technological and industrial development' rather than with the aircraft industry of other countries. The employment figures in table 11.17 suggest that the British industry was far from small by international standards in the interwar period. Furthermore, Britain was probably the largest exporter of aircraft until the mid-1930s (Edgerton, 1991: 25). The fact is that in the interwar period there simply was no large market for civil aircraft and production occurred in small firms using labour-intensive, customised methods in all countries.

Edgerton (1991: 33–5) notes that claims of British technological backwardness during the interwar period are also much exaggerated. Here he builds on the argument of Robertson (1975: 649) that appearances can be deceptive. Robertson pointed out that the performance characteristics of many of the planes derided by Fearon were at least as good as those deployed in other air forces at the time. Edgerton (1991: 34) notes that the

Table 11.17. *Employment in aircraft production,*
1924–39 (000)

	UK	Germany	France	US
1924	12		13	
1929			18	19
1930	21		20	
1932		4		
1933		12		10
1934	24	46	22	
1935	35	84	24	
1936	60	188	32	
1937		229	33	
1938	120	293	47	
1939	140		110	64

Source: Edgerton (1991: 26).

Hawker Hurricane was fabric covered and the de Havilland Mosquito was made of wood, but nobody calls these aircraft out of date. Edgerton's discussion of the Supermarine monoplane designed by R.J. Mitchell, which won the Schneider Trophy with a speed of more than 400 m.p.h. in 1931, is instructive. Monoplanes had an advantage over biplanes in achieving high speed but this created problems for landing. Hence Mitchell's Supermarine was a seaplane, since seaplanes could land at higher speed than landplanes. It is therefore incorrect to see this as an early version of the Spitfire, since the difficult task of making a wing suitable for a wide range of speeds had not yet been solved. This all suggests that the issues of biplanes versus monoplanes and seaplanes versus landplanes were not as clear-cut at the time as they may seem with hindsight. Edgerton also points out that the Air Ministry was easily the largest R&D spending institution in Britain, even before rearmament. In 1935–6, for example, the Air Ministry spent £1.25 million on R&D, compared with £0.59 million at ICI, the largest industrial R&D performer (Edgerton, 1991: 35).

However, the labour productivity comparisons do seem to bear out Fearon's suggestion that the policy of encouraging competition in design had its costs. The US/UK comparison in table 11.16 suggests a substantial American labour productivity lead at the end of the 1920s, which can be seen as reflecting the absence of large repeat orders needed for learning effects to raise productivity in production. However, Barnett's (1986: 146) suggestion that labour productivity was also higher in the German aircraft industry is surely incorrect. As Edgerton (1991: 80) points out, Barnett's comparison with German data on output per man day is based

Table 11.18. *Rearmament and*
wartime production of aircraft in
Britain and Germany, 1935–44

	Britain	Germany
1935	893	3,183
1936	1,830	5,112
1937	2,218	5,606
1938	2,828	5,235
1939	7,940	8,295
1940	15,049	10,826
1941	20,094	11,424
1942	23,672	15,288
1943	26,263	25,094
1944	26,461	39,275

Sources: Central Statistical Office (1951)
Statistical Digest of the War (London: HMSO
and Longmans: 152–3); Postan (1952: 471).

on a conversion of British annual and monthly output per worker into daily figures by dividing through by 365 and 31, respectively, which assumes that no worker ever had a day off. In fact, as the production figures in table 11.18 show, Britain out-produced Germany during the crucial years 1940–3, after a later start in rearmament. Only after Speer's reorganisation during 1944 is there any evidence that Germany produced aircraft more productively than Britain (Overy, 1984: 148–85). As Edgerton (1991: 81) notes, 'Britain almost certainly produced more aircraft more efficiently for longer'.

Shipbuilding

The British shipbuilding industry was depressed throughout the interwar period, never regaining the 1913 level of output, as can be seen from the data in table 11.19. Labour productivity and TFP remained rather stagnant during the 1920s and the first half of the 1930s, although the cyclical recovery of output during the rearmament boom of the late 1930s led also to a strong recovery of productivity. The problem faced by British and other European shipbuilders was that world shipbuilding capacity had expanded during the First World War (Svennilson, 1954: 153). During the interwar period, however, world trade in primary products stagnated, which severely curtailed the demand for new ships (Parkinson, 1979: 79–80). With the decline in warship demand at the end of the war, this inevitably led to excess capacity and unemployment in the shipyards.

Table 11.19. *Output, employment and capital in the British merchant shipbuilding industry, 1907–51 (1924=100)*

	Output	Employment	Capital	Labour productivity	TFP
1907	126.9				
1913	156.5				
1924	100.0	100.0	100.0	100.0	100.0
1929	109.9	89.7	96.7	122.5	119.6
1930	95.8	79.5	95.1	120.5	113.8
1935	59.1	54.8	88.5	107.8	92.5
1937	117.8	78.3	88.5	150.4	144.7
1948	106.1				
1951	116.7				

Sources: Output: 1907–37: Lomax (1959: 192); 1937–48: Feinstein (1972: T115); 1948–51: *Annual Abstract of Statistics* (1952: 179); Employment: Chapman (1953: 98); Capital: Feinstein (1965: 116).

Table 11.20. *Merchant tonnage launched, 1909–13 to 1951 (000 gross tons)*

	UK	World	UK as % of world
1909–13	1,522	2,589	58.8
1924	1,440	2,248	64.1
1929	1,523	2,793	54.5
1930	1,479	2,889	51.2
1933	133	489	27.2
1935	499	1,302	27.2
1937	921	2,691	34.2
1948	1,176	2,310	50.9
1951	1,341	3,643	36.8

Source: Jones (1957: 64).

The figures in table 11.20, however, suggest that Britain continued to hold onto a large share of the world market until the slump of the 1930s, when protection and subsidies distorted what was left of the world ship-building market. As Parkinson (1979: 80) notes, in some ways the remarkable thing is that the industry managed to bounce back and resume production on such a large scale in such adverse circumstances.

Nevertheless, the industry has been criticised for being slow to tackle trade union restrictive practices, to adopt important innovations and to rationalise production (Svennilson, 1954: 155; Jones, 1957: 122–40, 158–76). Here, however, care must be taken to retain a balance. First, on the issue of trade union restrictive practices, as Pollard and Robertson (1979) note for the pre-1914 period, the secret of survival of the British ship-building industry was its reliance on skilled labour-intensive production methods. By keeping fixed overheads to a minimum, British firms were able to survive sharp downturns in demand, and there can be no sharper down-turn than that of the early 1930s. Craft unionism was one of the institutions that underpinned this labour-intensive style of production, and the benefits and costs must be considered together. Second, on the issue of innovations, it must be stressed that mass production techniques had still not been widely applied to shipbuilding at this time (Lorenz and Wilkinson, 1986: 118). Parkinson (1979: 93) argues that any premature widespread adoption of welding during the 1930s could have ruined British shipbuilders' repu-tation for quality. He also argues that the significance of the slower adop-tion of the diesel engine by British shipowners and shipbuilders has been exaggerated by Svennilson (1954: 155) with the benefit of hindsight, since there were also improvements in steamship technology at the time. Henning and Trace (1975), however, argue from a detailed examination of the Europe–Australia trade that the slow adoption of the diesel engine was an uneconomic lag, explained by a prejudice in favour of coal and the exces-sive claims of steam turbine producers. Third, on the issue of rationalisa-tion, National Shipbuilders' Security Ltd, formed in 1930 with the support of the Bank of England to purchase and scrap redundant shipyards, reduced capacity from 3.5 to 2.5 million gross tons (Jones, 1957: 136). As Parkinson (1979: 97) notes, however, this still left massive excess capacity. As in other industries, there was a reluctance on the part of independent firms to cease shipbuilding. Furthermore, the pressures to exit were eased from 1935 with the British Shipping (Assistance) Act, which instituted a 'scrap and build' scheme of subsidised loans to ship owners, with knock-on effects for shipbuilders (Jones, 1957: 150).

Parkinson (1979: 80) argues that the experience of the Depression of the 1930s was destructive of the long-term future of the industry, destroying managers' confidence in future market conditions and souring relations between workers and management. This is a theme taken up by Lorenz (1991b) in his discussion of the collapse of the British shipbuilding indus-try after the Second World War. In the short run, however, shipbuilding received a massive stimulus from rearmament and war production in the late 1930s and the 1940s. The warship production figures in table 11.21 are in tons of standard displacement, which cannot be compared directly with the gross and net tonnage measures used in merchant shipbuilding. As with aircraft production, it seems likely that Britain out-produced Germany at

Table 11.21. *Warship production,*
1936–7 to 1944 (000 displacement tons)

	Britain	Germany
1936–7	47.7	
1938	67.7	
1939	76.3	
1940	170.2	
1941	226.2	162
1942	233.9	193
1943	174.2	221
1944	171.0	234

Notes: British figures include battleships, aircraft
carriers, monitors, cruisers, destroyers and
submarines; German figures refer to submarines
only.
Sources: Central Statistical Office (1951),
Statistical Digest of the War (London: HMSO
and Longmans, 133); Kaldor (1945–6: 46).

the beginning of the war, although the figures are incomplete. In particular, the German figures refer to submarine production only, while the British figures include all major warships. However, German production was concentrated on U-boats and Britain was also producing a lot of escorts and landing craft at this time, so the comparison is probably not too inaccurate (Postan, 1952: 287–94).

The comparative US/UK labour productivity figures in table 11.16 suggest an important role for capacity utilisation, with the stagnant labour productivity in British shipbuilding during the 1920s leading to the opening of a productivity gap of the order of 50 percentage points. However, this had been all but eliminated by the late 1940s. At the end of the Second World War, then, before the era of mass production in shipbuilding, Britain still retained a comparative advantage in shipbuilding, continuing to supply about half of world tonnage (table 11.20).

Electrical engineering

As was noted in chapter 10, electrical engineering was slow to develop in Britain before 1914, along with electricity supply. As with the chemical industry, however, the First World War provided a stimulus to British production, as the supply of imports from Germany was cut off. In table 11.22 it can be seen that the growth of output accelerated during the interwar

Table 11.22. *Output, employment and capital in the British electrical engineering industry, 1907–48 (1924=100)*

	Output	Employment	Capital	Labour productivity	TFP
1907	44.3				
1913	64.6				
1924	100.0	100.0	100.0	100.0	100.0
1929	120.2	126.4	111.1	95.1	99.1
1930	121.6	130.2	111.1	93.4	98.2
1935	181.0	163.5	122.2	110.7	121.5
1937	219.0	203.2	133.3	107.8	123.3
1948	352.4	306.4	327.9	115.0	112.6

Sources: Output: 1907–37: Lomax (1959: 192); 1937–48: Feinstein (1972: T115); Employment: 1924–37: Chapman (1953: 98); 1937–48: *Historical Record of the Census of Production*, 33; Capital: Feinstein (1972: T101).

period, rising to 6.0 per cent per annum over the period 1924–37, as the national grid was established. It should be noted, however, that this rapid growth of output was achieved largely through the growth of factor inputs, with labour productivity growing at the modest rate of 0.6 per cent per annum and TFP at the rate of 1.6 per cent per annum. Rapid output growth continued across the Second World War, again driven largely by factor input growth.

As in the pre-1914 period, experience varied across the branches of the electrical engineering industry. The electrical machinery branch of the British industry (generators, motors, convertors, transformers, control and switchgear and switchboards) had lagged behind America and Germany before the First World War, as electricity supply was less widely diffused in Britain (Byatt, 1979: 213–19; Hannah, 1979: 37). However, during the inter-war period there was much progress in this section of the industry as the national grid was constructed, giving British producers an opportunity to catch up and overtake foreign rivals in the production of high voltage and large capacity equipment (Catterall, 1979: 256). The construction of the national grid during the Depression of the 1930s provided an unforeseen counter-cyclical boost to domestic demand to offset the fall in export demand (Hannah, 1979: 119). Figures for the US/UK relative labour productivity position in electrical machinery are unavailable for the 1930s, but the 1950 figure of 239 in appendix table A2.1 suggests that this was one of Britain's best performing engineering industries.

Electric wires and cables had been a relatively successful branch of British industry before the First World War, as noted in chapter 10.

Between the wars there was buoyant domestic demand with the construction of the national grid, but exports slumped. Catterall (1979: 258–60)
argues that the behaviour of trade associations, particularly the Cable
Makers' Association (CMA), restricted competition and output, and thus
contributed to the slow productivity growth in this sector. The CMA par-
ticipated in international restrictive agreements through the International
Cable Development Corporation. Cartels were also prevalent in electric
lamp making, where the figures in table 11.16 suggest an enormous labour
productivity gap of the order of 5:1 between Britain and the United States
between the wars. Furthermore, electric lamp making was one of the few
areas of electrical engineering protected by tariffs before the General Tariff
of 1932. The McKenna Duties of 1915 applied to electric lamps for motor
vehicles, and the Safeguarding of Industries Act of 1921 extended protection to tungsten and lamp-blown glassware (Catterall, 1979: 269). The
Electric Lamp Manufacturers' Association (ELMA) operated a resale price
maintenance scheme, supported by a register or 'black list' to prevent dis-
counting (Catterall, 1979: 268). ELMA members also introduced limited
quantities of a 'Type B' lamp in 1935 to counter competition from non-
members (Monopolies and Restrictive Practices Commission, *The Supply
of Electric Lamps*, London: HMSO, 1951). These cheap, non-branded
lamps were sold in low-priced stores as 'fighting brands'. ELMA's success
in maintaining effective barriers to entry and high prices was cited by the
Board of Trade in its 1946 *Survey of International Cartels and Internal
Cartels,* (vol.2: 126), where the price of lamps in Britain compared with the
United States (2.5 times as high) was regarded as excessive.

There was also a substantial labour productivity gap between Britain and
the United States in the production of radios during the 1930s and 1940s,
as the figures in table 11.16 show. In this branch of the industry there was
a three-tiered structure. The first tier consisted of a small number of large
multi-product firms, such as Marconi, Radio Communications,
Metropolitan–Vickers, BTH, GEC and Western Electric, who were responsible for the most important product and process innovations. The second
tier consisted of radio set makers who carried out development work and
built up a reasonably strong patent position. The third tier consisted of set
assemblers using circuit diagrams supplied by valve makers or even par-
tially assembled chassis. The low productivity of the British industry as a
whole resulted from the fact that the third tier was the largest numerically
(Catterall, 1979: 264).

The contribution of the radio industry to the war effort during the late
1930s and the 1940s is singled out for particular attention by Postan (1952:
358–70). Of particular importance was the development of centimetric
radar after the invention in early 1940 of the 'cavity magnetron' valve,

which permitted the radar pulses to travel along a narrow beam. The increased demand for equipment and components placed a great strain on the radio industry, and despite an enormous increase in output, some demands had to be met with imports from America. Postan (1952: 370) concludes that '[t]he great build-up in the production of communications equipments, of valves and of components was an industrial undertaking of the first magnitude'.

The demand for household appliances, such as refrigerators, washing machines, electric cookers, hair dryers, electric fans, electric irons, electric fires and vacuum cleaners, grew rapidly during the interwar period. Nevertheless, diffusion in general occurred later in Britain than in the United States (Bowden and Offer, 1994: 731). As with motor vehicles, then, the possibilities of mass production were much more limited in Britain. Although there are no available data on comparative productivity in this branch of electrical engineering during the 1930s, the 1950 figure of 412 for the US/UK labour productivity ratio in household appliances, seen in appendix table A2.1, is suggestive of economies of large-scale standardised production that were not available to British producers.

It seems likely that some of the difference in labour productivity between Britain and the United States in electrical engineering between the wars can be explained in terms of the greater opportunities for mass production for the affluent, homogeneous American market. However, it also seems likely that the collusive behaviour of the major British companies helped to foster a culture of complacency. Jones and Marriott (1970) are highly critical of the 'cosy' system of cartels which took root at this time and continued into the postwar period, with damaging consequences.

Mechanical engineering

Output, employment and capital stock trends in the British mechanical engineering industry are shown in table 11.23. Output, labour productivity and TFP all grew relatively slowly over the period 1924–37. However, as Gourvish (1979: 130) notes, this does not tell the whole story, because fluctuations were considerably larger in mechanical engineering than in the rest of manufacturing. Although this instability raises problems concerning the extraction of trend growth, there seems little doubt that mechanical engineering fared worse than manufacturing as a whole. This can be attributed to the export orientation of the industry, which exported 60 per cent of its output by value before 1914. In the hostile, protectionist world economy of the interwar period, this export ratio fell to about 25 per cent (Gourvish, 1979: 131).

As in electrical engineering, however, experience in mechanical engi-

Table 11.23. *Output, employment and capital in the British mechanical engineering industry, 1907–48 (1924=100)*

	Output	Employment	Capital	Labour productivity	TFP
1907	85.0	96.6		88.0	
1913	103.0				
1924	100.0	100.0	100.0	100.0	100.0
1929	120.9	108.2	100.5	111.7	114.4
1930	107.2	98.1	100.9	109.3	108.3
1935	110.4	97.7	101.8	113.0	111.5
1937	128.0	126.2	105.9	101.4	107.3
1948	205.2	178.8		114.8	

Sources: Output: 1907–37: Lomax (1959: 192); 1937–48: Feinstein (1972: T115); Employment: 1907–24 and 1937–48: *Historical Record* of the the *Census of Production*, 25; 1924–37: Chapman (1953: 98); Capital: Feinstein (1965: 116).

neering varied by branch. Textile machinery, once the most important branch, declined in relative importance. The plight of the depressed British textile industry reinforced the dependence on overseas markets, and here British producers had to face growing competition from German and Japanese machine builders (Gourvish, 1979: 134). Large companies such as Platt Brothers, Mather & Platt and Dobson & Barlow continued to retain a strong position in world markets (Musson, 1978: 312). Nevertheless, Britain's share of the exports of the six major exporting countries fell from 49 per cent during 1923–9 to 39 per cent during 1930–8, while Germany's share rose from 31 to 36 per cent. Furthermore, as Russia and America became increasingly self-sufficient and Japan made inroads in the Far East, British exports became increasingly dependent on Empire markets, especially India (Gourvish, 1979: 135).

In prime movers and boilers, there was a decline in demand for reciprocating steam engines, although this was offset by a rise in demand for turbines (including steam turbines) and diesel engines (Musson, 1978: 312). Gourvish (1979: 137) argues that Britain's share of world markets probably did not decline markedly before the 1930s, although reliable data are only available for locomotives. Here, Britain accounted for 50 per cent of the value of exports of the four major exporting countries between 1923 and 1938, and there was no significant downward trend.

Machine tools grew in relative importance within mechanical engineering during the interwar period. British manufacturers continued to supply about 70 per cent of the growing home demand, while retaining a little over 10 per cent of the value of exports from the major producing countries.

Table 11.24. *International exports of machine tools, 1913–38*

A. Export values (£000)			
	UK	Germany	US
1913	1,013	4,004	3,309
1923	1,508	2,521	2,864
1924	1,362	2,769	3,304
1929	2,153	8,939	8,401
1937	2,152	14,825	13,001
1938	4,476	14,247	19,892

B. Shares of world export market (%)			
	UK	Germany	US
1913	11.5	45.5	37.6
1923	19.7	32.9	37.3
1924	15.9	32.2	38.5
1929	10.2	42.2	39.6
1937	6.6	45.7	40.1
1938	10.7	34.4	47.8

Note: World export market is obtained as the sum of exports from the five major producers: UK, Germany, US, France and Switzerland.
Source: Aldcroft (1966: 284).

Although the figures in table 11.24 suggest that Britain's export performance improved during the early 1920s, this was not sustained as German producers recovered from the war. The argument is sometimes made that British firms were too small, but it must be remembered that production tended to occur in small firms in all countries and there were some large British producers such as Alfred Herbert (Musson, 1978: 315).

British performance in agricultural machinery was generally weak. Although it was not strictly classified with agricultural machinery in the *Census of Production*, there was a strong performance in tractors to set against the weaknesses in ploughs, lawnmowers and other grass cutters, reapers and binders, threshers, sheep shearers and clipping machines (Gourvish, 1979: 142).

The comparative labour productivity position in mechanical engineering as a whole can be evaluated from the data in table 11.16. In general, during the interwar period, the US/UK labour productivity gap was smaller in mechanical engineering than in total engineering, but was larger than for manufacturing as a whole. The 1950 US/UK comparative labour productivity ratio of 412 for agricultural machinery, seen in appendix table

A2.1, suggests a very weak British performance, although it should be noted that this excludes tractors. In machine tools, by contrast, the Anglo-American productivity ratio in 1950 was only 221, which can be explained by the continued importance of customised production in small firms, limiting the importance of the economies of standardised mass production. The limits to the spread of standardised mass production in Germany during the interwar period can also be seen in table 11.16, with German levels of labour productivity only slightly above British levels in mechanical (and electrical) engineering.

Tin cans

The demand for tin cans grew rapidly during the interwar period with the rising demand for processed foods (Reader, 1976: 67–71). Nevertheless, the comparative productivity figures in table 11.16 show cans and metal boxes as Britain's worst performer, with US labour productivity nearly six times higher than in Britain. Broadberry and Crafts (1992: 548) attribute this poor productivity performance to the abuse of monopoly power by Metal Box (MB), formed in 1921 from the four major British producers. In the 1920s MB followed an expansionary policy of acquisitions, but without effective rationalisation. In 1929 the American Can Company set up a subsidiary in Britain, which threatened the MB near-monopoly (Reader, 1976: 52). However, MB turned to American Can's major US rival, the Continental Can Company. MB and Continental signed an agreement giving MB exclusive rights for 15 years to use Continental's equipment, processes, patents and methods. A market-sharing agreement ensured that neither company would manufacture in the other's territory (Wagner, 1980: 23–4).

In 1931 the American Can Company gave up trying to fight MB's entrenched position and agreed to stay out of the UK market for 21 years. Thus MB effectively obtained a monopoly between 1931 and 1958, when American Can re-entered the British market. The monopoly was enforced through long-term leasing for can closing machines, with discounts offered to customers who used only MB's products (Wagner, 1980: 26).

The very poor British productivity performance in this sector dominated by MB would not be expected by a reader of Chandler (1990: 316–20), who praises MB's transformation into a modern industrial enterprise of world class. Yet Reader (1976: 72–82, 143–50) notes that MB failed to establish effective managerial control in the interwar period and remained little more than a collection of individual companies carving up a monopoly market. In 1943, after serious personality conflicts in the boardroom, a management consultants' report was damning in its criticism of MB's management. Reader (1976: 148–50) claims that the deficiencies were speedily corrected, but the persistence of the huge productivity gap into the post-1945 period suggests otherwise.

Conclusions

The engineering industries illustrate a number of the themes highlighted in chapters 6–9. The importance of demand factors can be seen in a number of industries. First, the lack of a mass market for motor vehicles limited the potential for the adoption of mass production technology in Britain. Second, in aircraft production the Air Ministry policy of spreading orders across a wide range of design teams meant few of the large repeat orders necessary for learning effects to raise productivity. Third, the collapse of the world market in a period of depression and protectionism severely hit the highly export oriented shipbuilding and mechanical engineering industries. And fourth, the construction of the national grid during the early 1930s provided a useful counter-cyclical boost for the electrical engineering industry.

The continued parallel development of British craft-based flexible production methods and American mass production methods can be seen in most of the engineering sector. However, in shipbuilding, mass production techniques could still not be applied and British labour productivity levels remained close to American ones. Aircraft production also continued to utilise skilled labour-intensive methods on both sides of the Atlantic, but labour productivity remained lower in Britain because of the lack of large repeat orders. Problems of labour conflict over technology, emphasised by Lewchuk (1987) in motor vehicles, remained relatively subdued in a world of persistent excess supply of labour. This only became a more serious problem after the Second World War, as firms moved more decisively to Americanise production methods.

Competition can also be seen to have played an important role in a number of engineering industries. In tin cans, collusion between the major British and American producers secured an effective monopoly of the British market for MB. In electrical engineering collusion and restrictive practices to limit competition were widespread. Most British engineering industries secured a substantial degree of protection during the 1930s and concentrated on Empire markets, avoiding head-to-head competition with American and German producers.

Textiles and clothing

Cotton: Lancashire 'under the hammer'

The collapse of the Lancashire cotton industry between the wars is clearly evident in table 11.25. The standard indicator of output is cotton consump-

Table 11.25. *British cotton consumption and exports,
1907–51*

	Cotton consumption (m lb)	Cotton yarn exports (m lb)	Cotton piece goods exports (m lin. yd)
1907	1,985	241.1	6,297.7
1913	2,178	210.1	7,075.3
1924	1,369	163.1	4,585.1
1929	1,498	166.6	3,764.9
1930	1,272	137.0	2,490.5
1935	1,261	141.7	2,013.4
1937	1,431	159.0	2,023.1
1948	977	59.0	765.7
1951	1,024	65.5	857.8

Source: Robson (1957: 332–3).

tion, which fluctuated between 45 per cent and 74 per cent of its 1913 peak during the interwar period. Thus Bowker (1928) conjures up the graphic phrase 'Lancashire under the hammer' in an otherwise unmemorable, polemical book. Although home demand rose above pre-1913 levels during the 1930s, the export position only worsened. The collapse of export demand was greatest in piece goods, with Britain retaining a strong position in the world market for yarns.

To a large extent Britain's loss of preeminence in cotton can be seen as inevitable. The product cycle model predicts that industries migrate to low wage countries as they mature and products and processes become standardised and simplified. Sandberg (1974) takes this position, seeing Lancashire's decline as inevitable in the face of competition from low wage countries like Japan, India and China. Nevertheless, as was noted in chapter 10, this view has been disputed strongly by Lazonick (1986), who castigates the British cotton industry for failing to develop a modern corporate structure using high throughput techniques. However, as Saxonhouse and Wright (1984: 119) note, the speed of collapse of the vertically integrated New England cotton industry between the wars casts serious doubt on this argument.

Thus I would argue that the underlying trend of decline in the Lancashire cotton industry should be seen as an inevitable shift of comparative advantage. It should be noted, however, that this does not preclude the possibility that the actions of the Lancashire producers *between the wars* helped to accelerate the process of decline. Indeed, such a view is consistent with the standard treatment of the interwar cotton industry (Kirby, 1974; Porter,

1979). However, this should be distinguished from the claim of Lazonick and Mass (1984: 2) that the *pre-1914* actions of British cotton entrepreneurs were to blame for the subsequent decline. The standard account also allows for the detrimental effects of the First World War, since with the interruption of supplies from Britain, overseas countries began to produce their own cotton textiles to substitute for imports from Britain and then began to compete with British exports in third markets (Musson, 1978: 318–19).

Criticisms of the British cotton industry between the wars centre on labour market inflexibilities, the postwar financial reconstitution and the slowness of rationalisation. In the labour market, the hourly real wage increased substantially during the 1919–20 postwar boom as the standard working week was reduced for a constant weekly wage (Dowie, 1975). A similar rise in real wages occurred in the cotton industry of the US South with the same adverse consequences, so that the major gainers in world markets were the Japanese rather than the Americans (Wright, 1981: 623). Also in the labour market, Lazonick (1986: 28–30) details the attempts of employers to escape from the rigidities of union imposed restrictions on work practices. Disputes were particularly severe and protracted in weaving, where weavers opposed attempts to increase the number of looms tended per worker.

The problems arising from the collapse of demand were exacerbated by a major financial reconstitution of the industry during the postwar boom of 1919–20 (Daniels and Jewkes, 1928: 167–80). While Continental European production was disrupted, British cotton producers faced strong demand and high profits. For a while it looked as if prewar prosperity might return to the Lancashire cotton industry. Given the rapidity of the rise in profits and the disruption of the building and equipment industries, the response took the form of a speculative financial reconstitution of existing mills rather than net investment. This financial reconstitution affected 46 per cent of spindles and 14 per cent of looms (Daniels and Jewkes, 1928: 174).

The most common method of financial reconstitution was reflotation, where speculators bought the shares of an existing company, hoping to recapitalise it on the basis of the exceptional profits, which they hoped might continue. An alternative method of financial reconstitution was to recapitalise by the issue of new bonus shares. Both methods had detrimental effects for the industry because of the practice whereby shareholders were normally required to pay up only half of the purchase price, with the balance found by the acceptance of loans on deposit and advances from banks. Thus the new companies were largely financed by overdrafts and loans bearing fixed interest and requiring payment even in the absence of

Table 11.26. *Cotton spindles and looms in Lancashire, 1907–51*

	Spindles (m)	Looms (000)
1907	52.6	726
1913	58.5	787
1924	60.0	800
1929	60.0	740
1930	58.0	704
1935	47.1	517
1937	43.1	472
1948	35.6	422
1951	34.0	383

Source: Robson (1957: 340).

profits (Daniels and Jewkes, 1928: 177). Many companies were thus at the mercy of the banks as profits disappeared after the collapse of the postwar boom. This increasingly became the case as unpaid share capital was called up, because many shareholders were also loanholders and had to withdraw their deposits when called upon for their unpaid share capital (Bamberg, 1988: 86).

Attempts at rationalisation during the 1920s were limited to schemes for restricting output and hence raising prices. The figures in table 11.26 show that the number of spindles remained stable throughout the 1920s and the decline in the number of looms was minimal. Only during the 1930s was there substantial disinvestment in the industry. The attempts to restrict output and raise prices during the 1920s were not very successful, as might be expected in an industry characterised by an atomistic structure (Porter, 1979: 39; Lazonick, 1986: 31–2). As well as the temptation for an individual spinning or weaving concern to cheat on quotas, there was a conflict of interest between the vertically separated spinners and weavers, since to the extent that spinners were successful in restricting output, weavers had to pay a higher price for their main input.

By the end of the 1920s, it was clear that more drastic action was required if the banks were to extricate themselves from the problem of bad debts. However, the banks themselves were reluctant to act as they lacked the expertise and were worried that enforced liquidations or amalgamations would lead to a loss of solvent customers who were opposed to bank interference in general (Bamberg, 1988: 86). Action awaited the intervention of the Bank of England, which intervened because of fears that a collapse of one of the banks in Lancashire could lead to a general banking

Table 11.27. *Productivity in the British cotton industry, 1907–51*
(1924=100)

	Output	Employment	Capital	Labour productivity	TFP
1907	145.0	108.4		133.8	
1913	159.1				
1924	100.0	100.0	100.0	100.0	100.0
1929	109.4	95.2	96.5	114.9	114.4
1930	92.9	72.5	94.6	126.9	117.7
1935	92.2	72.3	73.1	126.1	127.0
1937	104.5	74.8	67.4	139.7	144.5
1948	71.4	57.5		124.2	
1951	74.8	64.6		115.8	

Sources: Output: Mitchell (1988: 332–3); Employment: 1907–24 and 1937–48: *Census of Production*; 1924–37: Chapman (1953: 99); Capital: Feinstein (1965: 107).

collapse. Montagu Norman, the Governor of the Bank of England, played an active part in persuading the creditor banks to force many of the indebted companies into a large amalgamation, the Lancashire Cotton Corporation (LCC). Between 1929 and 1932 the LCC took control of 96 companies and 109 mills (Bamberg, 1988: 87). However, during its early years, the LCC was unable to develop an effective managerial structure, as vested interests blocked effective rationalisation. Only after a reorganisation of the Board in 1932, with Frank Platt emerging as the dominant figure, did effective rationalisation take place (Bamberg, 1988: 94). A scheme for the elimination of spindles with compensation funded from a compulsory levy on operating firms was implemented, and capacity declined sharply during the 1930s, as can be seen in table 11.26. Nevertheless, as Kirby (1974: 158) notes, the adjustment to excess capacity was only partial. In 1938, only 75 per cent of the much reduced spinning capacity and 66 per cent of the remaining weaving capacity was utilised.

The implications for productivity can be seen in table 11.27. The decline in output across the First World War was much greater than the decline in employment, so that there was a fall in labour productivity. It is clear that this fall in labour productivity was too large to be accounted for solely by the reduction in the working week. Kirby (1974: 147) argues that productivity was adversely affected by a trend away from specialisation and standardisation in the scramble for orders that followed such a precipitous decline in demand. Spinning and weaving concerns were prepared to quote for yarns and cloths outside their normal production ranges just to keep

Table 11.28. *Comparative labour productivity in textiles and clothing,*
1925/24 to 1947/48 (UK=100)

US/UK	1925/24	1929/30	1937/35	1947/48
Rayon	169	162	185	
Cotton	180	194	150	162
Linen	188	202		
Woollen & worsted	103	131	131	
Jute	200	148		169
Rope & twine	205	209		151
Hosiery	186	178	156	
Carpets		223		315
Boots & shoes	136	143	141	151
Germany/UK	*1924*	*1930*	*1935*	*1937*
Rayon		135	109	
Cotton spinning	114		100	90
Cotton weaving			69	52
Jute		121	116	100
Leather		95	99	
Boots & shoes		129	121	

Notes: US/UK figures based on output per operative; Germany/UK figures based on output
per employee.
Source: Appendix tables A2.1, A2.2.

going. Clearly, amalgamation could help here, and some of the rise in
labour productivity during the 1930s can undoubtedly be attributed to this
(Kirby, 1974: 150).

Bamberg's (1988) account of the rationalisation process in cotton
between the wars bears many similarities to Tolliday's (1987a) analysis of
steel, with interactions between shareholders, banks and the state acting to
frustrate improvements. Nevertheless, as in steel, the productivity outcome
was about the average for manufacturing. Output per worker in cotton grew
at 2.6 per cent per annum over the period 1924–37, compared with 2.4 per
cent per annum in manufacturing as a whole. Similarly, TFP growth in
cotton of 2.8 per cent per annum was above the average for manufacturing
of 2.5 per cent. On an international comparative basis, moreover, cotton
remained one of Britain's better performers. In table 11.28 we see that the
US/UK labour productivity ratio remained below 2:1 between the wars,
while the Germany/UK comparison shows Britain's position improving,
with a sizeable British labour productivity advantage in weaving. Only with
the further decline in output across the Second World War did the external

economies of scale disappear and productivity in cotton move close to the average for manufacturing.

Although the Second World War saw increased demand from the Services, and there were limits to the reduction of civilian demand, cotton output fell substantially during the war. Initially the problem was a shortage of raw cotton supplies, which meant that it was impossible to support prewar capacity at acceptable levels of utilisation. This led to a drive to concentrate production during 1940–1, which resulted in the closure of 200 out of 550 spinning mills and 400 out of 1400 weaving sheds (Hargreaves and Gowing, 1952: 364). As the raw materials shortage eased, the problem became one of shortage of manpower, as the industry had lost 112,000 workers during the concentration process, or about one-third of the prewar labour force (Hargreaves and Gowing, 1952: 366).

Although many in the industry thought that wartime techniques such as bulk buying and the standardisation of demands through the utility scheme had improved efficiency, there is little doubt that labour productivity fell across the Second World War (Hargreaves and Gowing, 1952: 477–9; Lacey, 1947; Shaw, 1950). The figures in table 11.27 suggest a fall in output per worker of 1.4 per cent per annum over the period 1937–51. Concern in London and Washington that joint textile supplies would be too low to meet Allied needs led to the establishment of a Cotton Textile Mission to the United States, led by the Cotton Controller, Sir Frank Platt, to see if British productivity could be raised by adopting some of the American methods. The findings of substantially higher American labour productivity documented in the 1944 *Report of the Cotton Textile Mission to the United States of America, March–April 1944* (London: HMSO) confirm the position shown in table 11.28, and can be seen as forming part of the backdrop to discussions about the need for postwar reconstruction and reequipment.

Courtaulds and the rise of rayon

Rayon is the name given to textile fibres and fabrics based on cellulose. The earliest process for drawing out filaments from a cellulose solution was the nitro-cellulose process, patented in 1883–4 by Sir Joseph Swan in Britain and Count Hilaire de Chardonnet in France (Harrop, 1979: 277). Since rayon was originally seen as a substitute for silk it was known for a long time as artificial silk, and was often classified in production statistics with silk. The second major rayon-producing process was the cuprammonium process, discovered in 1890 by the Frenchman Despaissis, but improved and commercially developed in Germany. Here, the cellulose was dissolved in a solution of copper oxide in ammonia (cuprammonium hydroxide)

Table 11.29. *Production of rayon filament yarn and staple fibre, 1919–51 (m lb)*

	UK	Western Europe	US	Japan	World
1919	5	15	8		28
1924	25	73	36	1	138
1929	55	223	122	27	442
1934	91	324	210	157	823
1939	173	1,053	380	540	2,241
1946	180	495	854	30	1,691
1951	374	1,355	1,294	369	4,030

Source: Robson (1958: 27).

(Coleman, 1969, vol.II: 6). However, the nitro-cellulose and cuprammonium processes were soon largely displaced by the viscose process, patented in 1892 by C.F. Cross, E.J. Bevan and C. Beadle. Cellulose was treated with aqueous caustic soda and then with carbon bisulphide to create cellulose sodium xanthate, a golden yellow, viscous liquid which the inventors called 'viscose' (Coleman, 1969, vol.II: 10). In addition to the viscose process, Cross and Bevan also patented the cellulose acetate process, although the commercial development was carried out by the Swiss Brothers Henry and Camille Dreyfus in Britain during 1918–20 for the British Cellulose and Chemical Manufacturing Company, later British Celanese Ltd (Harrop, 1979: 277). Whereas in the nitro-cellulose, cuprammonium and viscose processes the original cellulose is regenerated, in the acetate process a chemically modified cellulose is produced (Robson, 1958: 1).

If continuous filament rayon served as a substitute for silk, discontinuous filament, or staple fibre as it was known, became useful as a substitute for cotton and wool. Originally, waste from continuous filament rayon was chopped and mixed with cotton or wool for spinning or weaving on conventional machinery. Gradually, however, it became clear that staple fibre had advantages of uniformity and regularity compared with natural fibres, and staple fibre began to be produced in its own right (Hague, 1957: 52).

Production data for continuous filament rayon and staple fibre are given in table 11.29. The United States was the largest rayon producer during the 1920s and early 1930s, although Japan emerged as the major producer in the late 1930s. Although Britain was the largest European producer in the early 1920s, by 1929 Italy produced more. Germany also overtook Britain during the mid-1930s, although France continued to lag behind (Harrop, 1979: 281). Thus although output growth in Britain was rapid compared with other industries, in international terms it can be seen only as 'satisfactory rather than startling' (Coleman, 1969, vol.II: 173).

Table 11.28 suggests that labour productivity in the British rayon industry was close to German levels by the mid-1930s, with both Britain and Germany lagging behind the United States. Coleman (1969, vol.II: 457–8) suggests that demand factors may be important in explaining the difference between the two sides of the Atlantic, since American customers were more willing to accept standardised yarns and large orders, providing the advantage of long runs. This argument is strengthened by data showing substantial productivity differences between Courtaulds' plants in Britain and plants of the American Viscose Corporation (AVC), set up by Courtaulds to work the viscose patents in America.

Nevertheless, Coleman (1969, vol.II: 458) is prepared to accept that some of the British productivity gap in rayon may have been the result of poor performance rather than just demand constraints. Here, it should be noted that rayon was an oligopolistic industry, protected by duties from 1925 and Imperial Preference from 1932 (Harrop, 1979: 295). The British industry was dominated by Courtaulds, with a virtual monopoly in viscose production, and British Celanese, strong in acetate (Harrop, 1979: 289). In Britain, ICI stayed out of rayon production as a result of a restrictive agreement with Courtaulds to keep out of each other's sphere of activity. ICI stuck to the supply of materials (caustic soda and sulphuric acid) while Courtaulds stuck to the manufacture of the final product (rayon) (Reader, 1975: 365–9). In America, however, AVC had to face competition from chemical corporations like Du Pont (Harrop, 1979: 288). Nevertheless, although Courtaulds were able to make good profits throughout the 1920s, and never failed to pay a dividend during the 1930s, there were limits to the monopoly power that they could exercise, since rayon was in competition with other fibres.

Woollen and worsted and carpets

The woollen and worsted industry suffered a setback in the 1920s, but on a much smaller scale than the cotton industry. Indeed, by the end of the decade, output was back to pre-war levels, as the data in table 11.30 show. This greater stability in woollen and worsted was due largely to the fact that the industry was much less dependent on exports than cotton. Although exports declined, as can be seen from table 11.31, Britain retained a high world market share, with 30 per cent of international trade in yarns and nearly 50 per cent in tissues during the late 1930s (Musson, 1978: 321). The export decline was much stronger in yarns and tissues than in tops, where exports were back to pre-war levels by the end of the 1930s. In general, the recovery of output was based on the home market, with protection leading

Table 11.30. *Output, employment and capital in the British woollen and worsted industry, 1907–51 (1924=100)*

	Output	Employment	Capital	Labour productivity	TFP
1907	120.1	96.4		124.6	
1924	100.0	100.0	100.0	100.0	100.0
1929	119.1	88.5	95.8	134.6	131.2
1930	125.3	72.7	95.1	172.4	127.3
1935	138.7	83.6	93.7	165.9	160.0
1937	136.5	85.3	95.1	160.0	154.6
1948	120.6	72.6		166.1	
1951	100.6	75.4			

Sources: Output: Mitchell (1988: 336, 341–2); Employment: 1907–24: *Census of Production*; 1924–37: Chapman (1953: 99); 1937–51: *Historical Record of the Census of Production*, 46–7; Capital: Feinstein (1965: 109).

Table 11.31. *British woollen and worsted exports, 1912 to 1935–9 (annual averages)*

	Tops (m lb)	Yarn (m lb)	Tissues (m sq yd)
1912	45	63	218
1920–4	36	42	194
1925–9	35	46	173
1930–4	36	39	98
1935–9	43	33	112

Source: Porter (1979: 31).

to a decline in imports of woollen tissues from 46 million square yards in 1931 to 4 million per annum during 1934–7 and the virtual elimination of worsted tissue imports (Porter, 1979: 31). Within the domestic market woollens made some gains at the expense of worsted as demand shifted away from serges to grey flannel trousers and tweed jackets (Porter, 1979: 31).

Employment in woollens and worsted fell during the 1920s before staging a slight recovery during the 1930s, as can be seen in table 11.30. Thus there was a substantial upward trend in labour productivity between the wars, with output per worker growth of 3.6 per cent per annum during 1924–37, compared with 2.4 per cent per annum in manufacturing as a whole. Taking

Table 11.32. *Output and employment in the British carpet industry, 1912–37*

	Output (m sq yd)	Insured Employees (000)	Labour Productivity (1924=100)
1912	28.5		
1924	21.6	25.5	100.0
1930	21.5	22.4	113.3
1934	33.0	28.5	136.7
1935	36.6	27.8	155.5
1937	40.6	30.1	159.3

Source: Williams (1946: 282).

account of the small decline in the capital stock, TFP grew at a rate of 3.4 per cent per annum, also substantially above the rate for manufacturing as a whole. The decline in the capital stock would help to account for the slowness with which the automatic loom was adopted, since it is necessary for the total costs of new technology to be less than the variable costs of the old technology (where capital costs are sunk) to justify replacement investment. This argument is reinforced by the recognition that existing wool weaving sheds were often inadequate for the new looms, with the British Northrop Loom Company recommending the building of new sheds (Porter, 1979: 37).

The woollen and worsted industry remained highly atomistic during the interwar years, with only a small amount of merger activity (Porter, 1979: 41). The industry also remained highly localised, with the largest concentration of production and employment remaining in the West Riding, but the West of England, the Scottish Border counties, the Hebrides and other areas still retaining their distinctive products. Marshall's (1920) external economies of scale continued to be reaped. Hence the figures in table 11.28 show only a small British labour productivity shortfall relative to the United States in the 1920s and 1930s.

The carpet industry was classified as a sub-section of the woollen and worsted industry in the British *Census of Production*, since the primary materials were woollen and worsted yarns, together with jute and cotton. Output data in table 11.32 show rapid growth during the 1930s, after a depressed decade during the 1920s. This period of growth was based on the home market, with the housing boom of the 1930s playing an important role. Exports stagnated at between 6 and 7 million square yards, balanced by a similar level of retained imports (Williams, 1946: 297).

Table 11.33. *British consumption of*
jute, flax and hemp, 1907–51 (000 tons)

	Jute	Flax	Hemp
1907	225	109	74
1913	221	107	86
1924	170	45	78
1929	202	52	67
1930	127	42	63
1935	152	38	80
1937	170	44	93
1948	93	32	93
1951	114	35	102

Source: Mitchell (1988: 348–9).

Insured employment data in table 11.32 show a growth rate of 1.3 per cent per annum during 1924–37, yielding a labour productivity growth rate of 3.6 per cent per annum over the same period. Labour productivity nevertheless remained substantially below US levels, as can be seen from table 11.28. Williams (1946: 81) attributes this to the fact that American producers had gone further than British producers in standardising production for stock rather than producing to custom, although he also mentions labour market restrictions, such as the number of looms per worker.

Jute, flax and hemp

As in cotton, the British jute industry relied completely on imported fibres and exported a high proportion of its output (Menzies and Chapman, 1946: 249, 255). Hence the industry was badly hit by the loss of export markets in the interwar period, with growing competition from Calcutta on the basis of cheap labour (Musson, 1978: 323). Proxying output by the consumption of jute (i.e. retained imports) in table 11.33, there was a fall in output from pre-1914 levels in the 1920s, with further reductions during the 1930s. Accordingly, the number of insured employees fell from 41,220 in 1924 to 27,980 in 1938 (Menzies and Chapman, 1946: 247). Since the industry was almost entirely concentrated around Dundee, this had serious consequences for the region, which was almost entirely dependent on jute (Menzies and Chapman, 1946: 240). Attempts to counter Indian competition in the coarser jute packing with moves towards more skilled labour-intensive jute cloth, particularly for linoleum backing, could only delay the inevitable, and further decline occurred across the Second World War (Menzies and Chapman, 1946: 252, 260).

Flax and hemp were also largely imported and transformed into products highly dependent on export markets (Musson, 1978: 210). Flax was spun into yarn and woven into linen cloth in an industry highly localised around Belfast. The decline in linen output between the wars can be inferred from the data on consumption of flax in table 11.33. As in jute, the fall in linen output was accompanied by a fall in the number of insured workers from about 83,000 in 1924 to 74,000 in 1938 (Musson, 1978: 323). Hemp was largely used for the production of rope, twine and net, which declined with the decline of the sailing ship (Musson, 1978: 210).

The comparative labour productivity position in jute, linen and rope and twine was relatively favourable to Britain during the first half of the twentieth century, as can be seen in table 11.28. In jute, the American productivity lead was as low as 48 per cent at the end of the 1920s, while by 1937 British productivity was on a par with German levels. In linen and in rope and twine, the American lead barely rose above 2:1, and at times was much smaller. The localisation of production undoubtedly helped to yield external economies of scale, as firm size tended to remain relatively small (Menzies and Chapman, 1946: 243; *Census of Production for 1935, Final Report*, part I: 129, 227).

Hosiery and clothing

The transition from domestic to factory production in the hosiery industry was virtually complete by 1914 (Wells, 1972: 169). In contrast to the other established textile industries, output and employment continued to rise in hosiery across the First World War and into the interwar period, as can be seen in table 11.34. Although demand was curtailed through the rationing of clothing during the Second World War, prewar levels of output had been regained by 1948 (Wells, 1972: 178).

The continued growth of demand between the wars was partly the result of much less dependence on export markets than in other textile industries (Silverman, 1946a: 35). In the home market, the industry benefited from rising real incomes and changing fashions. Shorter skirts increased the demand for women's silk and rayon stockings and underwear, while the substitution of shoes for boots increased the demand for men's woollen socks. A growing demand for variety affected the demand for underwear and outerwear (Wells, 1972: 171).

The hosiery industry remained highly localised, with the East Midlands the main centre, although there were also significant concentrations in Lancashire, Greater London, Hawick and other Scottish centres where

Table 11.34. *Output and employment in the British*
hosiery industry, 1907–48 (1924=100)

	Output	Employment	Labour productivity
1907		52.3	
1912		64.2	
1924	100.0	100.0	100.0
1930	98.6	108.2	91.1
1935	142.9	120.5	118.6
1948	152.4	100.5	151.6

Sources: Output: 1924–35: *Census of Production*; 1935–48:
Brown (1954: vii); Employment: 1907–24 and 1935–48:
Historical Record of the Census of Production, 48–9; 1924–35:
Chapman (1953: 99).

there was abundant cheap female labour (Musson, 1978: 324–5). Establishments tended to be small, with 60 per cent of all establishments in 1935 employing less than 50 persons, but accounting for only 10 per cent of the net output of the industry (Silverman, 1946a: 14). There were, however, a few highly productive factories employing more than 1,000 workers, and these tended to supply more standardised products direct to retailers, especially chain and department stores (Musson, 1978: 325; Silverman, 1946a: 31–2). The higher level of labour productivity in the US hosiery industry, apparent from table 11.28, suggests that such standardised production was more prevalent in America than in Britain, as in so many other industries.

The hosiery industry is traditionally classified with textiles, but with the extension of the range of products between the wars in both underwear and outerwear as well as the new rayon stockings, the industry was becoming more like a section of the clothing industry (Musson, 1978: 325). After a setback during the First World War, the clothing industry returned to output growth at 2.1 per cent per annum during the period 1924–37. It should be noted that the data in table 11.35 include footwear, traditionally classified with clothing. Labour productivity grew at 2.0 per cent per annum as employment remained stable, while steady growth of the capital stock meant a somewhat slower rate of TFP growth at 1.4 per cent per annum. The growth of the capital stock reflected the growing use of power driven cutting and sewing machines as factory production spread.

Factory methods of production were established earlier in men's clothing and spread to women's clothing more slowly (Wray, 1957: 17–18;

Table 11.35. *Output, employment and capital in the British clothing industry, 1907–51 (1924=100)*

	Output	Employment	Capital	Labour productivity	TFP
1907	108.3	100.9		107.3	
1913	116.8				
1924	100.0	100.0	100.0	100.0	100.0
1929	114.1	99.3	112.0	114.9	110.6
1930	113.7	96.9	115.2	117.3	111.0
1935	123.8	98.4	121.7	125.8	117.6
1937	131.0	101.0	127.2	129.7	120.5
1948	95.3	80.7		118.1	
1951	105.8	89.5		118.2	

Sources: Output: Lomax (1959: 193); Employment: 1907–24: *Historical Record of the Census of Production*, 54–5; 1924–51: Feinstein (1972: T130); Capital: Feinstein (1965: 129).

Brockhurst, 1950: 4–10). The first difficulty to be overcome was the acceptance of ready-made outerwear, but even this cannot be taken as synonymous with factory production because of the persistence of home-workers making up garments cut in central warehouses by wholesale cloth-iers (Wray, 1957: 19). Moves against 'sweating' via the establishment of trade boards to regulate conditions and restrictions on the supply of cheap immigrant labour, together with simplification of women's fashions during and after the war and the experience gained from large-scale production of men's uniforms during the war, led to further growth of factory produc-tion of women's outerwear between the wars (Wray, 1957: 19–21). Wray (1957: 42) argues that these developments placed the British clothing industry technically in advance of any other country except the United States. The 1950 US/UK labour productivity ratio of 170, seen in appen-dix table A2.1, confirms the relatively small American lead in outerwear and underwear.

Footwear and leather

There was a modest growth of labour productivity in boots and shoes across the First World War, with both output and employment growing, as shown in table 11.36. A further increase in labour productivity between the wars was the result of a rise in output accompanied by a fall in employment. The growth of labour productivity was achieved through increased mechanisation, with a shift away from male towards female labour and a marked decline in the extent of outwork (Silverman, 1946b: 203).

Table 11.36. *Output and employment in the*
British footwear industry, 1907–48 (1924=100)

	Output	Employment	Labour productivity
1907	83.0	92.6	90.3
1924	100.0	100.0	100.0
1930	103.7	92.6	112.0
1935	122.0	90.3	135.1
1948	115.7	83.6	138.4

Sources: Output: 1907–35: *Census of Production*; 1935–48:
Brown (1954: vii); Employment: 1907–24 and 1935–48:
Census of Production; 1924–35: Chapman (1953: 100).

Machinery was generally leased on a rent or royalty basis from the British United Shoe Machinery Company, owned by the United Shoe Machinery Corporation of America, so that barriers to entry remained low (Silverman, 1946b: 218). This, together with the fact that varied sizes and patterns and changing fashions precluded long production runs, meant that the industry comprised largely small and medium-sized family firms (Musson, 1978: 327; Silverman, 1946b: 210). The industry remained geographically concentrated in Northamptonshire and Leicestershire, with lesser centres in London, Norwich, Bristol, Stafford and Leeds (Musson, 1978: 327). Exports were a small and declining share of production, so that the industry remained firmly oriented towards the domestic market, while imports remained relatively unimportant (Silverman, 1946b: 226).

The comparative labour productivity data in table 11.28 suggest relatively little difference between Britain, the United States and Germany between the wars. This largely reflects the fact that conditions were not very favourable to mass production, so that there were no large differences in technology and organisation. Henry Ford is reputed to have stated that he would undertake the production of shoes if he could concentrate on making 'men's black Oxfords, size 8' (Silverman, 1946b: 199).

Leather remained the basic material for footwear, and although rubber gained in importance, rubber footwear was classified separately as a subsection of the rubber industry in the *Census of Production*. Output in the leather trades grew modestly between the wars, while employment remained stable, as can be seen in table 11.37. Labour productivity thus increased modestly in Britain, rising slightly above German levels during the 1930s according to the figures in table 11.28.

Table 11.37. *Output and employment in the*
British leather industry, 1907–51 (1924=100)

	Output	Employment	Labour productivity
1907	79.3	88.4	90.3
1913	89.3		
1924	100.0	100.0	100.0
1929	94.3	97.0	97.2
1930	103.4	92.4	111.9
1935	117.2	102.0	114.9
1937	125.9	107.9	116.7
1948	116.5	100.5	115.7
1951	113.0	100.2	112.8

Sources: Output: Lomax (1959: 193); Employment:
1907–24 and 1937–51: *Historical Record of the Census of*
Production, 52–3; 1924–37: Chapman (1953: 99).

Conclusions

Demand factors played an important part in determining the fortunes of the textile and clothing trades. Drastic falls in export demand as the liberal world trading system disintegrated seriously worsened the problems of adjustment faced by the British cotton, jute and linen industries, as a result of competition from low wage economies. The clothing industries, more oriented towards the domestic market, were largely shielded from this catastrophic fall in demand.

Most of the British textile industries, however, continued to reap external economies of scale along classic Marshallian lines, based on localised production in small-scale firms, despite the widespread use of high throughput techniques in the United States. The textiles and clothing sector thus remained characterised by a high degree of competition, with the exception of rayon, where production in this new, science-based industry was concentrated in the hands of two British firms, Courtaulds and British Celanese. Although some writers have seen the atomistic structure of industries such as cotton textiles as hindering rationalisation by making coordination more difficult, the continued good productivity performance of these sectors suggests that these difficulties should not be overstated.

Food, drink and tobacco

Taking the sector as a whole in table 11.38, food, drink and tobacco showed output growth of 2.7 per cent per annum over the period 1924–37, a little

Table 11.38. *Output, employment and capital in the British food, drink and tobacco industry, 1907–51 (1924=100)*

	Output	Employment	Capital	Labour productivity	TFP
1907	82.9	81.9		101.2	
1913	94.1				
1924	100.0	100.0	100.0	100.0	100.0
1929	112.7	105.6	102.5	106.7	107.7
1930	113.8	103.8	102.5	109.6	110.1
1935	129.3	112.1	105.0	115.3	117.8
1937	142.7	119.7	107.5	119.2	123.3
1948	168.9	122.4	101.8	138.0	146.4
1951	177.5	136.2	117.2	130.3	136.7

Sources: Output: Lomax (1959: 193); Employment: 1907–24: *Historical Record of the Census of Production*, 2–3; 1924–51: Feinstein (1972: T130); Capital: Feinstein (1972: T101).

slower than for manufacturing as a whole, at 3.4 per cent per annum. Labour productivity and TFP growth were both relatively slow, at 1.4 per cent and 1.6 per cent per annum, respectively. The aggregate trends, however, mask relatively stagnant output and productivity in drink, offset by respectable output and productivity growth in food and tobacco (Dowie, 1969: 76).

Brewing

The First World War had a very serious effect on the output of the brewing industry, as is apparent from table 11.39. Output declined to about a third of its prewar level by 1918, measured in terms of standard barrels of 1055°, although the decline was less severe when measured in bulk barrels, since the average gravity was reduced. The reduction in the quantity of beer and the dilution of its strength arose both from official concern about drunkenness among munitions workers and pressure on the supply of materials. Lloyd George claimed in a speech at Bangor in February 1915 that

Drink is doing us more damage in the war than all the German submarines put together ... We are fighting Germany, Austria and Drink; and as far as I can see the greatest of these three deadly foes is Drink. (Gourvish and Wilson, 1994: 318)

The pressure on materials arose from the fact that they took up scarce shipping space if imported and used up land and labour if grown domestically (Vaizey, 1960: 23). Drastic measures were taken· by the government, including heavy excise increases, severe restrictions on licensing hours, an Output of Beer (Restriction) Act, a Compulsory Dilution Order, and even

Table 11.39. *Effects of the First World War on UK beer production,* *1913–20*

	Standard barrelage (m)	Bulk barrelage (m)	Bulk as % of standard	Average gravity (degrees)
1913	36.1	37.6	104	1052.80
1914	33.1	34.8	105	1052.35
1915	30.3	32.1	106	1051.88
1916	26.6	30.2	113	1048.54
1917	13.8	19.1	138	1039.81
1918	12.9	23.3	180	1030.55
1919	25.1	35.0	140	1039.41
1920	26.7	34.5	129	1042.61

Notes: Data on a financial year basis, e.g. 1919=year to 31 March 1920; Data for United Kingdom including Ireland.
Source: Gourvish and Wilson (1994: 320).

Table 11.40. *Output and consumption of beer in the United Kingdom,* *1919–51*

	Bulk output (000 bl)	Standard output (000 bl)	Average gravity (degrees)	Consumption per head (gal)
1919	31,543	22,604	1039.41	19.34
1924	26,827	20,954	1042.97	17.82
1929	25,062	19,551	1042.90	16.28
1930	23,900	18,488	1042.54	15.47
1932	17,950	12,899	1039.52	10.73
1935	21,970	16,387	1041.02	13.44
1937	24,206	18,056	1041.02	13.44
1948	26,990	16,410	1033.43	12.1
1951	25,156	16,959	1037.07	12.5

Notes: Data on a financial year basis, e.g. 1919=year to 31 March 1920; Consumption figures based on standard output; Consumption data after 1938 based on Net Duty Paid; Data for United Kingdom excluding Eire.
Source: Gourvish and Wilson (1994: 618–19).

nationalisation of licensed houses in some areas (Vaizey, 1960: 21–3). Nevertheless, despite the upheaval, brewing profits remained high as prices were raised to offset the decline in volume (Gourvish and Wilson, 1994: 330–5).

Consumption figures in table 11.40 show a further decline in the demand for beer during the 1920s and despite a recovery from 1932, prewar levels of output were not regained. The industry was thus faced with excess capacity and the need for rationalisation between the wars. The fall in demand can be explained by the effect of higher excise duties on the real price of beer, the growth of alternative leisure opportunities and the loss of 700,000 prime age males during the war (Gourvish and Wilson, 1994: 336–41). Strategies to deal with the situation included brewery amalgamations, advertising campaigns and investment in public house improvements. Concentration increased throughout the interwar period as the number of brewers fell from 2,464 in 1921 to 1,502 in 1928 and 840 in 1939 (Gourvish and Wilson, 1994: 346). In addition to the individual advertising campaigns of the individual companies, the Brewers' Society launched a collective advertising campaign in 1933 with the slogan 'Beer is Best' (Gourvish and Wilson, 1994: 352). Investment in pub improvements was helpful in countering the nationalisation lobby as well as offering better facilities to tempt consumers away from alternative leisure pursuits (Gourvish and Wilson, 1994: 418–37).

Conditions during the Second World War were in some ways similar to conditions during the First World War. There were shortages of raw materials and labour, higher taxation and pervasive government controls and higher prices (Gourvish and Wilson, 1994: 356). Nevertheless, there were also important differences. In contrast to the swingeing controls on output during the First World War from government leaders sympathetic to the temperance cause, the Second World War saw official sanctioning of the maintenance of the supply of beer to the armed forces, with the Brewers' Society establishing a Beer for Troops Committee in 1942 (Gourvish and Wilson, 1994: 359). As a result, the volume of output grew from 24.7 million bulk barrels in 1938 to 32.7 million in 1945, although the increase was much less in terms of standard barrels as the average gravity declined (Gourvish and Wilson, 1994: 360).

The figures in table 11.41 suggest that labour productivity in the British brewing industry fell across the First World War and then stagnated with the further decline in output. This could be taken to support the view that the interwar brewing industry was a quiescent, conservative and generally unenterprising backwater, facing no major technological changes and cushioned by its tied trade (Turner, 1969: 271). However, as Gourvish and Wilson (1994: 378, 389) note, the larger firms increasingly recruited from outside the founding families and professionalised executive management, while the smaller firms must have required some enterprise to survive and prosper in a declining market. International comparisons of labour productivity in table 11.42 continue to show the British brewing industry in a favourable light between the wars. Although no comparison with the United States is possible during the 1920s due to Prohibition, the American

Table 11.41. *Output and employment in the British brewing industry, 1907–48 (1924=100)*

	Output	Employment	Labour productivity
1907	149.7	125.9	118.9
1913	156.3		
1924	100.0	100.0	100.0
1930	94.3	93.8	100.5
1935	81.3	85.3	95.3
1948	108.0	106.8	101.1

Sources: Output: 1907–24: Hoffmann (1965: table 54B); 1924–35: *Census of Production for 1935*, part III, 180; 1935–48: Brown (1954: vii); Employment: 1907–24: *Historical Record of the Census of Production*, 8–9; 1924–35: *Census of Production for 1935*, part III, 176; 1935–48: Brown (1954: vii).

Table 11.42. *Comparative labour productivity in food, drink and tobacco 1925/24 to 1947/48 (UK=100)*

US/UK	1925/24	1929/30	1937/35	1947/48
Grain milling	212	206	173	194
Biscuits		352	345	204
Fish curing	46	39	50	95
Butter & cheese	266	239		
Sugar				128
Beet sugar	108	95	102	97
Cocoa/sugar confection.	307	273		
Margarine	104	145	152	121
Manufactured ice	263	172	219	75
Brewing & malting			201	198
Tobacco	127	134	160	

Germany/UK	1924	1930	1935
Beet sugar			33
Margarine			52
Brewing & malting			62
Tobacco	27		26

Source: Appendix tables A2.1, A2.2.
Notes: US/UK figures based on output per operative; Germany/UK figures based on output per employee.

Table 11.43. *Output, potable consumption and exports of the UK spirits industry, 1913–35 (000 proof gal)*

	Distilled	Potable retained for consumption	Exports
1913	46,693	25,286	9,984
1918	37,141	10,325	5,132
1924	37,323	12,897	8,032
1929	34,790	11,272	7,381
1930	40,669	10,630	8,247
1932	30,447	8,855	5,779
1935	51,839	8,344	5,898

Note: Figures from 1924 exclude Eire.
Source: Wilson (1940: 350).

productivity lead in the 1930s remained relatively low, while the Anglo-German comparison for 1935 suggests that the German brewing industry can hardly be seen as a model of efficiency.

Spirits

The First World War had a serious impact on the British spirit distilling industry. As in brewing, pressures to curtail the production of potable (or drinkable) spirits, principally whisky, arose from problems of drunkenness among industrial workers and shortages of materials (Daiches, 1976: 112). However, the serious decline in the production of potable spirits was to some extent offset by an increase in industrial alcohol, so that the fall in the total volume of spirits distilled was much less, as can be seen in table 11.43.

The downward trend in the domestic demand for whisky and other spirits which had been apparent since 1900 continued during the 1920s and 1930s. Although the industry had been successful in increasing exports in the decade before the First World War, there were limits to further expansion in overseas markets in the interwar period due to Prohibition in the United States and growing taxation and protection world-wide (Weir, 1989: 379). The response of the whisky industry to these trends was a combination of rationalisation and diversification. In 1925 Buchanan–Dewar and John Walker & Sons amalgamated with the Distillers Company Limited (DCL). This was the second largest merger by value in British manufacturing between the wars and made DCL the sixth largest manufacturer by market valuation in 1930 (Weir, 1989: 381). DCL were also successful in

Table 11.44. *Output and employment in the British spirit distilling industry, 1907–48 (1924=100)*

	Output	Employment	Labour productivity
1907	124.6	134.4	92.7
1913	135.1		
1924	100.0	100.0	100.0
1930	83.5	74.4	112.2
1935	117.6	66.3	177.4
1948	148.1	87.8	168.7

Sources: Output: 1907–24: Hoffmann (1965: table 54B); 1924–35: *Census of Production for 1935*, part III, 192; 1935–48: Brown (1954: vii); Employment: 1907–35: *Census of Production for 1907*, 527; *Census of Production for 1935*, part III, 176; 1935–48: Brown (1954: vii).

diversifying into alcohol-based and yeast-based chemicals as the demand for whisky fell. This successful diversification into related product areas, based on the application of scientific knowledge, the benefits of large scale and marketing skills, contrasts with the failed diversification at Mackie & Co. into a bizarre range of products including 'Highland tweeds, carragheen moss, concrete slabs and partitions and a branded flour sold under the initials "B.B.M", which allegedly stood for "Brain, bones and muscle"' (Weir, 1989: 383).

The output growth of the spirit distilling industry shown in table 11.44 was due largely to the growth of the demand for industrial alcohol as a feedstock for the chemical industry (Weir, 1989: 383). The rapid output growth of the 1930s was accompanied by an even more rapid rise in labour productivity, fully justifying Weir's (1989: 393) claim that the significant changes in the organisation, technology and composition of output in the distilling industry have been masked by aggregative work on the drink industry as a whole. Although there are no available comparative labour productivity data for spirit distilling, largely due to the disruption caused by American Prohibition, it seems likely that the British industry at least maintained its favourable pre-1914 position, given its own rapid labour productivity growth.

Tobacco

Tobacco consumption per head of population rose during the First World War, providing a boost to morale for soldiers and civilians. One padre, the

Table 11.45. *Sales of tobacco in the United Kingdom, 1907–51*

	Total sales (m lb)	Cigarette sales (m lb)	Consumption per head (lb)
1907	97.6	29.9	2.23
1913	104.1	45.5	2.28
1924	135.9	75.1	3.03
1929	155.8	101.4	3.41
1930	161.0	107.1	3.51
1935	173.9	126.9	3.71
1937	192.5	146.9	4.07
1948	226.9	183.9	4.54
1951	228.5	191.0	4.54

Sources: Tobacco Sales: Alford (1973: 476–7); Population: Feinstein (1972: T121).

Reverend G.A. Studdert-Kennedy earned the nickname 'Woodbine Willie' as he discovered among the carnage and suffering of the trenches that a Woodbine could often provide more immediate comfort than a prayer (Alford, 1973: 322). Tobacco consumption continued to rise throughout the first half of the twentieth century, as can be seen in table 11.45. There was also a steady rise in the proportion of tobacco being sold as cigarettes. In these favourable conditions output and productivity grew rapidly, as can be seen in table 11.46. Labour productivity growth of 2.8 per cent per annum during 1924–37 and TFP growth of 2.6 per cent per annum were above the average for manufacturing.

During the interwar period the British market continued to be dominated by Imperial, although within Imperial, Wills' Woodbines lost some ground to Player's Weights. Wills also faced growing competition from Godfrey Phillips, Carreras and J. Wix and Sons outside Imperial (Alford, 1973: 334–335). In addition to cutting prices, the new competitors issued coupons and cigarette cards. Although Imperial initially held aloof from coupon schemes, by 1932 they were forced to respond with the introduction of a coupon brand, Four Aces (Alford, 1973: 350). By the end of 1933, however, Imperial and the six next largest manufacturers had signed the Martin Agreement which ended coupon trading and moved towards the maintenance of retail prices (Alford, 1973: 352).

The comparative labour productivity figures in table 11.42 suggest that tobacco continued to be one of Britain's best performing industries between the wars. Productivity in Britain was substantially higher than in Germany

Table 11.46. *Output, employment and capital in the British tobacco industry, 1907–51 (1924=100)*

	Output	Employment	Capital	Labour productivity	TFP
1907	59.7	91.9		65.0	
1913	69.9				
1924	100.0	100.0	100.0	100.0	100.0
1929	130.2	112.9	106.3	115.3	117.6
1930	131.8	113.1	106.3	116.5	118.8
1935	136.9	105.9	112.5	129.3	126.8
1937	155.7	108.1	118.8	144.0	139.8
1948	184.5	119.1		154.9	
1951	191.0	113.0		169.0	

Sources: Output: Lomax (1959: 93); Employment: 1907–24 and 1937–51: *Historical Record of the Census of Production*, 10–11; 1924–37: Chapman (1953: 100); Capital: Feinstein (1965: 123).

where production continued to be organised on a very small scale (Broadberry and Fremdling, 1990: 415). Although the United States pulled ahead of Britain during the 1920s and 1930s, the scale of the US lead remained relatively small. Although it seems likely that the volume of tobacco processed per worker was substantially higher in the United States in the specialised cigarette branch due to greater standardisation, the British industry benefited by facing demand patterns more oriented towards cigarettes (Rostas, 1948a: 206). Only as US demand became more dominated by cigarettes did the productivity gap become large.

Grain milling

Total output of the grain milling industry grew slowly during the first half of the twentieth century, as can be seen in table 11.47. Indeed, the output of the principal product, wheat flour, stagnated at about 3.9 million tons per annum (Edwards, 1948: 28). Overall growth was dependent on rapid expansion in the less important animal feedstuffs, maize, barley and rice products (*Census of Production for 1935*, part III: 32). The stagnation in the demand for flour can be seen in turn as a result of stagnation in the demand for bread, a product with a negative income elasticity of demand (Maunder, 1970: 15–18).

The First World War interrupted the trend towards concentration in large- scale port mills since the supply of imported wheat was disrupted and country mills received a boost as a result of inland transport restrictions

Table 11.47 *Output and employment in the British grain milling industry, 1907–48 (1924=100)*

	Output	Employment	Labour productivity
1907	83.6	97.1	86.1
1913	89.5		
1924	100.0	100.0	100.0
1930	94.3	87.7	107.5
1935	113.6	99.7	113.9
1948	99.3	90.3	110.0

Sources: Output: 1907–24: Hoffmann (1965: table 54B); 1924–35: *Census of Production for 1935*, part III, 32; 1935–48: Brown (1954: vii); Employment: 1907–24: *Historical Record of the Census of Production*, 2–3; 1924–35: *Census of Production for 1935*, part III, 23; 1935–48: Brown (1954: vii).

(Smith, 1940: 21–2). This led to a problem of excess capacity between the wars and the need for rationalisation. Although the National Association of British and Irish Millers attempted to regulate prices during the 1920s, the scheme met with little success. Only after the elimination of many of the weaker firms were the large producers able in 1929 to form an effective cartel, the Millers' Mutual Association (Musson, 1978: 329). Although the Cooperative Wholesale Society (CWS) remained outside, the cartel embraced the two major producers, Ranks and Spillers, and covered about 80 per cent of flour output by 1939 (Edwards, 1948: 52). The Millers' Mutual Association operated a quota scheme and bought up and closed down redundant capacity. These measures were reflected in the rising margin of the average ex-mill flour price over the average imported wheat price, with the margin expressed as a percentage of the wheat price doubling from 16 per cent in 1929 to 32 per cent in 1938 (Edwards, 1948: 56).

Concentration in grain milling was growing throughout the interwar period as Ranks and Spillers expanded. However, Chandler (1990: 370) argues that whereas Spillers effectively rationalised their acquisitions, Ranks allowed many of their smaller mills to carry on much as before, with little effective reorganisation. Furthermore, the process of concentration was reversed across the Second World War due to the bombing of the major port mills (Evely and Little, 1960: 289). Although there were some pressures to integrate vertically into baking to secure tied outlets, as in brewing, this occurred only on a small scale in the interwar flour industry (Maunder, 1970: 23).

Labour productivity growth in grain milling was relatively slow between the wars, as can be seen in table 11.47. Nevertheless, the data in table 11.42 suggest that the British industry held its own against the US industry, with the comparative labour productivity position in the late 1930s on a par with the position before the First World War. The small deterioration in the British productivity performance during both world wars would be expected given the adverse effects on the port mills.

Sugar refining

In contrast to the demand for flour-based products, the demand for sugar and sugar-based products such as jam, syrup and confectionery grew rapidly during the first half of the twentieth century (Smith, 1940: 203). Furthermore, British sugar refiners were well placed to meet that rising demand after the dramatic changes in government policy across the First World War. Before the war, Britain had adopted a free trade stance, in the belief that sugar would always be cheap and abundant (Chalmin, 1990: 158). The outbreak of war showed the disadvantages of being dependent on imports from Continental Europe. A Royal Commission on Sugar Supplies was created and took control of sugar supplies and the domestic refining industry (Chalmin, 1990: 117). Early panic buying by the Commission raised world prices, and since Britain was cut off from the major beet sugar-producing countries, the refiners faced problems in switching to cane sugar, which is harder to filter and has lower yields (Chalmin, 1990: 123).

Between the wars all governments followed a policy of encouraging raw sugar supplies from the Empire through Imperial Preference and even subsidising domestic beet sugar production (Chalmin, 1990: 159). Furthermore, the government gave its blessing to the merger in 1921 between the two major producers, Henry Tate and Sons and Abram Lyle and Sons, to create a major force on the world sugar market (Chalmin, 1990: 132). From 1928, the British refiners received tariff protection, and even benefited from export bounties in a complete turn-round from the pre-1914 period, when they had campaigned against German and Austrian bounties (Chalmin, 1990: 184).

Tate and Lyle also moved from refining into beet sugar production before the beet sugar producers were effectively nationalised in 1936 with the formation of the British Sugar Corporation (Chalmin, 1990: 177). They then turned their attention to the acquisition of raw cane sugar in the West Indies (Hugill, 1978: 111). Tate and Lyle also acquired interests in transport in an attempt to integrate their complex overland transport system (Chalmin, 1990: 203). As Chalmin (1990: 211) notes, however, the firm remained very traditional in terms of its financial management and the

Table 11.48. *Output and employment in the British sugar industry, 1907–48 (1924=100)*

	Output	Employment	Labour productivity
1907	63.4	51.2	123.8
1913	88.8		
1924	100.0	100.0	100.0
1930	181.6	134.1	135.4
1935	204.1	131.0	155.8
1948	226.3	134.2	168.6

Sources: Output: 1907–24: Hoffmann (1965: table 54B); 1924–35: *Census of Production for 1935*, part III, 136; 1935–48: Brown (1954: vii); Employment: 1907–24: *Historical Record of the Census of Production*, 4–5; 1924–35: *Census of Production for 1935*, part III, 131; 1935–48: Brown (1954: vii).

human side of its management. Indeed, it seems clear that contrary to the strictures of Chandler, the company strengthened the role of the founding families in the business (Chalmin, 1990: 211). Despite this, table 11.48 suggests that the British sugar refining industry experienced rapid output and labour productivity growth between the wars, while table 11.42 shows British labour productivity well ahead of German levels and on a par with levels in the United States. Clearly M-form managerial structures were not essential for good performance.

The Second World War saw a resumption of government control in the sugar industry, this time in a more orderly fashion than at the start of the First World War. In line with prewar planning, a Ministry of Food was set up at the outbreak of war, with a Sugar Division to maintain supplies and supervise a rationing scheme for sugar consumption (Chalmin, 1990: 220).

Biscuits and confectionery

The British biscuit industry exhibited rapid growth during the interwar period, as can be seen in table 11.49. This growth was based largely on the home market, as the export trade, which had been dominated by Huntley and Palmers of Reading, never regained prewar levels (Corley, 1972: 220). Although output growth was rapid, labour productivity grew only slowly between the wars. Even the major national producers such as Associated Biscuit Manufacturers Ltd (formed in 1921 from a merger between Huntley and Palmers and Peek Freans), Jacobs, Crawfords, Macfarlane Lang and McVitie & Price, tended to produce a huge range of highly

Table 11.49. *Output and employment in the British biscuit industry, 1924–48 (1924=100)*

	Output	Employment	Labour productivity
1924	100.0	100.0	100.0
1930	130.2	129.9	100.2
1933	152.8	136.6	111.9
1934	173.6	149.5	116.1
1935	188.7	158.3	119.2
1948	231.1	109.2	211.6

Sources: Output and employment: 1924–35: *Census of Production for 1935*, part III, 55, 58; 1935–48: Brown (1954: vii).

differentiated products which set limits to the gains from mechanisation (Corley, 1972: 174, 238–43). Accordingly, the data in table 11.42 show a relatively large US labour productivity advantage during the 1930s. However, the dramatic improvement in British labour productivity across the Second World War shown in table 11.49 resulted in a substantial improvement in Britain's comparative productivity position by 1947/48. As Corley (1972: 243) notes, the wartime experience showed what vast economies postwar biscuit manufacturers could hope to achieve through standardisation and concentration of production, although the limited and austere range of wartime biscuits could not be maintained once peace returned.

Output of the British cocoa, chocolate and sugar confectionery industry also grew rapidly between the wars, as shown in table 11.50. Although labour productivity also grew rapidly, table 11.42 shows that British labour productivity levels were low compared with the United States in this industry. This partly reflects the fact that small companies were very important in sugar confectionery to set alongside the large companies like British Chocolate and Cocoa Ltd, (formed in 1919 from a merger between Cadbury and Fry) and Rowntree in cocoa and chocolate manufactures (Leak and Maizels, 1945: 193). However, it also reflects the large variety of differentiated products produced even by the large manufacturers. Thus Cadbury Brothers noted the much more rapid labour productivity growth in block chocolate than in assortments between the wars and the large wartime savings from the reduction in the number of lines and packings from 237 in 1939 to 29 in 1942 (Cadbury Brothers, n.d.: 16, 39).

Table 11.50. *Output and employment in the British chocolate and sugar confectionery industry, 1907–48 (1924=100)*

	Output	Employment	Labour productivity
1907	43.7	76.1	57.4
1913	51.3		
1924	100.0	100.0	100.0
1930	113.2	93.6	120.9
1935	147.1	95.4	154.2
1948	123.1	69.6	176.9

Sources: Output: 1907–24: Hoffmann (1965: table 54B); 1924–35: *Census of Production for 1935*, part III, 71; 1935–48: Brown (1954: vii); Employment: 1907–24: *Historical Record of the Census of Production*, 6–7; 1924–35: *Census of Production for 1935*, part III, 66; 1935–48: Brown (1954: vii).

Table 11.51. *Output of dairy products and margarine in Britain, 1924–35 (000 cwt)*

	Butter	Cheese	Margarine
1924	723.0	80.0	3,663.5
1930	1,025.5	386.6	4,033.0
1933	1,191.3	391.2	3,451.4
1934	1,534.1	536.0	3,036.5
1935	1,722.8	719.5	3,528.2

Sources: Census of Production for 1935, part III, 120.

Dairy produce and margarine

Despite rising demand, British butter and cheese manufacturing had been declining rapidly before the First World War due to the availability of cheaper imports from the Empire and Scandinavia (Taylor, 1976: 590–1). Although production on the farm from surplus milk had continued into the 1920s, during the 1930s manufacturers received a boost from the differential pricing policy of the Milk Marketing Board, with the price of milk for manufacturing sometimes little more than one-third of the liquid wholesale price (Smith, 1940: 41). The rapid growth of output during the 1930s can be seen in table 11.51. Nevertheless, by 1938 imports still made

Table 11.52. *Output of canned and bottled fruits and vegetables in Britain, 1924–35 (000 cwt)*

	Fruits in syrup	Fruits without sugar	Vegetables	Total
1924	58	59	40	157
1930	190	125	314	629
1932	484	205	945	1,634
1934	417	158	1,345	1,920
1935	363	103	1,532	1,998

Sources: Reader (1976: 68); *Census of Production for 1935*, part III, 84–5.

up more than 90 per cent of butter and 75 per cent of cheese consumption (Smith, 1940: 48). The figures in table 11.42 show that the small British butter and cheese manufacturing industry was not a good performer in labour productivity terms compared with the United States.

The growing availability of cheap butter inevitably hit the margarine industry, where output fell during the 1930s, as can be seen in table 11.51. The pressure of this competition from butter was an important factor behind the rationalisation of margarine production in Britain, beginning with the formation in 1929 of Unilever from Lever Brothers and the two major Dutch producers, Jurgens and van den Berghs, and culminating in the closure of half of the 10 Unilever plants in Britain between 1930 and 1937 (Wilson, 1954, vol.I: 336). The British margarine industry was thus a relatively good labour productivity performer, as the figures in table 11.42 show. British labour productivity was nearly twice the German level in 1935, and never lagged too far behind the United States.

Other processed foods

The British food canning industry grew very rapidly between the wars, with the number of factories increasing from half a dozen to about 80 (Musson, 1978: 330). The output of canned and bottled fruits and vegetables rose from 157,000 hundredweight (cwt) in 1924 to nearly 2 million cwt by 1935, although as can be seen in table 11.52, most of the growth was in vegetables. In fruits, it was difficult to compete directly with imports from the tropics, although local canners built up a market for strawberries, raspberries, etc. and also packed imported fruit salad. In vegetables, growth was

Table 11.53. *Product structure of the UK and US fish curing industries, 1935–9 (%)*

	UK (1935)	US (1939)
Herring	72.6	29.6
Cod	13.6	15.3
Haddock	8.1	5.0
Salmon	0.2	15.2
Other	5.5	34.9

Source: Rostas (1948a: 220).

spectacular, particularly with processed peas (Reader, 1976: 69). Nevertheless, the British industry lagged quite a way behind its American counterpart, with the figures in appendix table A2.1 suggesting a US/UK comparative labour productivity ratio of 235 in 1950.

Fish curing stands out in table 11.42 as the only industry in which Britain consistently recorded higher labour productivity than in the United States. Table 11.53 shows that the British industry was heavily dominated by herring, whereas the American output was more varied. This confirms the importance of demand factors, since where there was less variety in Britain, British producers could have higher labour productivity. The British ice industry was also closely related to the fish industry and again, with no product differentiation, British producers could attain American labour productivity levels in 1947/48, as can be seen in table 11.42. The volatility of the comparative productivity position for this industry arose largely from cyclical fluctuations in the United States.

Conclusions

A good productivity performance in food and tobacco was offset to some extent by stagnation in drink. The problem in drink was caused largely by a decline in demand, which was itself the result of taxation and government regulation. Although output in Britain declined, however, in the United States a policy of Prohibition had an even more catastrophic effect. In food and tobacco, British firms continued to follow a successful strategy of adopting mass production methods to the extent that demand patterns allowed. Hence labour productivity gaps with the United States remained relatively small in most industries, and productivity was substantially higher than in Germany, where demand patterns prevented mass production and mass retailing.

Table 11.54. *Output and employment in the British paper industry, 1907–48 (1924=100)*

	Output	Employment	Labour productivity
1907	57.9	79.8	72.6
1913	75.0		
1924	100.0	100.0	100.0
1930	125.4	104.5	120.0
1935	169.5	116.6	145.4
1948	200.0	134.2	149.0

Sources: Output: 1907–24: Hoffmann (1965: table 54B);
1924–35: *Census of Production for 1935*, part IV.II, 19; 1935–48:
Brown (1954: vii); Employment: 1907–24: *Historical Record of
the Census of Production*, 66–7; 1924–35: *Census of Production
for 1935*, part IV.II, 11; 1935–48: Brown (1954: vii).

Miscellaneous industries

Paper

The paper industry experienced rapid growth during the first half of the twentieth century, as can be seen from table 11.54. This growth was in turn sparked off by the rapidly rising demand for newspapers, magazines and books being produced by the printing industry and the packaging revolution in the consumer goods industries (Musson, 1978: 333). As was noted in chapter 10, however, there is little doubt that Britain had lost her comparative advantage in paper production with the switch from rags to wood pulp as the basic raw material, and imports continued to rise (Reader, 1981: 351). Bowaters, which had transformed itself from a paper merchant into the largest British newsprint producer during the interwar period, invested in North American production capacity during the late 1930s.

During the Second World War British paper production was drastically reduced due to raw material shortages (Reader, 1981: 157). The decline in British production was exacerbated by the actions of the newspaper proprietors in persuading the government to import newsprint rather than pulp from Canada, to avoid giving Bowaters monopoly power (Reader, 1981: 160). With the loss of most of their newsprint business, Bowaters turned to making containers for war stores from kraft liner board (Reader, 1981: 165).

The comparative productivity position in paper and board between the wars remained much as it had been in the pre-First World War period, with

Table 11.55. *Comparative labour productivity in miscellaneous industries,*
1925/24 to 1947/48 (UK=100)

US/UK	1925/24	1929/30	1937/35	1947/48
Bricks	235	213	132	166
Glass containers	235	208	264	287
Cement	241	167	99	115
Paper & board	258	293	247	
Rubber tyres & tubes	353	337	285	176
Linoleum & oilcloth	197	231	170	
Germany/UK	*1924*	*1930*	*1935*	
Cement	99	109	87	
Rubber tyres & tubes			112	

Notes: US/UK figures based on output per operative; Germany/UK figures based on output
per employee.
Source: Appendix tables A2.1, A2.2.

a US labour productivity level 2½–3 times the British level, as can be seen
in table 11.55. Although the British industry produced a larger proportion
of newsprint Rostas' (1948a: 158) calculations of comparative output reval-
ued at British and American prices show that this had no significant effect
on the calculation of the comparative productivity position in the 1930s.

Cement and bricks

As was noted in chapter 10, the fortunes of the British building materials
industries such as cement and bricks have mirrored the fortunes of the
construction sector. The data in table 11.55 show the importance of cyclical fluctuations in the three countries for comparative labour productivity
levels. Whereas the British building industry benefited from a housing
boom during the 1930s, the American industry remained depressed from
the late 1920s and the German industry exhibited very low levels of activity during the 1920s and the first half of the 1930s (Kendrick, 1961: 498;
Hoffmann, 1965: 393). During the housing boom of the 1930s, the British
cement industry eliminated the labour productivity gap with the United
States and pulled ahead of Germany, while in bricks the US lead was substantially reduced.

Output trends in the British cement and brick industries were similar,
as can be seen in tables 11.56 and 11.57. However, whereas the expansion
of output brought enormous labour productivity gains in the cement

Table 11.56. *Output and employment in the British cement industry, 1907–48 (1924=100)*

	Output	Employment	Labour productivity
1907	89.1	108.3	81.9
1924	100.0	100.0	100.0
1930	149.1	81.4	183.2
1935	175.4	75.7	231.7
1948	251.0	75.6	332.0

Sources: Output: 1907–24: *Census of Production for 1907*, 753; 1924–35: *Census of Production for 1935*, part IV.I, 76; 1935–48: Brown (1954: vii); Employment: 1907–24: *Historical Record of the Census of Production*, 62–3; 1924–35: *Census of Production for 1935*, part IV.I, 73; 1935–48: Brown (1954: vii).

Table 11.57. *Output and employment in the British brick and fireclay industry, 1907–48 (1924=100)*

	Output	Employment	Labour productivity
1907	89.2	98.9	90.2
1924	100.0	100.0	100.0
1930	110.9	110.4	100.5
1935	156.3	134.5	116.2
1948	133.4	106.4	125.4

Sources: Output: 1907–24: Rostas (1948a: 117), taken from *Census of Production*; 1924–35: *Census of Production for 1935*, part IV.I, 37; 1935–48: Brown (1954: vii); Employment: 1907–35: Rostas (1948a: 117); 1935–48: Brown (1954: vii).

industry, labour productivity growth was rather more modest in bricks. This different productivity experience of the two industries can be related to demand and organisational factors. On the demand side, there were limits to the possibility of substituting the more easily produced Fletton (semi-dry) bricks for other types because of differences of appearance (Bowley, 1960: 166). And on the supply side, the London Brick Company appears to have acted as an effective price leader, allowing the survival of a large number of relatively inefficient small producers (Bowley, 1960: 189–90).

By contrast, cement was a relatively homogeneous product, and a period

Table 11.58. *Output and employment in the British glass industry, 1924–48 (1924=100)*

	Output	Employment	Labour productivity
1924	100.0	100.0	100.0
1930	116.1	107.3	108.2
1933	132.3	107.9	122.6
1934	150.0	118.0	127.1
1935	161.3	125.2	128.8
1948	317.4	167.6	189.4

Sources: Output: 1924–35: *Census of Production for 1935*, part IV.I, 64; 1935–48: Brown (1954: vii); Employment: 1924–35: *Census of Production for 1935*, part IV.I, 58; 1935–48: Brown (1954: vii).

of cut-throat price competition during the 1920s and early 1930s led to the elimination of inefficient plant before the industry was effectively cartelised in 1934 (Rostas, 1948b: 77; Cook, 1958a: 63–96). Hence, although the cartel was successful in raising profit margins, it did not result in the preservation of a long tail of low productivity firms (Broadberry and Crafts, 1992: 552). This example illustrates the importance of distinguishing between structure and conduct when examining competition. For although the cement industry had a more concentrated structure than the brick industry, its conduct before 1934 was more competitive.

Glass

The output of the glass industry grew rapidly during the 1930s with the booming construction and car industries, as can be seen in table 11.58. The flat glass industry was dominated by Pilkingtons between the wars, although their position was much weaker in sheet glass than in plate glass, where they were the only British producer. In plate glass Pilkingtons developed a continuous grinder so that the glass could pass under a series of grinding heads instead of being bedded down on a circular grinding table. In addition, a continuous flow process was developed in liaison with the Ford Motor Company in America, with a continuous flow direct from the tank to replace the casting of plate glass from pots (Cook, 1958b: 304). Sales trends in panel *A* of table 11.59 show steady growth in exports as well as home sales during the 1920s, but increasing dependence on the home market during the 1930s. Even with a modest tariff, however, imports continued to grow during the 1930s (Barker, 1977a: 253).

Table 11.59. *Pilkingtons' glass sales and UK imports of glass,*
1920–37 (000 sq ft)

A. Plate glass	Home sales	Exports	Total sales	Imports
1920	6,440	3,458	9,898	6,924
1924	8,689	8,830	17,519	7,260
1929	14,852	10,638	25,490	10,351
1930	13,111	9,609	22,720	7,966
1935	17,434	5,552	22,986	14,559
1937	19,088	6,139	25,227	15,835
B. Sheet glass	Home sales	Exports	Total sales	Imports
1920	51,801	12,178	63,979	34,601
1924	43,560	16,491	60,051	51,246
1929	39,298	10,072	49,370	88,786
1930	37,946	6,281	44,227	93,155
1935	75,744	13,946	89,690	90,093
1937	84,977	20,687	105,664	94,881

Source: Barker (1977a: 251, 254).

In sheet glass, Pilkingtons were in a much weaker position, being slow to introduce the flat-drawn process to replace the cylindrical-drawn process, which required cylinders to be opened and flattened (Cook, 1958b: 298). After losing sales during the 1920s, particularly to Belgian imports, Pilkingtons improved their position after they began to work the Pittsburgh Plate Glass patents for drawing flat glass in 1930. The improvement in Pilkingtons' position in sheet glass is clearly visible in the sales trends in panel *B* of table 11.59, with home sales and exports increasing rapidly and imports stabilising.

Although there are no comparative labour productivity figures for the flat glass section of the industry between the wars, US/UK data on the glass container section are available in table 11.55. This section accounted for about one-third of the value of glass output in both countries. Rostas' (1948a: 166) figures suggest that the substantially lower labour productivity in Britain was associated with the existence of a large number of small plants with less than 100 employees. Again, the larger scale of activity in the American industry is suggestive of the economies of standardisation.

Table 11.60. *Output and employment in the British rubber industry, 1907–48 (1924=100)*

	Output	Employment	Labour productivity
1907	54.7	49.7	110.1
1913	91.2		
1924	100.0	100.0	100.0
1930	192.1	109.8	175.0
1935	263.2	117.0	225.0
1948	487.0	187.7	259.5

Sources: Output: 1907–24: Hoffmann (1965: table 54B); 1924–35: *Census of Production for 1935*, part III, 471; 1935–48: Brown (1954: vii); Employment: 1907–24: *Historical Record of the Census of Production*, 70–1; 1924–35: *Census of Production for 1935*, part III, 461; 1935–48: Brown (1954: vii).

Rubber

Output of rubber products grew rapidly from the early twentieth century, as can be seen in table 11.60. The rise of the car created what Woodruff (1955: 382) describes as a new phase in the history of the industry, and just as Britain lagged behind the United States in the motor vehicle industry, so a transatlantic gap opened up in the rubber industry. Woodruff (1955: 380) shows a US labour productivity advantage of more than 3:1 during the 1920s, when tyres and tubes accounted for a much larger proportion of American output. In the United States, tyres and tubes accounted for 74 per cent of the value of gross output in 1914, rising to 87 per cent in 1919 before falling to 73 per cent in 1925. In Britain, by contrast, the share of tyres and tubes was 38 per cent in 1912 and 44 per cent in 1924 (Woodruff, 1955: 385). Although this difference in product structure had largely disappeared by the mid-1930s, however, the productivity gap remained, suggesting that it was more than simply a product composition effect.

In fact, it is clear from the figures in table 11.55 that there was also a substantial US labour productivity advantage in tyres and tubes, which is attributed by Donnithorne (1958: 52–3) to the greater size of the American home market, coupled with the greater degree of standardisation in the United States. Fort Dunlop, for example, produced around 400 different types and sizes in the early 1950s, and this after a period of standardisation (Donnithorne, 1958: 53).

The importance of market demand in explaining the Anglo-American

Table 11.61. *Output and employment in the British linoleum and oilcloth industry, 1924–48 (1924=100)*

	Output	Employment	Labour productivity
1924	100.0	100.0	100.0
1930	98.6	104.0	94.8
1933	120.8	97.6	123.8
1934	134.7	98.3	137.0
1935	138.9	100.8	137.8
1948	146.4	98.9	148.0

Sources: Output: 1924–35: *Census of Production for 1935*, part III, 535; 1935–48: Brown (1954: vii); Employment: 1924–35: *Census of Production for 1935*, part III, 530; 1935–48: Brown (1954: vii).

productivity gap is also suggested by the similarity of labour productivity levels in Britain and Germany in 1935, shown in table 11.55. Furthermore, although the principal British producer, Dunlop, has been criticised for a lacklustre performance between the wars, both at home and abroad, much of the output produced in Britain came from multi-national companies that set up after the imposition of a 33.3 per cent tariff in 1927 (McMillan, 1989: 52–76; Jones, 1984: 52). These included the American companies Goodyear and Firestone, as well as Michelin from France and Pirelli from Italy (Donnithorne, 1958: 49).

Linoleum and oilcloth

Output and labour productivity grew rapidly in the British linoleum and oilcloth industry during the housing boom of the 1930s, having stagnated during the 1920s, as can be seen in table 11.61. Furthermore, the data in table 11.55 suggest that the labour productivity gap between Britain and the United States was significantly reduced during the 1930s. However, a cartel was established in 1934, in the form of the Linoleum and Floorcloth Manufacturers' Association. The common price system, which continued into the post-Second World War period, led to a referral to the Monopolies and Restrictive Practices Commission in 1953. Although the 1956 *Report on the Supply of Linoleum* argued that the common price scheme had not operated against the public interest, the deterioration in the comparative productivity position across the Second World War casts doubt on this conclusion.

Conclusions

A number of industries in the miscellaneous sector examined here show strong cyclical links to the construction industry. This includes cement, bricks, glass and even linoleum, which received a strong boost from the housing boom of the 1930s. There were nevertheless different supply side responses, depending on the organisation of the industries. Collusion under the price leadership of the London Brick Company limited productivity gains in the brick industry, in contrast to cement, where a period of cut-throat price competition eliminated inefficient producers before a cartel was established in the mid-1930s. There was also rapid productivity growth in linoleum, where a cartel was established only in 1934. In the rubber industry, the rise of the car created a new phase, with a surge in demand for rubber tyres and tubes. A strong US labour productivity lead developed as a result of both the greater proportion of the industry devoted to tyres and the greater standardisation of demand within the tyre section in the United States.

Econometric analysis

The above case studies can be complemented by an econometric investigation of the cross-sectional variation in comparative labour productivity for an Anglo-American sample from the 1930s. Following the approach set out in Broadberry and Crafts (1990a, 1992), we begin with a Cobb–Douglas production function and take logarithms:

$$\ln Q = \ln A + \alpha_1 \ln K + \alpha_2 \ln L \qquad (11.1)$$

where Q, K and L are output, capital and labour, respectively, and A is the efficiency parameter. Subtracting $\ln L$ from both sides and manipulating (11.1) gives us labour productivity as the dependent variable:

$$\ln Q - \ln L = \ln A + \alpha_1 (\ln K - \ln L) + (\alpha_1 + \alpha_2 - 1) \ln L \qquad (11.2)$$

Taking the difference between labour productivity in the United States and labour productivity in the United Kingdom yields:

$$\ln RELPROD = \ln RELA + \alpha_1 \ln RELCAP$$
$$+ (\alpha_1 + \alpha_2 - 1) \ln RELLAB \qquad (11.3)$$

where *RELPROD* is relative labour productivity, *RELA* relative efficiency, *RELLAB* relative employment and *RELCAP* relative capital per worker. This formulation allows an explicit consideration of the impact of capital intensity through *RELCAP* and also scale effects through *RELLAB*. If human capital is included as a separate factor endowment, we arrive at the specification:

$$\ln RELPROD = \ln RELA + \alpha_1 \ln RELCAP$$
$$+ \alpha_3 \ln RELHUMCAP + (\alpha_1 + \alpha_2 + \alpha_3 - 1) \ln RELLAB \quad (11.4)$$

where *RELHUMCAP* is relative human capital on a per worker basis. The approach taken so far focuses on factor endowments and scale as the key determinants of relative labour productivity. As was noted in chapter 9, however, many authors have stressed Britain's inadequate response to the challenge of the Second Industrial Revolution, with 'vested interests, established positions, and customary relations among firms and between employers and employees' limiting the possibilities of catch up growth (Abramovitz, 1986: 389). Capital and/or product market conditions must, of course, be permissive for such failure to persist. In this case it might be supposed that barriers to entry, collusion and strong unions would be important determinants of relatively weak performance in and slow catch up by British industry. These factors can be seen as affecting the relative efficiency term ln *RELA*:

$$\ln RELA = \beta_0 + \beta_1 \ln CR3 + \beta_2 \ln UNION + \beta_3 TARIFF \quad (11.5)$$

where *CR3* is the 3-firm concentration ratio, *UNION* is trade union density and *TARIFF* is the rate of protection, entered linearly because the tariff rate was zero in some industries. Note that these variables are included for the United Kingdom only, rather than on a relative US/UK basis. This reflects the fact that I do not wish to argue for a general relationship between relative labour productivity and relative concentration (nor protection, nor union density). Rather, I wish to allow for the possibility that, in British industries shielded from competitive forces, painful changes could be avoided and the process of catch up retarded. Substituting from (11.5) into (11.4) yields:

$$\ln RELPROD = \beta_0 + \alpha_1 \ln RELCAP + \alpha_3 \ln RELHUMCAP$$
$$+ (\alpha_1 + \alpha_2 + \alpha_3 - 1) \ln RELLAB + \beta_1 \ln CR3 + \beta_2 \ln UNION$$
$$+ \beta_3 TARIFF \quad (11.6)$$

This equation contains both factor endowments and competitive variables. In practice, the measurement of relative capital is difficult, so that relative power input (*RELPOWER*) is used as a proxy:

$$\ln RELPROD = \gamma_0 + \gamma_1 RELPOWER$$
$$+ \gamma_2 \ln RELHUMCAP + \gamma_3 RELLAB$$
$$+ \gamma_4 \ln CR3 + \gamma_5 \ln UNION + \gamma_6 TARIFF \quad (11.7)$$

This is the general specification used by Broadberry and Crafts (1992).

Turning to the issue of data, for relative labour productivity the 31-industry sample of Rostas (1948a) for 1937/35, which has already been

Table 11.62. *US/UK productivity regressions, 1937/35*

| | (1) | | (2) | |
Variable	Coeffi-cient	Std error	Coeff-cient	Std error
CONSTANT	−2.14	(0.92)	−0.92	(0.43)
ln RELPOWER	0.20	(0.15)		
ln RELHUMCAP	1.07	(0.42)	1.26	(0.35)
ln RELLAB	0.091	(0.12)		
ln CR3	0.29	(0.11)	0.24	(0.099)
ln UNION	0.33	(0.23)		
TARIFF	−0.00024	(0.0078)		
Adj. R^2		0.373		0.342
SE		0.412		0.423
N		31		31

Notes: The dependent variable is ln *RELPROD* (relative labour productivity). The method of estimation is ordinary least squares.
Source: Broadberry and Crafts (1992: 544).

discussed in chapter 2, was used. For the explanatory variables, the difficulty of measuring relative capital per worker has already been mentioned. As a proxy for machinery the ratio of power costs per operative converted at Rostas' purchasing power parity of £1 = $4.94 has been used. This was preferred to the alternative measure of horse-power per worker because the latest estimates for the latter in Britain were for 1930, after which the information was no longer gathered. For human capital data on earnings per operative from the censuses, converted in the same way have been used. The potential problems raised by the use of this variable will be examined when discussing the results. The scale variable is the ratio of US to UK employment, taken from Rostas (1948a).

In addition to these economic fundamentals of factor endowments and scale a number of variables have been included to capture the distortions to the competitive environment in Britain. These variables were not collected on a comparative basis, as discussed above. The 3-firm employment concentration ratio is taken from Leak and Maizels (1945), while the bargaining power of labour is captured by the trade union density from Bain and Price (1980). The nominal tariff rate is from Hutchinson (1965).

The results for an ordinary least squares estimation of (11.7) are reported in table 11.62. Positive signs would be expected on all variables. Greater US physical and human capital endowments should raise the US/UK labour productivity ratio, as should a greater US scale of operation. Barriers to competition in the form of a higher concentration ratio, higher tariffs and greater union density in the United Kingdom should also raise the US/UK productivity ratio.

Equation (1) in table 11.62 includes all the explanatory variables. The tariff variable (*TARIFF*) was incorrectly signed and statistically insignificant, whereas the power input (*RELPOWER*), scale (*RELLAB*) and union strength (*UNION*) variables were correctly signed but statistically insignificant. Hence a second equation (2) is also reported, that eliminates statistically insignificant variables, leaving a parsimonious specification that explains the variation of the US/UK productivity ratio across the sample in terms of human capital and concentration. The *F*-test for the validity of the restrictions necessary to move from (1) to (2) in table 11.62 is easily satisfied, with $F(4,24)$ equal to 2.78.

The correct interpretation of the human capital variable, which is measured by relative earnings, requires some discussion. It may be thought that the direction of causality runs from high productivity to high wages rather than vice versa (Carruth and Oswald, 1989). However, it should be noted that on that view, the relationship is between wages and revenue productivity. As Salter (1960) notes, over the period 1924–50 there was no correlation over time between growth in physical productivity and wages by industry; industries that grew faster had larger price falls, so that there was no extra revenue for workers to bargain over. As Salter notes, this would be expected with a unified market for labour. It should be stressed that the interpretation of (11.7) as a productivity rather than a wage equation hinges on the use of a single aggregate price ratio to compare wages in the two countries. If own product prices were used, this would indeed be a wage equation since, effectively, revenue productivity would be introduced.

Whereas Salter found no relationship between wages and physical productivity over time, the results in table 11.62 do suggest a strong relationship in an international comparison at a point in time. This is quite consistent with Salter's analysis, however, because Salter does not predict equal wages across industries. Rather, arbitrage ensures that differentials reflect human capital differences; workers with different skills are paid different wages. Although differentials may also be expected to reflect compensation for less agreeable jobs, this is unlikely to be important here because the same industries are being compared across countries. The role of unions in modifying wage differentials based on human capital is allowed for by the inclusion of the variable for trade union density. It therefore seems reasonable to use wage differentials as a proxy for human capital in a cross-section analysis.

The other significant variable is the concentration ratio, included to capture the effect of imperfect competition in product markets. An alternative specification using the price–cost margin instead of the concentration ratio produced very similar results.

Although the results from table 11.62 are suggestive of a role for factor endowments and the competitive environment in explaining the cross-sectional variation of the US/UK productivity gap in the 1930s, there is much that is left unexplained. The residuals are often large, and as can be seen from Broadberry and Crafts (1992: 543), these large residuals are usually associated with industries where the productivity ratio is a long way above or below the average. Hence the econometric approach should be seen as a complement to rather than a substitute for the case studies that have formed the bulk of this chapter. Issues such as the importance of mass production technology and the nature of competition, which are difficult to quantify, require a more detailed examination of the circumstances specific to each industry.

Conclusions

The years between 1914 and 1950 were highly disturbed, covering two world wars, a world slump of unprecedented severity and the collapse of the pre-First World War liberal international trading environment. British adjustment to the new circumstances took the form of an increase in dependence on Empire relations. Also, policies of protection and acceptance of collusion among firms were followed to counter the trend of falling prices. These policies undoubtedly enjoyed some success in the short run, limiting the impact of the world slump on Britain. However, they also had some adverse consequences in the long run, exacerbating problems of adjustment in the post-Second World War period.

Between the wars, there were further problems of adjustment to the innovations of the Second Industrial Revolution. The movement away from competition meant that pressures on firms to adjust were reduced, and the period is usually seen as one of failed rationalisation. Apart from a temporary cyclical narrowing during the slump of the 1930s, the US/UK labour productivity gap widened compared with the pre-1914 period. However, it should be noted that Germany also failed to close the gap on the United States in these turbulent times; Britain and Germany were much more evenly matched in manufacturing before the Second World War than a reader of Chandler (1990) would expect.

12 Changing markets and technology, 1950–1990

Introduction

British industry emerged from the Second World War highly dependent on home and Commonwealth markets, as was noted in chapter 7. The continued belief in the importance of the Commonwealth was an important part of the business environment in postwar Britain. It coloured the attitudes of businessmen, keen to return to the prewar cartels and to avoid direct competition with the United States and Germany. It also coloured the attitudes of politicians, who remained ambivalent about participation in supra-national European institutions such as the European Coal and Steel Community (ECSC) and the European Economic Community (EEC). Thus until Britain joined the EEC in 1973, British industry was to some extent shielded from international competition. Since anti-trust policy was also applied rather hesitantly during this period, domestic competition was also relatively restrained. The strengthening of competitive forces in Britain on both the international and domestic fronts during the 1970s and 1980s represents a major change in the business environment.

The Second World War also left its mark on technology in British industry. During the war, many British industrialists were brought face to face with the much higher labour productivity achieved in American industry, as the two economies were integrated in the Allied war effort. Wartime visits by British industrialists to the United States were followed up after the war by the Anglo-American Council on Productivity (AACP), which sponsored visits by productivity teams made up of managers and trade unionists in a wide range of industries. However, attempts to adopt American technology in British conditions were not very successful. As well as meeting the inevitable opposition of craft workers, who saw the value of their skills being eroded, American technology was unpopular with managers, who were not used to exercising the degree of shopfloor control required to make it profitable. The antagonistic industrial relations that emerged during this period of technological upheaval formed an important part of the postwar British industrial culture, and came to be seen as one of the major symptoms of the 'British disease' in the literature on economic decline.

These two problems of markets and technology came to a head in the 1970s. Although Imperial Preference had been removed and tariffs reduced under GATT during the 1950s and 1960s, EEC entry in 1973 produced a severe competitive shock. Industrial relations, which had been simmering throughout the postwar period, exploded in a wave of militancy. The situation was exacerbated by the oil shocks of 1973–4, when the price of oil was quadrupled, and 1979–80, when it was doubled again (known as OPEC I and II, respectively, after the international oil cartel). The increase in the price of a major input inevitably hit manufacturing profitability, already reeling from the effects of increased competition within the EEC. Furthermore, OPEC II had an additional damaging effect through exchange rate appreciation. Since Britain was a net exporter of oil by the end of the 1970s, the increase in the price of oil improved the current account of the balance of payments and hence put upward pressure on the pound (Bean, 1987).

After the recession of the early 1980s, British manufacturing emerged substantially reduced in size, but as the decade progressed, it became clear that much of the deterioration in comparative labour productivity that had occurred in the 1970s was being reversed. By the end of the 1980s, labour productivity in British manufacturing was once again approaching German levels. Manufacturing now accounts for about 20 per cent of employment in Britain, which is about average for Europe. Germany and Japan, with substantially larger shares of employment in manufacturing, are outliers in this respect.

The manufacturing industry that is now left in Britain achieves labour productivity levels close to the European average. Furthermore, there is evidence of a return to a more European approach to technology, with an emphasis on the skills of the labour force. The shake-out of labour that occurred during the recession of the early 1980s was largely unskilled. However, although there is now a renewed emphasis on shopfloor labour force skills, Britain still lags behind much of Continental Europe in the provision of intermediate level qualifications (Prais, 1993). Nevertheless, Britain now competes effectively in a number of skilled labour-intensive sectors, including general chemicals, pharmaceuticals, aerospace, motor vehicles and electronics.

Chemicals

Output, employment and capital stock trends for chemicals and allied products during the post-Second World War period are shown in table 12.1. The growth pattern in chemicals is in many ways typical of manufacturing as a whole, with a period of very rapid output and productivity growth to

Table 12.1. *Productivity in the British chemical industry, 1951–89*
(1973=100)

	Output	Employment	Capital	Labour productivity	TFP
1951	23.0	91.0	30.1	25.3	34.1
1954	28.8	97.7	36.6	29.5	38.5
1958	38.3	106.3	48.6	36.0	44.4
1963	55.3	108.2	63.8	51.1	59.0
1968	73.4	104.7	82.7	70.1	74.7
1973	100.0	100.0	100.0	100.0	100.0
1979	104.9	103.4	119.0	101.5	97.6
1986	116.4	80.0	138.3	145.5	125.5
1989	143.2	84.5		169.5	

Note: Industrial classification numbers: 1951–79: 1968 SIC Order V; 1979–89: 1980 SIC Groups 251–260.
Sources: Output and Employment: 1951–70: derived from *Historical Record of the Census of Production* and *Annual Abstract of Statistics*; 1970–89: derived from *Census of Production* and *Annual Abstract of Statistics*; Capital: derived from Oulton and O'Mahony (1994).

1973, followed by stagnation during 1973–9 and a strong recovery after 1979. However, output growth has been rather faster in chemicals than in total manufacturing during all three phases. Labour productivity also grew substantially faster in chemicals than in total manufacturing during 1951–73 and 1979–89. TFP growth performance has been better in chemicals than in total manufacturing in all three phases. Thus TFP growth was 4.9 per cent per annum in chemicals compared with 3.4 per cent in total manufacturing during 1951–73, −0.4 per cent per annum in chemicals compared with −0.9 per cent in total manufacturing during 1973–9, and 3.6 per cent per annum in chemicals compared with 1.9 per cent in total manufacturing during 1979–86.

General chemicals: ICI, the awakening giant?

The postwar British chemical industry continued to be dominated by ICI. Even with the growth of petrochemicals, the chemicals divisions of the major oil companies remained small relative to ICI. Thus Grant and Martinelli (1991: 81) note that during the early 1980s ICI still accounted for about 35 per cent of the output of the British chemical industry, while turnover at the chemicals division of BP, the next largest British producer, was less than one-fifth of turnover at ICI.

Pettigrew (1985) characterises ICI in the early postwar period as an underperforming large company, badly in need of a shake-up. First, with the break-up of the international cartels that dominated the industry between the wars, ICI needed to shift the distribution of its assets from the United Kingdom and the Empire and confront international competition directly in North America and Western Europe. Second, the company needed to become more market oriented in general. One manager in Mond Division told Pettigrew (1985: 333) that 'Marketing was sales control literally, we told the customer how much he could have and how much he would have to pay for the privilege of having the product'. Third, technology needed to be improved to best-practice levels, with the United States having emerged from the Second World War with a decisive technological lead. Fourth, there was a perception of the need to improve labour productivity in the British operations, particularly as a result of exposure to American methods via wartime economic cooperation and the early postwar Anglo-American Council on Productivity (AACP).

The AACP reports found substantially higher output per worker in the United States. In *Heavy Chemicals* (1953) labour productivity in the United States was estimated at between two and three times the British level (para. 25.2). The key factor singled out in the summary related to human capital; the team found that the Americans had one technically qualified man for every six workers while in Britain the ratio was one to 16 (para. 1.5). Unions and management both came in for criticism in the recommendations, in ways strongly linked to human capital. Unions were criticised for inflexible attitudes to apprenticeships (para. 2.13), while management were urged to make available facilities for training (para. 2.18).

In *Superphosphates and Compound Fertilisers* (1953) the summary emphasised differences in the conditions facing the British and American industries (paras. 2.1–2.16). Differences in raw materials (para. 2.3), standardisation (para. 2.11) and capital intensity (paras. 2.15–2.16) were all stressed. Again, there was some mention of research, with an important role attributed to state sponsored agricultural research stations in educating farmers in the use of fertilisers and thus stimulating demand (para. 2.6). Union organisation was noted to be in its infancy in the United States, but where it did exist, the report noted that all employees were in one union, irrespective of trade (para. 2.29). Finally, because it made firms reluctant to disclose information on costs, the report made a passing reference to the tough anti-trust laws in the United States (para. 2.41). This illustrates one of the key differences between the conduct of business on the two sides of the Atlantic at this time. Reader (1975: 419–27) draws a strong contrast between the British government's permissive policy on cartels after the war and the American government's anti-trust offensive during and after the war in the context of the chemical industry.

Table 12.2. *ICI sales, by region, 1973–82 (%)*

	1973	1976	1979	1982
UK	59	55	57	55
Western Europe	12	15	15	12
Americas	13	14	13	15
Australasia	10	9	9	13
Other	6	7	6	5

Source: Pettigrew (1985: 77).

Nevertheless, the backwardness of the British chemical industry after the Second World War should not be exaggerated. Indeed, if the comparison is made with the rest of Europe, the position does not look nearly so bleak. As Chapman (1991: 85) notes, the first petrochemical plants in Western Europe were all established in the United Kingdom.

As Pettigrew (1985: 82) notes, by the early 1960s the ICI Board had evolved a corporate strategy to deal with the four problems of dependence on British markets, poor marketing, technological backwardness and low labour productivity. Nevertheless, progress was not always rapid. First, as the figures in table 12.2 show, sales remained highly concentrated on the United Kingdom and Australasia into the 1970s. Western Europe and the Americas continued to take a small proportion of sales. Second, the company remained technology-led, without developing much in the way of marketing skill. Before the emergence of John Harvey-Jones as Chairman in 1982, the company was dominated by distinguished scientists, who were less experienced at developing new markets (Grant and Martinelli, 1991: 77).

Third, however, progress was made in closing the technological gap that had opened up across the war. Kennedy (1986) paints a picture of successful innovation in a number of areas, including fibres (terylene, the first polyester), plastics (polythene), dyestuffs ('Procion' reactive dyes), paints (Dulux alkyd-based paints), pharmaceuticals (fluothane anaesthetic, beta-blocker heart drugs, Nolvadex cancer therapy) and agricultural chemicals (diquat and paraquet herbicides, 'Pruteen' artificial protein).

Fourth, however, labour productivity problems persisted through the 1960s and worsened during the 1970s. Linking time series of output and labour inputs for Britain and Germany to the benchmark estimates for 1987 from O'Mahony (1992a), reported in appendix table A2.2, O'Mahony and Wagner (1994) show the serious deterioration in Britain's comparative productivity position in chemicals during the 1970s. The figures, on an output per hour basis, are shown here in table 12.3. During the 1960s, attempts

Table 12.3. *Comparative labour productivity in chemicals, 1950–89 (UK=100)*

US/UK	1950	1967/68	
Seedcrushing		277	
Mineral oil refining		224	
General chemicals	372	258	
Pharmaceuticals		305	
Soap & detergents	249	259	
Plastics, synthetics		216	
Fertilisers		196	
Matches	376		
Germany/UK	1973	1979	1989
General chemicals	103	128	103
Mineral oil refining	88	123	108
Plastic products	117	126	110

Notes: US/UK benchmark figures based on value added per employee; Germany/UK time series extrapolations from 1987 benchmarks based on value added per hour worked.
Sources: Appendix table A2.1; O'Mahony and Wagner (1994: 7).

were made to improve the utilisation of labour through the Manpower Utilisation and Payment Structure/Weekly Staff Agreement (MUPS/WSA). This was an example of productivity bargaining, following on from the 'Fawley Agreement' at Esso, which will be discussed below in the section on mineral oil refining. Given the productivity outcome reflected in table 12.3, it is not surprising that most writers have concluded that MUPS/WSA was not very successful (Pettigrew, 1985; Roeber, 1975). The inspiration for MUPS/WSA came from the United States, and it was seen by its advocates within ICI as holding out the prospect of attaining American levels of labour productivity, which the figures in table 12.3 suggest were about three times the British level. The company relied largely on American social scientists brought in as external consultants. The scheme met strong resistance, particularly from the craft unions at the large Wilton and Billingham sites. The problems which plagued large-scale plants in other British industries at this time also occurred in chemicals. Craft unions were suspicious of 'flexibility' aims, seen as an attack upon their skills and high earnings, while many managers were wary of assuming detailed supervision of the workforce (Pettigrew, 1985: 229–31). It may even be that the attempts to impose MUPS/WSA had by the 1970s increased the resistance of the workforce and management to change (Pettigrew, 1985: 115).

The improvement of Britain's comparative productivity position in chemicals during the 1980s, shown in table 12.3, wiped out the deterioration of the 1970s. Undoubtedly, one factor here was the change in the external environment. Faced after 1979 with a sharp domestic recession, a steep rise in the price of oil, rapid sterling appreciation and excess capacity in European petrochemicals, ICI moved into loss for the first time in its history (Pettigrew, 1985: 377). Rationalisation was clearly called for.

Nevertheless, there were also technological trends favouring the British chemical industry during the 1980s. As in other industries, British chemical companies found it difficult to compete in large-scale production of standardised items. The size of newly commissioned plant in petrochemicals, which had risen slowly during the 1960s and then increased very sharply during the early 1970s, stabilised in the mid-1970s and even began to fall during the 1980s (Chapman, 1991: 123). More importantly, though, as the market for industrial chemicals matured, with the end of the major thrust of chemical substitution for natural products such as wood and paper, further growth depended on specialty products (Pettigrew, 1985: 411). In these areas, where large scale was less important, British firms were not hampered by industrial relations problems.

Accordingly, ICI has reduced its presence in commodity chemicals and strengthened its presence in specialty chemicals. Between 1982 and 1985, industrial chemicals fell from 49 per cent to 44 per cent of ICI sales, while over the same period specialty products rose from 22 per cent to 28 per cent (Grant and Martinelli, 1991: 62). In 1987, the Chairman, Sir John Harvey-Jones divided ICI into two distinct arms, comprising the traditional bulk commodity sectors and the specialty growth sectors (Grant and Martinelli, 1991: 78). Kennedy (1986: 177) quotes Harvey-Jones as saying that

ICI has always wanted to invent big things like polythene and polyester, but I think we've realised over the last few years that you can make a lot of money out of quite small inventions; the effort now is to link the market place with the research base to produce relatively small things you can make money from.

Mineral oil refining

The period from the end of the Second World War to 1973 was characterised by rapid growth in the demand for energy, with cheap oil taking a growing share of that market (Hartshorn, 1993: 1). The world oil industry was dominated by a small group of companies, known as the 'Seven Sisters', including British Petroleum (formerly the Anglo-Persian Oil Company) and Royal Dutch-Shell. These vertically integrated 'major' companies dominated the three stages of production, refining and marketing (Hartshorn, 1993: 114). The 1970s saw a major restructuring of the indus-

Table 12.4. *Productivity in the British mineral oil refining industry, 1951–89 (1973=100*

	Output	Employment	Capital	Labour productivity	TFP
1951	14.6	81.3	34.5	18.0	22.6
1954	24.6	98.8	48.0	24.9	30.3
1958	28.5	112.8	59.3	25.3	30.1
1963	46.8	110.9	58.1	42.2	50.3
1968	72.7	94.2	78.6	77.2	81.0
1973	100.0	100.0	100.0	100.0	100.0
1979	85.5	93.0	97.3	91.9	90.9
1986	69.9	55.6	109.7	125.7	104.6
1989	76.8	57.5		133.6	

Notes: Industrial classification numbers: 1960–79: 1968 SIC Minimum List Headings 262–263; 1979–89: 1980 SIC Group 140; Output measured by volume indices due to erratic fluctuations in value data.
Sources: Output: *Digest of UK Energy Statistics*; Employment: *Historical Record of the Census of Production* and *Census of Production*; Capital: derived from Oulton and O'Mahony (1994).

try, which now became dominated by national oil companies, linked together through OPEC. As the OPEC cartel exercised control over supply, the era of cheap oil came to an abrupt end and the demand for oil stabilised. The simple flow of oil through the three stages in the 'majors', with a small role for 'independents' was replaced by a more complex web of relations between the national oil companies, the majors and the independents (Hartshorn, 1993: 122).

Although the 1970s also saw the emergence of the United Kingdom as an oil producer with the exploitation of the North Sea reserves, this had little effect on refining capacity in Britain, which was largely dependent on demand factors. With the surge in demand from the late 1960s to 1973, refining capacity had been greatly extended, which led to massive overcapacity during the rest of the 1970s. After the second oil price shock in 1979, major refinery closures were inevitable and capacity shrank sharply during the early 1980s. Figures from the *Digest of UK Energy Statistics* show a reduction of capacity from 132.9 million tonnes per annum in 1979 to 100.7 million tonnes by 1982 and 89.9 million tonnes by 1986.

The figures in table 12.4 confirm this picture of rapidly rising activity to a peak in 1973, followed by decline and stagnation. During the period 1951–73, output grew at an annual rate of 8.7 per cent, while labour productivity and TFP grew at 7.8 per cent and 6.8 per cent respectively. During

1973–9 labour productivity and TFP declined as output fell, while between 1979 and 1989, although output registered a further fall, labour productivity grew rapidly. Positive TFP growth was also resumed over the period 1979–86.

At first sight, the figures in table 12.4 appear to offer support for Flanders' (1964) optimistic interpretation of the experience of productivity bargaining at Esso Fawley in the early 1960s. Esso, an affiliate of Standard Oil of New Jersey (Exxon), made an attempt in 1960 to sweep away restrictive working practices in return for a substantial increase in basic wage rates. The initiative came from the American parent company, and can be seen as an attempt to Americanise the industrial culture. Prior to the introduction of the 'blue book' agreement in 1960, the labour force was organised on a craft basis, with shop stewards playing an important informal role in managing the plant (Flanders, 1964: 46). Part of the aim of the scheme was to get managers to take the initiative and play a more active role in the determination of working practices (Flanders, 1964: 100).

One of the perceived problems had been a rapid growth in overtime during the 1950s. The problem here was that a temporary shortage would lead to an increase in overtime for a small group of workers, whose earnings were thus boosted. This would then be followed by demands for overtime from other workers to boost their earnings. This then meant that power was transferred from union officials to shop stewards, who had increasing power to determine individual workers' earnings through the allocation of overtime (Flanders, 1964: 61–3).

The 1960 agreement was successful in the short run in reducing the amount of overtime, and Flanders (1964: 193) sees it as resulting in a 50 per cent labour productivity increase in plant and maintenance between 1960 and 1962, and a 45 per cent increase among shift workers. However, there was a major unofficial strike within a month of the introduction of the agreement, and progress on flexibility was limited. Indeed, in the 1962 wage negotiations the management made a further attempt to improve flexibility with the offer of a new 'orange book' agreement. Although an agreement was reached, the negotiations were drawn out and difficult (Flanders, 1964: 183).

The US/UK comparative labour productivity position in mineral oil refining can be seen in table 12.3 and appendix table A2.1. Although the American productivity lead diminished from 302 in 1947/48 to 224 in 1967/68, the gap remained above 2:1. Thus for some authors, Flanders (1964) is too optimistic. A more pessimistic interpretation of the Fawley experience is offered by Ahlstrand (1990), who retraced Flanders' steps in 1983. He notes that in addition to the lack of tangible progress on flexibility, the reduction of overtime working rapidly evaporated, and Fawley remained plagued by low productivity compared with Exxon's other

Table 12.5. *Productivity in the British soap and detergent industry, 1951–89 (1973=100)*

	Output	Employment	Capital	Labour productivity	TFP
1951	41.9	157.5	52.1	26.6	35.9
1954	59.2	145.1	57.1	40.8	52.5
1958	77.1	146.4	65.0	52.7	65.6
1963	99.0	143.8	82.4	68.8	80.0
1968	95.2	104.6	93.5	91.0	93.8
1973	100.0	100.0	100.0	100.0	100.0
1979	152.2	108.5	104.6	140.3	141.7
1986	189.2	92.7	124.1	204.1	188.6
1989	204.3	103.3		197.8	

Note: Industrial classification numbers: 1951–79: 1968 SIC Minimum List Heading 275; 1979–89: 1980 SIC Group 258.
Sources: Output and Employment: 1951–70: derived from *Historical Record of the Census of Production* and *Annual Abstract of Statistics*; 1970–89: derived from *Census of Production* and *Annual Abstract of Statistics*; Capital: derived from Oulton and O'Mahony (1994).

refineries. Ahlstrand argues that management lacked commitment to the high wage/high productivity strategy, doubting their ability to extract the required level of effort from the labour force. He also sees the bureaucratic proliferation of rules to define working practices as heightening worker awareness of demarcation. Nevertheless, the time series extrapolation in table 12.3 suggests that relative to Germany, Britain's oil refining industry still retained a productivity advantage in 1973. Although Germany forged ahead during the 1970s, most of the German productivity lead had been eliminated by 1989.

Seedcrushing, soap and detergents: Unilever

Figures of output, employment and capital stock in the British soap and detergent industry are shown in table 12.5. Output of soap and detergents grew steadily at 4.0 per cent per annum during the period 1951–73. This was followed by an acceleration of growth during the period 1973–9, with a return to moderate growth from 1979. Labour productivity and TFP grew rapidly throughout the postwar period, with employment falling during the periods of moderate output growth. The comparative labour productivity data in table 12.3 and appendix table A2.2 show a stable US/UK productivity ratio of the order of 2.5:1 between 1950 and 1967/68, but with Germany at only 71 per cent of the British productivity level in 1987.

The key firms in the British industry were the Anglo-Dutch company Unilever and Hedleys, owned by the American company Procter & Gamble. Although Corlett (1958: 202) argues that the reason for the dominance of large- scale producers in this industry had more to do with economies of marketing than economies of scale in production, Edwards (1962: 254) sees the soap and detergents industry as characterised by effective or 'workable' competition. The price of soap and detergents rose less than the retail price index, consumption and output rose more quickly than during the 1930s, labour productivity grew rapidly as employment declined, and profits remained about average for industry as a whole, although a large proportion of sales revenue was spent on advertising.

Wilson (1968: 5) sees the postwar development of Unilever as based on scientific research and not just on marketing, which had been the main source of the company's success during the interwar period. The company had a secure base in Western Europe, unusual among British firms in the early postwar period. The more usual links with the Commonwealth, inherited from Lever Brothers, remained but became proportionately less important (Fieldhouse, 1978). Unilever faced strong competition world-wide from Procter & Gamble and Colgate-Palmolive, marketing global brands. This produced tensions within the company between advocates of a centralised managerial approach to support global brands, and a decentralised managerial style to allow adjustment to individual market demands (Reader, 1980: 104). The emphasis on decentralisation of the 1950s gave way to a more centralised approach as competition intensified during the 1960s, with the appointment of 'coordinators' to deal with the proliferation of local brands (Wilson, 1968: 96).

The importance of both scientific research and marketing can be seen in the competition between Unilever and Hedleys after the end of soap rationing in 1950. Drawing on American research through Procter & Gamble, Hedleys immediately introduced a synthetic detergent Tide, based on an alkyl-aryl sulphonate base, with phosphate builders (Edwards, 1962: 220). It took two years for Unilever to respond with Surf, and in the meantime Hedleys gained market share. The launch of Surf in 1952 was accompanied by a massive marketing campaign, but this was initially countered by Hedleys. It was only after 1954 that Unilever were able to regain the market share lost in the early 1950s, by undercutting Hedleys on price (Edwards, 1962: 231).

As well as investing large amounts in R&D, Unilever were one of the pioneers in systematic recruitment of graduates into British industrial management (Wilson, 1968: 49). Furthermore, once recruited, managers could expect to receive regular management training (Reader, 1980: 111).

Unilever were also heavily involved in seedcrushing, to provide oils for their soap making and margarine businesses. In addition to improvements in crushing technology, with old hydraulic presses being replaced by high pressure expellers, a 'solvent extraction' process was developed to extract oil from the seeds by dissolving the latter (Wilson, 1968: 78). With growing competition from seed growing countries wishing to process their produce and export oil rather than seeds, oil production in Britain declined and the oil and cake mills increasingly concentrated on the production of animal feedstuffs (Wilson, 1968: 164). The comparative US/UK labour productivity figures in table 12.3 suggest that by the late 1960s what was left of the British seedcrushing industry was no longer on a par with its American counterpart.

British success in pharmaceuticals

Pharmaceuticals has been one of the major growth industries of the postwar period, accompanied by a revolution in health care. The 1940s saw the commercial development of penicillin, leading on to the introduction of broad spectrum antibiotics in the early 1950s. This was followed in the late 1950s and 1960s by anti-hypertensive preparations for high blood pressure and psychotherapeutic medicines for mental disorders, including the major tranquillisers. The 1960s also saw the introduction of oral contraceptives, anti-inflammatory medicines for rheumatism and arthritis and beta-blockers for heart disease. During the 1970s and 1980s developments have included drugs for the treatment of ulcers (including Glaxo's Zantac, the all-time pharmaceutical best-seller to date) and new generation antibiotics (Reekie and Wells, 1988: 96; Foreman-Peck, 1995: 103).

The figures in table 12.6 show output growing at an annual rate of 8.7 per cent during 1951–73, slowing down to 5.5 per cent during 1973–79 and 5.6 per cent during 1979–89. Employment has continued to rise slowly, generating rapid labour productivity growth. Although the capital stock has grown rapidly, TFP growth in pharmaceuticals has been faster than in chemicals as a whole.

Despite relatively low levels of *per capita* consumption of drugs in Britain compared with other rich industrialised countries, Britain has sustained a position as one of the four major pharmaceutical exporting nations (Earl-Slater, 1993: 79, 92). In table 12.7 we see that the United Kingdom, United States, Germany and Switzerland, despite increased competition from other industrialised countries, have continued to hold on to more than half of world exports, although this is down from about three-quarters in 1938 and 1955. Britain's proportion has remained stable over this period as a whole, but with a boost in the early postwar period following disruption in Germany. The early postwar gain in market share was rather more

Table 12.6. *Productivity in the British pharmaceutical industry, 1951–89* *(1973=100)*

	Output	Employment	Capital	Labour productivity	TFP
1951	14.9	84.2	26.5	17.7	24.2
1954	17.8	75.6	28.9	23.5	30.5
1958	26.3	90.7	37.7	29.0	36.7
1963	41.0	98.2	51.6	41.8	49.7
1968	61.6	90.9	67.8	67.8	73.3
1973	100.0	100.0	100.0	100.0	100.0
1979	138.9	107.5	130.8	129.2	122.6
1986	176.4	98.8	189.7	178.5	149.7
1989	242.1	110.2		219.7	

Note: Industrial classification numbers: 1951–79: 1968 SIC Minimum List Heading 272; 1979–89: 1980 SIC Group 257.
Sources: Output and Employment: 1951–70: derived from *Historical Record of the Census of Production* and *Annual Abstract of Statistics*; 1970–89: derived from *Census of Production* and *Annual Abstract of Statistics*; Capital: derived from Oulton and O'Mahony (1994).

Table 12.7. *National shares of world exports of pharmaceutical products,* *1938–88 (%)*

	1938	1955	1963	1975	1980	1988
UK	12	16	14	12	12	11
US	13	34	25	12	14	14
Germany	39	10	15	16	16	15
Switzerland	7	14	14	14	13	12

Sources: Cooper (1966: 249); Ballance *et al.* (1992: 64–5).

exaggerated in the United States with the commercial exploitation of penicillin and the first broad spectrum antibiotics.

Despite its relatively good performance, the British pharmaceutical industry has suffered from a poor image, along with drug companies the world over. Pharmaceutical companies are often portrayed as parasitic, making huge profits out of the misfortune of others. Teeling Smith (1992) attributes this to a misunderstanding of the workings of competition in a high risk business, where the possibility of high profits on a successful drug is needed to justify the huge research expenditure on products which may never come to market. Despite the attempts of economists such as Cooper (1966), Reekie (1975) and Teeling Smith (1992) to provide an analysis of the workings of the pharmaceutical industry along such Schumpeterian lines, criticism of the companies has recurred throughout the postwar period. Teeling Smith (1992: 71) identifies three periods when the outcry against drug company profits reached fever pitch. The first was in the wake of high profits on the broad spectrum antibiotics during the 1950s, which led to the critical Kefauver Report in the United States, and the introduction of the Voluntary Price Regulation Scheme (VPRS) in Britain in 1957 (Davenport-Hines and Slinn, 1992: 167). The deformities as a result of Thalidomide in the early 1960s did not help the drug companies with their image (Teeling Smith, 1992: 67). The outcry against the drug companies at this time can also be seen as ultimately resulting in the establishment of the Sainsbury Committee under the 1964 Labour government to examine the possibility of nationalisation of the industry, although this option was rejected when the Committee reported in 1967.

The second outcry resulted from high profits on benzodiazepine tranquillisers in the late 1960s and early 1970s, which culminated in a Monopolies and Mergers Commission investigation in 1971. The Swiss manufacturers Roche were reluctant to cooperate under the VPRS since they claimed that legitimate patents and product monopolies were undermined by compulsion to grant licences after three years under section 41 of the 1948 Patents Act. In this case the 1973 *Report on the Supply of Chlordiazepoxide and Diazepam* recommended price reductions of 40 per cent for Librium and 75 per cent for Valium, but within a short space of time the original prices were restored, in return for a financial agreement between the company and the government (Teeling Smith, 1992: 72).

The third outcry came in the early 1980s with profits from the anti-ulcer drugs Tagamet and Zantac. In this case, however, criticism within Britain was more muted, since most of the profits were earned on overseas sales. Furthermore, the process of 'creative destruction' could be seen clearly as Tagamet's markets were taken by Zantac and generics following the expiry of patents (Teeling Smith, 1992: 73). Nevertheless, drug price controls in Britain have been progressively tightened during the 1980s as the National Health Service (NHS) has sought to contain costs (Taggart, 1993: 235). This may not have the disastrous consequences for R&D predicted by some British companies because of the global nature of the industry (Taggart, 1993: 236).

Table 12.3 presents data on US/UK comparative labour productivity in pharmaceuticals for 1967/68. Although Britain does not come out of this comparison particularly well, it should be noted that success in the pharmaceutical industry does not depend primarily upon high labour productivity in production, but rather upon prowess in R&D. Ballance *et al.* (1992: 120) find that among the developed market economies during the late 1980s, labour costs accounted for only 16.5 per cent of gross output, or 28.5 per cent of value added.

Conclusions

Although the British chemicals sector grew rather faster than total manufacturing, its performance initially left much to be desired compared with overseas competitors. Chemicals shared many of the problems that affected British industry after the war, including lack of competition in domestic markets and dependence on Commonwealth export markets. Here, Unilever provides a noteworthy exception, building upon its strong European position inherited from the interwar period. There were also industrial relations problems in the bulk chemicals sector and oil refining, leading to attempts at 'productivity bargaining' in the 1960s. After the oil shocks and EEC entry of the 1970s, many of these problems were addressed successfully during the 1980s, and Britain entered the 1990s with a relatively strong position in chemicals. A noteworthy British success has been the pharmaceutical industry, built up on the back of a sustained R&D effort. Here, however, the industry has suffered from a bad image over what are seen by consumers as unjustified monopoly profits on successful patented drugs, but which the industry sees as necessary to cover the high cost of research, much of which will never bear fruit.

Metals

Iron and steel

Iron and steel, as a mature industry, grew relatively slowly during the postwar period, as can be seen in table 12.8. Output grew at an annual rate of only 1.3 per cent during 1951–73 so that, coupled with only a slow decline of the labour force and a fairly rapid rise in the capital stock, labour productivity and TFP also grew slowly, at 1.9 per cent and 0.7 per cent per annum, respectively. The iron and steel industry was adversely affected in most countries by the first oil shock in 1973, which plunged the industrialised world into recession and encouraged substitution away from energy-intensive products like steel (Cockerill, 1988: 70; Hudson and Sadler, 1989: 18). However, the period 1973–9 was particularly disastrous for the British iron and steel industry, with output declining rapidly at 10.2 per cent per annum, and with very strongly negative growth of labour productivity and TFP. The dramatic decline in Britain's labour productivity position relative to Germany between 1973 and 1979 can be seen in table 12.9. Equally, this table shows the remarkable turn-round during the 1980s, with British

Table 12.8. *Productivity in the British iron and steel industry, 1951–89 (1973=100)*

	Output	Employment	Capital	Labour productivity	TFP
1951	75.4	113.8	42.9	66.2	86.3
1954	74.5	112.6	48.6	66.2	83.1
1958	75.7	116.5	62.1	65.0	77.0
1963	84.0	116.1	87.4	72.4	78.1
1968	98.4	109.7	86.7	89.7	95.6
1973	100.0	100.0	100.0	100.0	100.0
1979	54.2	83.9	114.4	64.6	59.4
1986	58.2	34.0	93.8	171.2	130.2
1989	74.4	30.7		242.3	

Note: Industrial classification numbers: 1951–79: 1968 SIC Minimum List Headings 311–313; 1979–89: 1980 SIC Groups 221–223.
Sources: Output and Employment: 1951–70: derived from *Historical Record of the Census of Production* and *Annual Abstract of Statistics*; 1970–89: derived from *Census of Production* and *Annual Abstract of Statistics*; Capital: derived from Oulton and O'Mahony (1994).

Table 12.9. *Comparative labour productivity in metal manufacturing, 1950–89 (UK=100)*

US/UK	1950	1967/68	
Iron & steel (general)		259	
Blast furnaces	408		
Iron & steel smelt/roll	269		
Iron & steel foundries	202		
Aluminium		348	
Copper		245	

Germany/UK	1973	1979	1989
Iron & steel	125	263	89
Non-ferrous metals		120	113

Notes: US/UK benchmark figures based on value added per employee; Germany/UK time series extrapolations from 1987 benchmarks based on value added per hour worked.
Sources: Appendix table A2.1; O'Mahony and Wagner (1994: 7).

Table 12.10. *British crude steel production, by process, 1951–89 (%)*

	Open Hearth	Bessemer	Oxygen	Electric	Other
1951	86.6	7.1	0.0	5.2	1.1
1954	87.7	6.3	0.0	5.0	1.0
1958	87.6	6.0	0.0	5.8	0.6
1963	76.0	7.8	6.7	9.2	0.3
1968	54.9	3.9	25.0	16.1	0.1
1973	31.8	0.9	47.3	19.9	0.1
1979	5.4	0.0	60.1	34.4	0.1
1986	0.0	0.0	71.7	28.3	0.0
1989	0.0	0.0	72.7	27.3	0.0

Sources: Mitchell (1988: 289–90); UK Iron and Steel Statistics Bureau, *Annual Statistics* (London).

Table 12.11. *Continuous casting of crude steel in Britain, 1951–89 (% of output)*

Year	(%)	Year	(%)
1951	0.0	1973	3.0
1954	0.0	1979	16.9
1958	0.0	1986	60.5
1963	0.4	1989	80.2
1968	1.6		

Source: UK Iron and Steel Statistics Bureau, *Annual Statistics* (London).

labour productivity above German levels by 1989. Returning to table 12.8, there was a return to positive output growth of 3.2 per cent per annum during 1979–89. With the labour force being cut back drastically, labour productivity grew at an annual rate of 13.2 per cent.

Clearly, such dramatic trends in productivity are bound up with changes in organisation and the large literature on the postwar steel industry reflects this. However, as in many other industries, these changes in organisation can be related to technology, with the performance of British industry improving as the emphasis shifted away from the production of bulk steel in large integrated plants to the production of more differentiated special steels and the production of common grades in smaller scale mini-mills (Cockerill, 1988: 79). The major technological changes during the postwar period are charted in tables 12.10 and 12.11.

In table 12.10 we see the dominance of open hearth furnaces in the 1950s, but with the growth of Basic Oxygen Steelmaking (BOS) from the 1960s. Since BOS uses no more than 30 per cent of scrap in the charge, compared with about 50 per cent scrap in open hearth furnaces, this has contributed to the economic viability of electric steelmaking, which uses 90 per cent or more scrap (Ray, 1984: 7). The diffusion of BOS drastically raised the minimum efficient scale of production in an integrated steel plant, with hot metal making up 70–75 per cent of the charge, and with tapping time being reduced from 8–10 hours in an open hearth furnace to 30–45 minutes in a basic oxygen converter (Ray, 1984: 6–8). The poor performance of the British steel industry during the transition from open hearth to basic oxygen production during the late 1960s and the 1970s is consistent with the difficulties experienced by many British industries attempting large-scale production at this time. It may also be seen as one of the factors explaining the relatively slow diffusion of BOS in Britain compared with other major steel producing countries (Ray, 1984: 16).

However, turning to table 12.11, we see that during the 1980s there has been a surge in the importance of continuous casting of steel. The continuous casting machine replaces three stages in the production of semi-finished products (Ray, 1984: 21). In the conventional technology, liquid steel is first transferred into ingot moulds and cooled. The ingots are then reheated in soaking pits at the second stage, and transferred to the blooming mill, where they are rolled into slabs, blooms or billets at the third stage. Continuous casting changes this intermittent process into a continuous one, with the liquid metal poured into a mould at the same rate as the solidified metal emerges at the other end (Schenk, 1974: 232). This has drastically reduced minimum efficient scale, and in combination with electric arc furnaces for the production of liquid steel, has allowed the growth of 'mini-mills'.

The rationalisation of the British iron and steel industry, which it was noted in chapter 11 was first mooted between the wars, was thus effectively achieved only during the 1980s. Much of the literature on the postwar industry is concerned with the barriers to change, which allowed the persistence of failure on such a grand scale. As in the interwar period, this is a story of political economy, with heavy government involvement. The industry moved between the private and public sectors with nationalisation in 1950, denationalisation in 1953, renationalisation in 1967 and privatisation in 1988. However, before the 1980s, public ownership failed to secure effective reorganisation and private ownership failed to inject effective competition.

The need for rationalisation was recognised in the AACP Report on *Iron and Steel* (1952), which reported US/UK labour productivity ratios between 186 and 292 for a number of products (para. 2.8). The existence of a large productivity gap at this time is confirmed by the figures in table 12.9, where we see US/UK labour productivity ratios of 408 in blast furnaces and 269 in steelworks and rolling mills in 1950. The summary chapter of the AACP Report outlines a version of the Rothbarth–Habakkuk thesis, emphasising the role of resource abundance and labour scarcity in America leading to the adoption of more capital-intensive methods, together with the standardisation of American demand allowing concentration in large units (Rothbarth, 1946; Habakkuk, 1962). In addition, there is some discussion of the benefits of the rapid wartime expansion in the United States, lowering the average age of the capital stock, a point emphasised by Frankel (1957) in his study of British and American manufacturing productivity. Although chapter 3 on conclusions and recommendations offers little more than platitudes on labour and management, the more detailed chapters on these matters in part III of the report are more critical. The American system of representation of all workers at one steelworks by a single union is contrasted favourably with the British fragmentation of union structures along craft lines (section 8.4), while chapters 9–12 on works size and layout, plant engineering, costing and statistical records, and marketing are broadly critical of a number of key management responsibilities.

The AACP Report on *Steelfounding* (1949) found labour productivity in the American foundries visited between 50 and 90 per cent higher than in Britain (para. 1.6). This compares with the US/UK productivity ratio of 202 in iron and steel foundries in 1950, shown in table 12.9. The key factors emphasised in the AACP Report summary are: good factory layout and tidiness of working; use of power and widespread acceptance of machines; economy in the use of labour; standardisation of output; and application of the results of research (para. 1.8). There is a great deal of emphasis on competition and incentives in creating a climate of productivity conscious-ness (paras. 1.7 and 1.24). Indeed, the idea that both sides of British indus-try had settled for a quiet life of low effort and low productivity is suggested by the question raised in para. 4.32: 'Is high productivity really desired by British steelfounders?' The supplementary question of 'Over what features of the British industrial system does the desire for high productivity take preference?' raises explicitly some of the barriers to change: 'Is high pro-ductivity more important than the organisation and customs of the trade association? Is high productivity to be sacrificed so as to retain intact the existing methods of the employers' associations? Are trade union practices, built up over the years before the present economic dangers, to remain unal-tered, at the expense of high productivity?' (para. 4.33). Note that American labour is seen as conspicuously unskilled by British standards (para. 1.10), emphasising the importance of the relationship between product market strategy and human capital accumulation.

The nationalisation of steel became a possibility with the election of a Labour government in 1945. However, there were divisions within the party on the desirability of nationalising steel, which was not a natural monopoly (unlike the electricity industry), was not suffering from the unwillingness of the owners to invest (unlike coal), and was not loss making (unlike coal and the railways) (Burk, 1988: 13). Hence the policy was implemented only very late in the life of the government, with the vesting date delayed until after the February 1950 election, when Labour were returned with a very small majority (Vaizey, 1974: 125–8). Since the Conservatives were returned to office in the autumn of 1951, the nationalised Iron and Steel Corporation of Great Britain (ISCGB) made little impact before it was given a standstill order, and the industry prepared for return to the private sector (Vaizey, 1974: 150). This was facilitated by the form which nationalisation had taken, with the ISCGB acting as a holding company and leaving the companies as the major operating units (Vaizey, 1974: 127). The Iron and Steel Holding and Realisation Agency (ISHRA) was set up in July 1953 to supervise the sale of shares to the public (Vaizey, 1974: 153). The sell-off continued until the return of a Labour government in October 1964, when only one company, RTB remained unsold (Vaizey, 1974: 156). However, state influence remained strong through a new statutory body, the Iron and Steel Board, which was established to supervise but not dominate a privately owned industry (Vaizey, 1974: 156).

Although for all but a brief period during 1951–3 the iron and steel industry was in private hands until 1967, it seemed almost to operate as part of a planned economy. A series of five year plans, beginning with the Franks Report in 1945, through to the fourth development plan of 1961 aimed to raise crude steel capacity from about 14 million tons in 1945 to 32 million tons by 1965 (Vaizey, 1974: 148, 162). The fifth development plan, begun under the shadow of renationalisation in 1964 aimed to stabilise capacity at this level. The plans generally aimed to patch up existing plant where possible and were heavily influenced by political factors when recommending new investments. Thus, for example, when a decision came to be taken on the location of a new strip mill in 1958, to be financed by public money, cabinet intervention ensured that two mills were built at Newport in South Wales and Ravenscraig in Scotland. Since there were insufficient funds for two mills, both were starved of resources and neither turned out satisfactorily (Vaizey, 1974: 169–76).

During the period of private ownership between 1953 and 1967, the industry remained largely shielded from competition. On the international front, although the Franks Report in 1945 had favoured a free trade policy, in practice there was a return to the protectionist policies of the interwar years, and imports and exports of iron and steel remained low relative to output (Rowley, 1971: 71–3). Britain remained outside the ECSC, formed in 1954 to eliminate tariffs between the six countries of Benelux, Germany, France and Italy, and to establish a common external tariff (Vaizey, 1974: 168). On the internal front, the industry operated a system of uniform delivered prices, sometimes known by economists as the postage stamp system, since the price did not vary with distance to delivery, as in a national postal system (Rowley, 1971: 91; Scherer, 1980: 326). The policy could be justified as an attempt to prevent the problem of cut-throat price cutting during downturns in an industry with high fixed costs, but of course it could also be seen as consistent with a quiet life for inefficient producers.

Although a Labour government was returned in 1964 with a small majority, the controversial renationalisation of steel was postponed until after the 1966 election, when Labour's majority increased substantially (Vaizey, 1974: 179–80). The British Steel Corporation (BSC) took control of the 14 major firms in the industry in 1967. Initially there were four regional groupings, as had been envisaged by the Bank of England in the 1930s, but in 1970 BSC eliminated the old company structure more completely by reorganising on a product basis (Vaizey, 1974: 181–3). In 1973 a 10 year development plan was unveiled, which envisaged an expansion of capacity from 27 million to 33–35 million tonnes (Hudson and Sadler, 1989: 62).

The new structures were soon put to the test when Britain encountered intensified competition from European producers upon EEC entry at the beginning of 1973. Then at the end of 1973 the first oil shock plunged the industry into crisis. As the industrialised world moved into recession and as the development of less energy-intensive substitutes hit the demand for steel, BSC began to make heavy losses (Hudson and Sadler, 1989: 65). With the imposition of public expenditure cuts as a condition for the IMF loan in 1976, BSC were forced to change their policy from expansion to savage retrenchment. Although the trade unions in BSC had cooperated over plant closures during the early 1970s, within an environment of planned expansion, by 1977 union policy had become firmly opposed to closures within an environment of general contraction (Hudson and Sadler, 1989: 64–5). There followed a period of bitter industrial relations, with campaigns to contest closures at Corby and Consett in 1979 and a national strike over wages in 1980 (Hudson and Sadler, 1989: 66–72). Ravenscraig continued to owe its survival to political intervention (Hudson and Sadler, 1989: 73).

The capacity reductions of the early 1980s took place within the context of a quota system introduced by the European Commission under the

Treaty of Paris, which established the ECSC (Hudson and Sadler, 1989: 33). Once introduced, this crisis measure proved difficult to remove, and continued to operate until 1988, when much improved demand conditions finally allowed the withdrawal of quotas. Cockerill (1993: 73) concludes that on balance the European Commission's intervention in the steel industry hindered rather than helped the process of adaptation to the structural crisis.

Along with the cut-backs at BSC, there emerged in the early 1980s plans for a rejuvenation of the steel industry in the private sector. The 1981 Iron and Steel Act exempted BSC from its previous statutory duty to provide the full range of steel products, permitted joint ventures between BSC and private companies and allowed for the eventual liquidation of BSC. The joint ventures were codenamed 'Phoenix' to designate an industry rising from the ashes (Hudson and Sadler, 1989: 78). These Phoenix companies, such as Allied Steel & Wire and Sheffield Forgemasters, were concentrated in particular in special steels, leaving BSC to concentrate on its core business of bulk steels. As BSC moved back into profit from the mid-1980s, the issue of privatisation moved onto the political agenda, and BSC returned to the private sector in 1988 as British Steel (Cockerill, 1993: 68). Once again, political guarantees had to be given to keep Ravenscraig open at least until the end of 1989 (Hudson and Sadler, 1989: 81).

As Aylen (1988: 3) notes, the remarkable turn-round of the British steel industry occurred while it was in public ownership. However, his conclusion that privatisation was therefore unnecessary does not follow, since it is highly unlikely that the changes in the structure of incentives faced by the management and workforce which he sees as responsible for the improved performance could have been implemented without the threat of an end to public ownership. As in many industries, the intensification of product market competition during the early 1980s was crucial in forcing managers and workers to address inefficient work practices. However, the fact that technology had changed to favour smaller- scale production methods also undoubtedly helped the British industry.

Non-ferrous metals

Output, employment and capital stock trends in non-ferrous metals are shown in table 12.12. British output and labour productivity grew rapidly as world consumption of non-ferrous metals boomed during the period 1951–73. However, since 1973, the British industry has been in decline with falling output and factor inputs, as world consumption has stagnated and processing of minerals has moved increasingly to countries where the ores are mined (Mikesell, 1988: 39). Labour productivity fell during the period

Table 12.12. *Productivity in the British non-ferrous metals industry,*
1951–89 (1973=100)

	Output	Employment	Capital	Labour productivity	TFP
1951	31.2	93.5	40.3	33.4	41.9
1954	41.3	92.7	42.7	44.6	54.9
1958	49.5	106.8	51.6	46.3	56.4
1963	63.6	114.4	61.5	55.6	65.8
1968	72.5	109.7	73.9	66.1	73.5
1973	100.0	100.0	100.0	100.0	100.0
1979	83.5	89.2	99.5	93.6	90.9
1986	70.8	50.5	91.2	140.2	119.6
1989	63.3	48.7		130.0	

Note: Industrial classification numbers: 1951–79: 1968 SIC Minimum List Headings 321–323; 1979–89: 1980 SIC Group 224.
Sources: Output and Employment: 1951–70: derived from *Historical Record of the Census of Production* and *Annual Abstract of Statistics*; 1970–89: derived from *Census of Production* and *Annual Abstract of Statistics*; Capital: derived from Oulton and O'Mahony (1994).

1973–9, as employment declined more slowly than output, but rapid labour shedding during the 1980s has led to a return of high rates of labour productivity growth.

Before the industrial reclassification in 1980, the data refer to the production of semi-manufactures in foundries as well as the refining of basic metals. Examination of the output of refined metals in table 12.13 makes it clear that the decline of the 1970s was concentrated in the foundry rather than the refinery. Indeed, output of refined aluminium and lead increased substantially at this time. Data on consumption of non-ferrous metals confirm the decline in foundry output at this time (Metallgesellschaft AG, *Metal Statistics*, Frankfurt am Main). Because of the reclassification, O'Mahony and Wagner's (1994) time series extrapolation is reported in table 12.9 only for the 1980s. This indicates a small German labour productivity advantage in non-ferrous metals, which might be expected given the greater scale of the German industry (OECD, *Mining and Non-Ferrous Metals Policies of OECD Countries*, Paris, 1994: 268, 278).

By and large, the British non-ferrous metals industry has been allowed to contract without attracting significant government intervention to counter market forces (OECD, 1994: 204). By 1988, significant shares of world production were held by Britain only in tin (7.5 per cent) and lead (6.5 per cent) (World Bureau of Metal Statistics, *World Metal Statistics Yearbook*, Ware, Herts,UK). Britain nevertheless plays an important role

Table 12.13. *British production of major non-ferrous metals, 1951–89 (000 tons)*

	Refined aluminium	Refined copper	Refined lead	Refined nickel	Refined tin	Slab zinc
1951	99.1	205.9	73.6	23.3	27.7	69.7
1954	115.7	219.1	82.1	23.9	28.0	81.2
1958	125.4	193.2	133.5	23.1	33.0	74.6
1963	191.7	197.4	156.7	37.5	18.7	99.0
1968	234.1	194.6	232.0	41.0	27.6	140.6
1973	453.9	168.2	260.9	36.2	22.7	82.5
1979	527.7	119.7	362.4	18.6	11.2	85.3
1986	386.1	123.6	323.4	30.4	14.7	84.5
1989	400.6	117.1	344.5	25.7	10.8	78.5

Source: Mitchell (1988: 311); World Bureau of Metal Statistics, *World Metal Statistics* (Ware, Herts, UK).

in the world non-ferrous metals industry through the participation of British mining houses such as Rio Tinto Zinc (RTZ) in overseas projects and the location of the world's major metal market, the London Metal Exchange (LME) in the City of London (OECD, 1994: 203).

Conclusions

The British iron and steel industry performed poorly during the 1950s and 1960s, being used as a political football, with nationalisation in 1950 followed by denationalisation from 1953 and renationalisation in 1967. However, there was little effective rationalisation while the industry was in public ownership and little effective competition while the industry was in private hands. After a disastrous performance during the 1970s, with output and productivity declining rapidly, the industry was effectively rationalised during the 1980s as the government left it to stand on its own two feet, culminating in privatisation in 1988. The turn-round in productivity performance was truly staggering, with the Germany/UK comparative labour productivity ratio falling from 263 in 1979 to 89 in 1989. Technology has also played a part in the turn-round of the industry, with British performance improving as the emphasis shifted away from the production of bulk steel in large integrated plants towards the production of more differentiated special steels and the production of common grades in smaller mini-mills. In non-ferrous metals, although the British industry shared to some extent in the world boom of the 1950s and 1960s, in the more depressed conditions of the 1970s and 1980s the industry has been

Table 12.14. *Productivity in the British motor vehicle industry, 1951–89*
(1973=100)

	Output	Employment	Capital	Labour productivity	TFP
1951	33.7	65.8	66.9	51.2	51.0
1954	42.8	63.4	64.5	67.5	67.2
1958	48.9	68.9	70.3	71.0	70.6
1963	80.7	88.2	82.5	91.5	93.2
1968	93.6	92.8	93.8	93.1	100.5
1973	100.0	100.0	100.0	100.0	100.0
1979	99.2	97.9	113.1	101.3	97.4
1986	82.5	52.0	123.5	158.7	125.6
1989	95.3	53.2		179.1	

Note: Industrial classification numbers: 1951–79: 1968 SIC Minimum List Heading 381; 1979–89: 1980 SIC Class 35.
Sources: Output and Employment: 1951–70: derived from *Historical Record of the Census of Production* and *Annual Abstract of Statistics*; 1970–89: derived from *Census of Production* and *Annual Abstract of Statistics*; Capital: derived from Oulton and O'Mahony (1994).

allowed to decline. Britain's role in non-ferrous metals is now much more concerned with the overseas activities of British-based multi-nationals such as RTZ and trading on the LME.

Engineering

Motor vehicles

The figures in table 12.14 show rapid growth of output and productivity in the British motor vehicle industry during the period 1951–73, with output growing at an annual rate of 4.9 per cent, and with labour productivity and TFP both growing at a little over 3 per cent per annum. Nevertheless, the comparative data in table 12.15 show the United States maintaining a roughly 4:1 labour productivity lead between 1950 and 1967/68, at the height of the Fordist era. During the period 1973–9 the expansion of output came to a halt and productivity stagnated. Although rapid labour productivity growth has occurred since 1979, this has been a result of massive labour shedding, with output still below its 1973 level in 1989 despite a sustained upturn since 1982.

The stagnation of output and productivity during the 1970s led to a serious deterioration in Britain's labour productivity position relative to Germany, as can be seen in table 12.15. Equally clearly, the shake-out of

Table 12.15. *Comparative labour productivity in engineering, 1950–89 (UK=100)*

US/UK	1950	1967/68
Agric. mach. (exc. tractors)	429	
Agric. mach. (inc. tractors)		146
Machine tools	221	162
Electrical mach.	239	155
Radio/electronic comp.		193
Electronic tubes	355	
Broadcast recept. eqt.		288
Radios	400	
Household appliances	412	239
Electric lamps	356	
Shipbuilding	111	185
Motor vehicles	466	438
Aircraft		381
Cans & metal boxes	561	466

Germany/UK	1973	1979	1989
Motor vehicles	149	186	124
Aerospace	131	200	101
Shipbuilding	145	144	105
Electrical engineering	84	102	98
Office mach.	101	108	87
Mechanical engineering	126	142	124

Notes: US/UK benchmark figures based on value added per employee; Germany/UK time series extrapolations from 1987 benchmarks based on value added per hour worked.
Sources: Appendix table A2.1; O'Mahony and Wagner (1994: 7).

employment during the 1980s has led to a dramatic turn-round, more than undoing the comparative deterioration of the 1970s.

Attention will be focused here on cars, the largest part of the motor vehicle industry. Data on registrations, production and trade are given in table 12.16. In the immediate postwar years, the increase in production was export-led. This was a part of the government's postwar export drive, needed to shore up the fragile balance of payments position. The predominance of exports was ensured through controls over steel supply, with allocations channelled to firms exporting at least 50 per cent of output, rising in 1947 to 75 per cent (Church, 1994: 43). Britain's share of world motor exports rose from 15 per cent in 1937 to 52 per cent in 1950. However, this position could not be sustained once US production was no

Table 12.16. *British registrations, production and trade in cars, 1946–89 (units)*

	Registrations	Production	Exports	Imports
1946	121,725	219,162	84,358	63
1951	138,373	475,919	368,101	3,723
1954	394,362	769,165	372,029	4,660
1958	566,319	1,051,551	484,034	10,940
1963	1,030,694	1,607,939	615,827	48,163
1968	1,144,770	1,815,936	676,571	102,276
1973	1,688,322	1,747,321	598,816	504,619
1979	1,731,882	1,070,452	410,118	1,060,645
1986	1,943,745	1,018,962	201,411	1,071,747
1989	2,373,391	1,299,082	339,006	1,370,589

Note: Registrations are not equal to production *plus* exports *minus* imports because of changes in stocks and small inconsistencies between customs and manufacturers' definitions.
Source: Society of Motor Manufacturers and Traders, *The Motor Industry of Great Britain* (London: SMMT).

longer held back by steel shortage and as production in Continental Europe recovered (Dunnett, 1980: 34). Britain's share of world trade in cars fell back to 24 per cent during 1957–62 and 19 per cent during 1963–7. From 1974, for the first time since 1914, car imports exceeded car exports (Church, 1994: 44). By the end of the 1970s imports were roughly equal to production, and continued to grow until the end of the 1980s. Despite an upturn in the late 1980s, exports were still below their 1979 level in 1989.

I would see technology as the fundamental factor underlying these dramatic trends. The British failure in the volume production of cars epitomises the general British poor performance in mass production. This conclusion is further underlined by the success of British producers in the smaller niche markets for luxury cars and 4-wheel drive vehicles (Adeney, 1989: 127–41). There was also British success in sports cars during the early postwar period, before the companies were absorbed in the ailing volume producer, British Leyland (Whisler, 1995). The failure in mass production was rooted in the difficulties of switching away from the domestic and Empire markets traditionally served by British producers and the industrial relations problems brought about by attempts to reorganise production in ways which wrested control away from the shopfloor labour force.

Dealing first with the issue of markets, as was noted in chapter 11, a mass market along American lines had not developed in Britain between the wars. Thus the postwar British industry inevitably inherited a structure which was more fragmented and produced many more models than its American rival (Dunnett, 1980: 21; PEP, 1950: 129–39). Furthermore, exports during the interwar period had been heavily oriented towards Empire markets because of protection in Europe and Imperial Preference. SMMT data in *The Motor Industry of Britain* show that in 1938 81.2 per cent of British motor vehicle exports went to Imperial markets. Whisler (1994) is nevertheless very critical of the marketing policies of the companies, in particular, their failure in the immediate postwar years to invest in an effective distribution system in Europe, which he sees as the outstanding potential market. However, it was by no means clear at the end of the war that Europe would be the outstanding growth market of the next two or three decades; indeed, the experience of the 1930s pointed in precisely the opposite direction.

Whisler (1994: 5) acknowledges the difficulties caused by the introduction of currency exchange restrictions and high tariffs on imported cars in Australia in 1952, which effectively closed off Britain's most important overseas market (Whisler, 1994: 5). He also recognises the difficulties posed by British government prevarication over participation in European supranational bodies such as the EEC, which shifts some of the blame onto government (Whisler, 1994: 10). Nevertheless, Whisler (1994: 4) is surely right to point to some of the problems stored up for the future by the shortsighted response of producers during the export drive of the late 1940s in selling cars in European and North American markets without adequate after-sales service. Here, again, however, government must share some of the blame, since spare parts were not included in the export quotas, and exchange restrictions would have made a decent after-sales service difficult to finance (Dunnett, 1980: 37).

The concentration on Empire markets can be seen as having the unfortunate consequence that British producers could avoid head-to-head competition with foreign producers in overseas markets, and these attitudes towards competition also spilled over into domestic markets to some extent. Thus although there was undoubtedly strong rivalry between firms, this did not lead to price competition in the early postwar period. Rather, competition tended to take the form of quality improvements, which took longer for competitors to match than price cuts (Cowling and Cubbin, 1971). The avoidance of head-to-head competition during the early postwar period was not a good preparation for the tough environment as trade policies were increasingly liberalised at home and abroad (Cowling *et al.*, 1980: 209).

Remaining with problems of markets, Dunnett (1980: 61–5) emphasises the role of stop–go policies in creating an environment of uncertainty, thus hindering investment. In particular, he stresses the damaging role played by

Buyers of labour time
estimated payoffs

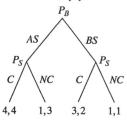

Sellers of labour time
estimated payoffs

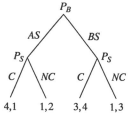

AS = American system

BS = British system

C = Cooperative workforce

NC = Non-cooperative workforce

P_B = Buyers move

P_S = Sellers move

12.1 Game-theoretic representation of technological choice in the postwar British vehicle industry
Lewchuk (1987: 225).

changes in hire purchase restrictions, which necessarily hit demand for consumer durables such as cars. However, as Prais (1981: 160) notes, there is little evidence to support this argument. With hindsight, it is clear that the early postwar period was one of outstanding stability compared with what was to come during the 1970s and 1980s. Furthermore, the German and American car industries showed much the same variability around a trend as the British car industry over the period 1955–75 (Prais, 1981: 356).

Even if all demand side problems could have been overcome, however, there remained on the supply side serious barriers to the successful introduction of mass production techniques in the British car industry. Here we return to the game-theoretic representation of the problem in Lewchuk (1987: 225). The strategy choices in post-1945 Britain are shown in figure 12.1. As in figure 11.1, managers, or buyers of labour time have to make the first move (P_B) in a two-stage game, with a choice between adopting the British system (*BS*) or the American system (*AS*). The choice the managers make depends on how they expect workers to behave. At the second stage of the game, when the technology has been installed, workers can be either cooperative (*C*) or non-cooperative (*NC*). The payoffs give the buyers' payoff first and the sellers' payoff second. The highest payoff is 4 and the lowest 1. Thus, for example, if managers invest in the American system and workers cooperate, the (4,4) payoff estimated by managers indicates that managers see this as yielding the highest possible payoff for both managers and workers.

As in the interwar case, Lewchuk assumes that managers and workers agree on how the managers rank the different strategy pairs, so that in both

Table 12.17. *Strike activity in the British motor vehicle industry, 1951–73*

	Number of strikes	Workers involved (000)	Working days lost (000)
1951	24	38.3	105
1954	16	15.5	35
1958	55	54.5	128
1963	120	137.2	298
1968	227	181.0	670
1973	297	442.6	2082

Source: Durcan *et al.*(1983: 315).

diagrams the buyers' rankings are the same. The change from the interwar position in figure 11.1 is that after the Second World War managers no longer see non-cooperation under the American system as any worse than non-cooperation under the British system (both ranked 1). This is because managers believe that automation provides an answer to their attempts to control effort norms (Lewchuk, 1987: 225).

Once again, however, Lewchuk assumes that there is disagreement and mistrust between managers and workers, which shows up in how buyers and sellers estimate the preference ranking of sellers. Managers believe if they can control effort levels through automation under the American system, this will deliver an increase in productivity which will allow them to raise wages enough to get labour to accept the bargain. Thus managers believe that workers rank the American system above the British system. However, in fact the postwar boom enhanced the ability of labour to control incentive payment systems, thus making the British system more attractive to workers.

Under these conditions, rational decision makers end up with non-cooperation under the American system. Using the left-hand side of figure 12.1, managers choose the American system because this yields possible outcomes of 4 or 1, compared with 3 or 1 if they choose the British system. But then at the second stage of the game workers use the right-hand side of figure 12.1. Given that managers have chosen the American system, workers get a higher payoff by not cooperating.

For Lewchuk, then, the central problem of the British car industry after the Second World War was a movement in the direction of American technology in an atmosphere of mistrust between management and unions. The deterioration of industrial relations can be seen in table 12.17, with the number of strikes, the number of workers involved and the working days lost all growing rapidly. When Michael Edwardes took charge of British Leyland in 1977, he was shown a daily list of disputes, which often ran to five sheets. He notes that it 'was to be three years before the daily dispute sheets dwindled to the point where I was able to discontinue them' (Edwardes, 1983: 15).

As the British firms made a switch to Fordist methods, all kinds of problems and anomalies cropped up. The British system of craft unionism meant that there was a huge multiplicity of unions to deal with. Thus, for example, in the early 1970s British Leyland had to deal with 36 unions, and Ford with 22 (Rhys, 1972: 445). The scope for inter-union disputes inherent in this structure was exacerbated by the two-tier nature of bargaining, with conflict between shop stewards and central union officials. Lewchuk (1987: 214) focuses on the difficulties caused by a shift from payment of piece rates under the British system to payment of fixed day rates under the American system. Under piecework, workers had a strong incentive to ensure that the plant ran smoothly, that parts were available when needed, that machinery was kept going, etc. otherwise they lost pay. Under measured day work, that direct incentive was removed, and management was ill-prepared to fill the coordination gap. As Prais (1981: 161) notes, industrial relations problems were concentrated in large plants, and this was particularly serious in the volume car industry, where large plants were essential.

The adoption of American production methods required a major reorganisation of the British motor vehicle industry, since economies of scale could only be reaped if many of the smaller producers merged and rationalised their range of models. The major mergers among the British owned motor vehicle producers, culminating in the formation of British Leyland Motor Corporation (BLMC) in 1968, are set out in Turner (1971). In 1952 Austin and Morris combined to form the British Motor Corporation (BMC), which in turn merged with Jaguar Group in 1966 to form British Motor Holdings (BMH). BMH combined with Leyland Motor Corporation in 1968 to form BLMC. Leyland had begun life as a commercial vehicle producer, but in 1961 acquired the car producer Standard-Triumph, formed in turn from the 1945 union of Standard and Triumph. Leyland had also acquired Rover in 1966.

The general verdict on the effects of these mergers has been highly negative (Cowling *et al.*, 1980: 170–90). As the figures in table 12.18 show, the British owned producers have tended to see their share of UK production decline, individually and collectively. During the early postwar years, Ford were very successful in increasing their share of UK production, while the principal gainers during the 1980s have been the Japanese producers, led by Nissan. British Leyland, renamed Rover Group in 1986, has continued to

Table 12.18. *Shares of UK car production by manufacturers, 1947–89 (%)*

	1947	1954	1967	1978	1985	1989
Standard	13.2	11.0	7.9			
Austin	19.2					
Morris	20.9					
BMC/BLMC/Rover Group		38.0	34.7	50.2	44.4	35.0
Rootes/Chrysler/Peugeot	10.9	11.0	11.7	16.1	6.4	8.3
Vauxhall	11.2	9.0	12.7	6.9	14.0	16.0
Ford	15.4	27.0	28.4	26.5	30.3	29.5
Nissan						5.9

Note: For a description of the major mergers in the industry, see text.
Sources: Dunnett (1980: 20); Church (1994: 79).

see its share of UK production shrink during the 1980s, although this can be interpreted more positively as a move towards higher quality niche markets rather than as a simple failure. Rootes, the other major British company at the beginning of the postwar period was taken over by Chrysler in 1964 (Young and Hood, 1977: 78). After a disastrous performance in the early 1970s and a government rescue in 1975, ownership passed to Peugeot in 1979 (Young and Hood, 1977: 287; Rhys, 1988: 165).

One issue raised by the above emphasis on technology is the much poorer performance of Britain relative to Germany. To some extent this can be explained by Britain's traditional emphasis on Empire markets compared with Germany's historical presence in European markets. It can also be noted that Germany's success tended to be at the higher quality end of the market, with companies like BMW and Mercedes. However, it must also be noted that during the early postwar years the success of Volkswagen was based on standardised mass production of a single cheap model, the Beetle. The difference between Britain and Germany here lies in the supply of unskilled labour from the countryside and overseas. Rather than persuading an established skilled labour force to accept dramatic changes in their working practices, Volkswagen could rely on rural migrants and guest workers who were more prepared to accept whatever working conditions were required to underpin relatively high earnings, since they did not intend to stay (Bardou *et al.*, 1982: 247–9). Guest workers and rural migrants played a vital role in the car industry in other Continental European countries from the end of the war to the 1960s (Bardou *et al.*, 1982: 249–51; Womack *et al.*, 1990: 47). By contrast, Britain lacked a supply of rural labour to draw upon, and allowed permanent settlement of immigrants rather than relying on transient guest workers (Church, 1994: 68).

The British attempts to switch to Fordist production methods ended disastrously. With losses mounting, in December 1974 British Leyland had to be given a £50 million guarantee, while a committee under the chairmanship of Sir Don Ryder, the head of the National Enterprise Board (NEB), prepared a report on the company (Church, 1994: 100). The rescue package agreed between the government and the company involved nationalisation of British Leyland and envisaged the injection of £1.4 billion of public money over eight years (Adeney, 1989: 281). However, NEB interference in the day-to-day running of the company and a new system of industrial relations machinery suggested by Ryder did not help the company to reach the unrealistic sales levels assumed in the Ryder Report, and poor performance persisted. The nationalisation of British Leyland was followed by a bail-out of Chrysler UK in December 1975, with the government making a commitment of £162.5 million over four years (Young and Hood, 1977: 287).

Most writers see American-style mass production techniques in the motor vehicle industry as encountering difficulties since the late 1960s (Womack *et al.*, 1990; Jürgens *et al.*, 1993). The emergence of modern flexible or 'lean' production techniques in the car industry is usually associated with Japan. However, as was noted in chapter 6, it is possible to see in modern flexible production techniques a return to some of the key features of the older British craft-based flexible production system; in particular, the use of skilled workers to produce differentiated products. Jürgens *et al.* (1993: 377) list six changes in the form of work: (1) task integration, (2) employee participation, (3) shopfloor self-regulation, (4) automation as much as possible, (5) reduction of line-paced jobs, (6) skilled workers for direct work. However, whereas Womack *et al.* (1990) see convergence among countries on a new standard of lean production, Jürgens *et al.* (1993: 17) take account of the role of history in shaping developments in different countries, accepting that 'the leopard cannot change its spots'. Thus, for example, they find more emphasis on the use of skilled workers in Germany than in Britain, reflecting the greater decline of the shopfloor skilled worker in Britain during the Fordist era (Jürgens *et al.*, 1993: 380).

In this changing environment, after a disastrous 1970s and a traumatic early 1980s, car production in Britain began to revive from the mid-1980s. This partly reflected inward investment from Japan, with Nissan, Toyota and Honda establishing plants in Britain (Jürgens *et al.*, 1993: 388). However, it also partly reflected a revival at British Leyland, which began under the leadership of Michael Edwardes, who was appointed Chairman and Managing Director in 1977. With a new model range and a change of name to Rover Group, the company has successfully repositioned itself as a producer of quality cars. With a return to wood panelling, leather upholstery and chrome grilles, by the end of the 1980s Rover was successfully pro-

Table 12.19. *Productivity in the British aerospace industry, 1951–89 (1973=100)*

	Output	Employment	Capital	Labour productivity	TFP
1951	25.5	73.2	84.3	34.8	33.6
1954	52.3	112.9	83.9	46.3	50.2
1958	62.3	127.6	88.7	48.8	53.8
1963	66.4	118.2	90.1	56.2	60.5
1968	86.6	109.9	96.1	78.8	81.7
1973	100.0	100.0	100.0	100.0	100.0
1979	64.5	89.2	107.6	72.3	68.8
1986	107.3	80.9	131.3	132.6	116.4
1989	130.4	79.2		164.6	

Note: Industrial classification numbers: 1951–79: 1968 SIC Minimum List Heading 383; 1979–89: 1980 SIC Group 364.
Sources: Output and Employment: 1951–70: derived from *Historical Record of the Census of Production* and *Annual Abstract of Statistics*; 1970–89: derived from *Census of Production* and *Annual Abstract of Statistics*; Capital: derived from Oulton and O'Mahony (1994).

jecting a distinctive (and positive) British image, rather than attempting to slavishly copy rivals. Jaguar was privatised in 1984, and in 1988 Rover Group was sold to British Aerospace (Church, 1994: 106–7). The industrial relations problems of the 1970s had largely been overcome, so that by the end of the 1980s the British car industry no longer faced a bleak future. The traumas of the early 1980s were thus a watershed, and few would now share the desire of Williams *et al.* (1987) for a return to protection so as to provide a secure home market base for mass produced British cars.

Aerospace

The aerospace industry embraces the manufacture of airframes, aero-engines, avionics (aviation electronics), missiles and space vehicles (Todd and Simpson, 1986: 1). Output and productivity trends in the British aerospace industry are shown in table 12.19. The period 1950–73 was character-ised by rapid growth of output and productivity (labour productivity and TFP), but this was followed during the period 1973–9 by declining output and productivity. This reflects the aftermath of a series of commercial fail-ures, including Concorde and the bankruptcy of Rolls Royce, as well as problems of adjustment to higher oil prices, which adversely affected the demand for air travel and hence aircraft orders. The period since 1979 has seen output and productivity growth even more rapid than during the 1950s

Table 12.20. *Western world aerospace sales, 1960 and 1975 ($billion)*

	1960	1975
UK	1.43	3.55
France	0.48	3.61
W. Germany	0.10	1.43
US	15.77	24.04
Western World	18.40	35.30

Source: Todd and Simpson (1986: 7).

and 1960s. This has been a period of rapid growth in civil air travel, with deregulation of the important US market and increasing liberalisation in other parts of the world. The 1980s also saw a strong demand for military aerospace equipment before the end of the Cold War (Todd, 1988: 4; Wulf, 1993: 3).

The close association between output and productivity growth in this industry reflects the importance of repeat orders and the economies of learning, with Klepper (1990: 777) noting a world-wide consensus that air-craft production exhibits a learning elasticity of 0.2, i.e. production costs decrease by 20 per cent with a doubling of output. The substantially higher labour productivity in the US aircraft industry in 1967/68, shown in table 12.15 should therefore come as no surprise, given the much greater size of the American industry. The Anglo-German comparative labour productivity figures, also in table 12.15, are also consistent with this view. German aerospace output continued to grow during 1973–9 while British output fell, and British output growth since 1979 has been faster than in Germany (O'Mahony and Wagner, 1994: 36–7). Accordingly, the Anglo-German labour productivity gap widened during the 1970s and closed during the 1980s. By 1989 labour productivity in the British aerospace industry was on a par with its German counterpart. The British industry also remained substantially larger, employing 169,000 workers in 1989, compared with 68,000 in Germany (O'Mahony and Wagner, 1994: 38–9).

Although the British aerospace industry grew rapidly from the end of the Second World War to the end of the 1960s, it remained small in global terms. In this respect, the British industry faced the same problem as other European producers, being simply too small to compete with the scale of resources available to the largest American producers. As the figures in table 12.20 show, even after rapid growth between 1960 and 1975, the British and French aerospace industries remained small compared with the US industry. Table 12.20 also shows that France rather than Germany emerged as the most serious European rival to Britain in aerospace. European producers resisted for a long time the need for cooperation to provide effective competition to the United States before collaborating on joint ventures. By the end of the 1980s, although European cooperation had produced a serious rival to the dominant American producer Boeing in civil aircraft (in the form of Airbus Industrie), national divisions remained more important in military aerospace (Taylor and Hayward, 1989: 14–15).

The early postwar history of the British aircraft producers is thus one of consolidation in an attempt to provide a serious all-British challenge to the American industry. Pressure to buy British planes was also put on the national airlines and the forces, sometimes leading counter-productively to parochial designs which did not appeal to overseas customers. In the civil field, the Bristol Brabazon and the Saunders-Roe Princess flying boat were early failures, conceived in the 1940s and cancelled in the early 1950s. The Brabazon was based on the prewar idea of a small number of people being transported in conditions of extreme comfort over long distances, while the Princess repeated this mistake with the addition of a second fallacy that water rather than land bases would be used (Reed, 1973: 16). The big disappointment of the 1950s, however, was surely the de Havilland Comet, the world's first jet airliner. When the Comet entered service with BOAC in 1952, Britain was a good three years ahead of US competitors. However, two unfortunate crashes in 1954, caused by structural failure in the fuselage, led to a withdrawal of the aircraft's air worthiness certificate at a crucial moment, and by the time the problem was sorted out the Boeing 707 was on its way to becoming the world standard (Hayward, 1983: 19–21). Given the network externalities associated with jet aircraft, via the arrangements for loading, servicing, etc. Reed (1973: 46) sees the Comet failure as an unlucky break which locked the British producers out of the market. However, a more realistic appraisal would surely be that the Comet failure underlines the fragility of an industry that simply was not big enough to withstand setbacks. The point is that the American industry, too, had its setbacks, but was big enough to survive.

In military aircraft, too, the small independent companies of the early postwar years were too small to withstand the failure of a major project. The most painful scar left in this field was the cancellation of the TSR2 in 1965. The TSR2 was conceived in the wake of the 1957 Defence White Paper, in which Duncan Sandys, the Minister of Defence, argued for the replacement of manned fighters by a ground-to-air missile system, and cancelled the development of the Avro 730 manned supersonic bomber, to be replaced by the Blue Streak Rocket (Reed, 1973: 53, 70–1). In the new setup, the RAF was seen as needing a multi-role, tactical strike and reconnaissance (TSR) aircraft. To meet the needs of tactical warfare in Germany and 'East of Suez', TSR2 required a short take-off capacity on rough airfields, supersonic speed, a low level bombing capacity, a high altitude reconnaissance capacity and a ferry range of 3,000 nautical miles to reach the far end of the Empire (Edgerton, 1991: 93). However, escalating development costs led to cancellation in April 1965, soon after the election of a Labour government committed to shifting scientific resources from defence to civilian projects (Reed, 1973: 57; Edgerton, 1996).

As the independent British producers failed to break into the global market in an effective way during the 1950s and 1960s, it gradually became clear that the resources needed to develop a successful aircraft were beyond the means of a small company, and with governmental encouragement, a series of mergers led to the emergence in 1960 of two groupings. The British Aircraft Corporation (BAC) brought together the airframe and guided weapons interests of Vickers, English Electric and Bristol, while Hawker Siddeley took over de Havilland and Blackburn to form Hawker Siddeley Aviation (HSA) (Edgerton, 1991: 96).

Although Anglo-French cooperation in aerospace first occurred on a sizeable scale during the 1960s, the early ventures were spectacularly unsuccessful. Although Concorde was a success technically, commercially it was a ruinous disaster, always hovering on the brink of cancellation (Reed, 1973: 93). The Anglo-French Variable Geometry (AFVG) fighter was on in a serious manner for less than six months between January and July 1967, when it was unilaterally cancelled by the French (Reed, 1973: 109). At this stage, the British and French companies still viewed each other more as rivals than as allies, which hampered effective cooperation (Reed, 1973: 108).

Wider cooperation in Europe began with the A300 Airbus project, which led to the signing of a protocol by Britain, France and Germany in 1967 (Reed, 1973: 116). However, doubts about the viability of even the smaller, less costly A300B, led the British government to withdraw from Airbus in 1969, although HSA continued to participate as a sub-contractor (Hayward, 1983: 94–5). At this stage, it seems clear that the British aerospace industry, backed by the government, was not prepared to see its role as merely one part of a wider European industry. In particular, the aero-engine manufacturer Rolls Royce seemed to lose interest in the Airbus when in 1968 it secured the contract to supply the engines for the American Lockheed Tristar (Reed, 1973: 119). However, the huge escalation of development costs for the RB211 engine led to the bankruptcy and nationalisation of Rolls Royce in 1971 (Hayward, 1983: 114). Following the slump in the airline market after the oil price shock in 1973, the industry was in disarray (Hayward, 1983: 159).

The new Labour government in 1974 announced plans to nationalise the struggling BAC and HSA, and in 1977 British Aerospace (BAe) came into being. After a consideration of the options, including the possibility of cooperation with Boeing on the 757, BAe decided that its future lay in European cooperation, and Britain rejoined Airbus (Hayward, 1983: 174–83). During the 1980s, Airbus finally emerged as a serious competitor to Boeing, and now provides a classic example for advocates of a strategic industrial policy (Klepper, 1990). Critics of the huge subsidies, however, point out that since Airbus failed to drive out Boeing, competition has driven down the price, so that most of the welfare gains have accrued to airline customers rather than to European producers (Pomfret, 1991).

British Aerospace was privatised between 1981 and 1985, although the government continued to provide launch aid to Airbus (Vickers and Yarrow, 1988: 161). BAe also continue to produce a number of all-British civil aircraft, including the ex-HSA 125, the ex-Scottish Aviation, ex-Handley Page Jetstream executive aircraft and its own BAe 146. In aero-engines, Rolls Royce returned to profitability in the 1980s and was privatised in 1987 (Vickers and Yarrow, 1988: 165).

As well as this brighter picture in civil aviation and aero-engines, the 1980s has also seen Britain retain an important role in military aerospace. Several of BAe's military aircraft have been commercially successful, particularly the Harrier and the Hawk, developed in collaboration with McDonnell Douglas of the United States (Taylor and Hayward, 1989: 14). European collaboration has led to the successful production of the Tornado, and work continues on the development of the European Fighter Aircraft (EFA) (Hayward, 1989: 179–83).

The case of aerospace suggests that the issue of markets is an important one. For there is little sign in aerospace of many of the supply side problems that plagued other British industries. Thus, for example, there was no problem of industrial relations, with the aerospace industry lying at the other end of the spectrum from the car industry. Whereas in the car industry workers faced monotonous production lines, becoming increasingly alienated from the ever more units of identical products they were turning out, in the aerospace industry workers were making fewer planes of ever more technological sophistication, putting something of themselves into each aircraft and feeling for it when it first flew (Edgerton, 1991: 100). The aerospace workforce remained a highly skilled élite, with high status, high wages and autonomy over a complex production process (Edgerton, 1991: 97). In short, mass production never reached aerospace.

Edgerton (1991) goes further and sees the aircraft industry as a paradigm case against the commonly held view of British decline as a result of anti-science attitudes widely held across the country, but particularly by the élite. In contrast to Barnett's (1986) picture of an Oxbridge arts graduate culture shaping a welfare state and neglecting science and industry, Edgerton sees an élite that put its faith in technology to shape a 'warfare state'. The huge amount of resources invested in the aircraft and other high technology industries, and the close involvement of the state are seen as refuting the idea that poor British industrial performance can be explained by the lack of a 'developmental state' (Edgerton, 1996). Indeed the Ministry of Technology is seen as attempting to play just such a role under the Labour government from 1964 to 1970.

However, the centrality of the aircraft industry in this process can also be seen as confirmation of the importance of Ergas' (1987) distinction between 'mission oriented' and 'diffusion oriented' technology policy that was discussed in chapter 8. The substantially smaller scale of the German aerospace sector meant that more resources were available to subsidise the diffusion of technology more widely across industry. Edgerton's analysis also raises questions about the incentive effects of interventionist government industrial policies. A culture of ineffective parliamentary monitoring, launch aid subsidies or direct government financing and even bail-outs from bankruptcy, can hardly have helped when difficult choices needed to be made (Hayward, 1983: 230–5).

Shipbuilding

The British shipbuilding industry data in table 12.21 refer to merchant and warship building and also to ship repairing and marine engineering. With the collapse of merchant shipbuilding in Britain from the mid-1970s, the industry has become increasingly defence oriented (Hilditch, 1990: 485). During the period 1951–73, output grew relatively slowly at 2.2 per cent per annum, but with falling employment, the industry experienced respectable labour productivity growth of 3.9 per cent per annum. With the capital stock expanding, TFP growth was somewhat lower at 2.6 per cent per annum. During this period, Britain failed to share in the world shipbuilding boom and lost its position as the world's leading shipbuilding nation (Lorenz, 1991a: 9). Between 1973 and 1979, the world shipbuilding boom came to an end, particularly with the contraction in the demand for oil tankers from 1975 (Todd, 1985: 9). British output contracted, so that despite declining employment, labour productivity stagnated, and with the capital stock continuing to expand, TFP growth was negative. During the 1980s output has continued to trend downwards, but with employment contracting more rapidly, labour productivity growth has improved.

The collapse of British merchant shipbuilding output is shown in table 12.22, along with output trends in the other major shipbuilding countries. In Britain, there was stagnation in merchant tonnage launched through the

Table 12.21. *Productivity in the British shipbuilding industry, 1951–89*
(1973=100)

	Output	Employment	Capital	Labour productivity	TFP
1951	62.2	147.4	49.9	42.2	56.5
1954	80.6	156.2	53.6	51.6	68.9
1958	84.2	151.5	65.0	55.6	69.8
1963	74.8	112.2	79.7	66.7	73.1
1968	84.0	103.1	87.9	81.5	85.0
1973	100.0	100.0	100.0	100.0	100.0
1979	88.3	86.1	125.4	102.6	92.7
1986	55.8	51.1	136.9	109.2	83.7
1989	75.5	44.5		169.7	

Note: Industrial classification numbers: 1951–79: 1968 SIC Minimum List Heading 370; 1979–89: 1980 SIC Group 361.
Sources: Output and Employment: 1951–70: derived from *Historical Record of the Census of Production* and *Annual Abstract of Statistics*; 1970–89: derived from *Census of Production* and *Annual Abstract of Statistics*; Capital: derived from Oulton and O'Mahony (1994).

Table 12.22. *Merchant shipbuilding tonnage launched, 1950–87 (m gross registered tons)*

	UK	West Germany	Sweden	Japan	South Korea	World
1950	1.32	0.16	0.35	0.35		3.49
1960	1.33	1.09	0.71	1.73		8.36
1970	1.24	1.69	1.71	10.48		21.69
1975	1.30	2.55	2.46	17.99	0.46	35.90
1980	0.24	0.46	0.34	7.29	0.63	14.33
1985	0.14	0.63	0.21	9.30	2.78	16.87
1987	0.05	0.22		4.17	2.30	12.34

Source: Lloyds Register of Shipping, *Statistical Tables* (London); Lorenz (1991a: 90).

1950s and 1960s as world output grew rapidly. Then as the world market collapsed from 1975, after the oil price shock of 1973–4, British output fell with British shipbuilders continuing to lose market share. Although other European producers such as West Germany and Sweden increased output during the boom to the mid-1970s, the biggest gainer was Japan. The subsequent collapse in West Germany and Sweden was even more dramatic than in Britain, with South Korea emerging since 1975 to threaten the dominance of Japan.

The period between 1950 and 1975 stands out as a time when Britain lost out relative to other West European producers. Once again, Britain seems to have faltered during the era of mass production, although the effects of the decline of the British merchant marine and the weakening of links between British shipowners and shipbuilders should not be ignored. In fact, as was noted in chapter 11, mass production techniques were applied only very slowly in shipbuilding, so that Britain was able to remain the world's dominant producer until the 1950s on the basis of a highly skilled craft labour force (Lorenz, 1991a: 80–3). During the post-Second World War period, however, mass production techniques were increasingly applied in shipbuilding, with shipyards adopting high throughput techniques to produce very large tankers or for series production of standard vessels. Burning and welding techniques increasingly replaced shearing and riveting, while prefabrication led to the replacement of traditional keel-up building methods with the flow conception of hull construction from simple standard components (Lorenz, 1991a: 78).

Lorenz (1991a: 103) echoes Lewchuk (1987) on the car industry by arguing that British shipbuilders were slow to adopt such mass production techniques because of a legacy of distrust between managers and workers. The problem of poor industrial relations in the shipbuilding industry goes back to the late nineteenth century, with demarcation disputes between trades as well as conflict between masters and men over machinery and manning levels (Lorenz and Wilkinson, 1986: 126–7). The early 1960s saw attempts to reform work practices through productivity bargaining, but as in many other industries, these attempts met with little success. Skilled craft workers were reluctant to give up their status, while managers had little experience of or desire for bureaucratic methods of control (Lorenz, 1991a, 117–22).

There is, however, an important difference between merchant shipbuilding and motor vehicles. Whereas the car industry is still dominated by the advanced industrialised countries, merchant ships are increasingly built by Newly Industrialised Countries (NICs), such as South Korea and Taiwan. Just as shipbuilding lagged in the adoption of mass production methods, so it has continued to lag in the return to flexible production methods. With the demand for ships remaining standardised and with relatively simple production techniques, production has shifted to countries with lower wages. These trends have particularly hit those countries such as Sweden and Japan that specialised in the production of very large tankers and standard bulk carriers (Stråth, 1986; Lorenz, 1991a: 89–90).

British producers would undoubtedly have suffered from the spread of mass production techniques to shipbuilding, but it seems likely that the decline of the British merchant marine and the pressure of competitive forces on the remaining British shipowners to purchase ships abroad exacerbated this trend (Todd, 1985: 15–19). Government attempts to stem the loss of orders from British and foreign shipowners via investment grants were notoriously exploited, with Hogwood (1979: 129) suggesting that 78 per cent of grants paid out between 1967/8 and 1977/8 were used to buy ships built outside the United Kingdom.

As in the car industry, attempts to switch to high throughput techniques during the 1960s and early 1970s were accompanied by government sponsored mergers. Also as in the car industry, the merged groupings continued to have problems, and after a series of high profile crises, the industry was nationalised in the mid-1970s. The incoming Labour government in 1964 set up an independent inquiry under Reay Geddes, managing director of the Dunlop Rubber Company (Hogwood, 1979: 66). This resulted in the *Shipbuilding Inquiry Committee 1965–1966 Report* (Cmnd. 2937), published in March 1966. A Shipbuilding Industry Board (SIB) was set up to aid reorganisation and facilitated a number of groupings, including Upper Clyde Shipbuilders (UCS) on the Upper Clyde, Scott Lithgow on the Lower Clyde, Swan Hunter on the Tyne and Tees and Austin and Pickersgill on the Wear (Hogwood, 1979: 99–110). Although the incoming Conservative government in 1970 were committed to a policy of industrial non-intervention, their resolve was soon tested with the collapse of UCS in 1971. Massive opposition to closure and an effective union campaign, including the famous 'work in', persuaded the government to back down and use public funds to establish Govan Shipbuilders, which took over the four UCS yards (Hogwood, 1979: 152–61). Large amounts of public money were also invested by the Conservative government in Harland and Wolff of Belfast and Cammell Laird of Birkenhead during the early 1970s (Hogwood, 1979: 163).

The Labour opposition at this time formulated proposals to nationalise the shipbuilding industry, and this was carried through when Labour returned to office, although vesting day was delayed until July 1977 due to strong opposition in Parliament (Hogwood, 1979: 192–7). The nationalised British Shipbuilders continued to struggle in a tough competitive environment, and when the Conservative government came to privatise the industry from 1983, relatively little revenue could be raised because of the unprofitability of the industry (Vickers and Yarrow, 1988: 166).

Despite the collapse of merchant shipbuilding, Britain has remained a major producer of warships (Todd, 1985: 312). As merchant shipbuilding has become a mass production industry, vulnerable to overseas competition on the basis of cheap labour, so naval shipbuilding has remained oriented towards customised production using highly skilled labour. Nevertheless, as Hilditch (1990: 493) notes, Britain has been slow to exploit the export

Table 12.23. *Productivity in the British electrical engineering industry,*
1951–89 (1973=100)

	Output	Employment	Capital	Labour productivity	TFP
1951	23.8	70.8	39.4	33.6	39.4
1954	30.7	74.2	43.8	41.4	47.7
1958	41.5	84.4	55.0	49.2	55.2
1963	62.5	99.0	66.9	63.1	70.1
1968	80.4	97.4	83.3	82.5	86.1
1973	100.0	100.0	100.0	100.0	100.0
1979	108.3	87.0	121.2	124.5	113.9
1986	125.5	68.6	150.9	182.9	147.8
1989	138.5	67.1		206.4	

Note: Industrial classification numbers: 1951–79: 1968 SIC Order IX; 1979–89: 1980 SIC
Class 34.
Sources: Output and Employment: 1951–70: derived from *Historical Record of the Census of
Production* and *Annual Abstract of*; *Statistics* 1970–89: derived from *Census of Production*
and *Annual Abstract of Statistics*; Capital: derived from Oulton and O'Mahony (1994).

potential of this sector. Hence doubts remain about the way this sector of
the industry is organised. Thus, for example, despite the recommendations
of the Geddes Report and subsequent inquiries that naval work should be
concentrated on a small number of specialised yards, governments have
continued to spread orders thinly across mixed merchant/naval yards
(Hilditch, 1990: 486–9).

Comparative labour productivity data in table 12.15 suggest that in 1950,
before the widespread adoption of mass production techniques, there was
still no substantial gap between Britain and the United States. Even by
1967/68, with the growth of standardised tanker production in the United
States, the productivity gap in shipbuilding overall remained relatively
small. Turning to the Anglo-German comparison, the German productivity advantage of the 1970s based on mass production of tankers and standard bulk carriers was not sustained into the 1980s, as the German industry
sustained an equally catastrophic collapse.

Electrical and electronic engineering

The British electrical and electronic engineering industry experienced rapid
expansion during the period 1951–73. The data in table 12.23 show output
growth of 6.5 per cent per annum over these years, with labour productivity and TFP growing at annual rates of 5.0 per cent and 4.2 per cent respec-

tively. This performance is nevertheless usually seen as disappointing when compared with other countries, particularly the United States, which came to dominate world markets (Owen, 1992: 1; Cowling *et al.*, 1980: 191–7; Morris, 1990: 111). Output growth slowed down to 1.3 per cent per annum between 1973 and 1979, but with employment falling, labour productivity grew at 3.7 per cent per annum. Employment continued to fall during the 1980s, leading to a recovery of labour productivity growth to 5.1 per cent per annum between 1979 and 1989 as output growth increased to 2.5 per cent per annum. TFP grew rather more slowly than labour productivity during the 1970s and 1980s as the capital stock continued to expand by more than 3 per cent per annum.

International comparisons in table 12.15 suggest a substantial labour productivity gap between Britain and the United States in 1950, particularly in consumer products such as household appliances, radios and electric lamps. The economies of scale associated with mass production of standardised products for the large home market gave American producers a huge advantage in these product areas. However, in the more customised capital goods sections of the industry, such as electrical machinery, the productivity gap was somewhat smaller. Although the figures for 1967/68 suggest some closing of the gap in the consumer goods and components sectors, a substantial productivity gap remained. However, the figures in table 12.15 suggest that the German industry was also constrained by a small home market, with labour productivity below the British level for most of the period.

The key problem faced by British producers in the early postwar period was one of markets. The traditional markets served by British companies, i.e. Britain and the Commonwealth, were not big enough, rich enough or homogeneous enough to allow volume production of standardised products on anything like the scale achieved by American producers. The situation was exacerbated by a hankering after the return of prewar international cartel agreements, which meant that opportunities to enter new markets, particularly in Western Europe, were forsaken (Jones and Marriott, 1970: 172). These defensive attitudes to international competition were also carried over to domestic competition, where there was a reluctance to abandon restrictive agreements between companies. Only after the Restrictive Practices legislation of 1956 and pressure from the Monopolies Commission did the domestic rings begin to break up (Jones and Marriott, 1970: 173).

The difficulties caused by growing international competition in the 1960s led to the round of mergers that occurred in many other industries, as an attempt was made to produce a national champion. The General Electric Company (GEC) took over Associated Electrical Industries (AEI) in 1967

Table 12.24. *Share of foreign owned firms in UK electronics, 1988 (%)*

	Share of employment	Share of gross value added
Data processing	40	45
Capital equipment	12	13
Telecommunications	7	4
Consumer electronics	49	39
Components	23	26
All electronics	21	25

Source: Owen (1992: 56).

and also absorbed English Electric (EE) in 1968 (Jones and Marriott, 1970: 265–313). The merger has generally been seen as a success, improving profitability and increasing efficiency (Cowling *et al.*, 1980: 198–209). Certainly, GEC has avoided the collapse of other national champions such as British Leyland. However, the company has continued to concentrate on sectors with captive domestic customers such as defence electronics, tele-communications equipment and electric power plant. In other sectors, in which GEC has chosen not to compete, the proportion of output produced by foreign owned firms has risen. The data in table 12.24 show that by 1988, foreign owned firms accounted for 25 per cent of gross value added in UK electronics, with the figure reaching 39 per cent in consumer electronics. In particular, Japanese firms have been highly successful in consumer elec-tronics during the 1970s and the 1980s (Morgan and Sayer, 1988: 66).

Although there were some difficulties concerning redundancies after the GEC mergers with AEI and EE in 1967–8, the industrial relations problems that plagued many of the more traditional engineering industries were much less severe in electrical and electronic engineering (Cowling *et al.*, 1980: 238–66). This can be attributed at least partly to the orientation of the British industry towards the more customised capital goods and defence equipment sectors, where large amounts of skilled labour were required (Morgan and Sayer, 1988: 128, 205). In consumer electronics, where volume assembly of standardised products with unskilled or semi-skilled labour accounted for most of the employment, recruitment of a largely female workforce avoided many of the problems encountered by deskilling in the traditional engineering industries (Morgan and Sayer, 1988: 133). However, the potential for conflict remained in an environment of boring, repetitive work. Thus, for example, Owen (1992: 17) mentions bad industrial relations as one factor in the closure of Thorn's Skelmersdale tube plant in 1976. During the 1980s, the working environment in consumer electronics has improved as Japanese firms have introduced flexible production techniques, such as autonomous work groups, job rotation, training, and quality circles, but even here the problem of assembly line boredom has not been eliminated completely (Trevor, 1988: 192, 209).

Owen (1992) argues that British performance in electronics during the postwar period has not been as poor as is often suggested. His assessment of Britain as a moderately successful niche player fits broadly with the interpretation offered here of Britain being 'locked out' of mass production because of the legacies of traditional markets and craft skills. Thus, for example, given the difficulties of other European electronics companies in television production, Owen (1992: 20) is surely right to conclude that the decision of British companies to exit this sector was rational. Similarly, in semiconductors, the failure of the state funded Inmos, conceived as a national hi-tech champion, can be seen as a vindication of the strategy of niche specialisation pursued by other British producers such as Ferranti, Plessey, GEC and Mullard (Morris, 1990: 112–23). Even in telecommunications, where Britain lagged in the transition from electromechanical to electronic exchanges because of difficult relations between the Post Office, Plessey and GEC, Owen (1992: 32) draws an optimistic conclusion that the privatisation of British Telecom (BT) and liberalisation of the telecommunications market in the 1980s should lead to an improvement of the situation.

Owen's work is a welcome counter to the pessimism of much of the literature on the British electronics industry. Nevertheless, care must be taken not to give too favourable an impression of the industry's performance. Given the importance of standards, network externalities and learning curves in many electronic products, a clear investment strategy based on the exploitation of a technological breakthrough can transform the fortunes of a company or a country (Arthur, 1989). Whilst it is true that all European countries experienced similar problems in competing with the United States and Japan, Germany did somewhat better than Britain. Thus by the end of the 1980s, West Germany accounted for 7 per cent of world electronics production, compared with 4 per cent in Britain and France and 3 per cent in Italy (Owen, 1992: 48).

Although it is not visible in the comparative productivity figures for the electronics industry as a whole, the literature is suggestive of the emergence of Marshallian regions benefiting from external economies of scale, particularly via higher level skilled labour (McCalman, 1988: 40–1; Morgan and Sayer, 1988: 221). The M4 Corridor around Newbury is particularly mentioned in this connection. However, the aggregate productivity figures caution against seeing every regional concentration of an industry in simple

Table 12.25. *Productivity in the British office machinery industry, 1951–89 (1973=100)*

	Output	Employment	Capital	Labour productivity	TFP
1951	16.6	54.9	29.4	30.2	35.8
1954	20.7	60.2	32.5	34.4	40.6
1958	30.8	78.1	42.1	39.4	46.6
1963	34.6	75.8	52.5	45.6	50.4
1968	58.9	93.4	77.0	63.1	66.4
1973	100.0	100.0	100.0	100.0	100.0
1979	131.7	75.5	121.1	174.4	153.5
1986	211.6	71.1	185.1	297.6	229.8
1989	304.1	89.8		338.6	

Note: Industrial classification numbers: 1951–79: 1968 SIC Minimum List Headings 338, 366; 1979–89: 1980 SIC Group 320.
Sources: Output and Employment: 1951–70: derived from *Historical Record of the Census of Production* and *Annual Abstract of Statistics*; 1970–89: derived from *Census of Production* and *Annual Abstract of Statistics*; Capital: derived from Oulton and O'Mahony (1994).

Marshallian terms. Thus, for example, it is doubtful if Silicon Glen in Scotland, with little concentration of higher level jobs, can be viewed in these terms (McCalman, 1988: 41).

Office machinery

The 1980 Standard Industrial Classification (SIC) brought together electronic computers and office machinery into a single group. Accordingly, the data in table 12.25 refer to both industries before 1980 as well as after. After rapid growth during the 1960s, electronic computers came to dominate office machinery by the early 1970s in terms of net output and employment. The overall industry experienced output growth at the very rapid rate of 8.2 per cent per annum during the period 1951–73. This was accompanied by labour productivity growth of 5.4 per cent and TFP growth of 4.7 per cent per annum. Although output growth declined to 4.6 per cent per annum during 1973–9, productivity growth accelerated as employment fell and the capital stock grew more slowly; labour productivity growth reached 9.3 per cent per annum, while TFP growth increased to 7.1 per cent per annum. During the 1980s, there has been a return to the rapid output growth of the 1950s and 1960s, although this has been accompanied by a reduction of productivity growth rates. Thus output grew at an average annual rate of 8.4 per cent during 1979–89, with a labour productivity growth rate of 6.6 per cent per annum.

Despite this dramatic growth, which was even more spectacular than in pharmaceuticals, the British computer industry is usually seen as a failure (Hendry, 1989; Kelly, 1987). As in electronics more generally, British computer companies failed to compete globally as volume producers. However, in this respect they were little different from other European producers. As in many other branches of the electronics industry, American companies had the enormous advantages of a large domestic market and considerable funding of R&D by the military (Owen, 1992: 5). Hence it is no surprise that European companies, with fragmented national markets and much smaller R&D budgets, were unable to compete seriously on a broad front with the likes of IBM.

The first real general purpose electronic computer was developed in secrecy during 1943–6 by Eckert and Mauchly at the University of Pennsylvania (Campbell-Kelly, 1989: 162). Their Electronic Numerical Integrator and Calculator (ENIAC) had a number of design shortcomings, which were appreciated before it was completed. Collaboration with the mathematician John von Neumann led to the development of the functional structure of the modern computer, or the 'von Neumann architecture' of a central processor, memory devices, input–output devices, and making use of sequential programming (Duysters, 1995: 47). After a conference at Pennsylvania in 1946, which was attended by two British delegates from Manchester and Cambridge, the race was on to produce a full-scale working machine. The British groups rapidly took the lead and had two working machines before any were completed in America, although Campbell-Kelly (1989: 163) notes that this may have been due to 'the modest scale of the projects in austerity Britain'.

However, British success at this level of pure research did not prevent the emergence of a gap in commercial applications. In 1949, an agreement between the British Tabulating Machine Company (BTM), the main British punched-card machine producer, and International Business Machines (IBM) was severed. This came in the same year as the ending of the agreement between Powers-Samas, the other major British punched-card machine producer, and Remington-Rand. The British companies were cut off from American R&D just as electronic accounting machines and computers called for unprecedented financial and technical resources (Campbell-Kelly, 1989: 143). The setback was compounded by the slowness of the British companies to perceive the threat posed to punched-card machines by electronic computers. Thus BTM and Powers-Samas were distinctly lukewarm towards early attempts by the National Research Development Corporation (NRDC) to stimulate the development of a commercial computer as a joint venture between punched-card machine and electronics manufacturers (Campbell-Kelly, 1989: 166).

Whereas the British computer industry had been on a par with its American counterpart in the early 1950s, at least in terms of technological capability, if not in scale, by the early 1960s a two–three year technological gap had opened up, and IBM had emerged as the dominant global producer. As in so many other industries, there then followed a series of mergers between the main British computer manufacturers in an attempt to produce a national champion that could compete across the full product range. Thus a merger between BTM and Powers-Samas in 1959 produced International Computers and Tabulators (ICT), which then absorbed the computer interests of GEC, EMI and Ferranti between 1961 and 1963. Between 1963 and 1967 the computer interests of English Electric merged with Leo Computers, the Marconi computer interests and Elliott-Automation to form English Electric Computers. Finally, in 1968 ICT and English Electric Computers merged to from International Computers Limited (ICL) (Campbell-Kelly, 1989: 217).

Although IBM's System/360 compatible range of computers, launched in the mid-1960s, left niches at the top and lower ends of the market, ICL initially aimed to compete across the full range, using a different architecture (Campbell-Kelly, 1989: 228, 265). As Owen (1992: 6) notes, other European 'flagship' companies followed a similar strategy, competing head-to-head with IBM in their national markets, rather than targeting specialised niches. During the 1970s and 1980s, however, ICL were gradually forced to adjust to commercial reality, as governments became increasingly reluctant to provide subsidies and preferential procurement policies (Owen, 1992: 7–8).

The first step towards commercial reality came after a financial crisis during 1971–2, as IBM cut prices (Campbell-Kelly, 1989: 286). The new managing director, Geoff Cross, head-hunted from Sperry Rand, redefined ICL as a 'systems supplier' rather than an integrated producer of the full range of electronic data processing equipment (Campbell-Kelly, 1989: 292). He also explored merger or other association possibilities within Europe, but negotiations were complicated here by government guidelines which insisted that control of the industry should remain in the United Kingdom (Campbell-Kelly, 1989: 298). When Cross left ICL in 1977, although the company's finances had improved markedly, there were still insufficient resources to support the wide range of the R&D portfolio (Campbell-Kelly, 1989: 325).

Another financial crisis during the recession of 1980–1 led to a further change of management, bringing in Robb Wilmot and Peter Bonfield from Texas Instruments, as managing director and marketing director, respectively (Campbell-Kelly, 1989: 337–9). Development costs were reduced by collaboration with the Japanese company Fujitsu on semiconductors, and the marketing effort was shifted away from mainframe computers towards distributed systems based on small and micro-computers (Campbell-Kelly, 1989: 340–2). Under the chairmanship of Sir Michael Edwardes (who, as we have seen, had earlier brought British Leyland 'back from the brink') ICL were taken over by Standard Telephone and Cables (STC) in 1984. At this stage the government were still worried about retaining British control, and the American company ITT had to reduce its shareholding in STC to 24 per cent (Campbell-Kelly, 1989: 348). However, the government took a more relaxed view of British sovereignty when STC sold 80 per cent of ICL to Fujitsu of Japan in 1990 (Owen, 1992: 7). By this stage, government technology policy had become more oriented towards diffusion rather than the support of national champions (Kelly, 1987: 103; Owen, 1992: 41). Given the enormous gains from the use of computers in the rest of the economy, it would be hard to justify a return to the restrictions and preferential procurement policies of the 1960s and 1970s, which hindered the diffusion of best-practice technology.

Kelly (1987: 230–3) clearly believes that the British government should have continued to pump money into ICL during the 1980s in support of the national champion. However, as Owen (1992: 8) points out, the experience of France, where continued government support for the state-owned Groupe Bull failed to bear fruit during the 1980s, suggests otherwise. In Germany, where Siemens has continued to receive substantial government support, although the office machinery industry is larger than in Britain or France, its productivity performance leaves something to be desired. Thus in table 12.15 it can be seen that German labour productivity was down to 86.6 per cent of the British level by 1989.

Mechanical engineering

Output and productivity trends in mechanical engineering are shown in table 12.26. The industry covers a wide range of activities including agricultural machinery, machine tools, industrial engines, textile machinery and other industrial machinery. During the period 1951–73 output in mechanical engineering grew at an annual average rate of 3.8 per cent compared with 4.4 per cent in manufacturing as a whole. Labour productivity and TFP in mechanical engineering grew at annual rates of 3.6 per cent and 2.9 per cent respectively over the same period. During 1973–9 output and productivity stagnated, and although there was a return to respectable productivity growth during the 1980s, this was achieved largely through labour shedding, as output growth was negative.

Turning to comparative productivity performance, the figures in table 12.15 suggest a relatively small Anglo-American labour productivity gap in

Table 12.26. *Productivity in the British mechanical engineering industry,*
1951–89 (1973=100)

	Output	Employment	Capital	Labour productivity	TFP
1951	43.4	95.7	52.2	45.4	53.4
1954	54.7	95.5	56.5	57.3	66.0
1958	58.5	100.6	67.5	58.2	64.8
1963	69.6	101.1	76.3	68.8	74.3
1968	94.2	107.3	90.5	87.8	91.9
1973	100.0	100.0	100.0	100.0	100.0
1979	102.2	97.0	117.0	105.4	100.2
1986	79.2	61.7	121.5	128.4	106.9
1989	87.8	59.2		148.3	

Note: Industrial classification numbers: 1951–79: 1968 SIC Order VII; 1979–89: 1980 SIC Class 32.
Sources: Output and Employment: 1951–70: derived from *Historical Record of the Census of Production* and *Annual Abstract of Statistics*; 1970–89: derived from *Census of Production* and *Annual Abstract of Statistics*; Capital: derived from Oulton and O'Mahony (1994).

machine tools during the 1950s and 1960s. The productivity gap was also relatively small in agricultural machinery including tractors (but relatively large excluding tractors). These figures are consistent with the persistence of small batch production in relatively small firms, which has continued to characterise much of mechanical engineering on both sides of the Atlantic. Despite the fact that mass production techniques could not be so extensively applied in this sector, it is clear that the process went further in the United States than in Britain or Germany, as a result of the large home market. Thus, for example, the AACP report on *Metalworking Machine Tools* (1953) notes that American firms were able to benefit from greater standardisation and longer production runs (para. 1.5). Similarly, large differences in batch sizes between the two sides of the Atlantic are noted by Mason and Finegold (1995) in pumps, valves and springs during the late 1980s and early 1990s. However, table 12.15 suggests that British labour productivity performance still left something to be desired when compared with German levels. Even after the improved productivity performance of the 1980s, British labour productivity lagged German levels by more than 20 percentage points in 1989.

British performance in machine tools appears disappointing when compared with German success in world markets. The figures in table 12.27 show Germany accounting for about a third of world exports of machine tools throughout much of the postwar period, falling back to about a

Table 12.27. *Shares of world exports of machine tools, 1955–90 (%)*

	UK	Germany	US
1955	12	35	30
1965	13	31	22
1975	8	36	12
1985	5	23	10
1990	5	25	8

Sources: Prais (1981: 167); United Nations, *Yearbook of International Trade Statistics* (New York: UN).

quarter during the 1980s with the rise of Japan and the NICs. Britain's share has declined from 12 per cent in 1955 to 5 per cent in 1990, while US machine tool exports have also collapsed dramatically in the postwar period. To understand these trends it is necessary to distinguish between the major machine tool types. General purpose machine tools allow a degree of flexibility and are appropriate for customised production, while special purpose machine tools are designed for a specific use and are appropriate for mass production (Sciberras and Payne, 1985: 20). Ironically, the general purpose machine tools are more standardised, and hence can themselves be produced by less flexible methods. The problem for Britain in the postwar period was the weakness of indigenous mass production, which meant that machine tool builders tended to specialise in the more standard general purpose tools (UNIDO, 1984: 63). Furthermore, this specialisation in the standard types was reinforced by Britain's reliance on Commonwealth countries for export markets. Parkinson (1984, 97–8) stresses the importance of customer–supplier interaction in new product development, although he sees weaknesses on the supplier side as well as on the customer side.

Prais (1981: 179–86) suggests that the British machine tool industry was hampered by an inadequate supply of skilled labour, which forced the specialisation in the more standard types. Although this specialisation has clearly occurred, I would see this primarily as a result of the demand factors discussed above, and leading to an inevitable weakening in the training effort, which Prais picks up. As was noted in chapter 8, however, it is by no means clear that the British labour force was less skilled than its German counterpart in the early postwar period.

Perhaps surprisingly, given the nature of the production processes, the machine tool industry was subjected to the standard remedy of the 1960s for underperformance, government encouraged mergers. As Cowling *et al.*

(1980: 114) note, prior to the merger wave of the second half of the 1960s, compared to other European countries the British machine tool industry was already made up of large firms, although this was not matched by large establishments. A detailed investigation of the Coventry Gauge–Tube Investments merger in 1969 showed little or no gain in efficiency by 1975 (Cowling et al., 1980: 118). However, the most spectacular failure was surely the expansion by merger of Alfred Herbert, which with the encouragement of the government sponsored Industrial Reorganisation Corporation (IRC) absorbed a number of other machine tool producers, including in 1966 the machine tool department of BSA (Prais, 1981: 177). By 1974 the Herbert Group was on the verge of bankruptcy, but was bailed out by the government to the tune of £26 million. Further injections of public money were required before the Group went into receivership in 1980. By this stage, the policy of concentration had been reversed, with the Group being split in 1979 into four main operating plants with separate design departments, but retaining centralised marketing. However, this move came too late to save the Group (Prais, 1981: 179).

Industrial trends during the late 1980s may be seen as improving the outlook for the British machine tool industry. In particular, the revival of the British car and aerospace industries, which have been the most important users of the more sophisticated machine tools in the past, holds out the prospect of a better domestic demand environment. However, against this, in both aerospace and cars there is increasing use of composites and ceramics, which lessens the need for metal machining, while in cars there has also been an acceleration in the move towards flexibility, and thus away from special purpose machine tools (Sciberras and Payne, 1985: 151). Furthermore, the strategy of specialisation in standard types during the 1960s and 1970s has had its impact on the stock of workforce skills, so that skill shortages may now act as a constraint on the production of more specialised machine tools, as envisaged by Prais (1981).

Conclusions

In the engineering sector, Britain tended to do best in industries where skilled labour was required to produce a customised product. Where attempts were made to Americanise production and to deskill the labour force to produce a standardised product, disaster ensued. Thus performance was worse in volume cars than in sports cars or 4-wheel drive vehicles, collapse occurred in merchant but not in naval shipbuilding, and companies withdrew from consumer electronics while maintaining a presence in industrial and defence electronics. Nevertheless, there were some areas, such as aircraft and computers, where the application of mass production technology remained limited but where the resources needed to build up a successful competitor to the United States proved beyond British means. In these areas, Britain did about as badly as other European countries. Although effective European cooperation has been secured in civil aircraft production, it remains limited in military aircraft and most other high-tech areas.

Attempts to Americanise production methods failed largely because on the demand side Britain lacked the large homogeneous home market of the United States, while on the supply side workers opposed the deskilling of shopfloor labour processes, leading to a serious deterioration of industrial relations in large plants. This did not happen to the same extent in Continental Europe, where large mass production factories were manned by workers recruited from rural areas and temporary 'guest worker' immigrants. In many industries, government encouragement to merger and the adoption of Fordist methods was followed by collapse, subsidisation and ultimately wholesale nationalisation. Although the problems were to some extent resolved in the 1980s with the retreat from Fordism, British engineering then faced skill shortages as a result of the decline of the apprenticeship system during the Fordist era.

Texiles and clothing

Reorganisation in textiles

Although output in the British textile industry grew relatively slowly during the postwar period, productivity growth was more rapid than in manufacturing as a whole. Figures in table 12.28 show that textile output grew at an annual average rate of 3.6 per cent during 1951–73, compared with 4.4 per cent in total manufacturing. Over the same period, labour productivity grew at 6.0 per cent per annum in textiles compared with 4.4 per cent in total manufacturing, while TFP grew at 4.7 per cent per annum in textiles and 3.4 per cent in total manufacturing. During the period 1973–9 textile output began to fall in absolute terms and productivity stagnated. During the 1980s, rapid productivity growth returned, but largely as a result of labour shedding and capital scrapping rather than rising output.

For previous periods, we have distinguished between the different branches of textiles according to fibre. However, this distinction has become less meaningful during the postwar period, as man-made fibres have increasingly been used together with natural fibres on the same machinery. Between 1950 and 1980, the share of man-made fibres in total fibre production increased from 17.9 per cent to 47.0 per cent in the world as a whole, and from 22.6 per cent to 67.3 per cent in the United Kingdom

Table 12.28. *Productivity in the British textile industry, 1951–89*
(1973=100)

	Output	Employment	Capital	Labour productivity	TFP
1951	45.3	169.6	58.5	26.7	35.6
1954	62.6	165.0	63.0	37.9	49.2
1958	61.0	143.4	68.6	42.5	51.9
1963	75.6	128.2	75.4	59.0	68.0
1968	93.5	114.0	89.8	82.0	87.5
1973	100.0	100.0	100.0	100.0	100.0
1979	80.3	77.6	97.5	103.5	97.3
1986	69.5	48.3	83.8	143.9	124.1
1989	72.4	45.5		159.1	

Note: Industrial classification numbers: 1951–79: 1968 SIC Order XIII; 1979–89: 1980 SIC Class 43.
Sources: Output and Employment: 1951–70: derived from *Historical Record of the Census of Production* and *Annual Abstract of Statistics*; 1970–89: derived from *Census of Production and Annual Abstract of Statistics*; Capital: derived from Oulton and O'Mahony (1994).

(Anson and Simpson, 1988: 7; Mitchell, 1988: 354). Over the same period, within man-made fibres, there was a shift from cellulosic fibres such as rayon and acetate to true synthetic fibres such as nylon, polyester and acrylic (Anson and Simpson, 1988: 7).

There have also been significant changes in technology. In spinning, the postwar period finally saw the widespread adoption of the ring spindle in Lancashire, an issue to which we shall return below. Since the mid-1970s, however, ring spinning has itself been increasingly replaced by open ended spinning using rotors (Cable and Baker, 1983: 30). In fabric manufacture, the most important development has been the use of cheaper yarns made from synthetic fibres and capable of withstanding the strains placed on them by new high speed knitting machines. Hence knitting, which was previously restricted largely to hosiery, has been used for a much wider range of fabrics (Anson and Simpson, 1988: 31). Spurred on by greater competition from knitting, weaving technology has also seen major improvements, particularly the development of the shuttleless loom (Anson and Simpson, 1988: 32; Ray, 1984: 38–41).

These changes in raw materials and technology were accompanied by major changes in organisation, leading to the emergence of a British textile industry that was highly concentrated by international standards (Anson and Simpson, 1988: 44). The high degree of concentration arose from a strategy of forward integration pursued by Courtaulds after a disappointing company performance during the 1950s and early 1960s. The problem for Courtaulds was that although it had a dominant position in the supply of rayon to the British market, its position was being undercut by the more rapid growth in demand for synthetic fibres. The acquisition of British Celanese in 1957 secured a virtual monopoly in rayon, but Courtaulds' position in synthetics remained weak because of early neglect and later problems in relations with ICI (Coleman, 1980: 151). Although Courtaulds had a 50 per cent stake in British Nylon Spinners (BNS), together with ICI, there was little technical spin-off as the independent BNS management team kept all information to themselves (Knight, 1974: 22).

A diversification strategy, involving acquisitions in paints, packaging, plastics, steel tyre cord and glass fibre, failed to improve the company's performance (Knight, 1974: 30–2). After an unexpected hostile bid by ICI, which was successfully fought off by the Courtaulds board in 1962, the company's options were limited (Coleman, 1988: 201–37). A future based wholly on fibres was ruled out by weakness in synthetics and bad relations with ICI, while unfocused diversification had been tried and failed. Thus after 1962, Courtaulds developed as a vertical fibre–textile group (Knight, 1974: 37). There were three strands to the verticalisation strategy, based around Lancashire, acrylic fibre and filament yarn.

The Lancashire strand originally envisaged the merger into one group of the Lancashire Cotton Corporation (LCC), Fine Spinners and Doublers (FSD), English Sewing Cotton (ESC), Tootals and Combined English Mills (CEM) (Knight, 1974: 51–2). Having cleared the first hurdle of securing ICI agreement to the proposal, the grand scheme collapsed when one of the five companies demanded a larger share of the equity in the new company. Concentration nevertheless occurred in a different way. In 1963 ESC bought Tootals with money provided by Courtaulds and ICI, and CEM was acquired by the outsider Viyella with financial backing from ICI. In 1964 Courtaulds acquired LCC and FSD (Turner, 1969: 407). In weaving, the small scale meant that most companies were privately owned and thus not susceptible to acquisition, and most sheds were unsuitable for re-equipment with the latest looms. Hence Courtaulds preferred to establish their own weaving operations on greenfield sites (Knight, 1974: 55). By 1970, Courtaulds accounted for 34 per cent of the cotton-type spinning market in the United Kingdom and 10 per cent of the weaving market (Knight, 1974: 55). The other two strands, based on acrylic fibre and filament yarn also involved substantial acquisitions (Knight, 1974: 56–60).

The emergence of a vertically integrated industry during the 1960s under the leadership of Courtaulds, however, did not stem the decline of British textiles. Lazonick (1986: 39) claims that this does not invalidate his thesis that vertical specialisation was the key constraint faced by the British cotton industry. He argues that because it originated with raw material suppliers, the process of integration did not go far enough downstream. In fact, however, this is highly doubtful. Indeed, if vertical integration had proceeded further downstream, it would surely have had adverse consequences. For with the introduction of computer technology and automation, and the need for quick response by producers and retailers to rapid changes in fashion, smaller-scale flexible production techniques have become increasingly important in clothing (Anson and Simpson, 1988: 252).

As in many other British industries, then, a merger boom in the 1960s leading to the adoption of high throughput methods came at the wrong time, when flexible production methods were about to become more important. The most successful European country across the full range of textiles and clothing has been Italy, where a large number of small firms have offered flexibility, and large integrated groups have been deverticalised (Anson and Simpson, 1988: 231).

The postwar experience also sheds light on another aspect of Lazonick's (1986) work, the alleged constraint of vertical specialisation on the adoption of ring spinning in the cotton industry. As Higgins (1993) notes, vertically specialised firms were not constrained in adopting ring spindles and increasingly did so after 1945, when it became profitable to do so. The factors that encouraged the adoption of rings after 1945 included a shortage of mule labour and the imposition of purchase tax, which biased demand away from higher value fine counts towards coarse counts, where the advantage of rings was greater (Higgins, 1993: 354). It is important to note that the switch from mules to rings was already nearly complete by the beginning of the vertical integration process of the 1960s. Whereas in 1950 mules and rings running in cotton factories totalled 15.22 million and 8.16 million respectively, in 1962 there were only 1.80 million mules against 5.54 million rings (Mitchell, 1988: 371). These trends are consistent with profit-maximising behaviour, given Higgins' (1993: 358) demonstration of higher profit rates for firms using only ring spindleage.

It is difficult to avoid the conclusion that the continued decline of the British cotton industry after the Second World War was the result of further erosion of comparative advantage rather than constraints that 'stood in the way of the transformation of the British cotton industry along modern corporate lines' (Lazonick, 1986: 20). Indeed, Singleton (1991: 232) argues that the British economy would have benefited from a speedier rather than a more protracted contraction of the cotton industry. In his view, 'the complex schemes put forward, largely by the unions and the Labour Party, between the 1930s and the 1950s for the protection and re-equipment of the industry, would have led to an even worse misallocation of resources'. On this analysis, protective measures such as the Long-Term Arrangement of 1962 and its successors, the Multi-Fibre Arrangements of 1974, 1978, 1982 and 1986, were harmful to the British economy (Anson and Simpson, 1988: 109–10). Measures such as the 1959 Cotton Industry Act were probably fairly neutral, since they subsidised scrapping as well as reequipment (Miles, 1968: 46–65).

Singleton (1986) provides a chronology of 'Lancashire's last stand', based on an accounting procedure that begins with the definition of labour productivity (P) as output (Q) divided by employment (E). Hence:

$$E = Q/P \tag{12.1}$$

Now since domestic demand (D) is equal to output *minus* exports (X) *plus* imports (M), we have:

$$Q = D + X - M \tag{12.2}$$

Substituting for output from (12.2) into (12.1) yields:

$$E = (1/P)\,[D + X - M] \tag{12.3}$$

Taking first differences, we obtain:

$$\Delta E = (1/P_0)\,[\Delta D + \Delta X - \Delta M - E_t \Delta P] \tag{12.4}$$

where P_0 and P_t are productivity at the beginning and end of the period, respectively. The final term in the square bracket shows how employment falls with rising productivity, while the other three terms show how employment rises with output, split into its component parts of domestic and overseas demand.

The results of applying this accounting procedure to the weaving and spinning sections of the cotton and allied textile industries during the period 1950–70 are shown in table 12.29. The results are quite straightforward for weaving. During the period 1950–5, the bulk of the decline in employment can be attributed to a decline in cloth exports. However, imports became the most important factor during 1955–60, while the decline in home demand for cloth was more important after 1960. Rising labour productivity also accounted for a steady decline in employment throughout the period.

The picture is more complicated in spinning, because it is necessary to take into account the effects of changes in home and overseas demand for cloth on the demand for yarn and thus on employment in spinning. Thus in panel B of table 12.29, after the first four effects, which are directly analogous to the four effects in panel A, there are three terms for cloth exports, cloth imports and home demand for cloth. Finally, there is an effect from

Table 12.29. *Accounting for the decline of employment in the British cotton and allied textiles industry, 1950–5 to 1965–70*

A. *Weaving: change in employment (000)*				
	1950–5	1955–60	1960–5	1965–70
Due to changes in:				
Cloth exports	−15.3	−14.2	−3.0	−1.7
Cloth imports	−1.1	−19.1	4.5	1.7
Home demand for cloth	−0.6	6.3	−13.0	−16.7
Weaving lab. productivity	−2.1	−9.7	−5.0	−5.0
Total weaving employment	−19.1	−36.7	−16.5	−21.7
B. *Spinning: change in employment (000)*				
Due to changes in:				
Yarn/thread exports	−4.1	−2.0	−1.3	1.3
Yarn imports	0.0	−2.9	0.6	−1.4
Home demand for yarn	0.0	4.5	0.9	−1.3
Spinning lab. productivity	3.8	−12.1	−7.7	−4.7
Cloth exports	−9.0	−8.2	−1.7	−0.7
Cloth imports	−0.6	−11.1	2.5	0.7
Home demand for cloth	−0.4	3.6	−7.1	−7.4
Use of cont. filament yarn	−5.4	0.6	−5.0	1.3
Total spinning employment	−15.7	−27.6	−18.8	−12.2

Source: Singleton (1986: 103).

the growing use of continuous filament yarn in weaving, which circumvents the whole spinning process. Despite the additional complexity, in fact the results for spinning are very much in line with the results for weaving. The most important factor during the period 1950–5 was exports (of yarn/thread and cloth), while imports (of both yarn and cloth) became more important during 1955–60. Again, home demand (particularly for cloth) became more important after 1960, and labour productivity exerted a downward pressure on employment throughout most of the period. Singleton (1986: 105) uses these calculations to suggest that there was no simple policy that could have saved the Lancashire cotton industry. In particular, it seems clear that greater protection would have had a limited effect, since imports were the most important factor only briefly, during 1955–60.

The Anglo-American labour productivity comparisons in table 12.30 suggest that by 1950 the external economies of scale in British textile industries had largely evaporated. In cotton, for example, a comparative productivity ratio of 249 was not far below the figure of 273 for total

Table 12.30. *Comparative labour productivity in textiles and clothing, 1950–89 (UK=100)*

US/UK	1950	1967/68	
Man-made fibres		194	
Rayon	226		
Spinning		203	
Weaving		225	
Cotton	249		
Woollen & worsted	185	208	
Rope & twine		188	
Hosiery	187	209	
Carpets		250	
Leather	168	208	
Outer & underwear	170		
Weatherproof outerwear		204	
Men's & boys' outerwear		223	
Boots & shoes	171	173	
Germany/UK	*1973*	*1979*	*1989*
Textiles	88	111	101
Clothing	134	124	124
Leather & footwear	93	85	105

Notes: US/UK benchmark figures based on value added per employee; Germany/UK time series extrapolations from 1987 benchmarks based on value added per hour worked.
Sources: Appendix table A2.1; O'Mahony and Wagner (1994: 7).

manufacturing. Comparative productivity in textiles remained close to the average for manufacturing throughout the postwar period, in strong contrast to the prewar position. Turning to the Anglo-German labour productivity position in table 12.30, textiles conform to the familiar pattern of Germany gaining ground during the 1970s, but Britain recovering during the 1980s. By 1989, labour productivity was roughly equal in the two countries.

Clothing

Data on output and productivity in the British clothing industry are shown in table 12.31. Output of clothing grew relatively slowly during the period 1951–73, although as in textiles, productivity grew relatively rapidly. However, whereas in textiles output fell during the 1970s and 1980s, in clothing output continued to grow during the 1970s and merely remained

Table 12.31. *Productivity in the British clothing industry, 1951–89 (1973=100)*

	Output	Employment	Capital	Labour productivity	TFP
1951	43.6	130.3	74.8	33.5	38.9
1954	55.1	129.8	74.3	42.4	49.4
1958	57.7	118.9	75.8	48.5	54.8
1963	66.6	111.1	81.6	59.9	65.2
1968	77.7	98.6	90.2	78.8	80.7
1973	100.0	100.0	100.0	100.0	100.0
1979	115.3	84.9	107.8	135.8	127.3
1986	106.5	65.6	118.8	162.3	138.3
1989	114.0	61.8		184.5	

Note: Industrial classification numbers: 1951–79: 1968 SIC Minimum List Headings 441–449; 1979–89: 1980 SIC Groups 453–456.
Sources: Output and Employment: 1951–70: derived from *Historical Record of the Census of Production* and *Annual Abstract of Statistics*; 1970–89: derived from *Census of Production* and *Annual Abstract of Statistics*; Capital: derived from Oulton and O'Mahony (1994).

stable during the 1980s. Although productivity growth remained rapid in clothing during the 1970s, both labour productivity and TFP grew more slowly during the 1980s. Thus the decline in clothing has been less severe than in textiles. This is undoubtedly due to the growing importance of flexible production methods, which during the 1970s and 1980s have improved the competitiveness of clothing firms producing in developed countries (Anson and Simpson, 1988: 252).

Although the volatility of fashion and the instability of limp cloth as a working material set limits to the achievement of production economies of scale, during the 1950s and 1960s the clothing industry shared in the general trend towards mass production methods, with greater standardisation and deskilling mechanisation (Zeitlin and Totterdill, 1989: 156; Wray, 1957: 105). Inevitably, firm size was larger and production runs longer in menswear and workwear than in womenswear, where the dictates of fashion set stricter limits on the adoption of mass production methods. International comparisons suggest that the adoption of mass production methods went further in Britain than in any other European country. This development can, in turn, be linked to the much greater importance in Britain of multiple retailers and department and variety stores, which by 1977 accounted for 70.1 per cent of clothing sales, compared with 32.9 per cent in Germany and only 15.5 per cent in Italy (Zeitlin and Totterdill, 1989: 158).

Given the relatively simple technology and skills required for mass produced clothing, the clothing industries of the developed world became increasingly subject to strong competition from NICs such as Hong Kong, South Korea and Taiwan, where wages were much lower (Zeitlin and Totterdill, 1989: 161). However, technological changes during the 1970s and 1980s have led to a shift of competitive advantage back to the advanced industrialised countries. As in many other industries, it has become considerably easier to tailor supply to demand. Improved monitoring of sales, culminating in Electronic Point of Sale (EPOS) systems has enabled retailers to gather precise information on product performance and adjust orders accordingly. The application of computers to design, cutting, sewing, management information and production control has enabled producers to cope with the reduced lead times and shorter production runs inherent in the newer flexible production systems (Zeitlin and Totterdill, 1989: 165–76). These developments have all favoured domestic sourcing by retailers, because of both the higher skill requirements and the short lead times. Some authors remain sceptical of the ability of the British clothing industry to take advantage of these developments, seeing a continued emphasis on mass production of standardised products rather than a decisive shift to flexible production of higher valued articles (Steedman and Wagner, 1989; Walsh, 1991; Ram, 1992). Steedman and Wagner (1989: 45) see this specialisation by British firms at the low quality end of the market as a result of a lack of the appropriate skilled labour, in particular the 'lack of a stock of technician-level skills in pattern-making and production control'. Although taking a longer historical perspective I would tend to see the stock of skills as the result of the specialisation on standardised items rather than vice versa, it is nevertheless true that firms seeking to specialise at the high quality end of the market would now be likely to experience skill shortages as Steedman and Wagner suggest.

The pessimistic view receives some support from the scale of the Anglo-German labour productivity gap in table 12.30, which remained about 25 per cent at the end of the 1980s. Furthermore, it seems likely that the position would be worse if the full extent of the 'sweatshop' sector, including unregistered workshops and home working, were taken into account (Ram, 1992: 505). However, a more favourable view of the British clothing industry compared with its German counterpart emerges if account is also taken of trends in output and employment. Whereas table 12.31 shows that British output in 1989 was above its 1973 level, in Germany output had fallen by 1989 to 80.3 per cent of its 1973 level (O'Mahony and Wagner, 1994: 36). Furthermore, although employment had fallen more in Germany than in Britain over the same period, labour productivity had also grown faster in Britain (O'Mahony and Wagner, 1994: 38).

Table 12.32. *Productivity in the British leather and footwear industry,*
1951–89 (1973=100)

	Output	Employment	Capital	Labour productivity	TFP
1951	52.5	143.3	68.5	36.6	44.7
1954	63.0	142.5	69.6	44.2	53.7
1958	63.9	125.4	69.8	51.0	59.7
1963	80.3	123.9	80.2	64.8	72.9
1968	89.4	110.6	92.4	80.8	84.8
1973	100.0	100.0	100.0	100.0	100.0
1979	101.7	83.6	103.6	121.7	114.8
1986	85.7	60.3	109.6	142.1	120.9
1989	82.0	56.1		146.2	

Note: Industrial classification numbers: 1951–79: 1968 SIC Minimum List Headings
431–433, 450; 1979–89: 1980 SIC Groups 441–442, 451.
Sources: Output and Employment: 1951–70: derived from *Historical Record of the Census of*
Production and *Annual Abstract of Statistics*; 1970–89: derived from *Census of Production*
and *Annual Abstract of Statistics*; Capital: derived from Oulton and O'Mahony (1994).

Leather and footwear

The data in table 12.32 combine the leather industries (tanning and leather
goods other than footwear) with footwear made of leather and other
materials. Leather has declined in importance relative to footwear throughout the postwar period, accounting for 42 per cent of net output in 1951,
but only 32 per cent in 1989. The output of the combined leather and footwear industries grew relatively slowly during the period 1951–73 at an
annual rate of 2.9 per cent, compared with 4.4 per cent in manufacturing
as a whole. Productivity growth in leather and footwear compared favourably with total manufacturing at this time, however. After 1973 output
began to stagnate, and since 1979 it has declined in absolute terms.
Productivity growth has been much slower since 1973. On a comparative
basis, however, British labour productivity performance in leather and footwear has remained relatively favourable. The figures in table 12.30 show
that during the 1950s and 1960s, the productivity gap with the United
States remained less than 2:1, while by the end of the 1980s the productivity gap with Germany was less than 5 per cent.

Footwear production moved towards standardised mass production
methods during the 1950s and 1960s. As in clothing, fashion set limits to
this process, especially in women's footwear. Nevertheless, machinery was
widely substituted for skilled labour during this period. Injection moulding
of synthetic soles onto uppers eliminated 30 mainly skilled operations,

while in the production of conventional shoes specialised machines routinised formerly skilled work in roughing and lasting, substituting preset specifications for operative judgement and dexterity (Flaherty, 1985: 347).

However, this mass production technology could easily be transferred to third world countries where labour was cheaper, and footwear producers in developed countries faced strong competition in the lower quality ranges (Flaherty, 1985: 346). The problem was exacerbated in Britain by bad industrial relations arising from the disaffection of skilled workers (Flaherty, 1985: 346, 348). During the 1970s and 1980s, however, as in clothing the growing importance of fashion has created opportunities for domestic producers at the higher quality end of the market (OECD, *The Footwear Industry: Structure and Governmental Policies*, Paris, 1976: 38; Flaherty, 1985: 346). This requires the application of modern flexible production techniques, but as in other industries, after decades of deskilling there have inevitably been problems with labour force skills. Thus although British footwear producers have shifted production to higher quality shoes and to a higher proportion of women's fashion shoes, they have also fought competition from abroad at the lower quality end of the market through non-tariff barriers. Voluntary export restraints (VERs) were imposed on imports of leather footwear from Czechoslovakia and Poland from 1975, while quotas were imposed on non-leather footwear imports from Taiwan during 1977–80, but replaced by VERs from 1981. VERs were also applied to non-leather footwear imports from South Korea from 1979 (Winters and Brenton, 1991: 72).

Conclusions

Despite the emergence of a highly concentrated British textile industry in the 1960s, following a strategy of vertical integration by Courtaulds, the decline in market share continued at home and abroad. However, this should be seen as part of a general 'product cycle' pattern shared by all developed countries, with production shifting from the developed world to NICs to take advantage of cheap labour as technology is standardised and simplified. Although a similar decline in market share occurred in clothing, it was less severe as the volatility of fashion and the limpness of cloth as a raw material set limits to the use of mass production techniques. Furthermore, the revival of flexible production techniques in the 1970s and the 1980s has created new opportunities for developed world producers, particularly at the high quality end of the market. A decline in British market share at home and abroad has also occurred in leather and footwear, with the decline slower in footwear on account of fashion and the revival of flexible production techniques in the 1970s and 1980s.

Table 12.33. *Output and consumption of beer in the United Kingdom, 1951–89*

	Bulk output (000 bl)	Average gravity (degrees)	Consumption per head (pints)
1951	25,156	1037.07	147.2
1954	23,934	1037.13	139.2
1958	23,784	1037.52	137.0
1963	28,964	1037.66	158.3
1968	31,554	1037.14	167.8
1973	37,894	1037.14	201.9
1979	41,701	1037.56	217.0
1986	36,239	1037.97	193.1
1989	36,499	1038.0	194.4

Source: Gourvish and Wilson (1994: 619, 630).

Food, drink and tobacco

Brewing

Beer output and consumption data for the United Kingdom are shown in table 12.33. Given the high costs of transport, imports and exports have remained of little importance, so that consumption and output have continued to move together very closely (Gourvish and Wilson, 1994: 453). Output is here measured in bulk barrels, but as can be seen from the data on average gravity, there have been only minor fluctuations in strength during the postwar period. During the 1950s, output continued the downward trend of the first half of the twentieth century, in line with consumption per head. However, during the 1960s and 1970s consumption per head rose, and output growth resumed, at a rate of 2.7 per cent per annum between 1958 and 1979. During the 1980s, the declining trend of consumption and output reasserted itself.

In table 12.34 I have continued to use bulk barrelage as the output measure, since the net output data show erratic fluctuations. This is partly explained by the importance of excise duties, but also partly reflects the high degree of vertical integration in the industry, which creates problems in the apportionment of value added between brewing and distribution (Hawkins and Pass, 1979: 111). With employment fluctuating between about 70,000 and 80,000 between 1951 and 1973, labour productivity followed broadly the same path as output, falling to 1958 before rising to 1973. However, with the capital stock growing rapidly, TFP showed no growth

Table 12.34. *Productivity in the British brewing industry, 1951–89*
(1973=100)

	Output	Employment	Capital	Labour productivity	TFP
1951	66.4	99.9	21.7	66.5	100.5
1954	63.2	95.9	23.6	65.9	96.2
1958	62.8	110.8	28.0	56.7	82.2
1963	76.4	121.2	48.0	63.0	80.9
1968	83.3	112.3	74.0	74.2	83.1
1973	100.0	100.0	100.0	100.0	100.0
1979	110.0	78.1	115.8	140.8	126.6
1986	95.6	49.3	117.4	193.9	153.5
1989	96.3	46.2		208.4	

Notes: Industrial classification numbers: 1951–79: 1968 SIC Minimum List Heading 231;
1979–89: 1980 SIC Group 427; Output measured by volume due to erratic fluctuations in
value data.
Sources: Output: Gourvish and Wilson (1994: 619, 630); Employment: 1951–70: derived
from *Historical Record of the Census of Production* and *Annual Abstract of Statistics*;
1970–89: derived from *Census of Production* and *Annual Abstract of Statistics*; Capital:
derived from Oulton and O'Mahony (1994).

over the period 1951–73. After 1973, productivity performance improved
as labour was shed and capital stock growth slowed down.

The period of rising demand from the end of the 1950s was accompanied
by a massive merger wave in brewing. This was a dramatic acceleration of
a tendency towards concentration that had been occurring in brewing for a
long time. Since brewing is a process using large containers, there are
obvious scale economies with the capacity of a cubical container rising in
proportion to the cube of its length, but the volume of material needed for
its construction rising in proportion to the square of its length (Prais, 1981:
111). Offsetting this, however, is the importance of transport costs for a
product which is made up largely of water. Better roads and delivery vehicles in the postwar period increased the area that could be served by a single
brewery. The development of keg beer also helped to overcome the limita-
tions on travelling time and storage life (Prais, 1981: 112).

The major brewing mergers also took place against the backdrop of an
economy-wide merger boom, stimulated in part by the 1956 Restrictive
Practices legislation, which outlawed much collusive behaviour (Gourvish
and Wilson, 1994: 451). Also, the greater disclosure requirements of the
1947 and 1948 Companies Acts had led to the development of the hostile
take-over bid (Gourvish and Wilson, 1994: 459). As the discrepancy
between the historically- based book value and the realisable market value

of the breweries' tied estate became clear, the industry was bound to attract attention from outside interests (Hawkins and Pass, 1979: 65). The two most influential outside interests were Charles Clore, chairman of Sears Holdings, and the Canadian entrepreneur E.P. Taylor. Clore's 1959 bid for the country's largest brewer, Watney Mann, although successfully fought off, stimulated the latter to transform itself into a national brewer, while Taylor's dramatic expansion by acquisition through his United Breweries had a similar effect on other large brewers. The upshot was the emergence by the late 1960s of the 'Big Six' of Allied, Bass, Courage, Scottish & Newcastle, Watneys and Whitbread (Gourvish and Wilson, 1994: 460–74). The 5-firm concentration ratio (*CR*5) for net output in brewing increased from 18 per cent in 1954 to 64 per cent in 1968, while *CR*5 for employment rose from 19 per cent to 61 per cent over the same period (Hawkins and Pass, 1979: 64).

Most studies of the effects of the merger boom in brewing have been highly critical (Gourvish and Wilson, 1994: 501–2). Thus, for example, Cowling *et al.* (1980: 220) find that their *k*-statistic, the total factor requirement per unit of output, rose steadily between 1955 and 1972. They conclude that the restructuring of the brewing industry was not in the public interest.

Cowling *et al.* (1980: 223–36) argue that one of the adverse consequences of the merger boom was a narrowing of the range of choice available to consumers. As in so many other industries, brewers during the 1960s attempted to realise economies of scale through standardisation. The attempt to establish national brands of keg beer was the most obvious manifestation of this trend. Keg beer differs from traditional beer in that the former is pasteurised to kill the yeast and prevent further fermentation, filtered to remove all solids and then carbonated to force the beer out of the barrel. In addition, chemicals are added to the brew, for instance to alter the water quality or maintain the head (Cowling *et al.*, 1980: 226). Although the Monopolies Commission *Report on the Supply of Beer* (1969) was critical of the vertical restraints which restricted the ability of the consumer to switch brands, it did not recommend prohibiting the tied house because of worries about transitional dislocation in the property market ensuing from forced sales of public houses (Prais, 1981: 119).

This period of rationalisation and standardisation was also accompanied by poor industrial relations. The concentration of production at larger sites and the consequent rationalisation of working practices led to the same pattern of labour unrest that characterised so much of British industry at this time. The pattern in brewing was for a large number of relatively minor disputes, so that during 1970–5, for example, the number of work stoppages per 100,000 employees was 38.8 in brewing compared with 22.9 in manu-

Table 12.35. *Comparative labour productivity in food, drink and tobacco, 1950–87 (UK=100)*

US/UK	1950	1967/68
Grain milling	183	255
Biscuits		349
Milk & milk products		182
Sugar	148	169
Cocoa/sugar confection		299
Fruit/veg. products		248
Canned fruit & veg.	235	
Margarine		405
Brewing & malting	300	294
Tobacco	251	371

Germany/UK	1967/68	1987
Grain milling	65	82
Sugar	50	
Veg./animal fats; margarine	178	195
Margarine		96
Brewing & malting	105	70
Tobacco	114	83

Note: US/UK and Germany/UK benchmark figures based on value added per employee.
Sources: Appendix table A2.1, A2.2.

facturing, while the number of days lost per 1,000 employees was 484.6 in brewing compared with 819.7 in manufacturing (Gourvish and Wilson, 1994: 519). The process of standardisation thus met resistance from the labour force as well as the consumer.

While the 1960s saw the emergence of the Big Six through horizontal amalgamations, the 1970s saw the first conglomerate mergers in brewing. In 1972 Courage merged with Imperial Tobacco and Watney Mann was taken over by Grand Metropolitan Hotels, while in 1978 Allied Breweries acquired J.Lyons & Co., having failed to merge with Unilever in 1969 and with the hotel chain Trust House Forte in 1971 (Gourvish and Wilson, 1994: 474). These changes are seen by Gourvish and Wilson (1994: 479) as representing a shift from a production-led to a marketing-led strategy, emphasising the use of alcohol within a wider leisure context and exploiting fully the brewers' property assets.

The standardisation of the 1960s gradually came to be seen as having gone too far. One symbol of the change was the strong consumer resistance to Watney Mann's ill-fated 'Red Revolution', an attempt to promote a uniform brand of bitter, Red, and to create a brand out of its tied houses by painting them red (Gourvish and Wilson, 1994: 566). Another symbol was the establishment in 1971 of the Campaign for Real Ale (CAMRA), a consumer group which stressed the virtues of traditional draught ales and championed the cause of local and regional diversity. As well as bolstering the fortunes of a number of smaller regional brewers, CAMRA ultimately helped to bring about a re-orientation of the marketing strategies of the Big Six away from national products. By 1980, the Big Six had reintroduced local brand names and were selling about 80 brands of cask-conditioned beer (Gourvish and Wilson, 1994: 567–8).

Although output turned down in the 1980s, the improved productivity growth of the 1970s continued. Although there was a decline in overall alcohol consumption, the fall in beer consumption was much greater. The decline of manufacturing employment hit many of the high volume 'session' drinkers among the unskilled and semi-skilled, while tax changes radically changed the relative prices of beer and wine (Gourvish and Wilson, 1994: 582–3). Merger activity picked up again as brewers sought to maintain volume in the face of falling demand. Although many mergers were agreed between the parties, three bids involving the major nationals were referred to the Monopolies and Mergers Commission (MMC) (Gourvish and Wilson, 1994: 591). Then in 1986 an MMC enquiry into the trade was established, threatening the tied house system. In its report *The Supply of Beer* (1989), the MMC recommended radical reform: a ceiling of 2,000 on the number of tied houses for any brewing company or group, no new tied loans, and the right of public house tenants to buy at least one 'guest beer' from another brewer. These proposals were implemented in the Beer Orders of December 1989, albeit in a slightly watered down form (Gourvish and Wilson, 1994: 597).

Figures on comparative labour productivity in appendix tables A2.1 and A2.2 suggest that between the 1930s and the post-Second World War period, the United States pulled further ahead while Germany caught up on Britain. These figures would tend to support the generally critical view of the industry's performance in the 1950s and 1960s noted above. Although the United States achieved high productivity through concentration and standardisation, a similar strategy in Britain met resistance both from the labour force and from consumers, although the latter was muted by the nature of vertical integration in the industry. In Germany, as Prais (1981: 114) notes, median plant size remained small as brewers continued to serve traditional markets. Responding to consumer demands and moving to eliminate overmanning during the 1980s, British brewers have regained a substantial productivity lead over German brewers.

Table 12.36. *British production and sales of spirits,*
1951–89 (m litres of pure alcohol)

	Scotch whisky distilled	Scotch whisky exports	UK spirits consumption
1951	74.0	27.6	26.0
1954	88.8	35.5	28.6
1958	140.8	50.1	33.7
1963	244.2	82.5	44.9
1968	316.9	153.5	48.3
1973	471.1	203.6	78.1
1979	459.0	262.4	105.5
1986	264.9	236.2	97.1
1989	385.5	242.5	99.9

Note: Production data before 1973 refer to the preceding season, e.g.
1950–1 for 1951.
Sources: Moss and Hume (1981: 219, 231); Scotch Whisky
Association, *Statistical Report* (Edinburgh); CSO, *Annual Abstract of*
Statistics (London).

Spirit distilling

Scotch whisky has been the principal potable spirit produced in Britain
throughout the postwar period. Production and export trends for Scotch
whisky are shown in table 12.36 together with UK spirits consumption. The
overall growth of the Scotch whisky industry has been fuelled by a dramatic
rise in exports, although home sales of whisky also grew as home consumption of spirits increased, particularly after the end of 'rationing' in 1959
(Moss and Hume, 1981: 168). However, the industry has been hit during the
1970s and 1980s by changes in drinking habits, particularly in the important US market, where there has been a swing to vodka, white rum and
chilled white wine (Moss and Hume, 1981: 194).

Time series on productivity are available only for the whole spirit distilling industry, which includes other potable spirits besides whisky, and also
industrial alcohol. The figures for the whole industry in table 12.37 show
output and employment continuing to rise until 1979 before declining
through the 1980s. After growing rapidly during 1951–73, both labour productivity and TFP have stagnated since 1973.

The huge success of Scotch whisky in world markets during the period to
1973 is strikingly at variance with the poor performance of British manufactured products in general at this time. Rather than attempting to mimic
American production and marketing methods, Scottish distillers have

Table 12.37. *Productivity in the British spirit distilling industry, 1951–89*
(1973=100)

	Output	Employment	Capital	Labour productivity	TFP
1951	9.8	29.0	25.8	33.8	34.9
1954	21.6	49.8	28.3	43.4	50.5
1958	33.4	60.6	33.5	55.1	64.7
1963	48.6	·68.9	48.5	70.5	77.5
1968	64.2	82.6	68.7	77.7	81.7
1973	100.0	100.0	100.0	100.0	100.0
1979	104.2	112.9	132.9	92.3	88.3
1986	74.1	66.8	137.0	110.9	91.4
1989	66.8	55.6		120.1	

Note: Industrial classification numbers: 1951–79: 1968 SIC Minimum List Heading 239(1); 1979–89: 1980 SIC Group 424.
Sources: Output and Employment: 1951–70: derived from *Historical Record of the Census of Production* and *Annual Abstract of Statistics*; 1970–89: derived from *Census of Production* and *Annual Abstract of Statistics*; Capital: derived from Oulton and O'Mahony (1994).

continued to produce a wide variety of highly differentiated brands in small distilleries (Moss and Hume, 1981: 190). The linking of distilleries through mergers and acquisitions during the 1970s threatened this approach. However, after Guinness acquired Distillers in a keenly contested take-over battle in 1986, renewed emphasis was placed on product differentiation and the marketing of upmarket brands. By 1990, Weir (1994: 159) notes that the bad strategy of the early 1980s, when Scotch was sold at a low price in the quest for volume, had been reversed.

Tobacco

The output of the British tobacco industry continued to grow steadily, but not spectacularly until 1973, as can be seen in table 12.38. However, as the adverse health implications of smoking became increasingly accepted, and as taxes and restrictions on smoking increased substantially, demand and output stagnated during the 1970s and fell during the 1980s. Labour shedding during the 1980s led to a dramatic surge in labour productivity, particularly during the second half of the decade as output recovered.

Comparative labour productivity data in table 12.35 show the American labour productivity lead increasing during the 1950s and 1960s and Germany catching up and overtaking Britain by the late 1960s. The

Table 12.38. *Productivity in the British tobacco industry, 1951–89 (1973=100)*

	Output	Employment	Capital	Labour productivity	TFP
1951	41.7	117.3	30.5	35.5	51.2
1954	39.1	105.1	33.0	37.2	50.8
1958	49.8	112.4	41.6	44.3	58.0
1963	56.0	109.9	53.7	51.0	61.8
1968	63.1	103.6	70.8	60.9	67.5
1973	100.0	100.0	100.0	100.0	100.0
1979	101.8	94.7	113.3	107.5	102.4
1986	61.7	52.0	114.3	118.7	96.0
1989	77.3	36.3		212.9	

Note: Industrial classification numbers: 1951–79: 1968 SIC Minimum List Heading 240; 1979–89: 1980 SIC Group 429.
Sources: Output and Employment: 1951–70: derived from *Historical Record of the Census of Production* and *Annual Abstract of Statistics*; 1970–89: derived from *Census of Production* and *Annual Abstract of Statistics*; Capital: derived from Oulton and O'Mahony (1994).

American productivity advantage can be attributed at least partly to the greater degree of standardisation in the United States. Thus Prais (1981: 107) notes the much greater range of products produced in a typical British plant, with the consequent frequent change-overs on production lines leading to more downtime, lower productivity when restarting because of teething problems and less opportunity to improve the smooth running of production. Nevertheless, it seems unlikely that this can explain the increasing productivity gap, since the German tobacco industry was also characterised by product diversity. Although the closing of the gap by Germany can be attributed at least partly to a composition effect, with the decline in importance of the highly labour-intensive cigar sector which had been very large in Germany, it seems likely that the deterioration with respect to both the United States and Germany reflects poor performance in Britain by an oligopoly under the leadership of Imperial Tobacco (Prais, 1981: 99, 106).

This interpretation is given further weight by the improvement in Britain's performance during the 1980s. Table 12.35 shows that by 1987 Britain's labour productivity advantage over Germany had been restored in the tobacco industry. This follows the labour shedding of the 1980s, which can be seen as a response to increased competition after BAT entered the British market in 1978, thus bringing to an end the long-standing market sharing agreement noted in chapter 10 (Prais, 1981: 106).

Table 12.39. *British production of milled wheat,*
refined beet sugar and biscuits, 1951–89 (000 tons)

	Milled wheat	Refined beet sugar	Biscuits
1951	5,389	628	415
1954	5,080	616	472
1958	5,145	564	524
1963	5,038	711	567
1968	4,968	849	602
1973	5,002	823	614
1979	4,973	1,136	616
1986	5,224	1,297	698
1989	4,545	1,247	

Source: CSO, *Annual Abstract of Statistics* (London: HMSO).

Table 12.40. *Productivity in the British grain milling industry, 1951–89*
(1973=100)

	Output	Employment	Capital	Labour productivity	TFP
1951	72.1	171.8	54.3	42.0	57.3
1954	81.1	158.3	61.0	51.2	66.3
1958	116.6	164.6	70.0	70.8	89.2
1963	110.6	142.7	85.9	77.5	88.9
1968	114.7	114.6	97.7	100.1	104.5
1973	100.0	100.0	100.0	100.0	100.0
1979	103.2	80.6	107.0	128.0	118.6
1986	99.0	56.0	112.7	176.8	146.4
1989	114.6	53.4		214.6	

Note: Industrial classification numbers: 1951–79: 1968 SIC Minimum List Heading 211;
1979–89: 1980 SIC Group 416.
Sources: Output and Employment: 1951–70: derived from *Historical Record of the Census of Production* and *Annual Abstract of Statistics*; 1970–89: derived from *Census of Production* and *Annual Abstract of Statistics*; Capital: derived from Oulton and O'Mahony (1994).

Grain milling

Although the physical volume of wheat milled, shown in table 12.39, has fluctuated around a constant level of about 5 million tons since 1951, real value added in grain milling as a whole, shown in table 12.40, increased during the 1950s before stabilising through to the end of the 1980s. With employment following a stable downward path from about 35,000 to just over 6,000 between 1951 and 1989, labour productivity in grain milling grew steadily at a rate of 4.3 per cent per annum. With the capital stock continuing to expand, TFP grew steadily at an annual rate of 2.7 per cent between 1951 and 1986.

Table 12.35 shows that although the US/UK productivity lead increased between 1950 and 1967/68, it remained below the average for manufacturing as a whole. Furthermore, it can be seen that Britain retained a sizable labour productivity lead over Germany in grain milling, which had still not been eliminated by 1987. Although the industry was highly concentrated, competition, which as was shown in chapter 11 had been tightly controlled during the interwar period, returned effectively in the early 1950s (Sutton, 1991: 167–8).

In 1953, when wartime controls were relaxed, Allied Bakeries fell out with the two major flour producers Ranks and Spillers over discounts on their flour purchases. Although agreement was eventually reached, the impact of the disagreement was to encourage Allied to integrate backwards into grain milling and Ranks and Spillers to integrate forwards into baking. The three leading firms accounted for 70–75 per cent of flour production by 1972, rising slightly to 75–80 per cent by 1986 (Sutton, 1991: 168, 335). Gospel (1989: 93) also sees the Monopolies and Restrictive Trade Practices Act of 1948 and the later Restrictive Trade Practices Act of 1956 and the Resale Price Act of 1964 as important in undermining the market-sharing and price-fixing arrangements inherited from the interwar period and thus opening the industry up to effective competition. Gospel (1989: 93–4) also sees the growing product market competition as undermining the highly corporatist industrial relations structures established during the interwar period, and allowing a return to more flexible decentralised procedures, which can be seen in turn as underpinning the relatively good productivity performance.

Sugar refining

Data on the volume of refined beet sugar output in Britain are shown in table 12.39, while output and productivity trends in the British sugar industry (including refined cane and beet sugar, syrup and treacle, molasses and invert sugar) are shown in table 12.41. Output in the sugar industry overall grew at 4.4 per cent per annum during the period 1951–73, the same rate as in manufacturing as a whole. Overall sugar output grew more slowly during the 1970s and stagnated during the 1980s, although beet sugar increased its share of production after Britain joined the EEC sugar regime (Chalmin, 1990: 461–75). With employment falling throughout the period, labour

Table 12.41. *Productivity in the British sugar industry, 1951–89*
(1973=100)

	Output	Employment	Capital	Labour productivity	TFP
1951	37.9	147.7	49.0	25.7	34.6
1954	34.4	135.2	55.1	25.4	32.4
1958	28.0	146.9	65.3	19.1	23.7
1963	52.1	124.2	76.2	41.9	47.8
1968	67.0	117.2	87.9	57.2	61.8
1973	100.0	100.0	100.0	100.0	100.0
1979	118.9	93.0	120.4	127.8	119.3
1986	107.1	58.6	125.3	182.8	149.0
1989	120.8	52.3		231.0	

Note: Industrial classification numbers: 1951–79: 1968 SIC Minimum List Heading 216; 1979–89: 1980 SIC Group 420.
Sources: Output and Employment: 1951–70: derived from *Historical Record of the Census of Production* and *Annual Abstract of Statistics*; 1970–89: derived from *Census of Production* and *Annual Abstract of Statistics*; Capital: derived from Oulton and O'Mahony (1994).

productivity growth has been above the average for manufacturing, while TFP growth has also been relatively high.

The performance of the British sugar industry also looks impressive in terms of comparative labour productivity levels in table 12.35. The US labour productivity advantage was one of the smallest recorded in the study by Smith *et al.* (1982) for 1967/68, while German productivity was only half the British level at the same time. The British company Tate and Lyle, pursuing a strategy of vertical integration since the late 1930s, had become an international player in the global sugar economy of the early postwar period, although at this time its influence was largely confined to the Commonwealth (Chalmin, 1990: 257). Only after the break-up of what Chalmin (1990: 503) calls 'sugar colonialism' did Tate and Lyle transform itself into a modern multi-national company and emerge as a major force in the world industry.

After the experience of wartime control, and with state ownership of the beet sugar section of the industry, the postwar Labour government announced its intention to nationalise the whole sugar industry (Hugill, 1978: 145). However, Tate and Lyle mobilised public opinion behind its 'Tate not State' campaign with the help of a clever advertising campaign utilising 'Mr Cube', and when Labour's majority was reduced at the 1950 general election, the nationalisation of sugar was effectively dropped (Chalmin, 1990: 233–55).

During the 1950s and 1960s, British sugar policy faced a conflict between on the one hand the desire to deregulate the British sugar market, and on the other commitments to protect domestic beet producers and also to allow Commonwealth producers access to the British market on preferential terms. The various interests were balanced in the 1956 Sugar Industry Act, which set up a Sugar Board to administer a surtax on sugar consumption, which financed deficiency payments to beet producers under the 1947 British Agricultural Act, and purchases of Commonwealth sugar at guaranteed prices under the 1951 Commonwealth Sugar Agreement (Chalmin, 1990: 279–90).

The colonial system was threatened during the 1960s both by nationalisation of plantations and by the possibility of British entry into the EEC (Chalmin, 1990: 429). When British EEC entry finally came, preferential access of sugar from Asian, Caribbean and Pacific producers continued under the terms of the 1975 Lomé Convention. Subsidisation of British beet farmers now switched to the EEC sugar regime, with generous maintained prices rather than deficiency payments (Chalmin, 1990: 461–75). With a world sugar shortage and price explosion in 1973–4, the government aimed to increase domestic production of beet sugar, and the balance between cane and beet sugar now shifted more in favour of beet (Abbott, 1990: 218–21). The beet sugar producer British Sugar gained market share at the expense of the sole remaining cane sugar refiner Tate and Lyle, which had absorbed the other cane sugar refiner, Mambré and Garton, in 1976 (Chalmin, 1990: 490–9). Rationalisation in the cane sugar refining section included the closure in 1981 of Love Lane Refinery in Liverpool, where Henry Tate had started the business a little over a century earlier (Chalmin, 1990: 497).

When the British Sugar Corporation was privatised in the early 1980s it was acquired by the commodity trader S.W. Berisford after an epic stock market battle (Sutton, 1991: 390). When Berisford got into financial difficulties during the mid-1980s, a bid by Tate and Lyle was blocked by the Monopolies and Mergers Commission (as was a bid by the Italian company Feruzzi), and the British sugar industry remained a duopoly of two highly efficient companies (Chalmin, 1990: 711).

Biscuits and confectionery

The physical volume of biscuits produced in Britain is shown in table 12.39, while trends in real net output and productivity are shown in table 12.42. For the chocolate and sugar confectionery industry, trends in real net output and productivity are shown in table 12.43. Output in both the biscuit and confectionery industries has continued to grow throughout the

Table 12.42. *Productivity in the British biscuit industry, 1951–89*
(1973=100)

	Output	Employment	Capital	Labour productivity	TFP
1951	45.1	91.8	33.9	49.1	64.2
1954	55.7	121.1	41.1	46.0	61.5
1958	64.3	118.9	59.9	54.1	65.1
1963	77.8	100.5	70.6	77.4	85.1
1968	92.5	105.7	92.6	87.5	90.7
1973	100.0	100.0	100.0	100.0	100.0
1979	108.0	97.4	105.3	110.9	108.5
1986	113.5	60.4	103.7	187.9	162.4
1989	151.8	64.4		235.7	

Note: Industrial classification numbers: 1951–79: 1968 SIC Minimum List Heading 213;
1979–89: 1980 SIC Activity Heading 4197.
Sources: Output and Employment: 1951–70: derived from *Historical Record of the Census of
Production* and *Annual Abstract of Statistics*; 1970–89: derived from *Census of Production*
and *Annual Abstract of Statistics*; Capital: derived from Oulton and O'Mahony (1994).

Table 12.43. *Productivity in the British chocolate and sugar confectionery
industry, 1951–89 (1973=100)*

	Output	Employment	Capital	Labour productivity	TFP
1951	47.1	104.2	40.2	45.2	58.4
1954	67.3	134.4	48.4	50.1	66.0
1958	78.7	141.2	59.4	55.7	70.4
1963	89.7	127.6	75.1	70.3	81.1
1968	96.7	112.5	90.3	86.0	91.2
1973	100.0	100.0	100.0	100.0	100.0
1979	96.8	94.4	116.1	102.5	97.0
1986	109.6	62.2	138.7	176.2	142.0
1989	118.7	58.2		204.0	

Note: Industrial classification numbers: 1951–79: 1968 SIC Minimum List Heading 217;
1979–89: 1980 SIC Activity Heading 4214.
Sources: Output and Employment: 1951–70: derived from *Historical Record of the Census of
Production* and *Annual Abstract of Statistics*; 1970–89: derived from *Census of Production*
and *Annual Abstract of Statistics*; Capital: derived from Oulton and O'Mahony (1994).

postwar period, and although growth was slower than in manufacturing as a whole before 1973, it has been above average since 1973. The same is true of labour productivity growth and TFP growth, with both industries registering extremely rapid productivity growth during the 1980s. Thus, for example, labour productivity in the biscuit industry grew at an annual rate of 7.5 per cent between 1979 and 1989, compared with 4.2 per cent in manufacturing as a whole.

Turning to table 12.35 it can be seen that by the late 1960s the American labour productivity advantage over Britain was of the order of 3.5:1 in biscuits and 3:1 in chocolate and sugar confectionery. Prais (1981: 126) accepts that some of this productivity gap can be attributed to demand conditions in America, permitting greater standardisation. Attempts were made in Britain to standardise, but the number of varieties invariably remained large. Thus Huntley and Palmers of Reading continued to produce nearly 40 varieties of biscuit in 1968 despite a major rationalisation (Corley, 1972: 283).

Nevertheless, it seems clear that standardisation is not a complete explanation, for some calculations by Prais (1981: 126) show German labour productivity at 101 per cent of the British level in biscuits and 131 per cent in confectionery during the period 1967–72. Since standardisation had clearly proceeded further in Britain than in Germany, Prais (1981: 137) attributes this puzzling failure of the British industry to reap economies of large-scale production to the weakness of product market competition in Britain at this time. The rapid productivity improvements experienced in the British biscuit and confectionery industries during the fierce competitive battles of the 1980s would tend to support this view. In biscuits, Huntley and Palmer Foods was acquired by the American National Biscuit Company (Nabisco) in 1982, while in confectionery Rowntree Mackintosh was taken over by the Swiss firm Nestlé in 1988 (Sutton, 1991: 467, 483). In turn, British firms have extended their interests overseas, as food processing has become increasingly multi-national (Maunder, 1988: 197).

By 1990, in physical volume terms, labour productivity in the German biscuit industry was down to 80 per cent of the British level (Mason et al., 1994: 67). However, this finding of higher British labour productivity in biscuits is rejected by Mason et al. (1994: 69) on the grounds that the German product is of superior quality. However, as was noted in chapter 2, this seems to confuse horizontal and vertical product differentiation. An adjustment should only be made for vertical quality differences, which would be agreed by all consumers. Yet it is clear, since there is free trade in biscuits but few imports of German biscuits to Britain, that most British consumers are not prepared to pay the higher price for German biscuits, i.e. tastes differ. Such horizontal product differentiation should not be adjusted for.

Table 12.44. *Productivity in the British fruit and vegetable processing industry, 1951–89 (1973=100)*

	Output	Employment	Capital	Labour productivity	TFP
1951	38.1	82.5	27.2	46.2	62.4
1954	37.5	86.5	31.0	43.4	57.2
1958	53.2	93.8	40.5	56.7	71.1
1963	80.0	100.6	65.8	79.5	89.2
1968	92.1	93.2	85.7	98.8	101.1
1973	100.0	100.0	100.0	100.0	100.0
1979	84.8	82.9	114.8	102.3	93.7
1986	74.1	52.0	138.9	142.5	109.3
1989	79.1	50.6		156.3	

Note: Industrial classification numbers: 1951–79: 1968 SIC Minimum List Heading 218; 1979–89: 1980 SIC Group 414.
Sources: Output and Employment: 1951–70: derived from *Historical Record of the Census of Production* and *Annual Abstract of Statistics*; 1970–89: derived from *Census of Production* and *Annual Abstract of Statistics*; Capital: derived from Oulton and O'Mahony (1994).

Just as American tastes allow greater standardisation than in Britain, so British tastes allow greater standardisation than in Germany, and the unadjusted productivity figures accurately reflect these genuine differences in technology and organisation.

Fruit and vegetable processing

Output of the processed fruit and vegetable industry, shown here in table 12.44, grew at 4.4 per cent per annum during the period 1951–73, the same rate as in manufacturing as a whole. Of particular importance here was the rapid growth of the frozen food market, led in Britain by Unilever's Birds Eye subsidiary (Wilson, 1968: 171). After 1973 the industry as a whole was characterised by declining output. Productivity growth (both labour productivity and TFP) was below average to 1979, but above average during the 1980s.

Comparative labour productivity data in table 12.35 show US labour productivity at 248 per cent of the British level in 1967/68. Similar calculations by Prais (1981: 128), but utilising expenditure-based price ratios rather than production census-based unit value ratios, show German labour productivity at 69 per cent of the British level during the period 1967–72. These figures are broadly consistent with the known facts about differences in the degree of standardisation between the three countries. In

Table 12.45. *British production of margarine and
dairy products, 1951–89 (000 tons)*

	Margarine	Butter	Cheese
1951	447	6	44
1954	379	23	82
1958	329	30	95
1963	337	43	104
1968	298	51	118
1973	336	95	179
1979	353	158	230
1986	452	218	255
1989	481	128	275

Source: CSO, *Annual Abstract of Statistics* (London: HMSO).

fruit and vegetable processing, unlike biscuits and confectionery, British producers at this time were able to translate their greater degree of standardisation and larger plant sizes into higher productivity than in Germany. To some extent, this can be attributed to the exceptional importance in Britain of a single basic product, canned baked beans, accounting for about 40 per cent of expenditure on canned vegetables (Prais, 1981: 127).

It seems likely, given the rapid productivity growth of the 1980s, that increased competition played an important role in reducing overmanning in the British fruit and vegetable processing industry, as in biscuits and confectionery. However, in this case, the main source of increased competition was the growing importance of retailers' own brands. Thus own-label sales of frozen foods increased from a mere 6 per cent in 1972 to 35 per cent by the mid-1980s. Birds Eye's market share fell from 60 per cent in 1972 to 25 per cent in 1987, while the retailer Sainsbury's own brand accounted for more than 10 per cent of the market in 1987, outselling Ross and Findus (Sutton, 1991: 195).

Dairy produce and margarine

Table 12.45 shows the volume of margarine, butter and cheese produced in Britain. The volume of margarine production declined during the 1950s and 1960s, while butter production rose, reflecting falling consumption of margarine and rising consumption of butter (Mitchell, 1988: 713). However, butter production increased more rapidly than consumption, as the operation of the Milk Marketing Scheme made available cheap milk to manufacturers and thus encouraged import substitution (Hollingham and Howarth, 1989: 49).

It is difficult to obtain a reliable series for real net output in the postwar margarine industry due to erratic fluctuations in the price of the principal input, vegetable oil. However, relating the volume of production from table 12.45 to the number of employees from the *Census of Production* suggests that labour productivity stagnated between 1951 and 1973, with both output and employment falling by about a quarter. Wilson (1968: 161) notes that Unilever, the major producer in Britain, had already concentrated production in two plants by 1949, so that further large gains in productivity were not readily available. Hence table 12.35 shows the emergence of a large labour productivity gap between Britain and the United States by the late 1960s.

However, the British margarine industry enjoyed a strong revival during the 1970s and 1980s based on product innovation and a marketing campaign exploiting the growing medical consensus in favour of a low fat diet (Sutton, 1991: 440). The major product innovations were the introduction of soft margarine sold in tubs and products involving a mix of butter and margarine, and the successful innovators included Unigate and Dairy Crest as well as the Unilever subsidiary van den Berghs and Jurgens. The British firms undoubtedly gained an advantage over their Continental European or North American counterparts from a more permissive legal framework, since margarine has always been a highly regulated product (Sutton, 1991: 440; van Stuyvenberg, 1969: 281). With the return of output growth and with employment declining, the British margarine industry has shown strong labour productivity growth during the 1980s. By 1987, the figures in table 12.35 suggest that labour productivity was higher in the British margarine industry than in Germany.

Butter and cheese producers gained from the policy of price discrimination practised by the Milk Marketing Board (MMB). In the postwar liquid milk market, no imports were allowed and inelastic demand meant that prices could be raised without losing revenue. In the manufacturing milk market, however, prices were set so as to allow manufacturers to make a reasonable profit, given the low prices for butter and cheese that were determined by unrestricted imported dairy produce (Hollingham and Howarth, 1989: 36). Hence different prices were charged for manufacturing milk, with milk for butter attracting the lowest price since the market for butter was dominated by imports (Hollingham and Howarth, 1989: 40). This meant that milk for butter became the marginal market to supply, and was subject to greater seasonal fluctuations than other markets (Hollingham and Howarth, 1989: 65).

The incentives to expand British butter and cheese production continued under the Common Agricultural Policy of the EEC, since protection from non-EEC imports raised the price of dairy produce (Hollingham and Howarth, 1989: 82). Although harmonisation also lowered the liquid milk premium, the MMB continued to practise price discrimination in favour of domestic butter and cheese producers (Hollingham and Howarth, 1989: 146). However, this was bound to provoke opposition from other EEC producers and governments, and by the late 1980s the threat of decontrol was a very real possibility (Hollingham and Howarth, 1989: 104, 200–1).

Conclusions

Food, drink and tobacco has remained a relatively successful sector of British manufacturing, achieving high levels of labour productivity through standardisation of output to meet demands served by mass retailers. Even here, however, there were signs of excessive adoption of American-style standardised production methods in some sectors. In brewing, for example, a merger boom accompanied by the introduction of homogenised keg beer in the 1960s led to a consumers' 'campaign for real ale' and the reintroduction of local brands. The period of concentration and standardisation was also accompanied by bad industrial relations, as in so many other British industries. The brewing industry offers a striking contrast with Scotch whisky, where a strategy of retaining production in small distilleries with a high degree of product differentiation led to a tremendous breakthrough in export markets.

Injection of competition has had a favourable impact in a number of industries, acting as a spur to greater efficiency for an incumbent dominant producer. In tobacco, for example, Imperial were forced to rationalise after BAT entered the British market in 1978, bringing a long-standing market-sharing agreement to an end. In grain milling, the anti-trust legislation of the early postwar period was important in undermining market-sharing and price-fixing agreements inherited from the interwar period, while in sugar refining, Tate and Lyle transformed itself into a modern multi-national company only after the break-up of the colonial sugar system. And in processed fruit and vegetables, Unilever were forced to rationalise during the 1980s in the face of growing competition from retailers' own-label brands.

Miscellaneous industries

Paper

By the 1950s, paper was a widely used intermediate product, so that its final demand was strongly influenced by the level of overall economic activity (Zavatta, 1988: 108). Hence total consumption of paper grew relatively

Table 12.46. *Production and consumption of paper in Britain, 1951–89 (000 tons)*

	Total paper production	Newsprint production	Newsprint consumption
1951	2,720	527	596
1954	3,079	612	821
1958	3,502	626	945
1963	4,125	672	1,309
1968	4,628	724	1,422
1973	4,633	435	1,613
1979	4,155	358	1,374
1986	3,862	451	
1989	4,378	560	

Source: CSO, *Annual Abstract of Statistics* (London: HMSO).

slowly in postwar Britain, in line with the relatively slow average growth rate of the British economy. British production of paper grew more slowly still, as imports gained in importance while exports stagnated (Shorter, 1971: 182). Total paper tonnage produced in Britain, shown in table 12.46, grew at an annual average rate of just 2.4 per cent during 1951–73. Already by the late 1960s, the British paper industry was feeling the effects of competition from Scandinavia, with imports from EFTA countries entering duty free from 1967 (NEDC, *Paper and Board SWP: Progress Report*, London, 1978: 7). Lacking an indigenous supply of the basic raw material, wood pulp, British producers were at a clear disadvantage, particularly in the production of standardised bulk grades such as newsprint, where significantly lower costs could be attained in vertically integrated pulp and paper mills. Hence the growing consumption of newsprint shown in table 12.46 was supplied largely through growing imports, with home production falling from the late 1960s.

The trend of total paper production was clearly downwards from the 1973 peak, as the industry was squeezed by high energy costs and rising wood pulp prices. The rise in wood pulp prices occurred as Scandinavian firms increasingly integrated forward from wood pulp production into paper making, to maximise the value added from their now fully utilised forest resources (Zavatta, 1988: 115). The greater use of waste paper as an input could only offset the lack of domestic wood pulp supplies to a small extent (Zavatta, 1988: 116). Although output resumed an upward trend during the second half of the 1980s, tonnage remained below the 1973 level.

Table 12.47. *Productivity in the British paper and board industry, 1951–89*
(1973=100)

	Output	Employment	Capital	Labour productivity	TFP
1951	56.4	115.9	45.1	48.7	62.8
1954	71.5	120.4	48.5	59.4	75.9
1958	68.1	134.8	72.1	50.5	59.8
1963	94.1	145.2	83.8	64.8	75.2
1968	98.1	125.0	99.3	78.5	83.5
1973	100.0	100.0	100.0	100.0	100.0
1979	83.8	88.0	103.7	95.2	91.1
1986	78.3	53.7	104.2	145.8	122.0
1989	92.5	55.6		166.4	

Note: Industrial classification numbers: 1951–79: 1968 SIC Minimum List Heading 481; 1979–89: 1980 SIC Group 471.
Sources: Output and Employment: 1951–70: derived from *Historical Record of the Census of Production* and *Annual Abstract of Statistics*; 1970–89: derived from *Census of Production* and *Annual Abstract of Statistics*; Capital: derived from Oulton and O'Mahony (1994).

Turning to table 12.47, it can be seen that productivity growth performance was relatively poor during the period of slow output growth before 1973. Labour productivity in paper and board grew at an annual rate of 3.3 per cent during 1951–73, compared with 4.4 per cent in total manufacturing, while TFP grew at an annual rate of 2.1 per cent in paper and board compared with 3.4 per cent in total manufacturing. As in total manufacturing, labour productivity growth fell dramatically during the 1970s, while TFP growth became negative. However, during the 1980s, both labour productivity and TFP have grown much more rapidly in paper and board than in total manufacturing. For the period 1979–86, labour productivity grew at an annual rate of 6.1 per cent in paper and board, compared with 3.8 per cent in total manufacturing, while the figures for TFP growth were 4.2 per cent in paper and board and 1.9 per cent in total manufacturing.

International comparisons of labour productivity suggest a poor British performance in paper and board throughout the postwar period. Table 12.48 shows that the Anglo-American labour productivity gap was of the order of 3:1 during the 1950s and 1960s, a little higher than in manufacturing as a whole. However, there was also a substantial Anglo-German labour productivity gap, which reached more than 2:1 in 1979. Although the British industry narrowed the gap during the 1980s, German labour productivity remained more than 60 per cent above the British level in 1989.

Table 12.48. *Comparative productivity in miscellaneous industries, 1950–89 (UK=100)*

US/UK	1950	1967/68	
Bricks		169	
Glass		218	
Glass containers	274		
Cement	116	191	
Furniture		253	
Paper & board	338	290	
Rubber		224	
Rubber tyres & tubes	241		
Other rubber goods	250		
Linoleum & oilcloth	256	256	
Germany/UK	1973	1979	1989
Paper & board	148	215	160
Printing & publishing	159	189	145
Wood products	176	178	150
Mineral products	84	106	91
Glass	100	130	118
Rubber products	125	140	104

Notes: US/UK benchmark figures based on value added per employee; Germany/UK time series extrapolations from 1987 benchmarks based on value added per hour worked.
Sources: Table A2.1; O'Mahony and Wagner (1994: 7).

To some extent the poor British productivity performance during the late 1960s can be explained by the slow growth of domestic demand and the strength of competition from Scandinavia, which reduced the profitability of investment, and hence slowed the diffusion of new technology, such as special presses (Håkanson, 1974: 104). However, as in many other mass production industries, there were also industrial relations problems (Reader, 1981: 296; NEDC, *Paper and Board SWP: Progress Report*, London, 1978: 24). Although the paper industry shared in the improvement of Britain's productivity performance in the 1980s, a substantial productivity gap remains. Furthermore, it seems unlikely that this can be explained by a greater concentration on higher grades of paper in Britain. Indeed, Waitt (1994: 68–9) argues on the contrary that whereas German manufacturers have specialised since the 1980s in the higher value added paper grades, Britain has become a specialist supplier of bulk grades, including newsprint and semi-chemical fluting paper.

Table 12.49. *Productivity in the British printing and publishing industry,*
1951–89 (1973=100)

	Output	Employment	Capital	Labour productivity	TFP
1951	33.5	90.0	44.6	37.2	45.0
1954	50.1	89.9	47.7	55.7	66.1
1958	53.3	97.3	55.6	54.8	63.7
1963	69.7	105.0	71.8	66.4	73.5
1968	81.4	102.9	86.7	79.1	82.9
1973	100.0	100.0	100.0	100.0	100.0
1979	95.4	95.5	115.9	99.9	94.8
1986	98.3	85.2	152.1	115.4	98.7
1989	121.4	92.6		131.1	

Note: Industrial classification numbers: 1951–79: 1968 SIC Minimum List Headings 485,
486, 489; 1979–89: 1980 SIC Group 475.
Sources: Output and Employment: 1951–70: derived from *Historical Record of the Census of
Production* and *Annual Abstract of Statistics*; 1970–89: derived from *Census of Production*
and *Annual Abstract of Statistics*; Capital: derived from Oulton and O'Mahony (1994).

Printing

Output grew slightly more rapidly in the British printing and publishing
industry than in manufacturing as a whole during the 1950s and 1960s.
Thus table 12.49 shows output growing at an average annual rate of 5.0 per
cent in printing compared with 4.4 per cent in total manufacturing.
However, since employment continued to grow in printing, labour productivity growth in this industry at 4.5 per cent was even closer to the manufacturing average of 4.4 per cent per annum. During the 1970s, output and
TFP fell while labour productivity stagnated. Although positive output
growth returned in the second half of the 1980s, labour productivity and
TFP performance remained disappointing.

Comparative labour productivity figures in table 12.48 show the British
printing and publishing industry in a bad light during the 1970s and 1980s.
Even after a period of catch up growth in Britain during the 1980s, the
German labour productivity advantage remained more than 45 percentage
points in 1989. A study by Prais (1981) which focuses more narrowly on
newspapers and periodicals also provides some productivity figures for the
United States. Using the crude measure of newsprint consumption per
employee, Prais (1981: 196) found US labour productivity at 257 per cent
of the British level during 1975–7, while German labour productivity
was 215 per cent of the British level. The large productivity gap with
Germany was seen by Prais (1981: 196) as particularly serious, since British

newspapers had much larger circulations, and should therefore have been able to reap substantial economies of scale. Prais (1981: 201) concluded that the main problem was resistance to new technology by entrenched craft unions.

The printing industry has long been notorious for its poor industrial relations, attracting much critical attention throughout the postwar period. Even authors who are normally very sympathetic to unions find it difficult to avoid condemnation of the restrictive practices of the print unions (Tiratsoo and Tomlinson, 1994: 77). Zweig (1951: 187–214) describes the situation in the early postwar period as characterised by a very high degree of organisation by craft, with closed shops common in some areas, strict union control of entry through apprenticeships, craft control over manning levels, and persistent inter-union disputes over wage differentials. The leap-frogging between unions in wage negotiations during the early postwar period, described by Child (1967: 309–25) is a graphic illustration of the kind of sectional interest group bargaining seen by Olson (1982) as so damaging for long-run productivity performance. Sisson (1975: 165) sees the degree of control over the production process exercised by the union 'chapels' as so strong that he uses the term 'sub-contracting' to describe union–management relations in the early 1970s. After three Royal Commissions on the Press, established in 1947, 1961 and 1974, the industrial relations problems of the printing industry remained unsolved, and indeed even escalated during the late 1970s (Sisson, 1975: 2; Jenkins, 1979: 13).

Many of the problems of the 1970s concerned the introduction of new technology, based on electronic or computer devices, which threatened the traditional craft skills of the print workers (Gennard and Dunn, 1983). The old technology used 'hot' production methods, pouring molten metal into moulds to produce lines of type. New 'cold' production methods began to make inroads during the 1960s, and by the late 1970s it was technically possible for journalists to type directly onto VDUs linked to a computer, thus eliminating many of the old composing functions (Prais, 1981: 196–7).

The new cold production methods were introduced first in the provincial newspapers, meeting stronger resistance in Fleet Street. After a major dispute in 1978–9, during which *The Times* failed to appear for 11 months, new technology was installed but continued to be operated by craft printers (Prais, 1981: 201). However, in a series of high profile disputes during the 1980s, the power of the print unions was largely broken. An important factor here was the use of the provisions of the new employment legislation of the early 1980s, including the 1980 Employment Act, which outlawed secondary action and restricted picketing to the workers' own place of work, and the 1984 Trade Union Act, which required secret individual ballots before industrial action could be taken (Kessler and Bayliss, 1992: 79–86). In the Messenger Newspapers dispute of 1984, when Eddie Shah began to recruit non-union labour, the assets of the National Graphical Association (NGA) were sequestered for contempt of court after the union ignored injunctions against unlawful secondary action and secondary picketing (Kessler and Bayliss, 1992: 80–1). In the News International dispute of 1986, when Rupert Murdoch moved printing from Fleet Street to Wapping, the assets of the Society of Graphical and Allied Trades (SOGAT) were sequestered after a failure to hold a ballot, although an injunction might equally have been based on unlawful secondary action (Kessler and Bayliss, 1992: 81–2).

Another important factor behind the defeat of the print unions in the 1980s was a change in ownership of the major newspapers. Whereas many of the previous generation of press barons had been content to bask in the prestige of ownership and even to tolerate losses, the new owners demanded an economic rate of return (Jenkins, 1979: 14–15). In the harsh competitive climate of the 1980s, the restrictive practices of the print unions could no longer go unchallenged. The defeat of the print unions has clearly improved the productivity performance of the British printing industry, but the comparative data in table 12.48 suggest that by the end of the 1980s there was still a lot of ground to be made up.

Furniture

Output and productivity trends in the British furniture industry are shown in table 12.50. Imports and exports have remained relatively unimportant in an industry where transport costs are large, so that output has grown broadly in line with domestic demand for furniture (Prais, 1981: 139). Output and productivity growth in this sector have remained fairly close to the average for manufacturing for most of the postwar period, although the acceleration of productivity growth during the 1980s was rather more muted in furniture than in manufacturing as a whole.

The comparative productivity data in table 12.48 refer to the rather broader category of wood products, which includes shop and office fittings, wooden containers and baskets, miscellaneous wood and cork manufactures and brushes and brooms. Nevertheless, the picture of an already large Anglo-German labour productivity gap by the early 1970s is broadly consistent with the calculations of Prais (1981: 142) for the more narrowly defined furniture industry. For 1967/68, using purchasing power parities to convert census net output, Prais finds German labour productivity to be 198.8 per cent of the British level, with US labour productivity 232.4 per cent of the British level.

Table 12.50. *Productivity in the British furniture and upholstery industry,*
1951–89 (1973=100)

	Output	Employment	Capital	Labour productivity	TFP
1951	36.1	114.7	44.0	31.5	40.7
1954	44.8	107.8	45.9	41.6	52.3
1958	47.0	105.4	50.4	44.6	54.4
1963	58.7	105.6	59.8	55.6	64.8
1968	70.1	91.2	72.4	76.9	81.8
1973	100.0	100.0	100.0	100.0	100.0
1979	100.8	95.9	115.8	105.1	99.9
1986	95.6	77.2	127.4	123.8	108.1
1989	117.5	91.6		128.3	

Note: Industrial classification numbers: 1951–79: 1968 SIC Minimum List Heading 472;
1979–89: 1980 SIC Activity Heading 4671.
Sources: Output and Employment: 1951–70: derived from *Historical Record of the Census of*
Production and *Annual Abstract of Statistics*; 1970–89: derived from *Census of Production*
and *Annual Abstract of Statistics*; Capital: derived from Oulton and O'Mahony (1994).

The finding of such a large German labour productivity lead in this
industry is undoubtedly related to demand patterns, with German furniture
makers able to proceed much further with mechanisation than their British
counterparts, constrained to produce in smaller batches. The major
postwar innovation which has allowed the use of flow-line methods is the
use of chipboard, where soft wood chips are bonded together to produce a
dimensionally accurate board which can be finished with wood veneer or
plastic laminate (Reid, 1986: 168). Veneer panels can be folded after V-
grooving and quick-drying adhesives can be applied automatically, thus
saving on much difficult joinery and edge-finishing. In addition, plastic
mouldings have become widely used for things like door handles and chair
seats (Prais, 1981: 143). Many of these developments originated in
Germany, where labour productivity has been close to US levels.

Prais (1981: 143–4) notes that although the British furniture industry has
not been very successful in the production of knock-down self-assembly
furniture made from chipboard, it has been more successful in the more
labour-intensive production of traditional styles of furniture, commensu-
rate with British demand patterns. However, in contrast to his tendency to
praise high quality German production in other industries, Prais (1981:
144) is very dismissive of British production of high quality 'reproduction'
furniture, claiming that, 'beautiful and profitable as this activity may be, it
advances the country's standard of living only in the same way as the

Table 12.51. *Productivity in the British cement industry, 1951–89*
(1973=100)

	Output	Employment	Capital	Labour productivity	TFP
1951	41.6	83.7	26.4	49.7	67.9
1954	51.5	85.7	32.0	60.1	78.4
1958	47.4	87.1	37.8	54.4	68.2
1963	70.5	96.6	54.3	73.0	85.2
1968	76.9	94.6	86.7	81.3	83.2
1973	100.0	100.0	100.0	100.0	100.0
1979	84.0	94.6	102.6	88.8	86.9
1986	67.0	53.8	111.1	124.5	102.4
1989	78.6	52.6		149.4	

Note: Industrial classification numbers: 1951–79: 1968 SIC Minimum List Heading 464; 1979–89: 1980 SIC Group 242.
Sources: Output and Employment: 1951–70: derived from *Historical Record of the Census of Production* and *Annual Abstract of Statistics*; 1970–89: derived from *Census of Production* and *Annual Abstract of Statistics*; Capital: derived from Oulton and O'Mahony (1994).

continued production of hand-woven carpets in Persia'. The more recent study by Steedman and Wagner (1987) reinforces and extends the bias against British producers by looking only at kitchen furniture, the area of greatest German success.

Cement and bricks

Output and productivity trends in the British cement and brick industries are shown in tables 12.51 and 12.52 respectively. In cement, output and productivity (both labour productivity and TFP) grew slightly more slowly than in manufacturing as a whole during 1951–73. During the 1970s output and labour productivity fell sharply in cement, while during the 1980s productivity growth was more rapid than at any other time since the Second World War, despite static output. Output and productivity trends were very different in the brick industry: during 1951–73 output grew very slowly in bricks, while productivity growth was more rapid than in cement. Relative performance between the two industries has, however, been reversed since 1973; output has remained more stable in bricks than in cement, but with relatively disappointing productivity growth in bricks.

The different output trends in cement and bricks are consistent with changes in building technology. During the 1950s and 1960s the growing use of prefabricated concrete structural materials was a major factor

Table 12.52. *Productivity in the British brick industry, 1951–89*
(1973=100)

	Output	Employment	Capital	Labour productivity	TFP
1951	66.8	165.8	36.6	40.3	60.6
1954	73.1	169.5	42.4	43.1	62.7
1958	67.5	149.2	50.8	45.2	60.5
1963	81.1	139.5	65.2	58.1	71.4
1968	91.0	122.5	85.0	74.3	82.0
1973	100.0	100.0	100.0	100.0	100.0
1979	66.6	76.3	107.5	87.3	79.6
1986	58.7	59.6	109.0	98.5	83.6
1989	76.3	64.4		118.5	

Note: Industrial classification numbers: 1951–79: 1968 SIC Minimum List Heading 461; 1979–89: 1980 SIC Group 241.
Sources: Output and Employment: 1951–70: derived from *Historical Record of the Census of Production* and *Annual Abstract of Statistics*; 1970–89: derived from *Census of Production* and *Annual Abstract of Statistics*; Capital: derived from Oulton and O'Mahony (1994).

behind the rapid growth in the demand for cement and stagnation in the demand for bricks, although changes in the relative importance of different types of construction output should also be borne in mind, since cement is a very important material for civil engineering projects such as aerodromes, roads, etc. (Bowley, 1960: 205–6). However, poor design and erection procedures led to increasing dissatisfaction with 'industrialised building' and a return to more traditional brick structures during the 1970s and 1980s (Harvey and Ashworth, 1992: 90).

Comparative labour productivity data for bricks and cement are shown in table 12.48 and appendix table A2.2. For the US/UK comparison in table 12.48, it can be seen that British performance remained relatively good in bricks during the 1950s and 1960s, but deteriorated in cement. The deterioration in British productivity performance in cement is also apparent in the Germany/UK figures in appendix table A2.2. The 1967/68 comparison also suggests a sizeable Anglo-German productivity gap in bricks. Britain's position has, however, improved relative to Germany in both cement and bricks between 1967/68 and 1987. In non-ferrous mineral products more generally, however, the data in table 12.48 suggest that the improvement in Britain's productivity performance was confined to the 1980s, with a period of deterioration between 1973 and 1979.

In the brick industry, the lower level of labour productivity in Britain than in Germany, which has continued into the 1980s, can be seen largely as a result of differences in the product mix, affecting the choice of technology. The tunnel kiln, widely adopted in most west European countries and the United States by the late 1960s, was unsuitable for clays with a high carbon content, thus effectively ruling out the large British Fletton sector (Lacci et al., 1974: 115). Hence the British industry remained more dependent on the less capital-intensive Hoffmann kilns.

The poor productivity performance of the British cement industry from the 1950s through to the 1970s can be linked to restrictive practices. As was noted in chapter 11, a common marketing and pricing agreement in 1934 followed a period of intense competition, which had eliminated the inefficient plant. By the 1950s, however, the agreement was beginning to have adverse effects on productivity through the blunting of incentives. In 1961, the Restrictive Practices Court allowed the cement manufacturers to continue their common marketing and price arrangements on the grounds that the agreement kept down the overall price of cement to a level lower than it would have been under free competition by reducing the risk facing the industry and thus lowering the required rate of return on capital (Stevens and Yamey, 1965: 206). However, in the more competitive climate of the 1980s, this argument looked increasingly suspect, and the Office of Fair Trading began an investigation with a view to having the 1961 judgement re-examined.

Before the matter reached court, however, in February 1987 the Cement Makers' Federation abandoned the common marketing and price arrangements (Office of Fair Trading, *Annual Report of the Director General of Fair Trading, 1987*, London: HMSO: 31). The dramatic productivity improvement of the 1980s suggests that the break-up of the cement cartel has been beneficial. In some building materials, however, the Office of Fair Trading has had less success. Thus in ready mixed concrete, for example, despite undertakings given in 1977 after the discovery of unregistered agreements, and a Monopolies and Mergers Commission Report in 1981, *Ready Mixed Concrete* (Cmnd.8354) stating that there was no evidence of the continued existence of such agreements, a long-running legal battle between the Office of Fair trading and ready mixed concrete firms raged into the 1990s (*Annual Reports of the Director General of Fair Trading*, London: HMSO).

Glass

Output and productivity in the British glass industry, shown here in table 12.53, grew at about the average rate for manufacturing during the period 1951–73. During the 1970s, output and productivity declined more rapidly in glass than in total manufacturing, while the recovery was stronger in glass during the 1980s. Whereas the comparative labour productivity data

Table 12.53. *Productivity in the British glass industry, 1951–89 (1973=10*

	Output	Employment	Capital	Labour productivity	TFP
1951	39.8	99.4	31.5	40.0	54.6
1954	39.2	93.6	35.6	41.9	54.4
1958	47.1	100.9	43.2	46.7	58.7
1963	54.7	103.3	57.2	53.0	62.1
1968	71.4	104.0	78.8	68.7	74.0
1973	100.0	100.0	100.0	100.0	100.0
1979	84.4	85.4	116.5	98.8	90.9
1986	82.2	56.2	115.8	146.3	120.4
1989	104.3	64.0		163.0	

Note: Industrial classification numbers: 1951–79: 1968 SIC Minimum List Heading 463; 1979–89: 1980 SIC Group 247.
Sources: Output and Employment: 1951–70: derived from *Historical Record of the Census of Production* and *Annual Abstract of Statistics*; 1970–89: derived from *Census of Production* and *Annual Abstract of Statistics*; Capital: derived from Oulton and O'Mahony (1994).

in table 12.48 show a substantially smaller Anglo-American productivity gap in glass overall than in manufacturing as a whole in 1967/68, this is not the case for glass containers in the immediate post-Second World War period. Turning to the Germany/UK comparison, after a deterioration during the 1970s and a smaller improvement during the 1980s, the Anglo-German productivity gap was still 17.7 per cent in 1989.

The better British productivity performance in glass as a whole than in glass containers can be attributed to the flat glass section, where Pilkingtons were responsible for the development of the float glass process (Barker, 1977b). By contrast, in glass containers there is evidence of restrictive practices holding back productivity before the agreements were struck down by the Restrictive Practices Court in 1961 (Swann *et al.*, 1974: 185; Stevens and Yamey, 1965: 207).

The float glass process improved on previous plate glass production methods, where molten glass from a furnace was rolled into a continuous ribbon, but then needed to be ground and polished since the surfaces were marked by glass-to-roller contact (Ray, 1984: 52). In the new process, a continuous ribbon of glass moves out of the melting furnace and floats along the surface of a bath of molten tin. After the irregularities have melted out at high temperature, the ribbon is cooled until the surfaces are hard enough for it to be taken out of the bath without being marked by the rollers, thus eliminating the need for grinding and polishing (Ray, 1984: 52–3).

The float glass process was developed during the 1950s by a research team under the direction of Alastair Pilkington, who was actually no direct relation of the founding family, but was employed at such a high level because the Board felt that 'a member of the Pilkington Family, no matter how remote, could be accepted only as a potential Family Director' (Barker, 1977b: 191). Diffusion was very rapid in Britain, where Pilkingtons were the only producers of flat glass, and the process spread to other countries under licence (Ray, 1984: 55–6). An important clause in the licensing agreement gave licensees an incentive to innovate, since improvements made by Pilkingtons went automatically and free to all licensees, but any patented improvement made by a licensee could be sold to other licensees (but given free to Pilkingtons) (Ray, 1984: 53). Many improvements to the original process have now been incorporated, allowing significant reductions in the minimum thickness of the glass produced, the development of tinted glass, security glass used in cars, combinations of glass with synthetic materials, and coloured patterned glass with a smooth surface. Electronic control has been applied increasingly in the float glass process (Ray, 1984: 54).

In glass containers, restrictive pricing agreements were struck down by the Restrictive Practices Court in 1961 (Stevens and Yamey, 1965: 207). There were wide cost differences between firms before the judgement, and the ending of the agreement led to a price war, which Swann et al. (1974: 186) see as improving static efficiency through the elimination of excess capacity. However, they remain concerned that these gains were offset by an increase in merger activity, allowing greater scope for prices to depart from costs.

Rubber

The British rubber products industry continued to experience rapid demand growth during the third quarter of the twentieth century, continuing the trend of the first half of the century examined in chapter 11. During this period, synthetic rubber based on oil by-products largely displaced natural rubber as the chief raw material, so that the industry is now classified alongside plastics (Prais, 1981: 205). The figures in table 12.54 refer to both the tyre and other rubber products sections of the industry. Growth of output was strong in both sections, which were of roughly equal importance in terms of output and employment. During the period 1951–73 output grew at an annual rate of 6.0 per cent, with labour productivity and TFP growing at annual rates of 5.2 per cent and 4.3 per cent respectively. The oil price rise of 1973, however, ushered in a period of falling output during the 1970s and stagnation during the 1980s. As well as the inevitable substitution away from an oil-based product with very high

Table 12.54. *Productivity in the British rubber products industry, 1951–89*
(1973=100)

	Output	Employment	Capital	Labour productivity	TFP
1951	26.7	83.6	41.4	31.9	38.6
1954	40.0	89.0	42.5	44.9	54.9
1958	37.1	89.3	51.0	41.5	48.3
1963	60.3	97.1	56.8	62.1	71.8
1968	88.2	·102.7	78.2	85.9	92.5
1973	100.0	100.0	100.0	100.0	100.0
1979	88.6	89.4	93.6	99.1	97.9
1986	79.3	54.0	84.8	146.9	129.8
1989	93.3	54.6		170.9	

Note: Industrial classification numbers: 1951–79: 1968 SIC Minimum List Heading 491;
1979–89: 1980 SIC Group 481.
Sources: Output and Employment: 1951–70: derived from *Historical Record of the Census of
Production* and *Annual Abstract of Statistics*; 1970–89: derived from *Census of Production*
and *Annual Abstract of Statistics*; Capital: derived from Oulton and O'Mahony (1994).

energy conversion requirements, the industry faced additional problems in
the tyre section from the decline of the British car industry coupled with the
growing importance of radial-ply tyres. The decline of the British car industry hit original equipment orders, while the hard wearing properties of the
radial reduced the demand for replacement tyres (McMillan, 1989: 88, 90).
Although productivity growth was negative during the 1970s, the 1980s has
seen a return to the rapid productivity growth rates of the 1950s and 1960s.

Comparative labour productivity data in table 12.48 and appendix table
A2.2 suggest a relatively good British performance in rubber. The Anglo-
American productivity gap in rubber remained below the average for manufacturing during the 1950s and 1960s, while there was no substantial
productivity difference between Britain and Germany in the late 1960s or
late 1980s, although the time series extrapolations in table 12.48 suggest the
rise and fall of a substantial Anglo-German productivity gap between these
two dates.

The deterioration of performance in the 1970s and recovery in the 1980s
can be seen in the fortunes of Dunlop, the major British rubber company.
The transition from Commonwealth to European markets was hindered by
an unsuccessful link-up with Pirelli between 1971 and 1980 (McMillan,
1989: 146–66). Substantial cross-shareholdings were taken and there was
collaboration on R&D, but the two companies continued to market their
own brands (Prais, 1981: 213). In a mass production industry with large

plants, there were inevitably industrial relations problems, which came to a head in the 1970s (Prais, 1981: 216). As profitability declined, Dunlop were forced to make major plant closures at Speke on Merseyside in 1979 and Ichinnan in Scotland in 1981 (McMillan, 1989: 175). In 1983, the Dunlop tyre interests were sold to Sumitomo of Japan (McMillan, 1989: 184). Finally, despite an attempt to rescue the remaining Dunlop non-tyre business with the appointment of Sir Michael Edwardes as executive chairman in November 1984, in March 1985 the Board accepted an offer from BTR (McMillan, 1989: 193). Thus although the Dunlop brand name is still used, the company no longer exists as an independent entity. The shock of the plant closures and the demise of a major 'establishment' company undoubtedly had a salutary effect on productivity performance.

Conclusions

The issue of mass production versus flexible production looms large in the success and failure of a number of the industries in the miscellaneous sector. Poor British performance in the paper and rubber industries is readily explicable, since these were classic large-scale mass production industries, which suffered from bad industrial relations. The British paper industry was also disadvantaged with respect to the supply of raw materials, which gave a comparative advantage to North America and Scandinavia. Although the printing industry also suffered from bad industrial relations, this had more to do with demarcation disputes between entrenched craft unions than frustration and boredom arising from deskilling associated with mass production technology. As mass production methods became more prevalent in kitchen furniture, the British furniture industry increased its specialisation in reproduction furniture. Nevertheless, the glass industry shows how Britain was able to retain a comparative advantage in a mass production industry through successful innovation, with the development of the float glass process at Pilkingtons.

Econometric analysis

As in chapter 11, it is instructive to complement the case studies with an econometric investigation of the cross-sectional variation in comparative labour productivity. In addition to studies of the US/UK productivity comparison for 1950 and 1967/68, it is also possible to consider a study of the Germany/UK productivity comparison for 1987. In all three studies, the methodology is broadly the same as that discussed in chapter 11, which derives originally from the work of Davies and Caves (1987). Relative labour productivity is seen as a function of relative factor endowments via a production function, with competitive variables also having an effect via the efficiency term.

Broadberry and Crafts (1996) report results for a cross-section of 44 matched British and American industries in 1950. The equation takes the form:

$$\ln RELPROD = \alpha_0 + \alpha_1 \ln RELCAP + \alpha_2 \ln RELHUMCAP$$
$$+ \alpha_3 \ln RELLAB + \alpha_4 \ln CR3$$
$$+ \alpha_5 \ln UNION + \alpha_6 RESPRAC \qquad (12.5)$$

where the dependent variable *RELPROD* is comparative US/UK labour productivity from Paige and Bombach (1959). For the explanatory variables, relative capital per worker (*RELCAP*) is proxied by the ratio of power costs per worker as in the results for the 1930s reported in chapter 11. Again as for the 1930s, the human capital variable (*RELHUMCAP*) is the ratio of average earnings per worker from the census reports converted to a common currency at the average unit value ratio. Economies of scale are captured through the coefficient on the relative size of employment in the two countries (*RELLAB*).

In addition to the above variables on a relative US/UK basis, a number of variables are included to represent the bargaining environment in Britain, as in Broadberry and Crafts (1992). This reflects the possibility that vested interests acted to slow down the rate at which Britain caught up with the United States. The 3-firm employment concentration ratio (*CR3*) is taken from Evely and Little (1960) and trade union density (*UNION*) from Bain and Price (1980). In addition, since there is no satisfactory measure of the extent of collusion available in the published literature, Broadberry and Crafts (1996) construct a variable using the information collected by the Registrar of Restrictive Trading Agreements following the 1956 Act and available for inspection in the public register. Allocating price-fixing agreements by MLH category, they construct a 0,1,2 dummy variable (*RESPRAC*), where 2 reflects agreements struck down by the Restrictive Practices Court and sectors described by the Registrar in his annual reports as freed from price fixing agreements in the years after the 1956 Act. Sectors in which no price fixing agreements relating to the national market applied to principal products are assigned 0. It should be noted that the average *CR5* was very similar for sectors categorised 0,1,2 at 40.4, 44.6 and 44.0 respectively.

In equation (1) in table 12.55, the capital variable has a coefficient close to capital's share of income, as predicted by theory. Almost identical coefficient estimates can be obtained using investment per worker from the Census reports in place of power costs per worker, but these estimates are less precisely determined. The human capital variable shows up strongly, as

Table 12.55. *US/UK productivity regressions, 1950*

	(1)		(2)	
Variable	Coeff-icient	Std error	Coeff-icient	Std error
CONSTANT	−6.128	(2.296)	−6.463	(2.253)
ln RELCAP	0.403	(0.142)	0.443	(0.141)
ln RELHUMCAP	1.336	(0.366)	1.346	(0.357)
ln RELLAB	0.185	(0.091)	0.169	(0.089)
ln UNION	0.223	(0.187)	0.259	(0.184)
ln CR3	0.143	(0.063)	0.116	(0.063)
RESPRAC			0.094	(0.056)
Adj. R^2	0.364		0.393	
SE	0.298		0.292	
N	44		44	

Notes: The dependent variable is ln *RELPROD* (relative US/UK labour productivity). The method of estimation is ordinary least squares.
Source: Broadberry and Crafts (1996).

in Broadberry and Crafts (1992), and the coefficient on *RELLAB* indicates increasing returns of the order of 15 per cent. The bargaining variables *UNION* and *CR3* are correctly signed, although the former is not statistically significant. Equation (1) thus presents a picture similar to that for the 1930s, reported in chapter 11, with Britain's productivity gap in 1950 influenced by economic fundamentals including human capital and also by the bargaining environment. Equation (2) adds the restrictive practices variable *RESPRAC* defined above. This has a (numerically) positive effect on the size of the productivity gap, as predicted by theory, and is statistically significant at the 10 per cent level. This is further evidence in favour of the importance of the bargaining approach.

Moving on to the late 1960s, Davies and Caves (1987) provide an econometric analysis of the cross-sectional variation of comparative productivity for Britain and America. In this study, the United States is used as the numeraire country, so that relative variables are expressed in terms of the UK variable as a proportion of its US counterpart. The equation takes the form:

$$\ln VPM = \alpha_0 + \alpha_1 \ln CAP + \alpha_2 \ln CHECAP + \alpha_3 \ln ELCAP$$
$$+ \alpha_4 \ln BMCAP + \alpha_5 \ln TPK + \alpha_6 \ln ELTP + \alpha_7 PCF$$
$$+ \alpha_8 PART + \alpha_9 NOPS + \alpha_{10} ED + \alpha_{11} RD + \alpha_{12} BEL$$
$$+ \alpha_{13} UNION + \alpha_{14} IMEXK \tag{12.6}$$

where the dependent variable *VPM* is UK/US relative value added per worker, taken from the study by Smith *et al.* (1982). The availability of independent variables is much greater for the 1960s than for earlier periods, when data availability severely restricts choice. The basic production function variables are relative gross fixed capital per employee (*CAP*) and the relative size of the median plant (*TP*). Slope dummies are interacted with relative capital intensity in the chemical, electrical and building material sectors (*CHECAP, ELCAP, BMCAP*) and with relative median plant size in the electrical sector (*ELTP*). For the sample as a whole, the median plant size effect is captured on a UK-only basis (*TPK*), rather than on a relative basis. Human capital variables include the difference in the female proportions of the labour force (*PCF*), the difference in the proportions of the labour force employed on a part-time basis (*PART*), the difference in the proportions of the labour force not directly engaged in production (*NOPS*), the difference in the average number of years of formal education of the labour force (*ED*), and the difference between R&D expenditures as a proportion of sales in Britain and the American counterpart industry (*RD*). Variables relating to the bargaining environment include the relative bellicosity of the labour forces, measured as the difference between British and American residuals from a strike activity equation (*BEL*), the difference between proportions of employees who are union members (*UNION*), and the sum of imports and exports deflated by the value of domestic market size for the United Kingdom (*IMEXK*), the latter variable representing the degree of exposure of British industry to international competition, and thus affecting the rents available for bargaining over between firms and unions.

In table 12.56, equation (1) reports results for all plants. Capital per employee is positive and statistically significant as expected, but with evidence of a stronger effect in chemicals and weaker effects in the electrical and building material sectors. The association between relative median plant size and relative productivity is positive in electrical industries. However, the most important effect from plant size is the negative effect on relative UK/US productivity from large median plant size in the United Kingdom, which will be discussed further below. Turning to human capital variables, higher proportions of females, part-timers and non-production workers all have negative effects on productivity, as expected, while education and R&D affect productivity positively. Finally, dealing with bargaining variables, bellicosity and union density have negative effects on productivity, while exposure to international competition raises productivity.

Davies and Caves investigate further the finding of a negative relationship between median plant size in the United Kingdom and low relative UK/US productivity by re-estimating equation (1) for plants larger than median size

Table 12.56. *UK/US productivity regressions, 1968/67*

Variable	(1) All plants Coeff-icient	Std error	(2) Large plants Coeff-icient	Std error	(3) Small plants Coeff-icient	Std error
CONSTANT	−0.138	(0.12)	0.071	(0.15)	−0.347	(0.13)
ln CAP	0.150	(0.03)	0.182	(0.04)	0.098	(0.04)
ln CHECAP	0.352	(0.06)	0.386	(0.08)	0.315	(0.07)
ln ELCAP	−0.145	(0.04)	−0.265	(0.09)	−0.106	(0.08)
ln BMCAP	−0.134	(0.05)	−0.146	(0.06)	−0.085	(0.06)
ln TPK	−0.055	(0.02)	−0.077	(0.02)	−0.038	(0.02)
ln ELTP	0.371	(0.08)	0.617	(0.13)	0.224	(0.12)
PCF	−0.362	(0.18)	−0.137	(0.23)	−0.544	(0.21)
PART	−1.148	(0.29)	−1.451	(0.36)	−0.819	(0.32)
NOPS	−0.394	(0.21)	−0.323	(0.26)	−0.487	(0.23)
ED	0.156	(0.04)	0.180	(0.05)	0.113	(0.04)
RD	0.024	(0.01)	0.041	(0.01)	0.014	(0.01)
BEL	−0.396	(0.22)	−0.582	(0.28)	−0.215	(0.24)
UNION	−0.133	(0.06)	−0.114	(0.08)	−0.108	(0.07)
IMEXK	0.160	(0.05)	0.209	(0.06)	0.136	(0.06)
Adj. R^2	0.651		0.646		0.467	
F	10.73		10.01		5.32	
N	74		74		74	

Notes: The dependent variable is ln *VPW* (relative UK/US real net output per employee). The method of estimation is ordinary least squares.
Source: Davies and Caves (1987: 47, 67).

and for plants smaller than median size. This is possible given the presentation of data on the distribution of output across plants of different size in the production censuses. Equations (2) and (3) suggest that during the late 1960s, large British plants suffered from a serious industrial relations problem; bellicosity is strongly significant in large plants but insignificant in small plants. Similar results are obtained by Davies and Caves for a sample of industries in 1977. This relationship between large plant size and bad industrial relations in the United Kingdom during the 1960s and 1970s is examined by Prais (1981: 59–83), who sees it as a major problem hampering Britain's performance at this time in industries requiring large-scale production, such as motor vehicles. I would go one stage further and relate these industrial relations problems in large plants to the Americanisation of technology. In small plants, where craft workers were not being threatened with deskilling to the same extent, British industrial relations were generally good.

O'Mahony (1992b) reports the results of a similar exercise for Germany

Table 12.57. *Germany/UK productivity regressions, 1987*

Variable	(1) Coefficient	(1) Std error	(2) Coefficient	(2) Std error
CONSTANT	−0.18	(0.078)	−0.32	(0.133)
Rk	0.15	(0.090)	0.19	(0.086)
RL	0.07	(0.065)	0.07	(0.059)
RH	2.38	(0.912)		
RH*			0.67	(0.316)
RAGE	−0.37	(0.200)	−0.38	(0.022)
RRD	0.06	(0.018)	0.08	(0.022)
Adj. R^2	0.236		0.231	
SE	0.188		0.188	
N	52		52	

Notes: Dependent variable is Rq (relative Germany/UK labour productivity). The method of estimation is ordinary least squares.
Source: O'Mahony (1992b).

and the United Kingdom in 1987 for a sample of 54 industries. As in the other studies considered above, O'Mahony works with a production function including physical capital, labour and human capital, together with an efficiency term affected by industrial organisation variables:

$$Rq = \alpha_0 + \alpha_1 Rk + \alpha_2 RL + \alpha_3 RH + \alpha_4 RAGE + \alpha_5 RRD \qquad (12.7)$$

where R preceding a variable name denotes relative German to British values, and lower case letters denote variables in per worker terms. Thus Rq is relative output per worker, Rk is relative capital per worker, RL is relative employment, RH is relative human capital, $RAGE$ is relative average age of machinery and RRD is relative expenditure on R&D.

O'Mahony uses two approaches to the calculation of human capital. The first measure (RH) divides the labour force into three skill groups in each country and weights each skill group according to its relative wage (using unskilled workers as the numeraire). Since there are many more workers in Germany with intermediate level qualifications, human capital is rather higher than in Britain, where a higher proportion of the labour force has no qualifications. The second approach simply proxies human capital by dividing the workforce into two categories, skilled and unskilled, and using the proportion of skilled workers as an alternative measure (RH^*).

Results using the two measures of human capital are reported in table 12.57. In both equations physical capital enters with the correct sign, but takes a value somewhat below capital's share in income. The coefficient on labour indicates static scale economies of about 7 per cent, but is not statistically significant. Both measures of human capital are statistically significant. The efficiency variables, the average age of machinery and R&D are correctly signed, although *RAGE* is not statistically significant. Re-estimation by instrumental variables to take account of the joint determination of output and inputs does not drastically alter the results.

The results in tables 12.55–12.57 are suggestive of a role for factor endowments and the competitive environment in explaining the cross-sectional variation of Britain's productivity gap during the postwar period. However, as in chapter 11, much of the variation is unexplained. Again, it is clear that there are limits to the extent that regression analysis can capture the importance of variables such as mass production technology or the nature of competition. Hence it is necessary to complement the econometric approach with detailed case studies of individual industries, as in the bulk of this chapter.

Conclusions

There can be little doubt that British manufacturing as a whole performed badly during the period 1950–79. I would attribute this poor performance to a failure in standardised mass production. Opposition by craft workers to a technology which undermined their skills and took away control of the labour process from the shopfloor, coupled with a hesitancy among managers to assume the responsibilities required to operate the American methods profitably, led to a deterioration of industrial relations, one of the most visible aspects of what came to be labelled as the 'British disease'. There were also problems in securing markets to accept the high volume of standardised output produced by the new methods. Constraints imposed by the size and variability of the British market were compounded by fundamental changes in the world economy, leading to a decline in the importance of Britain's traditional Commonwealth markets and requiring a reorientation towards Continental Europe, traditionally seen as Germany's natural market. Adjustment to these trends, which would inevitably have been difficult, was delayed by a reluctance to allow competitive forces to affect the allocation of resources, a reluctance which was not fully overcome until the 1980s.

By the time that the corporatist approach was finally abandoned after 1979, technological trends had moved back in Britain's favour. In the era of information technology, American mass production techniques were no longer seen as appropriate, and manufacturing technology moved back in the direction of customisation and skilled shopfloor labour. By the end of the 1980s, British manufacturing was once again achieving labour productivity levels close to the European norm. Nevertheless, the decline of shopfloor labour force skills during the Fordist era meant that Britain had a large skills gap to make up compared with most European countries.

The failure in standardised mass production should not be allowed to blind us to all achievements during this period, however. Some industries, such as pharmaceuticals, Scotch whisky or other food and drink industries, were extremely successful throughout the period. Although the defence sector has been shielded from competition, this has also been the case in other countries, and Britain has been relatively successful in these industries where customised production has remained the norm. In other industries, some firms were successful in niche markets even if the mass production oriented national champion failed. Thus even in the most widely cited British disaster, the car industry, there were successful niches such as the sports car during the 1950s and 1960s or the 4-wheel drive vehicle during the 1980s.

13   Concluding comments

Overview

Part 1 of this book is concerned with setting out quantitatively the patterns of productivity performance in manufacturing for Britain compared with the United States and Germany. Whereas at the whole economy level there has been a substantial relative decline in Britain's labour productivity performance since the mid-nineteenth century, in manufacturing comparative labour productivity levels have remained stationary. Labour productivity in US manufacturing has fluctuated around a level of about twice the British level, while German manufacturing labour productivity has fluctuated around a level broadly the same as the British level. British relative economic decline cannot therefore be explained in terms of a deteriorating relative labour productivity performance in manufacturing, but must rather be due to trends in other sectors and the effects of structural change.

Part 2 of the book sets out to explain the persistent labour productivity gap in manufacturing between the United States on the one hand and Britain and Germany on the other. This is explained largely in terms of the parallel development of national technological systems, geared to local demand conditions and to resource and factor endowments. The origins of the gap lie in the abundance of land and natural resources in America compared with Europe. During much of the nineteenth century, technological leadership rested with British flexible production methods, producing customised output with skilled shopfloor labour. American manufacturers adapted these methods to local circumstances, economising on scarce skilled labour but utilising abundant natural resources. This led to the development of a distinctive American machine-intensive and resource-using technology that economised on skilled shopfloor labour. This 'American system of manufactures' could not simply be copied in Britain or Germany because of different resource and factor endowments.

As the American system developed into mass production during the twentieth century, it required Chandler's (1990) three-pronged investment in production, management and marketing. Throughout the period of American technological leadership during much of the twentieth century, successful technical development in Britain and Germany required adapting American methods to local circumstances, making use of abundant skilled shopfloor labour and customising output to meet heterogeneous demands. British and German 'flexible production' technology thus developed in different ways to American 'mass production' technology, despite the fact that all countries had access to the same common pool of knowledge.

Since technical change is a path dependent process and success requires the development of distinctive capabilities, technology moves in parallel in different countries. A small change, or 'micro invention' in one country requires adaptation in other countries. However, there are problems when there is a large, discontinuous 'macro invention' in one country, which undermines the viability of a technology in another country. Slavish copying is unlikely to be a viable response, given different local circumstances. One tempting alternative for firms under threat is to lobby the government for protection or subsidies. However, once cut off from the stimulus of international competition, there is a danger that firms will allow technology to stagnate and fall behind international rivals. Britain after the Second World War appears to offer examples of both types of unsatisfactory response; attempts to copy American methods in British circumstances were notoriously unsuccessful, while protection and subsidies allowed many inefficient British firms to survive. The neglect of shopfloor skills during the period of Americanisation left Britain in a poor position to take advantage of the rejuvenation of flexible production techniques from the late 1960s, as improvements in information technology drastically reduced the cost of customisation with skilled workers. The change of British government policy after 1979, with a renewed emphasis on market forces, led to a painful period of adjustment for British manufacturing.

Part 3 of the book provides a detailed survey of the performance of British manufacturing, compared with the United States and Germany. Case studies are provided for a wide range of industries, covering three periods, 1850–1914, 1914–50 and 1950–90. During the period before the First World War, British industry had to adjust to the rise of competition from abroad, particularly the United States and Germany. Britain nevertheless continued to do well in three types of industry. First, there were industries where despite the successful application of high throughput mass production methods in the United States, craft-based flexible production techniques remained competitive in British conditions. In textile industries such as cotton, linen, jute, and woollen and worsted, large numbers of small-scale producers reaped external economies of scale in classic Marshallian form.

The second type of industry in which Britain remained successful was where mass production techniques could not be successfully applied on either side of the Atlantic, so that Britain benefited from a large supply of skilled labour. Industries of this type, such as shipbuilding, also enjoyed Marshallian external economies of scale. The third type of industry where Britain was successful was where there was no lag in the adoption of high throughput techniques, due to the absence of demand constraints. These industries, such as seedcrushing, coke, sugar and tobacco (before cigarettes became the major product) produced relatively homogeneous products. Britain was a long way ahead of Germany in the application of high throughput techniques in food, drink and tobacco before 1914, as a result of the high level of urbanisation and the development of mass retailing in Britain. In most industries competitive forces could be relied upon to ensure that firms made correct technical choices, although there is some evidence that cartels hindered adjustment in the chemicals sector.

The period 1914–50 was characterised by a series of major negative shocks, including two world wars and a world slump of unprecedented severity. As a result, the liberal world economic system disintegrated. British adjustment to the new circumstances took the form of increased dependence on relations with the Empire. Policies of protection and cartelisation were also promoted to try to stem the fall in prices. Although these policies had some success in meeting their short-run counter-cyclical objectives, in the long run they worsened adjustment problems and productivity performance after the Second World War.

Further problems of adjustment arose between the wars as a result of the innovations of the Second Industrial Revolution in the United States. The growing acceptance of restrictions on competition meant that pressures on firms to adjust were reduced, and the period is usually seen in terms of failed rationalisation. Apart from a temporary cyclical narrowing during the 1930s, the Anglo-American productivity gap widened during 1914–50. However, if rationalisation failed in Britain, it also failed in Germany; Britain and Germany were much more evenly matched in manufacturing before 1950 than a reader of Chandler (1990) would expect.

British manufacturing performance between 1950 and 1979 was disappointing in comparison with the United States, Germany and most other industrialised countries. The poor performance occurred largely as a result of an unsuccessful attempt to apply American mass production techniques. A major factor behind the over-Americanisation of British manufacturing during this period was the wartime experience of the Allied war effort, when businessmen saw at first hand the high levels of labour productivity achieved in American manufacturing. Wartime visits by British industrialists to the United States were followed up after the war by the Anglo-American Council on Productivity (AACP), which sponsored visits by teams of managers and trade unionists in a wide range of industries. However, opposition by craft workers to a technology that undermined the value of their skills and took away control of the labour process from the shopfloor, coupled with a hesitancy among managers to assume the responsibilities required to operate the American methods profitably, led to a serious deterioration of industrial relations.

There were also problems on the demand side in securing markets for the high volume of standardised output that the new methods were capable of producing. Constraints imposed by the size and heterogeneity of the British market were compounded by fundamental changes in the world economy. As the world economy re-integrated, it was inevitable that there would be a decline in Britain's trade with far-flung Commonwealth countries, which had become so important under the regime of Imperial Preference between the wars. Adjustment to these trends, which would inevitably have been difficult and painful, was delayed by a reluctance to allow competitive forces to affect the allocation of resources. This mistrust of market forces also had its origins in the period between the wars, when policies of protection and cartelisation were seen as useful bulwarks against falling prices. Market forces were not enthusiastically embraced by a British government until the Conservatives were elected to office under Margaret Thatcher in 1979.

By the time that the corporatist approach was finally abandoned after 1979, technological trends had moved back in Britain's favour. Given dramatic falls in the cost of information processing, technological leadership now switched back to methods that customised output using skilled workers. Although this meant an end to the terrible industrial relations disputes of the 1960s and 1970s, however, it should be noted that the decline of shopfloor skills during the Fordist era meant that Britain was not in as good a position to take advantage of modern flexible production technology as Germany and other European countries that had continued to invest in training workers with intermediate level skills. Hence one of the consequences of the exposure of the British economy to market forces was a reduction in the size of the manufacturing sector. Although the share of the labour force in manufacturing remained substantially higher in Britain than in the United States and on a par with most industrialised countries, it was no longer at the unusually high level of Germany or Japan. By the end of the 1980s, however, British manufacturing was once again achieving levels of labour productivity close to the European norm.

Epilogue

Matthews *et al.* (1982: 547) warn that 'nothing dates a work of history more surely than an attempt to bring its coverage up to the moment of writing', and in the main body of the text I have tried as far as possible to avoid the temptation to continue the story beyond 1990. Nevertheless, it is appropriate at this point to note briefly some trends of the 1990s. Continuing the time series extrapolations from table 3.1, provisional figures for 1994 indicate a comparative US/UK labour productivity ratio of 186.0 and a Germany/UK ratio of 109.1 (for the territory of the former Federal Republic), much the same as in 1989. For British manufacturing, then, the improved comparative labour productivity performance of the 1980s has not been undone during the 1990s so far. Although there was a sharp recession during the period 1989–92, labour productivity growth remained strong and also continued during the recovery phase of the cycle into the mid-1990s. There has not, however, been any spectacular revival of output growth in British manufacturing. So although manufacturing should no longer be seen as a poor performing sector of the British economy, equally it has not become the dynamic engine of wealth creation in the 1990s that might have been hoped for in the late 1980s. Given the skill shortages resulting from the decline of shopfloor training during the Fordist era, this should not be seen as too surprising, but equally it cautions against too optimistic a re-interpretation of the performance of British manufacturing.

For the United States, there is evidence that manufacturing has begun to recover from some of the difficulties caused by the growth of flexible production in the 1970s and 1980s. Having largely eschewed the option of protection, firms have adjusted in the 1990s, while retaining a distinctive American approach. Thus, for example, Mason and Finegold (1995) provide evidence of American firms substituting for their lack of qualified intermediate level skilled labour on the shopfloor with intelligent use of graduate engineers.

The 1990s have been challenging for Germany, following re-unification in 1989. Data are still published for the territory of the former Federal Republic, and indicate a massive post-unification boom, but followed by a severe slump. Nevertheless, despite continual worries about a high cost base and inflexible labour markets, Germany has retained a strong position in manufactured export markets, on the basis of its highly skilled workforce.

Bibliography

OFFICIAL PUBLICATIONS AND REPORTS

Where no date is given, publication is annual unless otherwise stated.

UNITED KINGDOM

Annual Abstract of Statistics (Central Statistical Office, annual from 1948)
Annual Report of the Director General of Fair Trading (Office of Fair Trading)
Annual Statement of the Trade of the United Kingdom (Command Paper to 1920 then Customs and Excise)
British Labour Statistics: Historical Abstract 1886–1968 (Department of Employment, 1971)
British Labour Statistics Yearbook (Department of Employment, 1976)
Census of Production: Final Report (Board of Trade; Business Statistics Office, 1907, 1924, 1930, 1935, 1948, 1951, 1954, 1958, 1963, 1968, annual from 1970)
Digest of UK Energy Statistics (Department of Energy)
Economic Trends Annual Supplement (Central Statistical Office)
Historical Record of the Census of Production 1907 to 1970 (Business Statistics Office, 1978)
Industrial Research and Development Expenditure and Employment (Business Statistics Office)
Labour Force Survey (Office of Population Censuses and Surveys)
National Income and Expenditure (Central Statistical Office, annual from 1952)
Ready Mixed Concrete (Monopolies and Mergers Commission, Cmnd. 8354, 1981)
Report of the Committee on the Machinery of the United States (Sessional Papers, House of Commons, 1854–5)
Report of the Cotton Textile Mission to the United States of America, March–April 1944 (Board of Trade, 1944)
Report on the Supply of Beer (Monopolies Commission, 1969)
Report on the Supply of Chlordiazepoxide and Diazepam (Monopolies and Mergers Commission, 1971)
Report on the Supply of Linoleum (Monopolies and Restrictive Practices Commission, 1953)
Shipbuilding Inquiry Committee 1965–1966 Report (Cmnd. 2937)
Statistical Digest of the War (Central Statistical Office, 1951)
The Supply of Beer (Monopolies and Mergers Commission, 1989)
The Supply of Electric Lamps (Monopolies and Restrictive Practices Commission, 1951)

Survey of International Cartels and Internal Cartels (2 vols.) (Board of Trade, 1946)
Survey of the Metal Industries (Committee on Industry and Trade, 1928)

UNITED STATES

Annual Survey of Manufactures (Department of Commerce)
Census of Manufactures (Department of Commerce, 1909, 1914, 1921, 1923, 1925, 1927, 1929, 1931, 1933, 1935, 1937, 1939, 1947, 1954, 1958, 1963, 1967, 1972, 1977, 1982, 1987)
Historical Statistics of the United States: Colonial Times to 1957 (Department of Commerce, 1960)
Historical Statistics of the United States: Colonial Times to 1970 (Department of Commerce, 1975)
National Income and Product Accounts of the United States 1929–1982 (Department of Commerce, 1982)
National Income and Product Accounts of the United States, Vol.1, 1929–58 (Department of Commerce, 1992), *Vol.2, 1959–88* (Department of Commerce, 1993)
Producer Prices and Price Indexes (Bureau of Labor Statistics, monthly)
Statistical Abstract of the United States (Department of Commerce)
Survey of Current Business (Department of Commerce, monthly)

GERMANY

Berufs- und Betriebszählung vom 12. Juni 1907. Gewerbliche Betriebsstatistik, *Statistik des Deutschen Reichs*, Band 213 (Berlin, 1910)
Berufs- und Gewerbezählung vom 14. Juni 1895. Gewerbestatistik für das Reich im Ganzen, *Statistik des Deutschen Reichs*, Neue Folge, Band 113 (Berlin, 1898)
Konzentrationsstatistische Daten für den Bergbau und das Verarbeitende Gewerbe, 1954 bis 1982, Fachserie 4, Reihe S.9 (Statistisches Bundesamt, 1985)
Konzentrationsstatistische Daten für den Bergbau und das Verarbeitende Gewerbe sowie das Baugewerbe, Fachserie 4, Reihe 4.2.3 (Statistisches Bundesamt)
Lange Reihen zur Wirtschaftsentwicklung (Statistisches Bundesamt, 1982)
Statistisches Handbuch von Deutschland, 1928–1944 (Länderrat des Amerikanischen Besatzungsgebiets, München, 1949)
Statistisches Jahrbuch für die Bundesrepublik Deutschland (Statistisches Bundesamt)
Volks- Berufs- und Betriebszählung vom 16. Juni 1925, Gewerbliche Betriebszählung. Die Gewerblichen Betriebe und Unternehmungen im Deutschen Reich, Teil III, Die technischen Betriebseinheiten im Deutschen Reiche (Berlin, 1929)
Volks- Berufs- und Betriebszählung vom 1933. Das Personal der gewerblichen Niederlassungen nach der Stellung im Betrieb und die Verwendung von Kraftmaschinen (Berlin, 1935)
Volkswirtschaftliche Gesamtrechnungen 1950 bis 1990, Fachserie 18, Reihe S.15 (Statistisches Bundesamt, 1991)

OTHER COUNTRIES AND INTERNATIONAL ORGANISATIONS

Centraal Bureau voor de Statistiek, *Negentig Jaaren Statistiek in Tijdreeksan* (The Hague, 1989)

Central Bureau of Statistics, *Statistical Yearbook of the Netherlands* (The Hague)

Commonwealth Bureau of Census and Statistics, *Production Bulletin no.31, 1936–37, Part I – Secondary Industries (Canberra)*

Year Book of the Commonwealth of Australia (Canberra)

Commonwealth Bureau of Statistics, *Year Book Australia* (Canberra)

Danmarks Statistik, *Industristatistik* (Copenhagen)

Produktionsstatistik 1935 (Copenhagen)

Statistisk Arbog (Copenhagen)

Dominion Bureau of Statistics, *Canada Yearbook* (Ottawa)

Eurostat, Purchasing Power Parities and Gross Domestic Product in Real Terms: Results 1985 (Brussels)

Food and Agriculture Organisation, *Yearbook* (Rome)

Institut National de la Statistique et des Etudes Economiques, *Les Comptes Nationaux Trimestriels: Series longues, 1970–1988 en base 1980* , Inséé Résultats no.17 (Paris, 1989)

Comptes Trimestriels 1949–1959, Collections de l'inséé C70 (Paris, 1979)

Rapport sur les Comptes de la Nation (Paris)

Rétrapolation des comptes nationaux dans le nouveau système de comptabilité nationale française, Séries 1959–1970, Collections de l'inséé C67–68 (Paris, 1978)

International Energy Agency, *Energy Prices and Taxes* (Paris)

Istituto Centrale di Statistica, *Annuario Statistico Italiano* (Rome)

Statistiche Industriali, Anni 1986, 1987 (Rome, 1990)

Japan Statistical Association, *Historical Statistics of Japan, Vol.2* (Tokyo, 1986)

Organisation for Economic Cooperation and Development, *Basic Science and Technology Statistics* (Paris)

The Footwear Industry: Structure and Governmental Policies (Paris, 1976)

Labour Force Statistics (Paris)

Main Technology Indicators (Paris)

Mining and Non-Ferrous Metals Policies of OECD Countries (Paris, 1994)

National Accounts Vol.II: Detailed Tables (Paris)

Organisation for European Economic Cooperation, *Vocational Training in the Footwear Industry* (Paris, 1960)

Statistics Bureau, Management and Coordination Agency, *Japan Statistical Yearbook* (Tokyo)

Statistics Canada, *Canadian Economic Observer: Historical Statistical Supplement* (Ottawa)

Statistisk Sentralbyra, *Historisk Statistikk* (Oslo, 1978)

Norges Industri (Oslo, 1930, 1985)

Statistik Arbok (Oslo)

Statistiska Centralbyran, *Industrieproduktionsindex 1913–1974* (Stockholm, 1975)

Statistisk Arsbok (Stockholm)

United Nations, *Yearbook of International Trade Statistics* (New York)

OTHER REPORTS AND ARCHIVE SOURCES

Anglo-American Council on Productivity, *Food Canning* (London, 1950

Heavy Chemicals (London, 1953)

Iron and Steel (London, 1952)
Metalworking Machine Tools (London, 1953)
Packaging (London, 1950)
Simplification in British Industry (London, 1950)
Steel Founding (London, 1949)
Superphosphates and Compound Fertilisers (London, 1950)
Engineering Employers' Federation, 'Number of Workpeople Employed'; 'Total Number of Men, Apprentices and Boys and Youths Employed' (Modern Records Centre, University of Warwick: EEF MSS.237/13/3/1–56)
Lloyds Register of Shipping, *Statistical Tables* (London)
Scotch Whisky Association, *Statistical Report* (Edinburgh)
Society of Motor Manufacturers and Traders, *The Motor Industry of Britain* (London)
SV-Gemeinnützige Gesellschaft für Wissenschaftsstatistik mbH, *Wissenschaftsausgaben der Wirtschaft: Ergebnisse der Registrierungen des Stifterverbandes 1948–63* (Essen, 1966)
Forschung und Entwicklung in der Wirtschaft (Essen)
UK Iron and Steel Statistics Bureau, *Annual Statistics* (London)
World Bureau of Metal Statistics, *World Metal Statistics* (Ware, Herts, UK)

BOOKS AND ARTICLES

Abbott, G.C. (1990), *Sugar,* London: Routledge
Abramovitz, M. (1979), 'Rapid Growth Potential and its Realisation: The Experience of the Capitalist Economies in the Postwar Period', in Malinvaud, E. (ed.), *Economic growth and Resources, Proceedings of the Fifth World Congress of the International Economic Association, Vol.I* , London: Macmillan, 1–30
(1986), 'Catching Up, Forging Ahead and Falling Behind', *Journal of Economic History* , 46, 385–406
Acton Society Trust (1956), *Management Succession*, London: Acton Society Trust
Adeney, M. (1989), *The Motor Makers: The Turbulent History of Britain's Car Industry*, London: Fontana
Ahlstrand, B.W. (1990), *The Quest for Productivity: A Case Study of Fawley after Flanders*, Cambridge: Cambridge University Press
Aldcroft, D.H. (1964), 'The Entrepreneur and the British Economy, 1870–1914', *Economic History Review*, 17, 113–34.
(1966), 'The Performance of the Machine-Tool Industry in the Interwar Years', *Business History Review*, 40, 281–96
Alford, B.W.E. (1972), *Depression and Recovery? British Economic Growth, 1918–1939*, London: Macmillan
(1973), *W.D. & H.O. Wills and the Development of the U.K. Tobacco Industry, 1786–1965*, London: Methuen
Allen, R.C. (1979), 'International Competition in Iron and Steel, 1850–1913', *Journal of Economic History*, 39, 911–37
(1983), 'Collective Invention', *Journal of Economic Behaviour and Organization*, 4, 1–24
Altman, M. (1987), 'A Revision of Canadian Economic Growth: 1870–1910 (A

Challenge to the Gradualist Interpretation)', *Canadian Journal of Economics*, 20, 86–113

Ames, E. and Rosenberg, N. (1968), 'The Enfield Arsenal in Theory and History', *Economic Journal*, 78, 827–42

Anson, R. and Simpson, P. (1988), 'World Textile Trade and Production Trends' (Special Report no.1108, Economist Intelligence Unit, London)

van Ark, B. (1990a), 'Comparative Levels of Labour Productivity in Dutch and British Manufacturing', *National Institute Economic Review*, 131, 71–85

(1990b), 'Manufacturing Productivity Levels in France and the United Kingdom', *National Institute Economic Review*, 133, 62–77

(1990c), 'Comparative Levels of Manufacturing Labour Productivity in Postwar Europe', *Oxford Bulletin of Economics and Statistics*, 52, 343–74

(1992), 'Comparative Productivity in British and American Manufacturing', *National Institute Economic Review*, 142, 63–74

(1993), 'International Comparisons of Output and Productivity: Manufacturing Productivity Performance of Ten Countries from 1950 to 1990' (Groningen Growth and Development Centre Monograph Series, no.1)

van Ark, B. and Pilat, D. (1993), 'Cross Country Productivity Levels: Differences and Causes', *Brookings Papers on Economic Activity: Microeconomics, 2*, 1–69

Arthur, W.B. (1989), 'Competing Technologies, Increasing Returns and Lock-in by Historical Events', *Economic Journal*, 99, 116–31

Atkinson, A.B. and Stiglitz, J.E. (1969), 'A New View of Technological Change', *Economic Journal*, 79, 573–78

Audretsch, D.B. (1989), 'Legalized Cartels in West Germany', *Antitrust Bulletin*, 34, 579–600

Aylen, J. (1988), 'Privatisation of the British Steel Corporation', *Fiscal Studies*, 9(3), 1–25

Baily, M.N. (1993), 'Competition, Regulation, and Efficiency in Service Industries', *Brookings Papers on Economic Activity: Microeconomics*, 71–159

Baily, M.N. and Chakrabarti, A.K. (1988), *Innovation and the Productivity Crisis*, Washington DC: Brookings Institution

Bain, G.S. and Price, R. (1980), *Profiles of Union Growth: A Comparative Statistical Portrait of Eight Countries*, Oxford: Blackwell

Balderston, T. (1983), 'The Beginning of the Depression in Germany, 1927–30: Investment and the Capital Market', *Economic History Review*, 36, 404–5

Balke, N.S. and Gordon, R.J. (1989), 'The Estimation of Prewar Gross National Product: Methodology and New Evidence', *Journal of Political Economy*, 97, 38–92

Ballance, R., Pogány, J. and Forstner, H. (1992), *The World's Pharmaceutical Industries: An International Perspective on Innovation, Competition and Policy*, Aldershot: UNIDO and Edward Elgar.

Bamberg, J.H. (1988), 'The Rationalization of the British Cotton Industry in the Interwar Years', *Textile History*, 19, 83–102

(1994), *The History of the British Petroleum Company, Volume 2: The Anglo-Iranian Years, 1928–1954*, Cambridge: Cambridge University Press

Bardou, J.-P., Chanaron, J.-J., Fridenson, P. and Laux, J.M. (1982), *The Automobile Revolution: The Impact of an Industry*, Chapel Hill, NC: University of North Carolina Press

Barker, T.C. (1968), 'The Glass Industry', in Aldcroft, D.H. (ed.), *The Development of British Industry and Foreign Competition, 1875–1914*, London: Allen & Unwin, 307–25

—— (1977a), *The Glassmakers, Pilkington: The Rise of an International Company, 1826–1976*, London: Weidenfeld & Nicolson

—— (1977b), 'Business Implications of Technical Developments in the Glass Industry, 1945–1965: A Case-Study', in Supple, B.E. (ed.), *Essays in British Business History*, Oxford: Oxford University Press, 187–204

Barnett, C. (1986), *The Audit of War: The Illusion and Reality of Britain as a Great Nation*, London: Macmillan

Barro, R.J. and Sala-i-Martin, X. (1991), 'Convergence Across States and Regions', *Brookings Papers on Economic Activity*, 1, 107–82

Batstone, E. (1986), 'Labour and Productivity', *Oxford Review of Economic Policy*, 2(3), 32–43

Baumol, W.J. (1986), 'Productivity Growth, Convergence and Welfare: What the Long Run Data Show', *American Economic Review*, 76, 1072–1159

Bean, C. (1987), 'The Impact of North Sea Oil', in Dornbusch, R. and Layard, R. (eds.), *The Performance of the British Economy*, Oxford: Oxford University Press, 64–96

Bean, C. and Crafts, N.F.R. (1996), 'British Economic Growth Since 1945: Relative Economic Decline ... and Renaissance?', in Crafts, N.F.R. and Toniolo, G. (eds.), *Economic Growth in Europe Since 1945*, Cambridge: Cambridge University Press, 131–72

Beard, C.A. and Beard, M.R. (1930), *The Rise of American Civilisation*, New York: Macmillan

Berghahn, V.R. (1986), *The Americanisation of West German Industry, 1945–1973*, Leamington Spa: Berg

Best, M.H. and Humphries, J. (1986), 'The City and Industrial Decline', in Elbaum, B. and Lazonick, W. (eds.), *The Decline of the British Economy*, Oxford: Oxford University Press, 223–39

Bolino, A.C. (1989), *A Century of Human Capital by Education and Training*, Washington, DC: Kensington

Booth, A. (1987), 'Britain in the 1930s: A Managed Economy?', *Economic History Review*, 40, 499–522

Borchardt, K. (1979), 'Zwangslagen und Handlungsspielräume in der grossen Wirtschaftskrise der frühen dreissiger Jahre', *Jahrbuch der Bayerischen Akademie der Wissenschaften*, 85–132. Reprinted in English translation as 'Constraints and Room for Manoeuvre in the Great Depression of the Early Thirties: Towards a Revision of the Received Historical Picture', in Borchardt, K. (1991), *Perspectives on Modern German Economic History and Policy*, Cambridge: Cambridge University Press, 161–83

Bowden, S.M. (1991), 'Demand and Supply Constraints in the Inter-War UK Car Industry: Did the Manufacturers Get it Right?', *Business History*, 33, 241–67

Bowden, S. and Offer, A. (1994), 'Household Appliances and the Use of Time', *Economic History Review*, 47, 725–48

Bowker, B. (1928), *Lancashire under the Hammer*, London: Hogarth

Bowley, M. (1960), *Innovations in Building Materials: An Economic Study*, London: Duckworth

Brinkmann, G. (1967), *Die Ausbildung von Führungskräften für die Wirtschaft*, Köln: Universitätsverlag Michael Wienand

Broadberry, S.N. (1986), 'Aggregate Supply in Interwar Britain', *Economic Journal*, 96, 467–81

(1990), 'The Emergence of Mass Unemployment: Explaining Macroeconomic Trends in Britain During the Trans-World War I Period', *Economic History Review*, 43, 271–82

(1993), 'Manufacturing and the Convergence Hypothesis: What the Long Run Data Show', *Journal of Economic History*, 53, 772–95

(1994a), 'Technological Leadership and Productivity Leadership in Manufacturing since the Industrial Revolution: Implications for the Convergence Debate', *Economic Journal*, 104, 291–302

(1994b), 'Comparative Productivity in British and American Manufacturing During the Nineteenth Century', *Explorations in Economic History*, 31, 521–48

(1997), 'Forging Ahead, Falling Behind and Catching-up: A Sectoral Analysis of Anglo-American Productivity Differences, 1870–1990', *Research in Economic History* (forthcoming)

Broadberry, S.N. and Crafts, N.F.R. (1990a), 'Explaining Anglo-American Productivity Differences in the Mid-Twentieth Century', *Oxford Bulletin of Economics and Statistics*, 52, 375–402

(1990b), 'The Implications of British Macroeconomic Policy in the 1930s for Long Run Growth Performance', *Rivista di Storia Economica*, 7, 1–19

(1992), 'Britain's Productivity Gap in the 1930s: Some Neglected Factors', *Journal of Economic History*, 52, 531–58

(1996), 'British Economic Policy and Industrial Performance in the Early Postwar Period', *Business History* , 38, 65–91

Broadberry, S.N. and Fremdling, R. (1990), 'Comparative Productivity in British and German Industry, 1907–37', *Oxford Bulletin of Economics and Statistics*, 52, 403–22

Broadberry, S.N. and Ritschl, A.O. (1994), 'The Iron Twenties: Real Wages, Productivity and the Lack of Prosperity in Britain and Germany Before the Great Depression', in Buchheim, C., Hutter, M. and James, H. (eds.), *Zerrissene Zwischenkriegzeit: Wirtschaftshistorische Beiträge, Knut Borchardt zum 65. Geburtstag*, Baden-Baden: Nomos Verlagsgesellschaft

(1995), 'Real Wages, Productivity, and Unemployment in Britain and Germany during the 1920s', *Explorations in Economic History*, 32, 327–49

Broadberry, S.N. and Wagner, K. (1996), 'Human Capital and Productivity in Manufacturing during the Twentieth Century: Britain, Germany and the United States', in van Ark, B. and Crafts, N.F.R. (eds.), *Quantitative Aspects of Postwar European Economic Growth*, Cambridge: Cambridge University Press, 244–70

Brockhurst, H.E. (1950), *British Factory Production of Men's Clothes*, London: London Clothing Designers' and Production Managers' Association

Bronowski, J. (ed.) (1966), *Technology: Man Remakes his World*, Englewood Cliffs, NJ: Lamp Light

Brown, B.C. (1954), 'Industrial Production in 1935 and 1948', *London and Cambridge Economic Bulletin*, December, v–vii

Burk, K. (1988), *The First Privatisation: The Politicians, the City and the Denationalisation of Steel*, London: The Historians' Press

Burn, D.L. (1940), *The Economic History of Steelmaking, 1867–1939: A Study in Competition*, Cambridge: Cambridge University Press

Burnett, R.G. (1945), *Through the Mill: The Life of Joseph Rank*, London: Epworth

Burnham, T.H. and Hoskins, G.O. (1943), *Iron and Steel in Britain, 1870–1939*, London: Allen & Unwin

Byatt, I.C.R. (1968), 'Electrical Products', in Aldcroft, D.H. (ed.), *The Development of British Industry and Foreign Competition, 1875–1914*, London: Allen & Unwin, 238–73

(1979), *The British Electrical Industry, 1875–1914: The Economic Returns of a New Technology*, Oxford: Oxford University Press

Cable, V. and Baker, B. (1983), 'World Textile Trade and Production Trends' (Special Report no.152, Economist Intelligence Unit, London)

Cadbury Brothers (n.d.), *Industrial Record, 1919–1939: A Review of the Interwar Years*, Bournville: Cadbury.

Calmfors, L. and Driffill, J. (1988), 'Centralisation of Wage Bargaining', *Economic Policy*, 6, 13–61

Campbell-Kelly, M. (1989), *ICL: A Business History*, Oxford: Oxford University Press

Capie, F. (1983), *Depression and Protectionism: Britain Between the Wars*, London: Allen & Unwin

(1994), *Tariffs and Growth: Some Insights from the World Economy, 1850–1940*, Manchester: Manchester University Press

Carruth, A.A. and Oswald, A. J. (1989), *Pay Determination and Industrial Prosperity*, Oxford: Oxford University Press

Carson, D. (1949), 'Changes in the Industrial Composition of Manpower since the Civil War', *Studies in Income and Wealth*, vol. 11, New York: National Bureau of Economic Research

Carter, C.F., Reddaway, W.B. and Stone, R. (1948), *The Measurement of Production Movements*, Cambridge: Cambridge University Press

Casson, M. (1983) (ed.), *The Growth of International Business*, London: Allen & Unwin

Catterall, R.E. (1979), 'Electrical Engineering', in Buxton, N.K. and Aldcroft, D.H. (eds.), *British Industry Between the Wars: Instability and Industrial Development, 1919–1939*, London: Scolar, 241–75

Chalmin, P. (1990), *The Making of a Sugar Giant: Tate and Lyle, 1859–1989*, Chur: Harwood

Chandler, A.D., Jr. (1977), *The Visible Hand: The Managerial Revolution in American Business*, Cambridge MA: Harvard University Press

(1980), 'The Growth of the Transnational Industrial Firm in the United States and the United Kingdom: A Comparative Analysis', *Economic History Review*, 33, 396–410

(1990), *Scale and Scope: The Dynamics of Industrial Capitalism*, Cambridge, MA: Harvard University Press

Channon, D.F. (1973), *The Strategy and Structure of British Enterprise*, London: Macmillan

Chapman, A.L. (1953), *Wages and Salaries in the United Kingdom, 1920–1938*, Cambridge: Cambridge University Press

Chapman, K. (1991), *The International Petrochemical Industry: Evolution and Location*, Oxford: Blackwell

Child, J. (1967), *Industrial Relations in the British Printing Industry: The Quest for Security*, London: Allen & Unwin

Church, R.A. (1968), 'The Effect of the American Export Invasion on the British Boot and Shoe Industry, 1885–1914', *Journal of Economic History*, 28, 223–54

(1971), 'The British Leather Industry and Foreign Competition, 1870–1914', *Economic History Review*, 24, 543–70

(1994), *The Rise and Decline of the British Motor Industry*, London: Macmillan

Clapham, J.H. (1938), *An Economic History of Modern Britain: Machines and National Rivalries (1887–1914), with an Epilogue (1914–1929)*, Cambridge: Cambridge University Press

Clark, C. (1940), *The Conditions of Economic Progress*, London: Macmillan

Clark, D.G. (1966), *The Industrial Manager: His Background and Career Pattern*, London: Business Publications

Clark, G. (1987), 'Why Isn't the Whole World Developed? Lessons from the Cotton Mills', *Journal of Economic History*, 47, 141–74

Clarke, R. (1993), 'Trends in Concentration in UK Manufacturing, 1980–9', in Casson, M. and Creedy, J. (eds.), *Industrial Concentration and Economic Inequality: Essays in Honour of Peter Hart*, Aldershot: Edward Elgar, 121–42

Clements, R.V. (1958), *Managers: A Study of their Careers in Industry*, London: Allen & Unwin

Cochran, T.C. (1969), 'Did the Civil War Retard Industrialization?', in Coats, A.W. (ed.), *Essays in American Economic History*, London: Arnold, 140–9

Cockerill, A. (1988), 'Steel', in Johnson, P. (ed.), *The Structure of British Industry* (2nd edn.), London: Unwin Hyman, 70–93

(1993), 'Steel', in Johnson, P. (ed.), *European Industries: Structure, Conduct and Performance*, Aldershot: Elgar, 52–74

Cocks, E.J. and Walters, B. (1968), A History of the Zinc Smelting Industry in *Britain*, London: Harrap

Coleman, D.C. (1969), *Courtaulds: An Economic and Social History* (2 vols.), Oxford: Oxford University Press

(1973), 'Gentlemen and Players', *Economic History Review*, 26, 92–116

(1980), *Courtaulds: An Economic History, Vol.III: Crisis and Change, 1940–1965*, Oxford: Oxford University Press.

Collins, M. (1991), *Banks and Industrial Finance in Britain, 1800–1939*, London: Macmillan

Cook, P.L. (1958a), 'The Cement Industry', in Cook, P.L. and Cohen, R. (eds.), *Effects of Mergers: Six Studies*, London: Allen & Unwin, 21–130

(1958b), 'The Flat-Glass Industry', in Cook, P.L. and Cohen, R. (eds.), *Effects of Mergers: Six Studies*, London: Allen & Unwin, 277–350

Cooper, M.H. (1966), *Prices and Profits in the Pharmaceutical Industry*, Oxford: Pergamon

Copeman, G.H. (1955), *Leaders of British Industry*, London: Gee & Co.

Corlett, W.J. (1958), *The Economic Development of Detergents*, London: Duckworth

Corley, T.A.B. (1972), *Quaker Enterprise in Biscuits: Huntley and Palmers of Reading, 1822–1972*, London: Hutchinson

Cornwall, J. (1977), *Modern Capitalism: Its Growth and Transformation*, London: Martin Robertson

Cowling, K. (1989), 'The Strategic Approach', in Industrial Strategy Group (ed.), *Beyond the Review: Perspectives on Labour's Economic and Industrial Strategy*, Edinburgh: University of Edinburgh, 9–19

Cowling, K. and Cubbin, J. (1971), 'Price, Quality and Advertising Competition: The UK Car Market', *Economica*, 38, 378–94

Cowling, K., Stoneman, P., Cubbin, J., Cable, J., Hall, G., Domberger, S. and Dutton, P. (1980), *Mergers and Economic Performance*, Cambridge: Cambridge University Press

Crafts, N.F.R. (1985), *British Economic Growth During the Industrial Revolution*, Oxford: Oxford University Press

(1989), 'British Industrialisation in an International Context', *Journal of Interdisciplinary History*, 19, 415–28

(1995), 'Exogenous or Endogenous Growth? The Industrial Revolution Reconsidered', *Journal of Economic History* , 55, 745–772

Crafts, N.F.R. and Thomas, M.F. (1986), 'Comparative Advantage in UK Manufacturing Trade, 1910–1935', *Economic Journal*, 96, 629–45

Daiches, D. (1976), *Scotch Whisky: Its Past and Present*, Glasgow: Fontana/Collins

Daniels, G.W. and Jewkes, J. (1928), 'The Post–War Depression in the Lancashire Cotton Industry', *Journal of the Royal Statistical Society*, 91, 153–206

Davenport-Hines, R.P.T. and Slinn, J. (1992*)*, *Glaxo: A History to 1962*, Cambridge: Cambridge University Press

David, P.A. (1975*)*, *Technical Choice, Innovation and Economic Growth*, Cambridge: Cambridge University Press

David, P.A. (1985), 'Clio and the Economics of QWERTY'*,* *American Economic Review Proceedings*, 75, 332–7

Davidson, W.H. (1976), Patterns of Factor Saving Innovation in the Industrialised World', *European Economic Review*, 8, 207–17

Davies, S. and Caves, R.E. (1987), *Britain's Productivity Gap*, Cambridge: Cambridge University Press

De Long, J.B. (1992), 'Productivity Growth and Machinery Investment: A Long Run Look, 1870–1980', *Journal of Economic History,* 52, 307–24

De Long, J.B. and Summers, L. (1991), 'Equipment Investment and Economic Growth', *Quarterly Journal of Economics*, 106, 445–502

Dertouzos, M.L., Lester, R.K., Solow, R.M. and the MIT Commission on Industrial Productivity (1989), *Made in America: Regaining the Productive Edge*, Cambridge, MA: MIT Press

Dimsdale, N.H., Nickell, S.J. and Horsewood, N. (1989), 'Real Wages and Unemployment in Britain During the 1930s', *Economic Journal*, 99, 271–92

Donnithorne, A.G. (1958), *British Rubber Manufacturing: An Economic Study of Innovation*, London: Duckworth

Dormois, J.-P. (1991), 'Anglo-French Labour productivity in Manufacturing in 1906/7 and 1911/12' (Research Paper in Economic History, European University Institute, Florence)

Dowie, J.R. (1969), 'Growth in the Interwar Period: Some More Arithmetic', in Aldcroft, D.H. and Fearon, P. (eds.), *Economic Growth in Twentieth-Century Britain*, London: Macmillan, 55–79

(1975), '1919–20 is in Need of Attention', *Economic History Review*, 28, 429–50

Drummond, I.M. (1974), *Imperial Economic Policy, 1917–1939: Studies in Expansion and Protection*, London: Allen & Unwin

Dunnett, P.J.S. (1980), *The Decline of the British Motor Industry: The Effects of Government Policy, 1945–1979*, London: Croom Helm

Dunning, J.H. (1958), *American Investment in British Manufacturing Industry*, London: Allen & Unwin

(1983), 'Changes in the Level and Structure of International Production: The Last One Hundred Years', in Casson, M. (ed.), *The Growth of International Business*, London: Allen & Unwin, 84–139

Durcan, J.W., McCarthy, W.E.J. and Redman, G.P. (1983), *Strikes in Post-War Britain: A Study of Stoppages of Work due to Industrial Disputes, 1946–73*, London: Allen & Unwin

Duysters, G. (1995), *The Evolution of Complex Industrial Systems: The Dynamics of Major IT Sectors*, Maastricht: Universitaire Pers Maastricht

Dyas, G.P. and Thanheiser, H.T. (1976), *The Emerging European Enterprise*, London: Macmillan

Earl-Slater, A. (1993), 'Pharmaceuticals', in Johnson, P. (ed.), *European Industries: Structure, Conduct and Performance*, Aldershot: Edward Elgar, 75–100

Easterly, W., Kremer, M., Pritchett, L. and Summers, L.H. (1993), 'Good Policy or Good Luck? Country Growth Performance and Temporary Shocks', *Journal of Monetary Economics*, 32, 459–83

Edgerton, D.E.H. (1991), *England and the Aeroplane: An Essay on a Militant and Technological Nation*, London: Macmillan

(1996), 'The "White Heat" Revisited: The British Government and Technology in the 1960s', *Twentieth Century British History*, 7, 53–82

Edgerton, D.E.H. and Horrocks, S.M. (1994), 'British Industrial Research and Development Before 1945', *Economic History Review*, 47, 213–38

Edquist, C. and Jacobsson, S. (1988), *Flexible Automation: The Global Diffusion of Technology in the Engineering Industry*, Oxford: Blackwell

Edwardes, M. (1983), *Back from the Brink: An Apocalyptic Experience*, London: Collins

Edwards, H.R. (1962), *Competition and Monopoly in the British Soap Industry*, Oxford: Oxford University Press

Edwards, H.V. (1948), 'Flour-Milling', in Fogarty, M.P. (ed.), *Further Studies in Industrial Organization*, London: Methuen, 21–100

Edwards, J.R. (1989), *A History of Financial Accounting*, London: Routledge

Eichengreen, B. (1996), 'Institutions and Economic Growth: Europe After World War II', in Crafts, N.F.R. and Toniolo, G. (eds.), *Economic Growth in Europe Since 1945*, Cambridge: Cambridge University Press, 38–72

Elbaum, B. (1989), 'Why Apprenticeship Persisted in Britain but not in the United States', *Journal of Economic History*, 49, 337–49

Elbaum, B. and Lazonick, W. (eds.) (1986), *The Decline of the British Economy*, Oxford: Oxford University Press

Engerman, S.L. (1971), 'The Economic Impact of the Civil War', in Fogel, R.W. and Engerman, S.L. (eds.), *The Reinterpretation of American Economic History*, New York: Harper & Row, 369–79

Ergas, H. (1987), 'The Importance of Technology Policy', in Dasgupta, P. and Stoneman, P. (eds.), *Economic Policy and Technological Performance*, Cambridge: Cambridge University Press, 51–96

Erker, P. (1990), 'Die Verwissenschaftlichung der Industrie', *Zeitschrift für Unternehmensgeschichte*, 35, 73–94

Evely, R. and Little, I.M.D. (1960), *Concentration in British Industry: An Empirical Study of the Structure of Industrial Production, 1935–51*, Cambridge: Cambridge University Press

Evers, H. and von Landsberg, G. (1982), *Qualifikation und Karriere*, Köln: Deutscher Instituts-Verlag

Fabricant, S. (1940*)*, *The Output of Manufacturing Industries, 1899–1937*, New York: National Bureau of Economic Research

Fama, E.F. (1970), 'Efficient Capital Markets: A Review of Theory and Empirical Work', *Journal of Finance*, 25, 383–417

Fearon, P. (1974), 'The British Airframe Industry and the State', *Economic History Review*, 37, 236–51

(1979), 'Aircraft Manufacturing', in Buxton, N.K. and Aldcroft, D.H. (eds.), *British Industry Between the Wars: Instability and Industrial Development, 1919–1939*, London: Scolar, 216–40

Feinstein, C.H. (1965), *Domestic Capital Formation in the United Kingdom, 1920–1938*, Cambridge: Cambridge University Press

(1972), *National Income, Expenditure and Output of the United Kingdom, 1855–1965*, Cambridge: Cambridge University Press

(1988), 'Sources and Methods of Estimation for Domestic Reproducible Fixed Assets, Stocks and Works in Progress, Overseas Assets and Land', in Feinstein, C.H. and Pollard, S. (eds.), *Studies in Capital Formation in the United Kingdom, 1750–1920*, Oxford: Oxford University Press, 257–471

Feldman, G.D. (1989), 'Foreign Penetration of German Enterprises after the First World War: The Problem of Überfremdung', in Teichova, A., Lévy-Leboyer, M. and Nussbaum, H. (eds.), *Historical Studies in International Corporate Business*, Cambridge: Cambridge University Press, 87–110

Ferrier, R.W. (1982), *The History of the British Petroleum Company, Volume 1: The Developing Years, 1901–1932*, Cambridge: Cambridge University Press

Fidler, J. (1981), *The British Business Elite: Its Attitude to Class, Status and Power*, London: Routledge & Kegan Paul

Field, A.J. (1985), 'On the Unimportance of Machinery', *Explorations in Economic History*, 22, 378–401

Fieldhouse, D.K. (1978), *Unilever Overseas: The Anatomy of a Multinational, 1895–1965*, London: Croom Helm

Fitzgerald, P. (1927), *Industrial Combination in England*, London: Pitman

Flaherty, D. (1985), 'Labor Control in the British Boot and Shoe Industry', *Industrial Relations*, 24, 339–59

Flanders, A. (1964), *The Fawley Productivity Agreements: A Case Study of Management and Collective Bargaining*, London: Faber & Faber

Florence, P.S. (1953), *The Logic of British and American Industry: A Realistic Analysis of Economic Structure and Government*, London: Routledge & Kegan Paul

Floud, R.C. (1974), 'The Adolescence of American Engineering Competition, 1860–1900', *Economic History Review*, 27, 57–71

(1976), *The British Machine Tool Industry, 1850–1914*, Cambridge: Cambridge University Press

Flux, A.W. (1924), 'The Census of Production', *Journal of the Royal Statistical Society*, 87, 351–75

(1933), 'Industrial Productivity in Britain and the United States', *Quarterly Journal of Economics*, 48, 1–38

Foreman-Peck, J.S. (1979), 'Tariff Protection and Economies of Scale: The British Motor Industry Before 1939', *Oxford Economic Papers*, 31, 237–57

(1982), 'The American Challenge of the Twenties: Multinationals and the European Motor Industry', *Journal of Economic History*, 43, 405–31

(1991), 'Trade and the Balance of Payments', in Crafts, N.F.R. and Woodward, N. (eds.), *The British Economy Since 1945*, Oxford: Oxford University Press, 141–79

(1995), *Smith & Nephew in the Health Care Industry*, Aldershot: Edward Elgar

Frankel, M. (1957), *British and American Manufacturing Productivity*, Urbana: University of Illinois Press

Franko, L.G. (1976), *The European Multinationals: A Renewed Challenge to American and British Big Business*, London: Harper & Row

Fraser, W.H. (1981), *The Coming of the Mass Market, 1850–1914*, London: Macmillan

Freeman, C. (1962), 'Research and Development: A Comparison between British and American Industry', *National Institute Economic Review*, 20, 21–39

Fremdling, R. (1986), *Technologischer Wandel und internationaler Handel im 18. und 19. Jahrhundert: Die Eisenindustrien in Grossbritannien, Belgien, Frankreich und Deutschland*, Berlin: Duncker & Humblot

(1991), 'The German Iron and Steel Industry in the 19th Century', in Abé, E. and Suzuki, Y. (eds.), *Changing Patterns of International Rivalry: Some Lessons from the Steel Industry*, Tokyo: Tokyo University Press, 113–36

Frickey, E. (1947), *Production in the United States, 1860–1914*, Cambridge, MA: Harvard University Press

Fua, G. (1965), *Notes on Italian Economic Growth 1861–1964*, Milan: Scuola Enrico Mattei di Studi Superiori sugli Idrocarburi

Gallman, R.E. (1960), 'Commodity Output, 1839–1899', in Parker, W.N. (ed.), *Trends in the American Economy in the Nineteenth Century, Vol.24, Studies in Income and Wealth*, Princeton: National Bureau of Economic Research, 13–71

(1966), 'Gross National Product in the US, 1834–1909', in Brady, D.S. (ed.), *Output, Employment and Productivity in the US After 1800, Vol.30, Studies in Income and Wealth*, New York: National Bureau of Economic Research, 3–76

Gemmell, N. and Wardley, P. (1990), 'The Contribution of Services to British Economic Growth, 1856–1913', *Explorations in Economic History*, 27, 299–321

Gennard, J. and Dunn, S. (1983), 'The Impact of New Technology on the Structure and Organisation of Craft Unions in the Printing Industry', *British Journal of Industrial Relations*, 21, 17–32.

George, K.D. and Ward, T. (1975), *The Structure of Industry in the EEC*, Cambridge: Cambridge University Press

Gerschenkron, A. (1962), *Economic Backwardness in Historical Perspective*, Cambridge, MA: Harvard University Press

Giersch, H., Paqué, K.-H. and Schmieding, H. (1992), *The Fading Miracle: Four Decades of Market Economy in Germany*, Cambridge: Cambridge University Press

Giffen, R. (1889), *The Growth of Capital*, London: Bell

Gilbert, M. and Kravis, I.B. (1954), *An International Comparison of National Products and the Purchasing Power of Currencies*, Paris: Organisation for European Economic Cooperation

Gillingham, J. (1986), 'The Deproletarianisation of German Society: Vocational Training in the Third Reich', *Journal of Social History*, 19, 423–32

Gomulka, S. (1971), *Inventive Activity, Diffusion and the Stages of Economic Growth*, Aarhus: Institute of Economics

Gospel, H.F. (1989), 'Product Markets, Labour Markets, and Industrial Relations: The Case of Flour Milling', *Business History*, 31(2), 84–97

(1995), 'The Decline of Apprenticeship Training in Britain', *The Industrial Relations Journal*, 25, 32–44

Gourvish, T.R. (1979), 'Mechanical Engineering', in Buxton, N.K. and Aldcroft, D.H. (eds.), *British Industry Between the Wars: Instability and Industrial Development, 1919–1939*, London: Scolar, 129–55

(1987), 'British Business and the Transition to the Corporate Economy: Entrepreneurship and Management Structures', *Business History*, 29, 18–45

Gourvish, T.R. and Wilson, R.G. (1994), *The British Brewing Industry, 1830–1980*, Cambridge: Cambridge University Press

Granick, D. (1972), *Managerial Comparisons of Four Developed Countries: France, Britain, United States and Russia*, Cambridge, MA: MIT Press

Grant, W. and Martinelli, A. (1991), 'Political Turbulence, Enterprise Crisis and Industrial Recovery: ICI and Montedison', in Martinelli, A. (ed.), *International Markets and Global Firms: A Comparative Study of Organized Business in the Chemical Industry*, London: Sage

Gribbin, J.D. (1978), 'The Postwar Revival of Competition as Industrial Policy' (Government Economic Service Working Paper no.19, London)

Griliches, Z. (1994), 'Productivity, R&D and the Data Constraint', *American Economic Review*, 84, 1–23

Grossman, G.M. and Helpman, E. (1991), *Innovation and Growth in the Global Economy*, Cambridge, MA: MIT Press

Habakkuk, H.J. (1962), *American and British Technology in the Nineteenth Century*, Cambridge: Cambridge University Press

Hacker, L.M. (1940), *The Triumph of American Capitalism*, New York: Macmillan

Hague, D.C. (1957), *The Economics of Man-Made Fibres*, London: Duckworth

Haig, B.D. (1975), 'Manufacturing Output and Productivity 1910 to 1948/49', *Australian Economic History Review*, 15, 136–61

(1986), 'The Comparative Productivity of Australian Industry' (Discussion Paper no.142, Centre for Economic Policy Research, Australian National University, Canberra)

Håkanson, S. (1974), 'Special Presses in Paper–Making', in Nabseth, L. and Ray, G.F. (eds.), *The Diffusion of New Industrial Processes: An International Study*, Cambridge: Cambridge University Press, 58–104

Handy, C., Gordon, C., Gow, I. and Randlesome, C. (1988), *Making Managers*, London: Pitman

Hannah, L. (1979), *Electricity Before Nationalisation: A Study of the Electricity Supply Industry in Britain to 1948*, London: Macmillan

(1983), *The Rise of the Corporate Economy* (2nd edn.), London: Methuen

(1990), 'Business Culture and the Changing Business Environment' (Discussion Paper EC8/90, Lancaster University Management School)

(1995), 'Delusions of Durable Dominance OR The Invisible Hand Strikes Back: A Critique of the New Orthodoxy in Internationally Comparative Business History' (unpublished, London School of Economics)

Hargreaves, E.L. and Gowing, M.M. (1952), *Civil Industry and Trade*, London: HMSO and Longmans

Harley, C.K. (1974), 'Skilled Labour and the Choice of Technique in Edwardian Industry', *Explorations in Economic History*, 2, 391–414

Harrop, J. (1979), 'Rayon', in Buxton, N.K. and Aldcroft, D.H. (eds.), *British Industry Between the Wars: Instability and Industrial Development, 1919–1939*, London: Scolar, 276–302

Hart, P.E. and Clarke, R. (1980), *Concentration in British Industry, 1935–75: A Study of the Growth, Causes and Effects of Concentration in British Manufacturing Industries*, Cambridge: Cambridge University Press

Hartmann, H. (1959), *Authority and Organisation in German Management*, Westport, CT: Greenwood

Hartmann, H. and Wienold, H. (1967), *Universität und Unternehmer*, Gütersloh: Bertelsman

Hartshorn, J.E. (1993), *Oil Trade: Politics and Prospects*, Cambridge: Cambridge University Press

Harvey, R.C. and Ashworth, A. (1992), *The Construction Industry of Great Britain*, Oxford: Newnes

Hawke, G.R. (1975), 'The United States Tariff and Industrial Protection in the Late Nineteenth Century', *Economic History Review*, 28, 84–99

Hawkins, K.H. and Pass, C.L. (1979), *The Brewing Industry: A Study in Industrial Organisation and Public Policy*, London: Heinemann

Hawley, E.W. (1966), *The New Deal and the Problem of Monopoly*, Princeton: Princeton University Press

Hayami, Y. and Ruttan, V.W. (1985), *Agricultural Development: An International Perspective* (2nd edn.), Baltimore, MD: Johns Hopkins University Press

Hayward, K. (1983), *Government and British Civil Aerospace: A Case Study in Post-War Technology Policy*, Manchester: Manchester University Press

Hayward, K. (1989), *The British Aircraft Industry*, Manchester: Manchester University Press

Head, P. (1968), 'Boots and Shoes', in Aldcroft, D.H. (ed.), *The Development of British Industry and Foreign Competition, 1875–1914*, London: Allen & Unwin, 158–85

Heller, R. (1970), 'Britain's Boardroom Anatomy', *Management Today*, September, 83–5.

Hendry, J. (1989), *Innovating for Failure: Government Policy and the Early British Computer Industry*, Cambridge, MA: MIT Press

Henning, G.R. and Trace, K. (1975), 'Britain and the Motorship: A Case of Delayed Adoption of New Technology?', *Journal of Economic History*, 35, 353–85

Henrekson, M., Jonung, L. and Stymme, J. (1996), 'Economic Growth and the Swedish Model', in Crafts, N.F.R. and Toniolo, G. (eds), *Economic Growth in Europe Since 1945*, Cambridge: Cambridge University Press, 240–89

Higgins, D.M. (1993), 'Rings, Mules and Structural Constraints in the Lancashire Textile Industry, c.1945–c.1965', *Economic History Review*, 46, 342–62

Hilditch, P.J. (1990), 'Defence Procurement and Employment: The Case of UK Shipbuilding', *Cambridge Journal of Economics*, 14, 483–96

Hobsbawm, E.J. (1968), *Industry and Empire*, Harmondsworth: Penguin

Hoffman, R.J.S. (1933), *Great Britain and the German Trade Rivalry*, Philadelphia: University of Pennsylvania Press

Hoffmann, W.G. (1955), *British Industry, 1700–1950*, Oxford: Blackwell

(1965), *Das Wachstum der deutschen Wirtschaft seit der Mitte des 19. Jahrhunderts*, Berlin: Springer-Verlag

Hogan, W.T. (1971) *Economic History of the Iron and Steel Industry in the United States, Vol.1 (Parts 1 and 2)*, Lexington: D.C. Heath

Hogwood, B.W. (1979), *Government and Shipbuilding: The Politics of Industrial Change*, Farnborough: Saxon House

Hollingham, M.A. and Howarth, R.W. (1989), *British Milk Marketing and the Common Agricultural Policy: The Origins of Confusion and the Crisis*, Aldershot: Avebury

Hounshell, D.A. (1984), From *the American System to Mass Production, 1800–1932*, Baltimore, MD: Johns Hopkins University Press

Howell, D.R. and Wolff, E.N. (1992), 'Technical Change and the Demand for Skills by US Industries', *Cambridge Journal of Economics*, 16, 127–46

Howson, S. (1975), *Domestic Monetary Management in Britain, 1919–38*, Cambridge: Cambridge University Press

Hudson, R. and Sadler, D. (1989), *The International Steel Industry: Restructuring, State Policies and Localities*, London: Routledge

Hugill, A. (1978), *Sugar and All That: A History of Tate & Lyle*, London: Gentry

Hutchinson, H. (1965), *Tariff-Making and Industrial Reconstruction*, London: Harrap

Hutton, G. (1953), *We Too Can Prosper*, London: Allen & Unwin

Irwin, D.A. (1993), 'Free Trade and Protection in Nineteenth-Century Britain and France revisited: A Comment on Nye', *Journal of Economic History*, 53, 146–52

Isserlis, L. (1938), 'Tramp Shipping Cargoes and Freights', *Journal of the Royal Statistical Society*, 101, 53–134

James, H. (1986), *The German Slump: Politics and Economics, 1924–1936*, Oxford: Oxford University Press

James, J.A. and Skinner, J.S. (1985), 'The Resolution of the Labor-Scarcity Paradox', *Journal of Economic History*, 45, 513–40

Jefferys, J.B. (1954), *Retail Trading in Britain, 1850–1950*, Cambridge: Cambridge University Press

Jenkins, D.T. and Malin, J.C. (1990), 'European Competition in Woollen Cloth, 1870–1914', *Business History*, 32(4), 66–86

Jenkins, D.T. and Ponting, K.G. (1982), *The British Wool Textile Industry, 1779–1914*, Aldershot: Scolar

Jenkins, S. (1979), *Newspapers: The Power and the Money*, London: Faber & Faber

Jeremy, D.J. (1992) (ed.), *The Transfer of International Technology: Europe, Japan and the USA in the Twentieth Century*, Aldershot: Edward Elgar

Johansen, H.C. (1984), *Dansk Historisk Statistik 1814–1980*, Copenhagen: Gyldendal

John, A.H. (1950), *The Industrial Development of South Wales*, Cardiff: University of Wales Press

Jones, E. (1981), *Accountancy and the British Economy 1840–1980: The Evolution of Ernst & Whinney*, London: Batsford

Jones, G. (1984), 'The Growth and Performance of British Multinational Firms Before 1939: The Case of Dunlop', *Economic History Review*, 37, 35–53

(1986)(ed.), *British Multinationals: Origins, Management and Performance*, Aldershot: Gower

(1988), 'Foreign Multinationals and British Industry before 1945', *Economic History Review*, 41, 429–53

Jones, G.T. (1933), *Increasing Return: A Study of the Relationship between the Size and Efficiency of Industries with Special Reference to the History of Selected British and American Industries, 1850–1910*, Cambridge: Cambridge University Press

Jones, L. (1957), *Shipbuilding in Britain: Mainly Between the Two World Wars*, Cardiff: University of Wales Press

Jones, R. and Marriott, O. (1970), *Anatomy of a Merger: A History of G.E.C., A.E.I and English Electric*, London: Cape

de Jong, H.J. (1992), 'Real Output and Productivity in Dutch Manufacturing 1921–1960' (unpublished, University of Groningen)

Jürgens, U., Malsch, T. and Dohse, K. (1993), *Breaking from Taylorism: Changing Forms of Work in the Automobile Industry*, Cambridge: Cambridge University Press

Kagomiya, N. (1993), 'A Comparison of British and Japanese Manufacturing Productivity' (M.Phil. Thesis, University of Warwick)

Kaldor, N. (1945–6), 'The German War Economy', *Review of Economic Studies*, 13, 33–52

Kay, J. (1993), *Foundations of Corporate Success: How Business Strategies Add Value*, Oxford: Oxford University Press

Kaysen, C. and Turner, D.F. (1959), *Antitrust Policy: An Economic and Legal Analysis*, Cambridge, MA: Harvard University Press

Keating, M. (1973), *The Australian Workforce*, Canberra: Australian National University

Keatley, W.S. (1976), *The Fertiliser Manufacturers' Association: The Second Fifty Years, 1925–1975*, London: Fertiliser Manufacturers' Association

Keeble, S.P. (1992), *The Ability to Manage: A Study of British Management, 1890–1990*, Manchester: Manchester University Press

Kelly, T. (1987), *The British Computer Industry: Crisis and Development*, London: Croom Helm

Kendrick, J.W. (1961), *Productivity Trends in the United States*, Princeton: National Bureau of Economic Research

Kennedy, C. (1986), *ICI: The Company that Changed Our Lives*, London Hutchinson

Kennedy, W.P. (1987), *Industrial Structure, Capital Markets and the Origins of British Economic Decline*, Cambridge: Cambridge University Press

Kessler, S. and Bayliss, F. (1992), *Contemporary British Industrial Relations*, London: Macmillan

Kirby, M.W. (1974), 'The Lancashire Cotton Industry in the Inter-War Years: A Study in Organizational Change', *Business History*, 26, 145–59

(1981), *The Decline of British Economic Power Since 1870*, London: Allen & Unwin

Klepper, G. (1990), 'Entry into the Market for Large Transport Aircraft', *European Economic Review*, 34, 775–98

Knight, A. (1974), *Private Enterprise and Public Intervention: The Courtaulds Experience*, London: Allen & Unwin

Krijnse Locker, H. and Faerber, M.D. (1984), 'Space and Time Comparisons of Purchasing Power Parity and Real Values', *Review of Income and Wealth*, 30, 53–83

Krugman, P.R. (1991), *Geography and Trade*, Leuven: Leuven University Press
(1994), *Peddling Prosperity: Economic Sense and Nonsense in the Age of Diminished Expectations*, London: Norton

Kruk, M. (1967), *Die oberen 30, 000*, Wiesbaden: Betriebswirtschaftlicher Verlag Gabler

Kuznets, S. (1946), *National Product since 1869*, New York: National Bureau of Economic Research
(1955), 'Economic Growth and Income Inequality', *American Economic Review*, 45, 1–28

Lacci, L.A., Davies, S.W. and Smith, R. (1974), 'Tunnel Kilns in Brick-Making', in Nabseth, L. and Ray, G.F. (eds.), *The Diffusion of New Industrial Processes: An International Study*, Cambridge: Cambridge University Press, 105–45

Lacey, R.W. (1947), 'Cotton's War Effort', *Manchester School*, 15, 26–74

Landes, D.S. (1969), *The Unbound Prometheus: Technological Change and Industrial Development in Western Europe from 1750 to the Present*, Cambridge: Cambridge University Press

Lawrence, P. (1980), *Managers and Management in West Germany*, London: Croom Helm

Lazonick, W. (1981a), 'Factor Costs and the Diffusion of Ring Spinning in Britain Prior to World War I', *Quarterly Journal of Economics*, 96, 89–109
(1981b), 'Production Relations, Labor Productivity and Choice of Technique: British and U.S. Cotton Spinning', *Journal of Economic History*, 41, 491–516
(1986), 'The Cotton Industry', in Elbaum, B. and Lazonick, W. (eds.), *The Decline of the British Economy*, Oxford: Oxford University Press, 18–50
(1990), *Competitive Advantage on the Shop Floor*, Cambridge, MA: Harvard University Press

Lazonick, W. and Mass, W. (1984), 'The Performance of the British Cotton Industry, 1870–1913', *Research in Economic History*, 9, 1–44

Leak, H. and Maizels, A. (1945), The Structure of British Industry', *Journal of the Royal Statistical Society*, Series A, 108, 142–207

Lebergott, S. (1960), 'Labor Force and Employment, 1800–1960', in Brady, D.S. (ed.), *Output, Employment and Productivity in the United States After 1800, Vol. 30, Studies in Income and Wealth*, New York: National Bureau of Economic Research, 117–204

Lee, C.H. (1986), *The British Economy Since 1700: A Macroeconomic Perspective*, Cambridge: Cambridge University Press

Levine, A.L. (1967), *Industrial Retardation in Britain, 1880–1914*, New York: Basic Books

Levy, H. (1927), *Monopolies, Cartels and Trusts in British Industry*, London: Cass (1968 reprint)

Lewchuk, W. (1986), 'The Motor Vehicle Industry', in Elbaum, B. and Lazonick, W. (eds.), *The Decline of the British Economy*, Oxford: Oxford University Press, 135–61

American Technology and the British Vehicle Industry, Cambridge: Cambridge University Press

Lewis, J.P. (1965), *Building Cycles and Britain's Growth*, London: Macmillan

Lewis, W.A. (1978), *Growth and Fluctuations, 1870–1913*, London: Allen & Unwin

Liepmann, H. (1938), *Tariff Levels and the Economic Unity of Europe*, London: Allen & Unwin

Liepmann, K. (1960), *Apprenticeship: An Enquiry into its Adequacy in Modern Conditions*, London: Routledge & Kegan Paul

Lindert, P.H. (1991), *International Economics*, Homewood, IL: Irwin

Lindert, P.H. and Trace, K. (1971), 'Yardsticks for Victorian Entrepreneurs', in McCloskey, D.N. (ed.), *Essays on a Mature Economy: Britain after 1840*, London: Methuen, 239–74

Lomax, K.S. (1959), 'Production and Productivity Movements in the United Kingdom Since 1900', *Journal of the Royal Statistical Society*, Series A, 122, 185–210

Lorenz, E.H. (1991a), *Economic Decline in Britain: The Shipbuilding Industry, 1890–1970*, Oxford: Oxford University Press

(1991b), 'An Evolutionary Explanation for Competitive Decline: The British Shipbuilding Industry, 1890–1970', *Journal of Economic History*, 51, 911–35

Lorenz, E.H. and Wilkinson, F. (1986), 'The Shipbuilding Industry, 1880–1965', in Elbaum, B. and Lazonick, W. (eds.), *The Decline of the British Economy*, Oxford: Oxford University Press, 109–34

Lucas, A.F. (1937), *Industrial Reconstruction and the Control of Competition: The British Experiments*, London: Longmans Green & Co.

Lucas, R.E., Jr. (1988), 'The Mechanics of Economic Development', *Journal of Monetary Economics*, 22, 3–42.

(1993), 'Making a Miracle', *Econometrica*, 61, 251–72

McCalman, J. (1988), *The Electronics Industry in Britain: Coping with Change*, London: Routledge

McCloskey, D.N. (1973), *Economic Maturity and Entrepreneurial Decline: British Iron and Steel, 1870–1913*, Cambridge, MA: Harvard University Press

(1981), *Enterprise and Trade in Victorian Britain: Essays in Historical Economics*, London: Allen & Unwin.

McCloskey, D.N. and Sandberg, L. (1971), 'From Damnation to Redemption: Judgements on the Late Victorian Entrepreneur', *Explorations in Economic History*, 9, 89–108

McKinsey Global Institute (1993), *Manufacturing Productivity*, Washington DC: McKinsey

McMillan, J. (1989), *The Dunlop Story: The Life, Death and Re-Birth of a Multi-National*, London: Weidenfeld & Nicolson

Maddison, A. (1952), 'Productivity in Canada, the United Kingdom and the United States', *Oxford Economic Papers*, 4, 235–42

(1964), *Economic Growth in the West*, London: Allen & Unwin

(1982), *Phases of Capitalist Development*, Oxford: Oxford University Press

(1987), 'Growth and Slowdown in Advanced Capitalist Economies: Techniques of Quantitative Assessment', *Journal of Economic Literature*, 25, 649–98

(1989), *The World Economy in the Twentieth Century*, Paris: Organisation for Economic Cooperation and Development

(1991), *Dynamic Forces in Capitalist Development*, Oxford: Oxford University Press

(1993), 'Standardised Estimates of Fixed Capital Stock: A Six Country Comparison', *Innovazione e Materie Prime*, April, 1–29

(1995), *Monitoring the World Economy, 1820–1992*, Paris: Organisation for Economic Cooperation and Development

Maddison, A. and van Ark, B. (1988), 'Comparisons of Real Output in Manufacturing' (Policy, Planning and Research Working Papers, WPS 5, World Bank)

Magee, G.B. (1994), 'Technology, Productivity and Performance in the British Paper Industry, 1861–1913' (D.Phil Dissertation, University of Oxford)

Mankiw, N.G., Romer, D. and Weil, D.N. (1992), 'A Contribution to the Empirics of Economic Growth', *Quarterly Journal of Economics*, 107, 407–37

Marrison, A.J. (1975), 'Great Britain and her Rivals in the Latin American Cotton Piece-Goods Market, 1880–1914', in Ratcliffe, B.M. (ed.), *Great Britain and her World, 1750–1914: Essays in Honour of W.O. Henderson*, Manchester: Manchester University Press, 309–48

(1996), 'Indian Summer, 1870–1914', in Rose, M.B. (ed.), *The Lancashire Cotton Industry: A History Since 1700*, Preston: Lancashire County Books, 238–95

Marshall, A. (1920), *Principles of Economics* (8th edn.), London: Macmillan

Mason, G., van Ark, B. and Wagner, K. (1994), 'Productivity, Product Quality and Workforce Skills: Food Processing in Four European Countries', *National Institute Economic Review*, 147, 62–83

Mason, G. and Finegold, D. (1995), 'Productivity, Machinery and Skills in the United States and Western Europe: Precision Engineering' (unpublished, National Institute of Economic and Social Research, London)

Mathias, P. (1959), *The Brewing Industry in England, 1700–1830*, Cambridge: Cambridge University Press

(1967), *Retailing Revolution: A History of Multiple Retailing in the Food Trades Based Upon the Allied Suppliers Group of Companies*, London: Longmans

(1969), *The First Industrial Nation: An Economic History of Britain, 1700–1914*, London: Methuen

Matthews, D. (1993), 'Counting the Accountants: A Trial Balance for 1911', *Accounting, Business and Financial History*, 3, 197–223

Matthews, R.C.O., Feinstein, C.H. and Odling-Smee, J.C. (1982), *British Economic Growth, 1856–1973*, Oxford: Oxford University Press

Maunder, P. (1970), *The Bread Industry in the United Kingdom: A Study in Market Structure, Conduct and Performance Analysis*, Loughborough: Department of Social Sciences and Economics, University of Technology, Loughborough

(1988), 'Food Processing', in Johnson, P. (ed.), *European Industries: Structure, Conduct and Performance*, Aldershot: Edward Elgar, 188–212

Mayer, C. (1993), 'Ownership: An Inaugural Lecture' (Warwick Economic Reseach Paper no.402)

Meeks, G. (1977), *Disappointing Marriage: A Study of the Gains from Merger*, Cambridge: Cambridge University Press

Melman, S. (1956), *Dynamic Factors in Industrial Productivity*, Oxford: Blackwell

Melrose-Woodman, J. (1978), 'Profile of the British Manager' (British Institue of Management Foundation, Management Survey Report no.38, London)

Mensink, G.J.A. (1966), *Comparisons of Labour Productivity in the United Kingdom and the Netherlands, 1958*, The Hague: Central Bureau of Statistics

Menzies, I.E.P. and Chapman, D. (1946), 'The Jute Industry', in Silverman, H.A. (ed.), *Studies in Industrial Organization*, London: Methuen, 235–63

Mercer, H. (1989), 'The Evolution of British Government Policy Towards Competition in Private Industry, 1940–1956' (Ph.D Thesis, London School of Economics)

Mikesell, R.F. (1988), *The Global Copper Industry: Problems and Prospects*, London: Croom Helm

Milgrom, P. and Roberts, J. (1990), 'The Economics of Modern Manufacturing: Technology, Strategy and Organisation', *American Economic Review*, 80, 511–28

Miles, C. (1968), *Lancashire Textiles: A Case Study of Industrial Change*, Cambridge: Cambridge University Press

Miller, M. and Church, R.A. (1979), 'Motor Manufacturing', in Buxton, N.K. and Aldcroft, D.H. (eds.), *British Industry Between the Wars: Instability and Industrial Development, 1919–1939*, London: Scolar, 179–215

Minchinton, W.E. (1957), *The British Tinplate Industry: A History*, Oxford: Oxford University Press

Mitchell, B.R. (1980), *European Historical Statistics* (2nd edn.), London: Macmillan
(1988), *British Historical Statistics*, Cambridge: Cambridge University Press

Mokyr, J. (1990), *The Lever of Riches: Technological Creativity and Economic Progress*, Oxford: Oxford University Press

Morgan, K. and Sayer, A. (1988), *Microcircuits of Capital: 'Sunrise' Industry and Uneven Development*, Oxford: Polity

Morris, P.R. (1990), *A History of the World Semiconductor Industry*, London: Peregrinus

Moss, M.S. and Hume, J.R. (1981), *The Making of Scotch Whisky: A History of the Scotch Whisky Distilling Industry*, Edinburgh: James & James

Mowery, D.C. (1986), 'Industrial Research, 1900–1950', in Elbaum, B. and Lazonick, W. (eds.), *The Decline of the British Economy*, Oxford: Oxford University Press, 189–222

Mueller, W.F. and Hamm, L.G. (1974), 'Trends in Industrial Concentration, 1947 to 1950', *Review of Economics and Statistics*, 56, 511–20

Musson, A.E. (1965), *Enterprise in Soap and Chemicals: Joseph Crosfield and Sons Limited, 1815–1965*, Manchester: Manchester University Press
(1978), *The Growth of British Industry*, London: Batsford

National Economic Development Council (1978), *Paper and Board SWP: Progress Report*, London: NEDO

National Institute of Economic and Social Research (NIESR) (1991), *Productivity, Education and Training: Britain and Other Countries Compared* (Reprints of studies published in the National Institute Economic Review with a Preface by S.J. Prais), London: NIESR

Neale, A.D. (1960), *The Antitrust Laws of the United States of America: A Study of Competition Enforced by Law*, Cambridge: Cambridge University Press

Nelson, R.R. (1993) (ed.), *National Innovation Systems: A Comparative Analysis*, Oxford: Oxford University Press

Nelson, R.R. and Wright, G. (1992), 'The Rise and Fall of American Technological Leadership: The Postwar Era in Historical Perspective', *Journal of Economic Literature*, 30, 1931–64

Newcomer, M. (1955), *The Big Business Executive*, New York: Columbia University Press

(1965), *The Big Business Executive/1964*, New York: Scientific American

Newell, E. (1990), 'Copperopolis: The Rise and Fall of the Copper Industry in the Swansea District, 1826–1931', *Business History*, 32(3), 75–97

Norton, W.E. and Aylmer, C.P. (1988), *Australian Economic Statistics, 1949–50 to 1986–87*, Canberra: Reserve Bank of Australia

Nye, J.V. (1991), 'The Myth of Free-Trade Britain and Fortress France: Tariffs and Trade in the Nineteenth Century', *Journal of Economic History*, 51, 23–46

O'Brien, P.K. and Prados de la Escosura, L. (1992), 'Agricultural Productivity and European Industrialisation', *Economic History Review*, 45, 514–36

O'Mahony, M. (1992a), 'Productivity Levels in British and German Manufacturing', *National Institute Economic Review*, 139, 46–63

(1992b), 'Productivity and Human Capital Formation in UK and German Manufacturing' (Discussion Paper no.28, National Institute of Economic and Social Research, London)

(1996), 'Measures of Fixed Capital Stocks in the Postwar Period: A Five Country Study', in van Ark, B. and Crafts, N.F.R. (eds.), *Quantitative Aspects of Postwar European Economic Growth*, Cambridge: Cambridge University Press, 165–214

O'Mahony, M. and Wagner, K. (1994), 'Changing Fortunes: An Industry Study of British and German Productivity Growth Over Three Decades (Report Series no.7, National Institute of Economic and Social Research, London)

O'Rourke, K.H., Taylor, A.M. and Williamson, J.G. (1996), 'Factor price Convergence in the Late 19th Century', *International Economic Review*, 37, 499–530

Ohkawa, K. and Shinohara, M. (1979) (eds.), *Patterns of Japanese Economic Development: A Quantitative Appraisal*, New Haven: Yale University Press

Oliver, N. and Wilkinson, B. (1988), *The Japanisation of British Industry*, Oxford: Blackwell

Olson, M. (1965), *The Logic of Collective Action: Public Goods and the Theory of Groups*, Cambridge, MA: Harvard University Press

(1982), *The Rise and Decline of Nations: Economic Growth, Stagflation, and Social Rigidities*, New Haven: Yale University Press

Oulton, N. and O'Mahony, M. (1994), *Productivity and Growth: A Study of British Industry, 1954–1986*, Cambridge: Cambridge University Press

Overy, R.J. (1984), *Goering: The 'Iron Man'*, London: Routledge & Kegan Paul

Owen, G. (1992), 'The British Electronics Industry from 1960 to the 1990s' (Working Paper no.324, Centre for Economic Performance, London School of Economics)

Owen Smith, E. (1994), *The German Economy*, London: Routledge

Paige, D. and Bombach, G. (1959), *A Comparison of National Output and Productivity of the United Kingdom and the United States*, Paris: Organisation for European Economic Cooperation

Paretti, V. and Bloch, S. (1956), 'Industrial Production in Western Europe and the United States 1901 to 1955', *Banca Nazionale del Lavoro Quarterly Review*, 39, 186–234

Parkinson, J.R. (1979), 'Shipbuilding', in Buxton, N.K. and Aldcroft, D.H. (eds.), British Industry Between the Wars: Instability and Industrial Development, 1919–1939, London: Scolar, 79–102

Parkinson, S.T. (1984), *New Product Development in Engineering: A Comparison of the British and West German Machine Tool Industries*, Cambridge: Cambridge University Press

Pashigian, B.P. (1968), 'Market Concentration in the United States and Great Britain', *Journal of Law and Economics*, 11, 299–319

Payne, P.L. (1968), 'Iron and Steel Manufactures', in Aldcroft, D.H. (ed.), *The Development of British Industry and Foreign Competition, 1875–1914*, London: Allen & Unwin, 71–99

(1979), *Colvilles and the Scottish Steel Industry*, Oxford: Oxford University Press

Peaker, A. (1974), *Economic Growth in Modern Britain*, London: Macmillan

Peden, G.C. (1985), *British Economic and Social Policy: Lloyd George to Margaret Thatcher*, Deddington: Philip Allan

Peppercorn, G. and Skoulding, G. (1987), *Profiles of British Industry: The Manager's View*, Corby: British Institute of Management

Perren, R. (1990), 'Structural Change and Market Growth in the Food Industry: Flour Milling in Britain, Europe, and America, 1850–1914', *Economic History Review*, 43, 420–37

Pettigrew, A.M. (1985), *The Awakening Giant: Continuity and Change in Imperial Chemical Industries*, Oxford: Blackwell

Phelps-Brown, E.H. and Handfield-Jones, S.J. (1952), 'The Climacteric of the 1890s: A Study in the Expanding Economy', *Oxford Economic Papers*, 4, 266–307

Pilat, D. (1994), *The Economics of Rapid Growth: The Experience of Japan and Korea*, Aldershot: Edward Elgar

Piore, M.J. and Sabel, C.F. (1984), *The Second Industrial Divide: Possibilities for Prosperity*, New York: Basic Books

Plummer, A. (1951), *International Combines in Modern Industry*, London: Pitman

Political and Economic Planning (PEP) (1950), *Motor Vehicles: A Report on the Organisation and Structure of the Industry, its Products, and its Market Prospects at Home and Abroad*, London: Political and Economic Planning

Pollard, S. (1989), *Britain's Prime and Britain's Decline: The British Economy 1870–1914*, London: Edward Arnold

Pollard, S. and Robertson, P. (1979), *The British Shipbuilding Industry, 1870–1914*, Cambridge, MA: Harvard University Press

Pomfret, R. (1991), 'The New Trade Theories, Rent–Snatching and Jet Aircraft', *World Economy*, 14, 269–77

Poole, M., Mansfield, R., Blyton, P. and Frost, P. (1981), *Managers in Focus: The British Manager in the Early 1980s*, Aldershot: Gower

Porter, J.H. (1979), 'Cotton and Wool Textiles', in Buxton, N.K. and Aldcroft, D.H.

(eds.), *British Industry Between the Wars: Instability and Industrial Development, 1919–1939*, London: Scolar, 25–47

Porter, M.E. (1990), *The Competitive Advantage of Nations*, London: Macmillan

Postan, M.M. (1952), *British War Production*, London: HMSO and Longmans

Prais, S.J. (1976), *The Evolution of Giant Firms in Britain: A Study of the Growth of Concentration in Manufacturing Industry in Britain, 1909–70*, Cambridge: Cambridge University Press

(1981), *Productivity and Industrial Structure: A Statistical Study of Manufacturing Industry in Britain, Germany and the United States*, Cambridge: Cambridge University Press

(1993), 'Economic Performance and Education: The Nature of Britain's Deficiencies' (Discussion Paper no.52, NIESR, London)

Pratten, C.F. (1976), *Labour Productivity Differentials within International Companies*, Cambridge: Cambridge University Press

Pross, H. and Bötticher, K. (1971), *Manager des Kapitalismus*, Frankfurt: Suhrkamp

Ram, M. (1992), 'The West Midlands Clothing Sector: A Suitable Case for Team Working', *Regional Studies*, 26, 503–9

Ray, G.R. (1984), *The Diffusion of Mature Technologies*, Cambridge: Cambridge University Press

Reader, W.J. (1960), *Unilever: A Short History*, London: Unilever

(1970), *Imperial Chemical Industries: A History, Vol.1: The Forerunners, 1870–1926*, Oxford: Oxford University Press

(1975), *Imperial Chemical Industries: A History, Vol.2: The First Quarter-Century, 1926–1952*, Oxford: Oxford University Press

(1976), *Metal Box: A History*, London: Heinemann

(1979), 'The Chemical Industry', in Buxton, N.K. and Aldcroft, D.H. (eds.), *British Industry Between the Wars: Instability and Industrial Development, 1919–1939*, London: Scolar, 156–78

(1980*)*, *Fifty Years of Unilever, 1930–1980*, London: Heinemann

(1981), *Bowater: A History*, Cambridge: Cambridge University Press

Reed, A. (1973), *Britain's Aircraft Industry: What Went Right? What Went Wrong?*, London: Dent

Reekie, W.D. (1975), *The Economics of the Pharmaceutical Industry*, London: Macmillan

Reekie, W.D. and Wells, N. (1988), 'Pharmaceuticals', in Johnson, P. (ed.), *The Structure of British Industry* (2nd edn.), London: Unwin Hyman, 94–118

Rees, M. (1922), *Trusts in British Industry 1914–21*, London: King

Reid, H. (1986), *The Furniture Makers: A History of Trade Unionism in the Furniture Trade, 1865–1972*, Oxford: Malthouse Press

Rhys, D.G. (1972), *The Motor Industry: An Economic Survey*, London: Butterworths

(1988), 'Motor Vehicles', in Johnson, P. (ed.), *The Structure of British Industry* (2nd edn.), London: Unwin Hyman, 164–87

Richardson, H.W. (1965), 'Over-commitment in Britain before 1930', *Oxford Economic Papers*, 17, 237–62

(1968), 'Chemicals', in Aldcroft, D.H. (ed.), *The Development of British Industry and Foreign Competition, 1875–1914*, London: Allen & Unwin, 274–306

Robertson, A.J. (1975), 'The British Airframe Industry and the State in the Interwar Period: A Comment', *Economic History Review*, 38, 648–57

Robson, M. (1988), 'The British Pharmaceutical Industry and the First World War', in Liebenau, J. (ed.), *The Challenge of New Technology: Innovation in British Business Since 1850*, Aldershot: Gower, 83–105

Robson, R. (1957), *The Cotton Industry in Britain*, London: Macmillan

(1958), *The Man-Made Fibres Industry*, London: Macmillan

Röber, J. (1975), *Social Change at Work: The ICI Weekly Staff Agreement*, London: Duckworth

Romer, P.M. (1986), 'Increasing Returns and Long Run Growth', *Journal of Political Economy*, 94, 1002–37

(1990), 'Human Capital and Growth: Theory and Evidence', *Carnegie–Rochester Conference Series on Public Policy*, 32, 251–86

(1994), 'The Origins of Endogenous Growth', *Journal of Economic Perspectives*, 8(1), 3–22

Röpke, W. (1931), *Der Weg des Unheils*, Berlin

Rosenberg, N. (1969) (ed.), *The American System of Manufactures*, Edinburgh: Edinburgh University Press

Rosenbluth, G. (1955), 'Measures of Concentration', in National Bureau of Economic Research, *Business Concentration and Price Policy: A Conference*, Princeton: Princeton University Press, 57–95

Rostas, L. (1943), 'Industrial Production, Productivity and Distribution in Britain, Germany and the United States', *Economic Journal*, 53, 39–54

(1948a), *Comparative Productivity in British and American Industry*, Cambridge: Cambridge University Press

(1948b), *Productivity, Prices and Distribution in Selected British Industries*, Cambridge: Cambridge University Press

Rothbarth, E. (1946), 'Causes of the Superior Efficiency of USA Industry as Compared with British Industry', *Economic Journal*, 56, 383–90

Rowe, D.J. (1983), *Lead Manufacturing in Britain: A History*, London: Croom Helm

Rowley, C.K. (1971), *Steel and Public Policy*, London: McGraw-Hill.

Rowthorn, R. (1986), 'The Passivity of the State', in Coates, D. and Hillard, J. (eds.), *The Economic Decline of Modern Britain: The Debate Between Left and Right*, Brighton: Wheatsheaf, 264–6

Rubinstein, W.D. (1993), *Capitalism, Culture and Economic Decline in Britain, 1750–1990*, London: Routledge

Salter, W.E.G. (1960), *Productivity and Technical Change*, Cambridge: Cambridge University Press

Sandberg, L.G. (1969), 'American Rings and English Mules: The Role of Economic Rationality', *Quarterly Journal of Economics*, 83, 25–43

(1971), 'Discussion', in McCloskey, D.N. (ed.), *Essays on a Mature Economy: Britain after 1840*, London: Methuen, 277–9

(1974), *Lancashire in Decline: A Study in Entrepreneurship, Technology and International Trade*, Columbus: Ohio State University Press

(1981), 'The Entrepreneur and Technological Change', in Floud, R. and McCloskey, D. (eds.), *The Economic History of Britain since 1700, Volume 2: 1860 to the 1970s*, Cambridge: Cambridge University Press, 99–120

Sanderson, M. (1972), 'Research and the Firm in British Industry, 1919–1939', *Science Studies*, 2, 107–51

(1988), 'Education and Economic Decline, 1890 to the 1980s', *Oxford Review of Economic Policy*, 4(1), 38–50

Saul, S.B. (1962), 'The Motor Industry in Britain to 1914', *Business History*, 5, 22–44

(1968), 'The Engineering Industry', in Aldcroft, D.H. (ed.), *The Development of British Industry and Foreign Competition, 1875–1914*, London: Allen & Unwin, 186–237

Sawyer, M.C. (1971), 'Concentration in British Manufacturing Industry', *Oxford Economic Papers*, 23, 352–83

Saxonhouse, G.R. and Wright, G. (1984), 'New Evidence on the Stubborn English Mule and the Cotton Industry, 1878–1920', *Economic History Review*, 37, 507–19

(1987), 'Stubborn Mules and Vertical Integration: The Disappearing Constraint?', *Economic History Review*, 40, 87–94

Schenk, W. (1974), 'Continuous Casting of Steel', in Nabseth, L. and Ray, G.F. (eds.), *The Diffusion of Industrial Processes: An International Study*, Cambridge: Cambridge University Press, 232–50

Scherer, F.M. (1980), *Industrial Market Structure and Economic Performance* (2nd edn.), Boston, MA: Houghton Mifflin

Schlote, W. (1952), *British Overseas Trade: From 1700 to the 1930s*, Oxford: Blackwell

Schmitz, C.J. (1986), 'The Rise of Big Business in the World Copper Industry, 1870–1930', *Economic History Review*, 39, 392–410

Sciberras, E. and Payne, B.D. (1985), *Machine Tool Industry: Technical Change and International Competitiveness*, Harlow: Longman

Shaw, D.C. (1950), 'Productivity in the Cotton Spinning Industry', *Manchester School*, 18, 14–30

Shepherd, G. (1961), 'A Comparison of Industrial Concentration in the United States and Britain', *Review of Economics and Statistics*, 43, 70–5

(1982), 'Causes of Increased Competition in the US Economy, 1939–1980', *Review of Economics and Statistics*, 64, 613–26

Shorter, A.H. (1971), *Paper Making in the British Isles: An Historical and Geographical Study*, Newton Abbot: David & Charles

Sigsworth, E.M. (1965), 'Science and the Brewing Industry', *Economic History Review*, 17, 536–50

Sigsworth, E.M. and Blackman, J.M. (1968), 'The Woollen and Worsted Industries', in Aldcroft, D.H. (ed.), *The Development of British Industry and Foreign Competition, 1875–1914*, London: Allen & Unwin, 128–57

Silverman, H.A. (1946a), 'The Hosiery Industry', in Silverman, H.A. (ed.), *Studies in Industrial Organization*, London: Methuen, 1–46

(1946b), 'The Boot and Shoe Industry', in Silverman, H.A. (ed.), *Studies in Industrial Organization*, London: Methuen, 199–234

Singleton, J. (1986), 'Lancashire's Last Stand: Declining Employment in the British Cotton Industry, 1950–70', *Economic History Review*, 39, 92–107

(1991), *Lancashire on the Scrapheap: The Cotton Industry, 1945–1970*, Oxford: Oxford University Press

Sisson, K. (1975), *Industrial Relations in Fleet Street: A Study in Pay Structure*, Oxford: Blackwell

Smith, A.D. and Hitchens, D.M.W.N. (1985), *Productivity in the Distributive Trades: A Comparison of Britain, America and Germany*, Cambridge: Cambridge University Press

Smith, A.D., Hitchens, D.M.W.N. and Davies, S.W. (1982), *International Industrial Productivity: A Comparison of Britain, America and Germany*, Cambridge: Cambridge University Press

Smith, C.(1940), *Britain's Food Supplies in Peace and War*, London: Routledge

Sokoloff, K.L. (1986), 'Productivity Growth in Manufacturing During Early Industrialisation: Evidence for the American Northeast, 1820–1860', in Engerman, S.L. and Gallman, R.E. (eds.), *Long Term Factors in American Economic Growth, Vol.51, Studies in Income and Wealth*, Chicago: National Bureau of Economic Research, 679–736

Solow, R.M. (1957), 'Technical Change and the Aggregate Production Function', *Review of Economics and Statistics*, 39, 312–20

Soltow, L. (1968), 'Long Run Changes in British Income Inequality', *Economic History Review*, 21, 17–29

(1969), 'Evidence on Income Inequality in the United States, 1866–1965', *Journal of Economic History*, 29, 279–86

(1990), *Distribution of Wealth and Income in the United States in 1798*, Pittsburgh: Pittsburgh University Press

Soskice, D. (1993), 'Product Market and Innovation Strategies of Companies and their Implications for Enterprise Tenure: A Comparative Institutional Approach of Some Cross–Country Differences' (unpublished, Wissenschaftszentrum, Berlin)

Stafford, G.B. (1981), *The End of Economic Growth? Growth and Decline in the UK Since 1945*, Oxford: Martin Robertson

Stanworth, P. and Giddens, A. (1974), 'An Economic Elite: A Demographic Profile of Company Chairmen', in Stanworth, P. and Giddens, A. (eds.), *Elites and Power in British Society*, Cambridge: Cambridge University Press, 81–101

Steedman, H. and Wagner, K. (1987), 'A Second Look at Productivity, Machinery and Skills in Britain and Germany', *National Institute Economic Review*, 122, 84–95

(1989), 'Productivity, Machinery and Skills: Clothing Manufacture in Britain and Germany', *National Institute Economic Review*, 128, 40–57

Stern, R.M. and Maskus, K.E. (1981), 'Determinants of the Structure of US Foreign Trade, 1958–1976', *Journal of International Economics*, 11, 207–24

Stevens, R.B. and Yamey, B.S. (1965), *The Restrictive Practices Court: A Study of the Judicial Process and Economic Policy*, London: Weidenfeld & Nicolson

Stopford, J.M. and Turner, L. (1985) *Britain and the Multinationals*, Chichester: Wiley

Stråth, B. (1986), 'Redundancy and Solidarity: Tripartite Politics and the Contraction of the West European Shipbuilding Industry', *Cambridge Journal of Economics*, 10, 147–63

van Stuyvenberg, J.H. (1969), 'Aspects of Government Intervention', in van Stuyvenberg, J.H. (ed.), *Margarine: An Economic, Social and Scientific History, 1869–1969*, Liverpool: Liverpool University Press, 281–327

Summers, R. and Heston, A. (1984), 'Improved International Comparisons of Real Product and its Composition: 1950–1980', *Review of Income and Wealth*, 30, 207–62

(1991), 'The Penn World Table (Mark 5): An Expanded Set of International Comparisons, 1950–1988', *Quarterly Journal of Economics*, 106, 327–68

Supple, B.E. (1994), 'Fear of Failing: Economic History and the Decline of Britain', *Economic History Review*, 47, 441–58

Sutton, J. (1991), *Sunk Costs and Market Structure: Price Competition, Advertising, and the Evolution of Concentration*, Cambridge, MA: MIT Press

Svennilson, I. (1954), *Growth and Stagnation in the European Economy*, Geneva: United Nations

Swann, D., O'Brien, D.P., Maunder, W.P.J. and Howe, W.S. (1974), *Competition in British Industry: Restrictive Practices Legislation in Theory and Practice*, London: Allen & Unwin

Szilagyi, G. (1984), 'Procedures for Updating the Results of International Comparisons', *Review of Income and Wealth*, 30, 207–62

Taggart, J. (1993), *The World Pharmaceutical Industry*, London: Routledge

Taussig, F.W. (1892), *The Tariff History of the United States*, New York: Putnam's

(1924), 'Labor Costs in the US Compared with Costs Elsewhere', *Quarterly Journal of Economics*, 39, 96–114

Taussig, F.W. and Jocelyn, C.S. (1932), *American Business Leaders*, New York: Macmillan

Taylor, D. (1976), 'The English Dairy Industry, 1860–1930', *Economic History Review*, 29, 585–601

Taylor, T. and Hayward, K. (1989), *The UK Defence Industrial Base*, London: Brassey's

Teichova, A., Lévy-Leboyer and Nussbaum, H. (1986) (eds.), *Multinational Enterprise in Historical Perspective*, Cambridge: Cambridge University Press

Teeling Smith, G. (1992), 'The British Pharmaceutical Industry: 1961–1991', in Teeling Smith, G. (ed.), *Innovative Competition in Medicine: A Schumpeterian Analysis of the Pharmaceutical Industry and the NHS*, London: Office of Health Economics, 67–83

Temin, P. (1966a), 'Labor Scarcity and the Problem of American Industrial Efficiency in the 1850s', *Journal of Economic History*, 26, 361–79

(1966b), 'The Relative Decline of the British Steel Industry, 1880–1913', in Rosovsky, H. (ed.), *Industrialization in Two Systems: Essays in Honour of Alexander Gerschenkron*, New York: Wiley, 140–59

(1971), 'Labour Scarcity in America', *Journal of Interdisciplinary History*, 1, 251–64

Thomas, B. (1973), *Migration and Economic Growth: A Study of Great Britain and the Atlantic Economy* (2nd edn.), Cambridge: Cambridge University Press

Tiratsoo, N. and Tomlinson, J. (1994), 'Restrictive Practices on the Shopfloor in Britain, 1945–60: Myth and Reality', *Business History*, 36(2), 65–82

Todd, D. (1985), *The World Shipbuilding Industry*, London: Croom Helm

(1988), *Defence Industries: A Global Perspective*, London: Routledge

Todd, D. and Simpson, J. (1986), *The World Aircraft Industry*, London: Croom Helm

Tolliday, S. (1986), 'Steel and Rationalization Policies, 1918–1950', in Elbaum, B. and Lazonick, W. (eds.), *The Decline of the British Economy*, Oxford: Oxford University Press, 82–108

(1987a), *Business, Banking and Politics: The Case of British Steel, 1918–1939*, Cambridge, MA: Harvard University Press

(1987b), 'The Failure of Mass Production Unionism in the Motor Industry, 1914–39', in Wrigley, C. (ed.), *A History of British Industrial Relations, Vol. II: 1914–1939*, Brighton: Harvester, 298–322

(1991), 'Competition and Maturity in the British Steel Industry, 1870–1914', in Abé, E. and Suzuki, Y. (eds.), *Changing Patterns of International Rivalry: Some Lessons from the Steel Industry*, Tokyo: Tokyo University Press, 20–72

Tolliday, S. and Zeitlin, J. (1991) (eds.), *The Power to Manage? Employers and Industrial Relations in Comparative Historical Perspective*, London: Routledge

Trevor, M. (1988), *Toshiba's New Company: Competitiveness through Innovation in Industry*, London: Policy Studies Institute

von Tunzelmann, G.N. (1982), 'Structural Change and Leading Sectors in British Manufacturing, 1907–68', in Kindleberger, C.P. and di Tella, G. (eds.), *Economics in the Long View, Vol.3: Applications and Cases, Part II*, London: Macmillan, 1–49

Turner, G. (1969), *Business in Britain*, London: Eyre & Spottiswoode

(1971), *The Leyland Papers*, London: Eyre & Spottiswoode

Tyson, R.E. (1968), 'The Cotton Industry', in Aldcroft, D.H. (ed.), *The Development of British Industry and Foreign Competition, 1875–1914*, London: Allen & Unwin, 100–27

United Nations Industrial Development Organization (1984), *World Non–Electrical Machinery: An Empirical Study of the Machine Tool Industry*, New York: United Nations

Urquhart, M.C. (1965), *Historical Statistics of Canada*, Cambridge: Cambridge University Press

Utton, M.A. (1982), 'Domestic Concentration and International Trade', *Oxford Economic Papers*, 34: 479–97

Vaizey, J. (1960), *The Brewing Industry, 1886–1951: An Economic Study*, London: Pitman

(1974), *The History of British Steel*, London: Weidenfeld & Nicolson

Veblen, T. (1915), *Imperial Germany and the Industrial Revolution*, New York: Macmillan

Vickers, J. and Yarrow, G. (1988), *Privatization: An Economic Analysis*, Cambridge, MA: MIT Press

Vincent, L.A. (1962), 'Evolution de la production intérieure brute en France de 1896 à 1938: Méthodes et premiers résultats', *Etudes et Conjoncture*, November, 300–33

(1965), 'Population active, production et productivité dans 21 branches de l'économie française (1896–1962)', *Etudes et Conjoncture*, February, 73–108

Wagenführ, H. (1931), *Kartelle in Deutschland*, Nürnberg: Krische Verlag

Wagner, K. (1980), 'Competition and Productivity: A Study of the Metal Can Industry in Britain, Germany and the United States', *Journal of Industrial Economics*, 29, 17–35

Waitt, G. (1994), 'Global Competition and the Nature of Trade in the European Community's Pulp and Paper Industry', *Economic Geography*, 70, 60–71

Walsh, J. (1991), 'The Performance of UK Textiles and Clothing: Recent Controversies and Evidence', *International Review of Applied Economics*, 5, 277–309

Warren, K. (1980), *Chemical Foundations: The Alkali Industry in Britain to 1926*, Oxford: Oxford University Press

Warner, W.L. and Abegglen, J.C. (1955), *Occupational Mobility in American Business and Industry, 1928–1952*, Minneapolis: University of Minnesota Press

Watson, J.A. (1973), *A Hundred Years of Sugar Refining: The Story of Love Lane Refinery, 1872–1972*, Liverpool: Tate and Lyle Refineries

Watson, K. (1990), 'Industrial Finance in the UK: The Brewing Experience, 1880–1913' (D.Phil Dissertation, University of Oxford)

Weir, R. (1989), 'Rationalization and Diversification in the Scotch Whisky Industry, 1900–1939: Another Look at "Old" and "New" Industries', *Economic History Review*, 42, 375–95

(1994), 'Managing Decline: Brands and Marketing in Two Mergers, "The Big Amalgamation" 1925 and Guinness–DCL 1986', in Jones, G. and Morgan, N.J. (eds.), *Adding Value: Brands and Marketing in Food and Drink*, London: Routledge, 139–61

Weiss, F.D. (1988) (ed.), *Trade Policy in West Germany*, Tübingen: Mohr

Wells, F.A. (1972), *The British Hosiery and Knitwear Industry: Its History and Organisation* (revised edn.), Newton Abbot: David & Charles

Wengenroth, U. (1994), *Enterprise and Technology: The German and British Steel Industries, 1865–1895*, Cambridge: Cambridge University Press

Whisler, T.R. (1994), 'The Outstanding Potential Market: The British Motor Industry and Europe, 1945–75', *Journal of Transport History*, 15, 1–19

(1995), *At the End of the Road: The Rise and Fall of Austin-Healey, MG, and Triumph Sports Cars*, Greenwich, CT: JAI Press

Wiener, M.J. (1981), *English Culture and the Decline of the Industrial Spirit 1850–1980*, Cambridge: Cambridge University Press

Wigham, E. (1973), *The Power to Manage: A History of the Engineering Employers' Federation*, London: Macmillan

Williams, C. (1946), 'The Carpet Industry', in Silverman, H.A. (ed.), *Studies in Industrial Organization*, London: Methuen, 264–301

Williams, G. (1957), *Recruitment to Skilled Trades*, London: Routledge & Kegan Paul

(1963), *Apprenticeship in Europe: The Lesson for Britain*, London: Chapman & Hall

Williams, I. (1931), *The Firm of Cadbury, 1831–1931*, London: Constable

Williams, K., Williams, J. and Haslam, C. (1987), *The Breakdown of Austin Rover: A Case Study in the Failure of Business Strategy and Industrial Policy*, Leamington Spa: Berg

Williams, K., Williams, J. and Thomas, D. (1983), *Why are the British Bad at Manufacturing?*, London: Routledge & Kegan Paul

Williamson, J.G. (1985), *Did British Capitalism Breed Inequality?*, London: Allen & Unwin

(1991), *Inequality, Poverty and History*, Oxford: Blackwell

(1995), 'The Evolution of Global Labor Markets since 1830: Background Evidence and Hypotheses', *Explorations in Economic History*, 32, 141–96

Wilson, C. (1954), *The History of Unilever: A Study in Economic Growth and Social Change* (2 vols.), London: Cassell

(1968), *Unilever, 1945–1965: Challenge and Response in the Post–War Industrial Revolution*, London: Cassell

Wilson, G.B. (1940), *Alcohol and the Nation (A Contribution to the Study of the Liquor Problem in the United Kingdom from 1800 to 1935)* London: Nicholson & Watson

Winters, L.A. and Brenton, P.A. (1991), 'Quantifying the Economic Effects of Non–tariff Barriers: The Case of UK Footwear', *Kyklos*, 44, 71–91

Womack, J.P., Jones, D.T. and Roos, D. (1990), *The Machine that Changed the World*, New York: Rawson Associates

Wonnacott, T.H. and Wonnacott, R.J. (1990), *Introductory Statistics for Business and Economics* (4th edn.), New York: Wiley

Woodruff, W. (1955), 'Growth of the Rubber Industry of Great Britain and the United States', *Journal of Economic History*, 15, 376–391.

(1958), *The Rise of the British Rubber Industry During the Nineteenth Century*, Liverpool: Liverpool University Press

Wray, M. (1957), *The Women's Outerwear Industry*, London: Duckworth

Wright, G. (1981), 'Cheap Labor and Southern Textiles, 1880–1930', *Quarterly Journal of Economics*, 96, 605–29

(1990), 'The Origins of American Industrial Success, 1879–1940', *American Economic Review*, 80, 651–68

Wrigley, J. (1986), 'Technical Education and Industry in the Nineteenth Century', in Elbaum, B. and Lazonick, W. (eds.), *The Decline of the British Economy*, Oxford: Oxford University Press, 189–222

Wulf, H. (1993), 'Arms Industry Limited: The Turning-Point in the 1990s', in Wulf, H. (ed.), *Arms Industry Limited*, Oxford: Oxford University Press, 3–26

Wuppermann, M. (1989), *Geschäftsführer in Deutschland*, Frankfurt: Campus

Yamada, S. and Ruttan, V.W. (1980), 'International Comparisons of Productivity in Agriculture', in Kendrick, J.W. and Vaccara, B.N. (eds.), *New Developments in Productivity Measurement and Analysis*, Chicago: Chicago University Press, 509–85

Yamey, B.S. (1966), 'United Kingdom', in Yamey, B.S. (ed.), *Resale Price Maintenance*, London: Weidenfeld & Nicolson, 249–98

Young, A. (1991), 'Learning by Doing and the Dynamic Effects of International Trade', *Quarterly, Journal of Economics*, 106, 369–406

Young, S. and Hood, N. (1977), *Chrysler U.K.: A Corporation in Transition*, New York: Praeger

Zapf, W. (1965), 'Die deutschen Manager: Sozialprofil und Karriereweg', in Zapf, W. (ed.), *Beiträge zur Analyse der deutschen Obersicht*, München: Piper.

Zavatta, R. (1988), 'The Paper Industry in the European Economic Community', in de Jong, H.W. (ed.), *The Structure of European Industry* (2nd revised edn.), Dordrecht: Kluwer, 105–25

Zeitlin, J. (1994), 'Re–Forming Skills in British Engineering, 1900–40: A Contingent Failure' (unpublished, University of Wisconsin-Madison)

Zeitlin, J. and Totterdill, P. (1989), 'Markets, Technology and Local Intervention: The Case of Clothing', in Hirst, P. and Zeitlin, J. (eds.), *Reversing Industrial Decline? Industrial Structure and Policy in Britain and Her Competitors*, Oxford: Berg, 155–90
Zweig, F. (1951) *Productivity and Trade Unions*, Oxford: Blackwell

Index

432